MULTICHANNEL RETAILING

fb

MULTI-CHANNEL RETAILING

LYNDA GAMANS POLOIAN

FAIRCHILD BOOKS
NEW YORK

**This book is dedicated to
Puppen and Wyck**

Executive Editor: Olga T. Kontzias
Acquiring Editor: Joseph Miranda
Editorial Development Director: Jennifer Crane
Development Editor: Donna Frassetto
Associate Art Director: Erin Fitzsimmons
Production Director: Ginger Hillman
Associate Production Editor: Andrew Fargnoli
Project Manager: Jeff Hoffman
Copyeditor: Ellen Howard
Text Design: Tom Helleberg

Copyright © 2009 Fairchild Books, A Division of Condé Nast Publications, Inc.

All rights reserved. No part of this book covered by the copyright hereon may be reproduced or used in any form or by any means—graphic, electronic, or mechanical, including photocopying, recording, taping, or information storage and retrieval systems—without written permission of the publisher.
Library of Congress Catalog Card Number: 2009925891
ISBN: 978-1-56367-630-7
GST R 133004424
Printed in the USA

TP09

Contents

Preface	xvii
Acknowledgments	xxi

Unit I > The Road to Multichannel Retailing — 1

Chapter 1 > Evolution and Impact of Multichannel Retailing	2
Chapter 2 > Components of Multichannel Retailing	36
Chapter 3 > Multichannel Customer Behavior	82
Multichannel Retail Profile > QVC	133
Multichannel Retail Profile > J. C. Penney	136

Unit II > Strategic Imperatives — 141

Chapter 4 > The Strategic Planning Process	142
Chapter 5 > Implementing Multichannel Strategies	176
Chapter 6 > Cross-Channel Collaboration	206
Multichannel Retail Profile > Red Envelope	242
Multichannel Retail Profile > L.L. Bean	244

Unit III > Technology Solutions — 249

Chapter 7 > Designing Effective Online Stores	250
Chapter 8 > Multichannel Customer Service	296
Chapter 9 > Synchronizing the Supply Chain	336
Chapter 10 > Business Intelligence and the Future of Multichannel Retailing	364
Multichannel Retail Profile > Amazon.com	396
Multichannel Retail Profile > Apple	400

Glossary	404
Index	415

Extended Contents

Preface xvii
Acknowledgments xxi

Unit I > The Road to Multichannel Retailing

Chapter 1 > Evolution and Impact of Multichannel Retailing 2

Objectives	2	**Impact of Multichannel Retailing**	15
Multichannel Retailing Defined	3	Worldwide Internet Usage	15
Understanding Electronic and		Online Performance Measures	15
Mobile Transaction Methods	3	*Annual Sales*	17
Bricks, Slicks, and Clicks	3	*Holiday Sales Significance*	17
Discerning Channels and Vehicles	4	*Other Performance Measures*	18
Organizational Structures	5	**Top Multichannel Retailers**	19
Pure-Play Retailers	5	Overview of Key Players	19
Dual-Channel Retailers	6	Deployment Strategies	23
Multichannel Retailers	6	**Factors Shaping the Retail Industry**	24
Electronic Spin-Offs	7	Technological Advances	24
Nontransactional Retail Sites	7	Customer Dynamics	25
Why Adopt Multichannel Retailing?	7	Industry Consolidation and	
Reasons for the Multichannel		Ownership Change	25
Approach	8	Merchandising Polarity	26
Justification for Multichannel		Supply Chain Initiatives	27
Retailing	9	Global Retail Expansion	27
Roots of Multichannel Retailing	11	Emergence of China	28
Early History and Origins of		Multichannel Emphasis	29
the Internet	12	Organized Retail Crime	29
From Isolation to Integration	13	Customer Privacy and Security	30
Obstacles to Multichannel Retailing		Sustainability	30
Development	13	**Summary**	31
Evolution of the Contemporary		Questions for Reflection and	
Business Model	14	Discussion	33
Current Status	14	Notes	33

Chapter 2 > Components of Multichannel Retailing — 36

Objectives	36
Brick-and-Mortar Retailing	37
Department Stores	38
Full-Line versus Limited-Line Stores	38
Target Market and Pricing Strategies	39
Department Store Weaknesses	39
Department Store Strengths	40
Specialty Stores	41
Target Market and Pricing Strategies	42
Specialty Store Strengths	42
Specialty Store Weaknesses	43
Discount Stores	44
Key Characteristics	44
Types of Discount Retailers	44
General Merchandise Discounters	44
Category Killers	45
Off-Price Discounters	46
Warehouse Clubs	46
Factory Outlet Stores	46
Deep Discounters	47
Brick-and-Mortar Retailers Encapsulated	47
Direct Marketing and Direct Selling	48
Direct Marketing versus Direct Selling	49
Direct Marketing Terminology	50
Direct Marketing Methods	52
Catalogs	52
Catalog Selling versus Store Retailing	52
Weaknesses of Catalog Selling	53
Direct Mail	54
Strengths of Direct Mail	56
Weaknesses of Direct Mail	56
Telemarketing	57
Strengths of Telemarketing	57
Weaknesses of Telemarketing	58
Direct Selling Methods	59
Face-to-Face Direct Selling	59
Individual Contact	59
Party Plan and Group Sales	60
Remote Selling	60
Electronic Retailing	61
Online Strategies: Reaching the Customer	62
Push and Pull Strategies	62
Merchandise Preferences	63
Shopping Options	63
Online Shopping Malls	63
Online Auctions	65
Comparison Shopping Sites	65
Tactics and Concerns of Online Retailers	66
Online Tactics	66
Optimizing Search Engine Efficiency	67
Increasing Conversion Rates	67
Reducing Shopping Cart Abandonment	67
Increasing Frequency of Purchase	68
Online Concerns	68
Customer Privacy	68
Sales Taxation	68
Updating Web Sites	68
Improving Customer Service	69
Electronic Retailing Options	69
Mobile Commerce	69
Usage and Reach	70
Strengths of M-commerce	71
Weaknesses of M-commerce	71
Electronic Kiosks	72
Strengths of Kiosks for Retailers	72
Weaknesses of Kiosks for Retailers	73
Television Retailing	74
Home Shopping Channels	74
Infomercials	74
Interactive Television	76
Summary	78
Questions for Reflection and Discussion	79
Notes	80

Chapter 3 > Multichannel Customer Behavior 82

Objectives 82
Ensuring Consumer Value Through Multiple Channels 83
  Brick-and-Mortar Retailing 83
  Catalog Retailing 84
  Online Retailing 85
A Primer on Customer Behavior 88
  Human Needs and Wants 89
    Biogenic and Psychogenic Needs 89
    Utilitarian and Hedonic Needs 89
    Aspirational Wants 89
  Major Shifts in Customer Behavior 90
    The Value/Price Equation 90
    Unrestrained Choices 90
    The Control Factor 91
    Perception of Time 92
    The Technology Revolution 92
  Marketing Principles and Customer Behavior 93
    Product Life Cycle 93
    Consumer Adoption Categories and the Diffusion of Innovation 94
    Classification of Purchasing Situations 95
      Shopping Goods 95
      Specialty Goods 95
      Convenience Goods 96
      Impulse Goods 96
    Decision-Making Process and Time Frame 96
Bases for Market Segmentation 98
  Demographic Segmentation 98
    Age 98
      Sterling Silver Seniors 98
      Baby Boomers 99
      Generation X 100
      Generation Y and Millennials 100
      'Tweens 100
      Children as Consumers 101
    Gender 101
      Gender Breakdown of Internet Users 101
      Gender Differences in Shopping 102
      Gay and Lesbian Segments 102
    Household Income 103
      Ramifications for Online Retailers 103
      Internet Usage in Mainstream and Low-Income Families 103
      The Wage Gap 104
    Ethnicity 104
    Family Life Cycle 104
    Social Class Stratification 105
  Geographic Segmentation 105
  Psychographic and Lifestyle *Segmentation* 106
    Fashion Orientation 107
    "Green" Orientation 110
  Behavioral Segmentation: New Parameters 110
    Time Spent on Top Web Sites 111
    Online Purchase Decision Time Frame 111
Customer Expectations of Multichannel Retailers 112
  What Customers Want 112
    Price and Value Commitment 112
    Integrated Services 113
      Cross-Channel Shopping 113
      Promotions 114
      Communication 114
      Gift Card Use 114
    Operational and Merchandising Efficiencies 115
      Consistent In-Stock Position 115
      Customization 115
      Purchase and Return Options 115
      Pick-Up and Delivery Services 116
    Human Interaction 116

Personal Shoppers	116	Word-of-Mouth (WOM)	121
Telephone and Internet Options	117	Viral Marketing	122
Online-Specific Amenities	117	Guerilla Marketing	122
E-mail Alerts and Follow-Up	117	Social Networking	122
Click-to-Chat Services	117	*Media*	123
Social Networking Availability	118	Inhibitors of the Multichannel	
Electronic Kiosks	118	*Customer Experience*	124
Secure Systems and Payment Options	118	*Intangibility and Perceived Risks of Online Shopping*	124
What Customers Do Not Want	119	*Privacy and Security Concerns*	125
Brick-and-Mortar Stores	119	Preference Services	125
Catalog Retailers	119	Payment Problems	125
Online Stores	120	Identity Theft	126
The Multichannel Customer		*Shopping Cart Abandonment*	126
Experience: Influencers and Inhibitors	120	*Technological Malfunctions*	127
Influencers of the Multichannel		**Economic Impact of Customer**	
Customer Experience	120	**Behavior on Retailers**	127
Groups and Individuals	121	**Summary**	128
Reference Groups	121	Questions for Reflection and Discussion	130
Opinion Leaders	121	Notes	130
Marketing and Communication Tools	121		

Multichannel Retail Profile > QVC — 133
Multichannel Retail Profile > J. C. Penney — 136

Unit II > Strategic Imperatives

Chapter 4 > The Strategic Planning Process — 142

Objectives	142	Recession	147
Steps of the Strategic Planning Process	143	Inflation	147
		Currency Volatility	149
Conducting a Situation Analysis	143	Interest Rate Fluctuations	150
Determining a Differential Advantage	144	*Economic Indicators*	151
		Implications for Multichannel Retailers	152
Developing a Vision Statement	145		
Preparing Goals and Objectives	145	Political Influences	154
Planning Detailed Strategies	146	*Trade Agreements*	154
Monitoring the Retail Environment	146	*Trade Restrictions*	155
Economic Impact	147	*Impact of Globalization*	156
Monetary Dynamics	147	Multichannel Retailing and the Law	156

Legislative Lobbying Practices	157	**Decision-Making Tools and Market**	
Legal and Ethical Issues	157	**Strategies**	167
Regulatory Laws Affecting Retailers	157	Growth-Share Matrix	167
Antitrust Laws	158	Product/Market Expansion Grid	168
Data Privacy Laws	158	*Understanding the Grid*	168
Product Safety Laws	158	*Using the Grid to Formulate*	
Population Dynamics	159	*Strategies*	169
Internal and External Competition	159	Market Penetration	169
Internal Tactics	160	Market Development	170
Scrambled Merchandising	160	Product Development	171
Advantageous Locations	161	Diversification	171
Product Differentiation	162	*Market Segmentation Strategies*	171
External Tactics	162	**Summary**	173
Acquisitions and Divestitures	162	Questions for Discussion and	
Market Share Growth	164	Reflection	174
Unpredictable Events	165	Notes	174

Chapter 5 > Implementing Multichannel Strategies   176

Objectives	176	E-mail Contact	186
Impact Areas for Strategic Decision		Blogging	187
Making	177	Digital Shopping Malls	187
Enabling Technologies	177	*Distribution and Fulfillment*	187
Store-Centered	177	Distribution Center Synergy	189
Catalog-Oriented	178	Conflicting Outcomes	189
Internet-Centered	178	**Overcoming Channel-Specific**	
Retail Expansion	179	**Limitations**	190
New Concept Development	179	Brick-and-Mortar Strategies	190
Global Expansion	181	*Supplementing Limited Store Space*	190
Cultural Differences	182	*Coping with Market Saturation*	191
Online Payment Differences	182	Catalog Strategies	191
International Shipping Issues	182	Online Strategies	192
Brand Building and Product		*Optimizing Search*	192
Development	183	Mechanics of Search	192
Brand Positioning	183	Visual Search Engines	194
Customizing Retail Locations	183	Expanding Search	195
Private Labeling	185	*Enhancing Apparel Sales and*	
Product Development at		*Services*	195
Amazon.com	185	Overcoming Fit Problems	195
Marketing and Communications	186	Color Management	196

Online Trunk Shows	196	Online Franchising	198
Improving Customer Conversion Rates	197	Online Resellers	199
		Brand Resurrection	199
Increasing Click-Through	197	**Evaluating Multichannel Best Practices**	200
Encouraging Repeat Purchases	197	**Summary**	201
Personalizing Contact	197	Questions for Discussion and Reflection	203
Offering Meaningful Incentives	198		
Alternative Multichannel Strategies	198	Notes	204

Chapter 6 > Cross-Channel Collaboration — 206

Objectives	206	Effective Distribution Practices	219
Elements of Cross-Channel Collaboration	207	*Customer Expectations*	220
		Fulfillment Strategies	220
Cross-Channel Organizational Design	207	Promotion in Perspective	222
Significance of Channel Synchronization	208	*Consistent Cross-Channel Exposure*	223
		Modern Media Trends	224
Solutions to Cross-Channel Collaboration Problems	209	Personalization	225
		Social Network Advertising	225
Synchronizing Information Technology	209	E-mail Customer Contact and Advertising	226
Sharing Customer Data	210	Banner Advertising Grows Up	227
Implementing Customer Service Procedures	210	Search Drives Sales	229
		Interchannel Promotion	230
Countering Limited Financial Resources	212	Customer Relationship Management	231
Developing Internal Expertise	213	*Database Development and Use*	231
Embracing Change	213	*Data Mining to Facilitate Advertising*	232
Integrated Marketing Strategies	215	*Cross-Channel Loyalty Programs*	234
Building Brand Equity Across Channels	215	Organizational Leadership	234
		Human Resource Management	235
Merchandise Selling and Pricing Tactics	217	*Profitability and Productivity*	236
		Summary	238
Cross-Channel Selling	217	Questions for Discussion and Reflection	239
Selling Luxury Goods	217		
Pricing Techniques	218	Notes	240

Multichannel Retail Profile > Red Envelope	242
Multichannel Retail Profile > L.L. Bean	244

Unit III > Technology Solutions

Chapter 7 > Designing Effective Online Stores — 250

Objectives — 250
Characteristics of Effective Retail Web Sites — 251
  Winning the Customer — 251
  Common Traits of Effective Sites — 252
Framework for Web Site Design — 255
  Web Page Layout and Design — 255
    Principles of Design — 255
      Balance — 255
      Emphasis — 257
      Proportion — 258
      Rhythm — 258
    Elements of Design — 258
      Line — 258
      Color — 258
    Selecting and Using Typography — 259
      Type Categories — 259
      Sizing Type — 260
      Using Type Effectively — 261
      Type and White Space — 261
  Essentials of Web Content — 262
    Product Information Content — 262
    Transactional Capabilities and Functionality — 262
      Site Maps — 262
      Menus — 263
      Links — 263
      Side Bars — 263
      Shopping Cart Functions — 263
    Online Communications — 264
    Web Site Performance — 264
Setting Up an E-commerce Site — 265
  Eight Steps of Web Site Planning — 265
    Step 1: Find the Best Address — 265
    Step 2: Construct the Site — 266
    Step 3: My Site or Yours? — 267
    Step 4: Safe and Secure — 267
    Step 5: Pay Me Now or Pay Me Later? — 267
    Step 6: Promote, Promote, Promote — 268
    Step 7: Sell, Sell, Sell — 269
    Step 8: Evaluate and Update — 269
  Advanced Graphic and Interactive Technologies — 270
    Rich Media and Web 2.0 — 270
      Three-Dimensional Graphics — 272
      360-Degree Rotation — 272
      Embedded Image Recognition Software — 274
      Mashup Applications — 274
      Content-Enhancing Microsites — 274
      Streaming Video — 275
      RSS Programs — 275
      Avatars — 276
    Web 3.0 Evolution — 277
Foundations of Online Communications — 278
  Copywriting Across Channels — 278
    Structure and Preliminary Activities — 278
      Types of Copy — 279
      Precopywriting Preparation — 279
    Hints for Creative Writing — 279
    Approaches to Copywriting — 280
    Online Copy Guidelines — 281
  E-mail Communication — 282
    E-mail, Text Messaging, and Twittering — 282
    Live Chat — 283
    Mobile Commerce Communication — 284
  Contemporary Personal Communication — 286
    Blogging — 286
    User-Generated Reviews — 287

Contents > **Extended Contents** xiii

Web Site Personalization	287	Making Search Work	290
Search Engine Selection and Maximization	288	**Summary**	291
		Questions for Discussion and Reflection	293
The Power of Search	288		
Types of Search	288	Notes	293

Chapter 8 > Multichannel Customer Service — 296

Objectives	296	*Personalization*	316
Parameters for Effective Customer Service Programs	297	In-Store Services	317
		Front-End and Back-End Services	317
Levels of Customer Service	297	*Selling Tactics*	318
Macro and Micro Views of Retail Service	297	Personal Shoppers	318
		Shoppertainment Features	319
Basic and Augmented Services	298	Fulfillment-Related Tactics	319
Customer Relationship Management Practices	299	**Online-Centered Services**	320
		Communication-Enhancing Services	320
S-E-R-V-I-C-E with a Smile	300	*Product Recommendations*	320
S: Superior Service Across Channels	300	*E-mail and Chat Services*	321
E: Exceptional Content	300	Online Community-Oriented Services	322
R: Relationship-Driven Programs	301	*Private Event Retailing*	322
V: Visionary Tactics	301	*Fan Networks*	322
I: Infallible Follow-Up	303	*Advertising Targeting*	322
C: Confidence-Building Communication	303	*Blogging*	323
		Impact of Crime on Customer Services	323
E: Empowered Customers	304	Organized Retail Crime	324
Leading Customer Service Providers	304	*Influence on Retailers*	324
Online Evaluation Using Mystery Shopping Reports	304	*Types of Organized Retail Crime*	325
		Cyber Intrusions	325
Online Assessment by Customer Reports	305	Credit Card Fraud	326
		Identity Theft	326
Evaluation Across Retail Formats	308	In-Store Criminal Activity	327
Excellence Across Business Disciplines	309	*Methods of Reselling Stolen Goods*	328
Optimizing Customer Service	309	Fencing	328
Cross-Channel Services	309	E-fencing	328
Loyalty Programs	309	Fraudulent Returns	329
Payment Options and Preferences	312	Retailers Fight Back	330
E-mail Payment Services	312	**Summary**	332
Mobile Payment Services	312	Questions for Discussion and Reflection	333
Other Payment Programs	313		
Self-Service Options	314	Notes	334

Chapter 9 > Synchronizing the Supply Chain 336

Objectives 336
Supply Chain Membership and Function 337
  Functional Areas and Participants 337
    Production 337
    Distribution 337
    Customer Interface 339
  Supply Chain Goals 339
Supply Chain Synergy 341
  Fulfillment 341
    Customer Service Standards 341
    Effect on Inventory Turnover 342
    Strategic Partnerships 343
  Collaborative Transportation Decisions 345
    Land Transportation Methods 345
    Sea Transportation 345
    Air Freight 345
  Inventory Control 346
    Inventory Management Applications 347
    Inventory Tracking Methods 347
      Periodic and Perpetual Systems 348
      Advanced Shipping Notification 348
Supply Chain Technology Initiatives 349
  Radio Frequency Identification (RFID) Technology 349
    Evolution of Product Recognition Technology 350
    How Does RFID Work? 350
    Benefits of RFID Over Bar Codes 351
    Challenges to RFID Adoption 352
    Present and Future Retail Applications 352
      Walmart's Involvement in Research 353
      Apparel Sector Progress 354
      Innovation and the Future 354
  Merchandise Management 355
  Strategic Partnerships and Direction 357
    Online Retail Exchanges 357
    B2C Disintermediation 357
      Viewpoints on Disintermediation 358
      New Partnerships 358
    Web-Based Private-Label Management 358
Summary 360
Questions for Discussion and Reflection 362
Notes 363

Chapter 10 > Business Intelligence and the Future of Multichannel Retailing 364

Objectives 364
Business Intelligence 365
  Adaptive E-commerce Architecture 365
  Performance Metrics 366
  Web Analytics 367
    Evaluating Web Site Performance 367
    Types of Assessment Tools 369
      A/B Split Testing 369
      Multivariate Testing 371
      Logistic Regression Analysis 371
      Cognitive Measures 371
    Selecting Web Metrics 372
    Measuring Online Advertising Effectiveness 372
    Assessing Web Video 373
    E-mail Effectiveness 373
    Mobile Metrics 374
  Catalog Fulfillment Measurement 375
  Brick-and-Mortar Productivity 376
  Maximizing Multichannel Return on Investment 378
Legal Impediments to Multichannel Retailing 378
  Online Sales Tax Legislation 379

Privacy Bills	379
Network Neutrality Debate	379
Retailer and Consumer Rebuttals	380
Environmental Influences Shaping the Future	381
Technological Innovations and Solutions	381
Hot Products and Cool Services	381
Mobile Phones: Designer to Discount	382
Touch Screen Displays	382
Eye Tracking	383
Holographic Sales Associates and Digital Signage	384
Taste Bud Tempters	384
Customization	384
Enterprise Solutions	385
Virtualization	385
Wine Online	385
Sustainability	385
Green Building	386
Green Products	386
Green Customers and Their Wallets	387
Economic Volatility	387
Impact of Social and Lifestyle Changes	388
Changes in Attitudes and Latitudes	389
Incongruence in Service Supply and Demand	389
Multichannel Retailing: A Final Word	391
Summary	392
Questions for Discussion and Reflection	393
Notes	394

Multichannel Retail Profile > **Amazon.com**	396
Multichannel Retail Profile > **Apple**	400

Glossary	404
Index	415

Preface

Rationale for *Multichannel Retailing*

The majority of retailers now sell through multiple channels. What was once a gradual evolution from core business formats to more complex organizations has become an established practice. Multichannel retailing is the way retail companies plan to thrive and grow in the twenty-first century. The practice is not new—Sears and J. C. Penney served customers through stores and catalogs decades before the multichannel approach became popular. Soon after the advent of the Internet, retailers and consumers embraced the multichannel concept. Its boundless commercial potential and its qualities as a global marketplace help perpetuate multichannel retailing as a significant strategy. That multichannel retailers perform better than those selling through only one channel certainly fuels this momentum. Balancing brick-and-mortar stores, catalogs, online stores, and mobile commerce operations is the mandate and the challenge.

Technology empowers selling platforms, performance metrics, and fulfillment processes that support the concept, but it is human innovation and intervention that make multichannel retailing possible. When it became evident that shopping malls and other traditional retail venues would not cease to exist as online stores grew in popularity, retailers turned their energies toward establishing effective supply chain practices to ensure consistent delivery of sales and services across all channels of distribution.

The academic world has embraced the concept, and annually more universities are adding multichannel retailing courses. Educators integrate material into other retailing, marketing, and fashion courses. As the business practice becomes an industry norm, multichannel retailing will be ever more central to higher education curriculums.

Objectives of the Text

Many new concepts can be embraced by the study of multichannel retailing. The following objectives reflect the scope of learning material presented in this text and preview key areas of discovery for readers.

> To trace the roots, current status, and future of multichannel retailing.
> To examine the strengths and weaknesses of major multichannel components (i.e., stores, catalogs, online, and other retail distribution methods).
> To analyze integrative multichannel strategies by highlighting concrete retail company examples.
> To describe the attributes and behaviors of multichannel customers.
> To discern cross-channel synchronization of customer service, fulfillment, marketing, and other key retail functions.
> To delineate the fundamentals of online store design.
> To highlight supply chain functions, synergies, and enabling technologies.
> To survey aspects of business intelligence, including performance metrics.

Organization

The text comprises ten chapters in three units. Unit I, "The Road to Multichannel Retailing," covers the history, organizational structures, economic significance, and environmental factors behind the emergence and implementation of multichannel retailing. Organizational models are evaluated and the development of multichannel systems is introduced. Brick-and-mortar retailers, catalogs and other direct marketing tactics, online, m-commerce, and other electronic means of reaching the customer are described and their benefits presented. The multichannel customer is profiled and behaviors, including shopping habits, preferences, and implications for affinity/loyalty, are covered. In a world where multitasking has become the behavioral norm, multichannel retailing answers the needs of time-starved consumers. Development of this concept rounds out the unit.

In Unit II, "Strategic Imperatives," the strategic planning process is reviewed and the implementation of integrative strategies is discussed in depth. Cross-channel collaboration and industry best practices are addressed. Specific examples of tactics used by high-performing companies are highlighted.

Unit III, "Technology Solutions," looks at the many ways technology is used to design, power, and manage multichannel retail systems. Web site design fundamentals are covered from aesthetic, communications, and developmental viewpoints. Attributes of effective cross-channel customer service programs are described, with a special section on the impact of organized retail crime on retail initiatives. Synchronizing the supply chain and facilitating fulfillment are emphasized. The gradual shift to radio frequency identification (RFID) technology throughout the supply chain is stressed. Business intelligence applications include performance metrics for major channels. Web analytics play a key role in this unit. The future of multichannel retailing and the companies that embrace this concept round out the unit. Practical applications take precedence throughout the textbook.

Pedagogical features include chapter learning objectives, highlighted glossary terms, as well as summary statements and review questions at the end of each chapter. Every chapter features *What's the Buzz?*—industry viewpoints brought to readers through synopses of trade publication articles. Each Unit features profiles of multichannel retailers: QVC and J. C. Penney follow Unit I, Red Envelope and L.L. Bean enhance material in Unit II, and Amazon.com and Apple round out Unit III. Retailers were chosen to represent different types of organizational structures, merchandise, size, and levels of performance as multichannel retailers.

An Instructor's Guide, Test Bank, and PowerPoint presentations accompany the textbook. Suggestions for interactive assignments and projects are included in the Guide.

This text is designed for undergraduate retailing, marketing, general business, and consumer science programs; it is also a resource for graduate students who require an overview of multichannel retailing. Training directors for retail companies may also find the material useful for executive training and professional enrichment programs.

Acknowledgments

Having completed other works with Fairchild, I was well acquainted with the depth of experience and high standards held by its executives, editors, and staff. From original concept discussions with Joe Miranda to completion of this book, it has been a privilege to work with such a competent—and patient—team. I thank senior development editor, Jennifer Crane, for selecting Donna Frassetto to guide me through the nitty-gritty of the editorial process. Both women brought a fresh viewpoint and a high level of professionalism to our partnership and worked diligently to bring out the best in this sometimes pedantic, but ever grateful, author. Ginger Hillman, Andy Fargnoli, and Jeff Hoffman saw me through production; Erin Fitzsimmons, the design. I appreciate Olga Kontzias's watchful eye and her faith in my abilities to wield the written word, value our mutual enchantment with global travel.

Reviewers provide objectivity, academic expertise, and insight during the development of a textbook. I greatly appreciate the time and work of Soyoung Kim, University of Georgia; Alena Minarovicova, The Art Institute of Philadelphia; and Amy J. Harden Leahy, Ball State University. Their suggestions have sharpened content and brought clarity to several critical areas.

Several students in my first multichannel retailing class served as a sounding board for new ideas, critiqued exercises, and delivered integrative final projects that exceeded my expectations for a new course. Jackie Copp, Meghan Dyer, Heather Hart, Chelsea Hills, and Rachel Platt—who all now work in retailing or marketing—deserve special thanks.

Colleagues from Southern New Hampshire University lent support during the planning and execution of this writing project. They include marketing professors Karen Stone and Marc Rubin who have unfailingly applauded my work as an educator. In addition, Marty Bradley, former Dean of the School of Business, facilitated access to research that was crucial to the completion of this book—even after my retirement from the University.

Several trade associations provided articles, statistics, industry contacts, and expertise that were indispensable to the authenticity of this text. The National Retail Federation, Shop.org, the Direct Marketing Association, and the Direct Marketing Educational Foundation are among those sources most cited. Special accolades go to Nancy Kyle, President of the Retail Merchants Association of New Hampshire, who not only provided valuable insight regarding organized retail crime but also invited me to attend an ORC symposium as her guest. Nancy served as "guest editor" for the ORC sections and, most importantly, is a supportive friend.

For many years the American Collegiate Retailing Association has sponsored retail industry study tours for members as part of its educational mission. Were it not for these opportunities to liaison with top retailers worldwide and to draw from the plentiful research done by the organization's members, this text would be less steeped in pertinent, current, and insightful examples.

To my family, friends, and animal companions who provided support despite working around my deadlines, rescheduling family gatherings, ordering dinner out too many nights, or being expelled from my office for sitting on the keyboard: I thank you.

THE ROAD TO MULTICHANNEL RETAILING

Unit I

Chapter 1

Evolution and Impact of Multichannel Retailing

Objectives

> To master key definitions and utilize appropriate terminology relating to multichannel retailing.
> To identify the major types of multichannel organizational structures.
> To list the reasons for multichannel retailing adoption.
> To highlight the history and development of multichannel retailing.
> To discern the impact of Internet usage and sales performance on retailers.
> To identify factors shaping the retail industry.

>

Today we barely remember a world without the option of ordering a pizza online for delivery, or using a cell phone to text Papa John's and request one of several favorites that we earlier stored in the company's database. Keying in "fav 1" means pepperoni and mushroom to Papa John's and us. We can forward e-mail from Zappos.com alerting friends to a shoe sale, or download a piece of music heard on the TV show *Heroes* to our iPod for only 99 cents. These examples all involve electronic retailing, a key component of multichannel retailing. For this reason the online sector commands extensive coverage in this text, but it is not the only driver of retail change. To appreciate the impact of multichannel retailing on retailers and consumers, we need to immerse ourselves in all of its dimensions.

Multichannel Retailing Defined

Before we travel to a new country, probe the depths of a culture, or tackle new technology, we try to learn some of the language. To begin our exploration of multichannel retailing, we'll look at the terms used to describe the electronic infrastructure followed by the vocabulary of multichannel retailing.

> Understanding Electronic and Mobile Transaction Methods

E-retailing involves online and other electronic transactions involving goods and services for personal, nonbusiness use. In comparison, **e-commerce** includes consumer and business sectors, encompassing all goods and services sold on the Internet and through other electronic means including business-to-business (B2B) as well as business-to-consumer (B2C) transactions. Manufacturers of consumer products that sell online are in the B2B category when they sell to retailers and in the B2C category when they sell directly to consumers. Epitomizing this approach, Del Monte set up a B2C Web site to support its Meow Mix cat food. Read about the company's campaign and retail involvement in Box 1.1. **Mobile commerce (m-commerce)** refers to selling through cell phones and personal digital assistants (PDAs) that are Internet equipped.

Online selling has become a magic carpet ride for retailers but its contribution to total retail sales is relatively small. Retail sales in the United States were $4.5 trillion in 2007.[1] In dollar terms online sales were expected to hit $176.9 billion in 2010.[2] By 2011 online sales will account for 9 percent of total retail sales in the United States.[3] Although 9 percent seems small, the online sector has been growing in double digits since its inception and sales growth is expected to continue.

> Bricks, Slicks, and Clicks

Multichannel retailing is a B2C model that integrates store, direct marketing, direct selling, online, and other electronic methods to transact business with customers globally. The practice of using two or more methods of retail selling concurrently is the minimum required to be a multichannel retailer. In fact, many retailers operate through three or more channels, selling through stores, catalogs, and online at the same time. To use the vernacular: bricks, slicks, and clicks form the core of multichannel retailing. Figure 1.1 illustrates the multichannel aspects of L.L. Bean.

> **Box 1.1 What's the Buzz?**

> ***Meow Mix Has Cat-Centric Site for Pet Lovers***

Del Monte Food's Meow Mix developed a new interactive Web site as part of its "Think Like a Cat" campaign for the cat food brand. The initiative behind the Web site was to reinforce the Meow Mix brand and to engage consumers in an interactive way. The entire Web site is written from the perspective of a cat, as a way to attract pet lovers.

The site at www.MeowMix.com brings the brand to life online. Videos of a variety of cats, humming the Meow Mix theme song, have been superimposed over a living room setting. The site also lets visitors scroll over the cats and play with them as the cats play with a ball of yarn, swat at a fish bowl, and eat Meow Mix food. Speech bubbles on each cat let viewers link to other pages on the site where they can see products, play games, and read cat facts on physiology, diet, behavior, and mythology. They can also get information from the Meow Mix Acatemy, a course aimed at creating a better understanding between cats and owners. Visitors can sign up for Meow Mail or enter a sweepstakes offer.

In addition to the Web site the campaign ran in radio, print, TV, and in-store promotions and events. Prior to the events in several cities, customers were sent invitations on their cell phones. In-store promotions included a display in selected Petco store branches. The goal of the campaign was to build brand awareness, but the goal of the retail promotion was to drive sales.

Source: Excerpted and condensed from Dianna Dilworth, DM News, *August 27, 2007.*

Catalogs, direct mail, e-mail, and outbound telemarketing are popular direct-marketing vehicles. Direct-selling techniques, including home parties and consultative selling, are other options. Online stores and their offshoots, including m-commerce, interactive television, e-mail, and electronic kiosks, are contemporary ways to reach customers. All are defined and discussed in Chapter 2.

> **Discerning Channels and Vehicles**

Differentiating channels from vehicles can be confusing. **Channels** are conduits through which sales are transacted. For example, going online, calling a catalog company, faxing a deli, or visiting a store to make a purchase involves using a channel. **Vehicles** are promotions or other techniques used to reach and inform customers. When customers browse direct mail pieces or call retailers to request catalogs, they are using a vehicle. In the latter instance, for example, a catalog serves as an advertising mechanism. If retailers e-mail customers about an upcoming sale, that, too, illustrates using vehicles. A retail store itself is both a vehicle (we can browse) and a channel (we can buy) because a store displays and advertises merchandise to a customer but also is where the customer makes the actual purchase. A telephone call regarding delivery confirmation from a customer to a retailer is a vehicle, but a telephone call initiated by a retailer for the purpose of selling involves both a vehicle and a channel.[4]

Businesses that practice multichannel retailing come in all shapes and sizes. There is no single pattern of evolution or organization. An overview of several popular formats alerts us to the strategic choices made by companies that choose to capitalize on their assets.

> Organizational Structures

Several organizational structures are used by single- and multiple-channel retailers. The choice of a multichannel organizational structure reflects company objectives, the nature of the business, shareholder preferences, perceived opportunities for growth, and the state of the economy. Most businesses fall into one or more of the following categories.

"Bricks, slicks, and clicks" is the vernacular used to describe retail stores, catalogs, and online selling channels. L.L. Bean became a multichannel retailer by expanding its stores, developing a catalog, and opening an online business. *[Source: LLBean.com.]*

Pure-Play Retailers

Companies that do business through one predominant channel are called **pure-play retailers**. The term *pure play* is usually attributed to online retailers that have never operated brick-and-mortar stores nor engaged in other types of nonstore distribution, but it is appropriate to use the term to describe any business using a single channel to trade. **Brick-and-mortar retailers** conduct business from traditional physically constructed facilities. Examples of pure-play online

1.2 Online electronics retailer Newegg.com is a pure-play company because it trades through a single channel. [Source: Newegg.com]

retailers include Amazon.com; Blue Nile, Inc., the jewelry retailer; and Newegg.com, the computer retailer. The Newegg.com home page is illustrated in Figure 1.2.

Dual-Channel Retailers

Companies that operate through two distinct channels are **dual-channel retailers**. Typically those that run brick-and-mortar stores and also maintain transactional Web sites or catalog divisions are in this category. Target and Walmart are brick-and-mortar retailers that also operate online stores.

Multichannel Retailers

Companies that sell through two or more channels are considered **multichannel retailers**. Frequently these businesses use traditional stores, catalogs, and online stores to reach their customers although many other options are possible. L.L. Bean and J. C. Penney each had catalog and store operations before opening online stores. Companies like these are sometimes called triple-plays in the industry. **Triple-plays** are retailers that trade through three channels such as stores, catalogs, and online.

Electronic Spin-Offs

Companies that originally traded through other electronic means before opening online stores are considered **electronic spin-offs**. For example, QVC.com was started by QVC, the cable shopping channel. QVC is also considered a triple-play retailer because it runs a studio store at its headquarters in West Chester, Pennsylvania. Further information about QVC appears in Chapter 2 and in the Multichannel Retail Profile at the end of Unit I.

Discovery Communications once operated stores, catalogs, and an online store in addition to its TV channels, Discovery Channel and Animal Planet. In late 2007 the company announced plans to acquire the Web site HowStuffWorks.com in order to enhance its Internet business. Discovery earlier had closed its brick-and-mortar store business.[5]

Nontransactional Retail Sites

Web sites used purely for information and promotion that do not sell online are called **nontransactional sites**. Using this format many retailers (generally smaller companies) provide location and educational and customer service material on their Web sites.

Occasionally large retail chains also use nontransactional sites. Pier 1, the home décor retailer, discontinued its catalog business and online store in 2007 in order to concentrate on its 1,100 brick-and-mortar stores. No longer considered a multichannel retailer, the company sustains a nontransactional site.[6] Building brand image and driving traffic to the store are major objectives of nontransactional sites.

As the examples in this section emphasize, many retailers experiment with different multichannel organizational structures as they find the most effective integrative strategies for their companies. Sales performance also affects the decision to expand or contract a business.

Why Adopt Multichannel Retailing?

Retailers that adopt the multichannel model state several advantages and reasons why the practice has become widespread. Simply put, multichannel retailing generates more revenue and profits for retailers by reaching more customers more effectively.

> Reasons for the Multichannel Approach

There are many reasons why retailers have embraced multichannel retailing. Some emphasize building a larger customer base and serving existing customers more efficiently. Others cite financial goals, a desire to gain advantages over competitors, or the wish to expand globally.

> *Reach More Customers* By using more than one channel, retailers are able to reach customers previously not served through their original channel in local, domestic, and global markets.

> *Provide Customer Convenience* Most stores are not open to the customer 24 hours per day, 7 days per week, and 365 days per year. Adding catalogs and online alternatives greatly extends the hours of operation and expands opportunities for customer interaction and service. Customers today have less time and higher expectations than ever before, owing to the stresses of contemporary life and the availability of seemingly endless product choices. Shaving precious moments from an already frantic day at home or at work is important to many multitaskers. Rapid changes in society today and their impact on shopping behavior cannot be underestimated.

> *Compete More Effectively* In an intensely competitive retail market, companies benefit from multichannel access to customers. Long-term survival may depend on a company's ability to utilize more than one channel. Virgin Megastores left its partnership with Amazon.com to launch its new site VirginMega.com in late 2007. By doing so, it has been able to create a comparable customer experience at both its brick-and-mortar and online stores, an important goal for the company. The Web site features music themes and boutiques, blogs, streaming videos, and fashion excitement similar to that in the stores.[7] The switch to an independent site has invigorated Virgin's competitive thrust.

> *Grow the Business* Few retailers can maintain the status quo. All are conscious of developing strategies that will ensure strong futures for their companies. Many retail markets in the United States are overstored. **Overstored** describes a retail area where too many stores are selling relatively similar products so that none captures significant market share. Nonstore sectors such as catalogs and online stores may provide the vehicles for sustained growth once retail markets become overstored and thereby less profitable. Walmart, the largest retailer in the world, is considering adding online grocery shopping to its

other formats.[8] It expects to expand its smaller, more upscale Marketside food stores to more than a thousand stores.[9] Although it covers most major markets in the United States, it is cognizant of the need to continue to offer new services to its customers and to identify new avenues of growth.

> *Balance Risk* During times of economic uncertainty, companies derive benefits from using multichannel options because they have flexibility to shift emphasis on sales from one channel to another. Two examples clarify this point. When postal rates increase or gasoline costs skyrocket, as they did in 2007, customers are encouraged to shop online more frequently rather than use catalog or store options. If viewers are not watching their favorite television shows because of a screenwriters' strike, that means potential customers are not seeing as many commercials. It was advantageous for retailers to intensify their online advertising or use e-mails to deliver their promotional messages until the strike ended.

> *Achieve Profitability* Increased sales and market coverage are important to retailers, but without profitability there is no reason to exist. Stockholders of publicly held companies hold high expectations regarding consistent high performance. Growing pressures on retailers compel them to find new growth models and operational tactics that save money. Some retailers that drive customers to online stores find that the tactic increases profitability by reducing brick-and-mortar store operating expenses.

> *Expand Globally* Before the advent of the Internet, retailers had to gain critical mass in terms of number of stores and revenue volume to expand globally. Now it is possible to reach customers worldwide through the Internet. Despite the associated challenges, which include communicating with customers in several languages, using various units of currency, identifying diverse needs, and dealing with logistical challenges, many online companies have expanded globally. Box 1.2 illustrates how Blue Nile, a global pure-play retailer, is expanding its online business internationally.

> **Justification for Multichannel Retailing**

There are several justifications for the adoption of multichannel retailing:

> The practice is a strategic necessity for retailers that are committed to growth and profitability.

Box 1.2 What's the Buzz?

> ***Blue Nile Uses Web to Extend Across the Atlantic***

Blue Nile, an online seller of diamonds and jewelry, is to become one of the first "pure-play" U.S. retailers to cross the Atlantic, in a move that reflects the growing interest of such companies in international expansion.

The potential of international sales for U.S. retailers has been demonstrated by Amazon, the world's largest retailing Web site. Amazon's sites in the United Kingdom, Japan, Germany, China, and France accounted for 46 percent of the company's $3 billion in sales in its first quarter, and sales in those countries rose faster than North American sales.

Scott Silverman, executive director of Shop.org, an association whose membership is made up of U.S. online retailers, said he had seen evidence of growing interest in international markets as his members become more confident.

Jim Okamura, partner at J.C. Williams retail consultancy, noted that online-led international expansion strategies are being explored by U.S. chains that have started to reach the limits of market growth at home. "It's not for everyone, but we've definitely seen a growing interest in international expansion strategies that use an e-commerce platform as an initial entry point," he said, citing efforts by J. C. Penney and Victoria's Secret to develop sales in Canada.

Blue Nile says its operation will be in Ireland and involve "only a handful of employees," with site technology handled from the United States. So far, it has sold goods worth about $3.3 million to United Kingdom customers using a trial site with products priced in dollars.

Source: Excerpted and condensed from Jonathan Birchall, Financial Times, *reported on www.MSNBC.com, May 14, 2007, © 2007 The Financial Times Ltd.*

> Multichannel retailers are more likely to reach customers at a time and place that is convenient for the customers.
> Operating from one channel is no longer effective for most retailers; the exploration of all multichannel alternatives is necessary.
> Multichannel customers spend more than those who shop through only one channel.

Let's look at how these considerations play out for retailers in a real-life example. As a prelude to product decision making, online research is important to customers, as are brand availability, customer service, and integrative online experiences. Homeowners who were researching new kitchen appliances first did rudimentary online research. Later, having had previous experience with the brand, they visited a Sears store looking for ideas. There, a sales associate approached the shoppers, directed them to suitable models, and suggested that they visit the Sears's Web site for more options. She mentioned that a model of their kitchen could be built virtually that would help with placement and design once they had taken measurements of their kitchen. The homeowners were encouraged to comparison shop and were told that Sears would meet any of its main competitors' prices. Orders could be placed online or in the store. Home delivery could be arranged or the appliances could be picked up at a nearby Sears's distribution center. Making shopping and the transaction convenient for customers was the goal.

Reinforcing the importance of an integrative approach, the results of a survey showed that 19.8 percent of customers intending to buy appliances do research online before making a purchase. When looking at all product categories, 89.4 percent of customers said they regularly or occasionally do research online.[10] Selling has become more complex, but the opportunity for customers to make more informed choices further cements the retailer–customer relationship through multichannel retailing.

Customers who shop through more than one channel spend significantly more money than those who shop only one channel. J. C. Penney found that the average annual purchases of its multichannel customers were $150 online, $195 in stores, and $201 via catalog.[11] In 2007, J. C. Penney reached online sales of $1.5 billion.[12] This is approximately 7.5 percent of its total annual sales. Incremental sales increases make the multichannel model even more attractive. One of the oldest retail companies in the United States, J. C. Penney is covered in more depth in the Multichannel Retail Profile at the end of Unit I. The next section provides a brief history of the Internet and the development of multichannel retailing.

Roots of Multichannel Retailing

The birth of multichannel retailing occurred earlier than we might think, yet its emergence as a principal strategy is relatively new. Let's review some of the milestones along the road to multichannel retailing since its rise in the late 1990s.

Although the term *multichannel retailer* has become popular in the last decade, the concept of multichannel retailing is more than 100 years old. By the late nineteenth century Sears, Roebuck and Co. had established one of the first major catalogs in the United States and also operated a chain of brick-and-mortar stores. Modem shopping was a precursor to online shopping and had been popular since 1984 when Prodigy and IBM partnered with Sears to bring CD-ROM shopping to customers.[13]

1.3 After a hiatus of 13 years, Sears reinstated its catalog prior to the 2007–2008 holiday season. Called the *"Wish Book,"* it was reminiscent of the multipage catalogs once published by the company. *[Source: AP Photo/PRNewsFoto/Sears, Roebuck and Co.]*

Sears's history as a multichannel retailer is rich in other respects. Fourteen years after discontinuing its famous full-size catalog the company brought back a 188-page version of its tome for the holiday season in 2007 under the appropriate title, *Wish Book*. The catalog was available electronically through its Web site and in hard copy.[14] The cover of the 2007 holiday edition is illustrated in Figure 1.3.

> Early History and Origins of the Internet

The development of the Internet can be traced to the Advanced Research Projects Agency (ARPA) of the U.S. Department of Defense, which in the late 1960s developed the ARPAnet, used by the U.S. government as a military research network. The first decentralized computer network worldwide, ARPAnet gained scores of other users including research agencies and universities. This progress paved the way for the development of the World Wide Web. Tim Berners-Lee developed this part of the Internet in Switzerland in 1989 as a means of sharing physics research. When users reached the one million mark, the Internet Society was formed; the first Web browser, called Mosaic, was developed; and, as they say, the rest is history.[15]

Mosaic formed the underpinnings of what became Netscape Navigator in the 1990s. Eventually Netscape was sold to AOL and ultimately ceased operating in early 2008 after 13 years of service.[16] By that time, the Internet had become an essential tool for communication, e-commerce, and information sharing. Let's look at how that transformation occurred.

> From Isolation to Integration

Actual commercial use of the Internet, including electronic retailing, did not occur in earnest until the mid-1990s when there was great speculation that electronic retailers would put stores and shopping centers out of business. This never happened but the competitive sphere certainly changed.

Some companies feared that online stores would cannibalize sales in their brick-and-mortar operations. **Cannibalization** is the erosion of sales from an original sales channel by the startup of a new channel. Early in the development of multichannel retailing, some retailers resisted developing Web sites for this reason.

> Obstacles to Multichannel Retailing Development

By the new millennium, several factors contributed to a climate of change. A failing economy worldwide, overinvestment in the dot-com sector, and perhaps inflated opinions of the supposed e-commerce takeover of the retail industry created an environment ripe for change. **Dot-com** is the contemporary term used to describe Web-based businesses that use the abbreviated *.com* domain-name suffix for "company" in their Universal Resource Locator (URL). During this period, retailers were compelled to adopt a more integrative approach as they planned for future growth and profitability. For some the motivation was simply survival.

The multichannel approach was adopted but brought internal problems to many brick-and-mortar retailers. Competition for resources was tight as online stores developed after the dot-com bubble burst early in the century. Turf wars between store and online divisions created conflict, resulted in poor communication, and emphasized the vulnerability and resistance to change of some retailers. According to a study done by Forrester Research, 60 to 70 percent of retailers communicate poorly and do not like to share resources.[17] Forrester Research is a leader in media and technology research and analysis and acquired a competitor, JupiterResearch, in 2008.[18] The work of both companies is cited throughout this text.

> Evolution of the Contemporary Business Model

Growing realization of the benefits brought by multichannel retailing preceded the evolution of a contemporary business model. In this new era, the greatest number of sales would go not to pure-play dot-coms but to brick-and-mortar retailers that sell through multiple channels.

Between 1996 and 1998, multichannel terminology became prevalent in retail trade publications and at industry conferences and presentations. Shop.org, a trade association for online retailers, was formed in 1996 and eventually acquired by the National Retail Federation (NRF) in 2001.[19] This acquisition shows support for multichannel retailing at the highest trade association level. The NRF is the largest retail trade association in the world.

By 1998 the early technologically skilled online customers were replaced by more sophisticated multichannel customers. More involvement with retailers by major consulting firms was noticeable during this period. Evidence of industry acceptance and adoption was apparent. In 2000, Retail Forward (now TNS Retail Forward), a major retail consulting group based in Columbus, Ohio, called multichannel retailing a "dominant business model in industry."[20] The specter of cannibalism faded somewhat as retailers embraced the new retail model.

Strategic partnerships were formed between retailers and suppliers representing diverse origins and all multichannel delivery systems. For example, Marks & Spencer teamed up with Amazon.com to provide hosting technology for the British retailer's Web site along with call center services. Marks & Spencer provides a fully cross-functional ordering system for its 24 million online visitors annually. This was Amazon's first team effort in the United Kingdom but the online company had previously partnered with Target and Borders Books in the United States.[21] By 2005 multichannel companies reached a high level of complexity and creativity.

> Current Status

It is safe to assume that online retailing never will totally displace other forms of commerce. Sales are growing but are expected to slow as the sector matures. E-retailing tactics are sharpening as businesses operate more efficiently, improve technologies, and reach customers worldwide. Multichannel companies are becoming industry leaders and will set the standards for retailing now and in the future.

Impact of Multichannel Retailing

Several measures are used to chart the growth of the Internet and performance of multichannel retailers. Data on Internet usage rates, language options, penetration, sales performance, Web site effectiveness, and customer service efficiencies are commonly gathered. More sophisticated measures involving Web analytics are discussed in Chapter 10.

When using statistics, care is taken to note what is being measured, who is gathering the information, and what sample of the population is being used. Several sources of information are used in this book and it is wise to remember that discrepancies in statistical reporting occur due to differences in research objectives, sampling techniques, measurement, and data analysis.

> Worldwide Internet Usage

In 2000 there were 350 million Internet users worldwide. At that time it was predicted that 765 million users would sign on by 2005.[22] By 2007 1.15 billion people worldwide were online.[23] In terms of Internet users, China topped the United States for the first time in 2008 with approximately 250 million people online compared with 220 million in the United States. However, these figures account for only 19 percent of China's population compared with 70 percent of Americans who are online.[24] This statistic is called the penetration rate. **Penetration rate** measures the percentage of the population that purchases a product or service. The United States has the highest penetration rate worldwide followed closely by Japan and South Korea.[25] The top 10 countries in Internet usage and penetration are listed in Table 1.1.

Another topic of interest is language availability on the Internet. Slightly more than 30 percent of Web sites use English as their language of choice. But if Chinese or Arabic is your native tongue, rest assured that the dot-com has been adapted to your language.[26] The Amazon.com homepage for Japanese customers illustrated in Figure 1.4 reinforces the global reach of pure-play Web sites.

> Online Performance Measures

In this section we'll look at how performance results are measured in terms of revenue growth over time. Annual sales, the impact of the holiday period, and an introduction to other online performance metrics are covered. Sales data and predictions included here have been culled from a variety of industry sources.

Table 1.1 Top 10 Countries in Internet Usage and Penetration

RANK	COUNTRY	INTERNET USERS	PENETRATION (% OF POPULATION)
1	United States	210,575,287	69.7
2	China	162,000,000	12.3
3	Japan	86,300,000	67.1
4	Germany	50,426,117	61.1
5	India	42,000,000	3.7
6	Brazil	39,140,000	21.0
7	United Kingdom	37,600,000	62.3
8	South Korea	34,120,000	66.5
9	France	32,925,953	53.7
10	Italy	31,481,928	52.9

Source: InternetWorld Stats.com, "Top 20 Countries With the Highest Number of Internet Users," June 30, 2007. User information from Nielson/Net Ratings and International Telecommunications Union. Copyright © 2000–2007, Miniwatts Marketing Group.

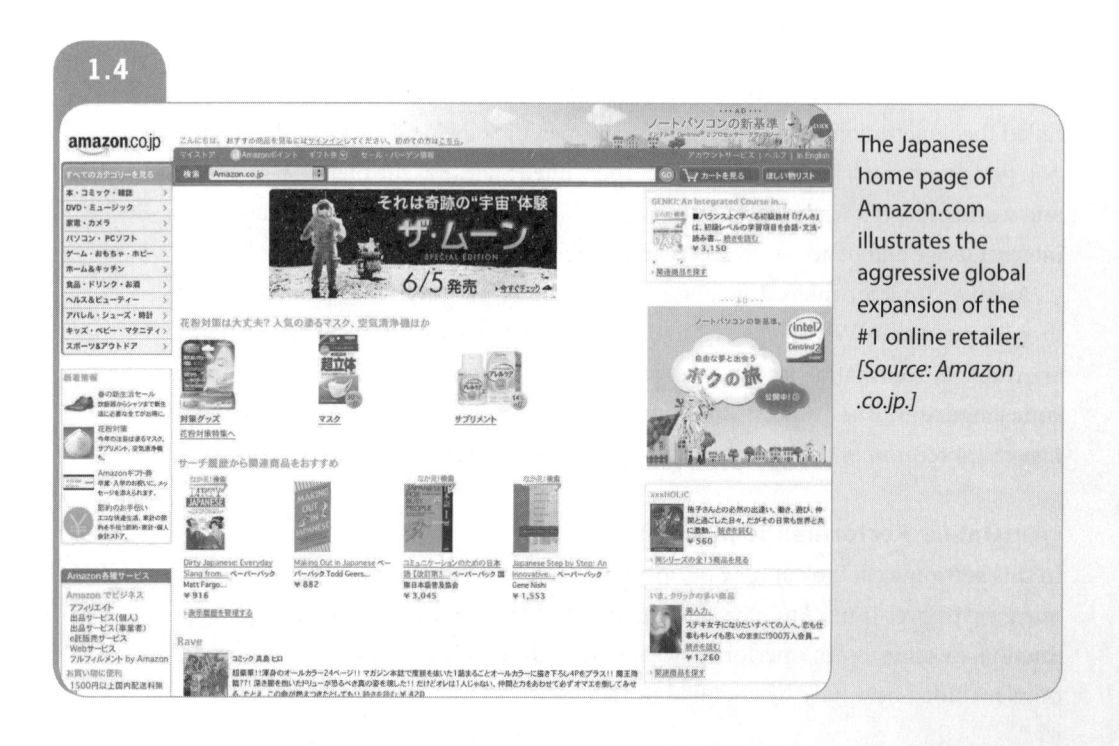

1.4 The Japanese home page of Amazon.com illustrates the aggressive global expansion of the #1 online retailer. [Source: Amazon.co.jp.]

Top 10 Web Retailers for 2007   Table 1.2

RANK	COMPANY	WEB SALES	TOTAL SALES	PERCENTAGE OF SALES FROM WEB
1	Amazon.com Inc.	$14,800,000,000	$14,800,000,000	100
2	Staples Inc.	5,600,000,000	19,371,000,000	29
3	Office Depot Inc.	4,900,000,000	15,500,000,000	32
4	Dell Inc.	4,200,000,000*	61,133,000,000	7
5	HP Home and Home Office	3,361,000,000*	104,300,000,000	3
6	OfficeMax Inc.	3,163,000,000*	9,082,000,000	35
7	Apple, Inc.	2,700,000,000*	24,006,000,000	11
8	Sears Holdings Corporation**	2,589,840,000*	50,703,000,000	5
9	CDW Corp.	2,001,372,000	6,800,000,000	30
10	Newegg.com	1,900,000,000	1,900,000,000	100

* *Internet Retailer* estimate.
** Sears Holdings Corporation includes Sears.com, Kmart.com, LandsEnd.com, Craftsman.com, and Kenmore.com.
Source: "Top 100 E-retailers," *Internet Retailer 2008 Top 500 Guide,* 42. © 2008 Vertical Web Media LLC.

Annual Sales

Retail sales revenue is an important measure of performance for all retailers and a useful tool for many types of analysis. Market share, performance of specific merchandise categories, and retail industry output are studied by extrapolating information from sales reports.

Internet Retailer, a trade publication for multichannel retailers, is a reputable source for sales performance information. The publication lists the leading online retailers annually, based primarily on sales. The *Internet Retailer* Top 500 Web Retailers generated 61.3 percent of all online sales, which accounted for $101.7 billion in 2007.[27] The annual sales of the Top 10 Web Retailers for 2007 are listed in Table 1.2.

Holiday Sales Significance

Sales during the November to January holiday period are important to all retailers because of their weight in determining annual performance. Traditionally the day after Thanksgiving is called "Black Friday" because it is one of the busiest shopping days in the holiday season, signifying the shift to profitability for many retailers. The newer term "Cyber Monday" was coined by the NRF in 2006 and indicates one of the most lucrative sales days for online retailers. Cyber Monday falls on the Monday immediately following Thanksgiving. In the 2007–2008 holiday season, the biggest sales day for online companies was December 10, dubbed "Green Monday" by the industry. None of these is the official benchmark day for all retailers, but each serves as a basis for year-to-year comparisons.

Predicted and actual online sales results for the 2007–2008 holiday season are included in the following statistics. Across all channels, 55.3 percent of retailers expected Thanksgiving to New Year's holiday sales to account for 25 percent of their annual sales. Holiday sales account for more than 50 percent of annual sales for 9.1 percent of retailers. For this reason, it is appropriate to scrutinize how retailers prepare for and perform during this important selling season. For the past several holiday seasons, online sales have grown by approximately 25 percent annually, but in 2007 the bulk of retailers surveyed expected to see increases of 20 percent or less.[28] Reasons for the negative forecast included increased energy costs, continued declines in the housing market due in part to the nonprime mortgage crisis in 2007, the ensuing credit crunch and turmoil in the financial sector, uncertainty in the economy, and concerns about the threat of recession.

To counter the expected downturn, retailers planned appropriate promotions, invested in more efficient technology infrastructures, and added customer services in time for holiday ordering. For example, Bath & Body Works, a division of Limited Brands, sent customer reviews on key skin care products to other customers via e-mail.[29] The power of testimonial advertising is strong because the message comes from fellow customers and is more believable and actionable. Many online retailers offered free shipping, discounts, and other incentives.

Online sales reports for the 2007–2008 holiday period were up 19 percent over 2006 figures and sales volume reached $29.5 billion.[30] For this selling period, expectations were close to reality, but this is not always the case.

Other Performance Measures

Other methods and different criteria are used to judge excellence. Some of these performance measures evaluate retail Web sites on the basis of design, services offered, click-through rates, and shopping cart abandonment figures. Click-through measures the number of times a link from one Web site to another is used. Some retailers rely heavily on consumer input regarding services offered and received as a measure of retail performance.

Statistics published in magazines, educational journals, and those that emanate from retailers, independent research firms, and trade organizations lend different perspectives and value to the study of multichannel retailing and the retail decision-making process.

Top Multichannel Retailers

Multichannel retailers fare well in an analysis of the top retail Web sites. In 1999 only 27 of the top 50 online retailers were multichannel. According to *Internet Retailer*, 41 of the top 50 were multichannel in 2006. Of the top 10 e-retailers, only two retailers—Amazon.com and Newegg.com—were pure-play sites in 2007.

> Overview of Key Players

Charting the performance of retailers over time gives dimension to statistics and introduces some of the key players in pure-play Internet and multichannel areas. The discussion that follows includes examples of pure-play Web retailers that appeared to be overnight successes and those that took years to become profitable. Time in the online marketplace is not a factor when evaluating a retailer in terms of sales performance alone. E-retailing history is full of companies that began strongly and then declined as competition stiffened.

Brief vignettes describing the top 10 online retailers listed in *Internet Retailer 2008 Top 500 Guide* appear next. Other examples demonstrate the delicate balance between success and failure and highlight strategies used to retain or upgrade online businesses.[31] Order of ranking is as it appears in the 2008 *Guide* and supporting information is culled from both the 2007 and 2008 editions.

1. **Amazon.com** went online in 1994 but showed no profits until the last quarter of 2001. A few roller-coaster years ensued before the online retailer was again profitable.[32] Sales continue to grow but investment in new technologies and content adversely affected net income by 2007. Over the past several years, Amazon announced the introduction of new departments before the start of the holiday season. The addition of health and beauty

lines, gourmet foods, apparel, and shoes in successive years brought the company well beyond books and music. By 2007 Amazon operated transactional Web sites in six countries. It had decreased its marketing costs and was doing more targeted promotions to lure its customers to the online store.[33] Evidently these tactics were successful as Amazon sales increased by 38 percent in 2007 and net income grew 150 percent.[34]

2. **Staples,** the office products company, operates stores internationally (in locations that include China and India), online, and through a direct-mail company in South America. The company netted 27 percent of total sales in 2006 from Web sales.[35] It expects to do one-third of its business on the Web eventually. Extensive research completed in 2007 helped Staples derive two key customer personas used for targeting distinct online shoppers. "Lisa Listmaker" describes an organized customer who is task-oriented, and "Sally Sales" signifies a shopper who wants to be directed to promotions expediently.[36]

3. **Office Depot,** another multichannel office products retailer, redesigned its Web site in 2006, added many personalized treatments, and extended services and online workshops for customers. In 2007 it added several technology tools including online customer reviews and text-messaged coupons. Office Depot offers members of its loyalty program discounts on its partner 1-800-Flowers Web site.[37]

4. **Dell, Inc.,** the online and catalog computer retailer, has survived ups and downs in recent years as it competes with Hewlett Packard (HP). Half of its sales come from its Web site, and Dell is known for its online troubleshooting service. The company departed from its vertical integration strategy in 2007 when it began distributing to several retailers, including Walmart and Sam's Club in the United States.[38] Dell also sells to Gome Electrical Appliances, China's largest electronics retailer.[39] Fashionable laptops promoted by Dell at Macy's are illustrated in Figure 1.5.

5. **HP Home and Office** is a key contender to oust Dell from its #4 position. Relying heavily on its advanced technological infrastructure, HP uses attribute-based navigation and click-to-call tools to serve online customers well.

6. **Office Max** has gained recognition by simplifying procedures for online customers. It has ceased using paper rebates for products in favor of instant discounts at the time of sale. The company advertises on Google to promote sales.

1.5 Dell is forming new partnerships with brick-and-mortar retailers as the company moves from its original catalog and online focus. Laptops in cutting-edge fashion colors were promoted by Macy's at a special in-store event. *[Source: Courtesy of Fairchild Publications, Inc.]*

7. **Apple Inc.** Moving up from position #15 in 2006, Apple made its first appearance in the top 10 in 2007, replacing Sears Holdings Corporation. Apple dazzles customers with its consistent upgrades in Web content and stores, as well as new options for its computer and iTunes customers.
8. **Sears Holdings Corporation.** By early 2008 company-wide sales for Sears had plummeted, causing some analysts to speculate about its future.
9. **CDW Inc.** carries computers and electronics. Its online business is 28 percent of its $2 billion annual sales.
10. **Newegg.com** is a pure-play retailer. Customers visiting the online store can use a unique product review system featuring "5 egg" ratings to acknowledge high performance.

Several retailers in the group that follows have overcome weaknesses or capitalized on strengths not apparent during their first years on the Web. Others have used seemingly appropriate and valid techniques and still do not perform well.

Chapter 1 > **Evolution and Impact of Multichannel Retailing** 21

> **Blue Nile** is #48 in the *Guide* and ranks first in the jewelry category.[40] This online specialist in diamond engagement rings has not significantly diversified its original merchandise selection since opening its online store in 1999. At the time, many shoppers believed an engagement ring was too expensive and important an item to be purchased online. Others found it hard to place their trust in a retailer without the familiar option of face-to-face interactions. The company built trust, defied merchandise sales trends, and is profitable. Blue Nile was featured earlier in Box 1.2.
> **Red Envelope Inc.,** the gift specialist, is ranked #132 in the *2008 Guide* after recording a 13.9 percent decline in online sales from 2007 when it was ranked #120.[41] The company had a stellar launch in 1999 as a pure-play company and in 2000 released its first print catalog. It has not been able to compete effectively with other online gift retailers despite having one of the more sophisticated search engine interfaces in the online marketplace. Red Envelope is featured in the Multichannel Retail Profile following Unit II.
> **Lillian Vernon**, #59 in the *2007 Guide,* dropped to #105 in the 2008 rankings. Rising printing and mailing costs teamed with price increases from its Chinese suppliers were listed as reasons for the decision to file for Chapter 11 bankruptcy protection in early 2008.[42] The company had been gradually paring down its core catalog business to concentrate more intensively on online sales, which were 65 to 75 percent of its business.[43] The seller of housewares, gadgets, jewelry, and children's items was sold to Current USA Inc.[44] Although sales remained strong through 2007, skyrocketing operating costs coupled with a poor economy forced Lillian Vernon to take action.

There are many lessons to be learned from the top retailers. Some perform well despite historic precedence in their merchandise category—for example, Blue Nile's innovation of selling expensive jewelry items when some prognosticators believed people would never purchase an intimate item like an engagement ring online. Others find that their sales do not keep pace with merchandising efforts despite aggressive use of new technologies. Still others find that the costs of doing business are prohibitive and that changes in channel focus must be made. More information about strategic planning and implementation is provided in Chapters 4 and 5.

> **Deployment Strategies**

It is important not only to know the major multichannel companies and their contributions to industry sales, but also to understand how they navigated the paths to success. Some started as brick-and-mortar retailers and later added online stores. Several originated online, then added catalog operations and eventually stores. Others began as catalog operations and then opened stores followed by online divisions. Most multichannel retailers that started as store chains continue to derive the majority of their annual sales from their brick-and-mortar operations. Tactically, retailers use various tools to keep them healthy in the face of internal and external pressures as the following examples suggest:

> > **Macy's** (formerly Federated Department Stores) is #28 in the *2008 Guide*.[45] The department store company has invested heavily in software and built new distribution facilities to support its online business while it nurtures its vast brick-and-mortar empire. Macy's had $450 million in online sales in 2005 and expected to earn more than $750 million by 2008.[46] Recently the company has experienced a slowdown due to the economic downturn and perhaps to overinvestment in acquisitions during the last several years. Despite this, its online sales continue to grow.
> > **H&M (Hennes and Mauritz)** is not yet listed in the *Guide*. The fast-growing specialty apparel chain has extended its reach in areas outside its homebase of Scandinavia. The company supplemented its store sales with online and catalog sales in its home markets and has penetrated the United States with its aggressive multichannel approach.[47]
> > **Restoration Hardware**, #83 in the *Guide,* sells through stores and direct marketing and reported that for the third quarter of 2007, it generated 56 percent of sales from its catalogs.[48] Although Sears, which owned shares in Restoration Hardware, was interested in increasing its stake in the company to improve its product offerings,[49] the economic downturn of 2007 overturned this plan. Instead, Restoration Hardware merged with the private equity firm, Catterton Partners, in early 2008.[50]

These companies used different deployment techniques in their efforts to achieve profitability as multichannel retailers. As their examples suggest, the experiences shaping company expansion or retrenchment are varied and no set of rules will apply in all situations.

1.6

Webkinz.com is directed to 'tweens who enjoy sharing virtual world experiences and purchasing related merchandise with their friends. *[Source: Webkinz.com.]*

Factors Shaping the Retail Industry

Every day, retailers of all kinds face challenges and change. Some of the major areas that are monitored by retailers include the following.

> ### Technological Advances

In tandem with improvements in hardware, software, and accessories have come ever-expanding applications on the Internet, including social networking sites like Facebook and MySpace, YouTube, virtual worlds, and Web analytics. Changes in technology occur at an unprecedented pace and will continue to do so. Changes in content and delivery make headlines every day. A few examples support this statement:

> Advances in 3-D technology mean that virtual stores now look much more similar to the real thing. The company Kinset has set up online stores for several retailers including Brookstone and Amazon-based LectroTown. The company expected to add ten to fifteen new retailers in 2008 and will build a 3-D online shopping complex in the future.[51]

> Virtual worlds such as Second Life and Webkinz are gaining a strong foothold by coupling strong marketing efforts and merchandising strategies. Gartner Research predicts that 80 percent of active Internet users will participate in virtual worlds by the end of 2011.[52] Through Webkinz.com, young people collect stuffed animals and other signature merchandise commemorating the characters they have met on the site. This virtual world targets preteen girls, and the site invests heavily in creative online activities that are to be shared with friends as illustrated in Figure 1.6.

> Storeadore.com is a shopping service geared to women who shop and share information about fashion products and venues. Visitors to the site can virtually tour 1,700 stores from all over the country.[53] Once users leave the domain

24   Unit I > **The Road to Multichannel Retailing**

of general search engines like Google, Yahoo!, and Ask.com, there are specialized search engines for every interest from fashion to fishing. Partnerships with special-interest search engines like Storeadore enable retailers to determine affinity groups, segment their markets, and sell products.

The greatest change in technological support is occurring in the areas of customer relationship management (CRM), database segmentation, and marketing automation.[54]

The causes, effects, interrelationships, and implications of new technology make a compelling argument for the "snowball effect." Our lives are affected by technology, and a change in one sector fuels change in another. Multichannel retailing is not exempt. The areas of technology most significant to multichannel retailing are discussed in Box 1.3.

> Customer Dynamics

The oldest baby boomers will turn 70 in 2016. These individuals already require deep study by retailers because they do not think or behave like the senior citizens of past generations. They are healthier, more active, and many are affluent. Near the other end of the age spectrum, technologically savvy young people think, act, talk, write, and otherwise communicate differently. The cyber-world is their space, and they consider privacy to be less important than connectedness. Both groups comprise the bulk of U.S. consumers; hence, their different attitudes toward shopping, customer service, locus of sales, and product and brand preferences are central to retail research.

Across many demographic and lifestyle groups, customers want value pricing, timeliness, extensive selections, and top customer service. Many customers are looking for individualized products whether in stores, online, or through catalogs and this trend is expected to grow.

> Industry Consolidation and Ownership Change

Mergers, acquisitions, and divestitures have been a hallmark of retail change for at least twenty years. Organizations have grown larger, but not necessarily stronger, as a result. In 2007, a shift in emphasis occurred as fewer U.S. companies changed hands and expansion plans of others were curtailed. However, the rate of company acquisitions by foreign investors grew significantly due to the declining dollar worldwide. As global economic conditions worsened in 2008, even foreign direct investment in American retail companies had declined.

Box 1.3 What's the Buzz?

> Marketing Technology: The Bridge to Multichannel Success

Here's a message to catalogers, e-commerce merchants, and retail storeowners: You aren't who you say you are.

Maybe a few years ago these old-fashioned distinctions still suited you. But today's complex selling environment no longer allows for such strict definitions. Catalogers have turned to the Internet as an order-taking channel. Brick-and-mortar retailers are adding catalogs to reinforce their brand and increase customer touchpoints. And even pure-play online retailers have moved offline in a move to broaden their product footprint.

In such a dynamic environment, virtually all retailers are multichannel retailers. And given the growing sophistication of today's consumers, for a group whose mastery of information and technology helped garner it *Time* magazine's 2006 Person of the Year honor, achieving meaningful differentiation required a coordinated, strategic approach to sales and product promotion.

Increasingly, that multichannel solution is rooted in technology. Driven initially by the introduction and advent of customer relationship management (CRM) tools, the technological landscape has expanded significantly. From the marketer's perspective, today's opportunity can broadly be divided into three functions:

> - CRM tools organize customer and prospect contact efforts and govern the usage of applicable data across the sales process.
> - Database segmentation tools provide a foundation for the storage and profitable use of customer and prospect data, whether for prospecting or for predictive modeling purposes.
> - Marketing automation platforms serve as a "highway" that organizes the flow of data, resources, and strategic intent throughout the marketing process.

The challenge facing today's marketers is to use these tools in such a manner that generates true incremental value. In the multichannel sales environment, gaining the attention of offer-savvy consumers demands more. Technology will play a role, but taking that last step toward profitable relationships will require marketers to build the strategies, initiate the campaigns, and react constantly and proactively to marketplace demand.

Source: Adapted from Michael Grant and Jonathan Margulies, Winterberry Group, DM News, www.dmnews.com, *posted February 26, 2007.*

> Merchandising Polarity

From luxury to "cheap chic," apparel assortments available through various channels range from ultraexpensive designers to very cost-conscious private-label and generic brands. Just as Prada and Coach successfully reach their upscale customers, so, too, do H&M and Target, with their midmarket clienteles.

Online retailers have followed suit, and pricey designers and discount Web sites abound. Bulgari traditionally flaunted high-end jewelry but offers more affordable prices on its bulgari.com Web site. The Italian company has also opened brick-and-mortar stores in Florida and in the U.S. Virgin Islands.[55]

Bluefly.com began as a pure-play online retailer serving up quantities of affordable trendy apparel. The company has experimented with temporary brick-and-mortar locations including a stint in New York City's SoHo district in 2004 and, more recently, a small shop at Underground-NYC, a marketplace in Manhattan for innovative designers and merchants.[56] The exposure is good for brand building but also might indicate an overture for permanent Bluefly stores. "The Tailor" is another initiative intended to draw more fashion-conscious, upmarket men to Bluefly's Web site. Featuring menswear from more than 350 designers, Bluefly expects to offer many of the services traditionally provided by a fine men's apparel store through its online store.[57]

> Supply Chain Initiatives

Shorter lead times for merchandise production and faster time to market are chief goals of all supply channel members. What decades ago took months to complete now takes weeks or days. Design and product specifications are routinely accomplished or tweaked over the Internet.

RFID technology is expected to eventually ensure that merchandise has a flawless, more cost-effective trip from suppliers to manufacturers to retailers to consumers. **Radio frequency identification (RFID)** uses radio wave technology to detect merchandise, people, and other discernable elements. Some of the retail applications include inventory control, user authentication, and asset protection. More on supply chain topics is in Chapter 9.

> Global Retail Expansion

Continued emphasis on the globalization of all business and nonbusiness sectors will continue. Countries are becoming increasingly dependent on each other for education, communication, sustainability, banking and finance, manufacturing, and retailing.

According to a survey completed by The Nielson Company, 85 percent of the world's Internet users have purchased something online. Books and apparel were the most popular merchandise categories purchased by shoppers globally.[58] This factor alone reinforces the great potential for retail companies that embrace global markets through multichannel tactics.

Table 1.3 Top 10 Global Retailers

RANK	COMPANY	COUNTRY OF ORIGIN	NUMBER OF COUNTRIES OF OPERATION	2006 RETAIL SALES
1	Walmart Stores Inc.	United States	15	$374,500,000,000
2	Carrefour S.A.	France	31	112,600,000,000
3	Tesco plc	United Kingdom	12	94,740,000,000
4	Metro AG	Germany	31	87,600,000,000
5	The Home Depot, Inc.	United States	6	77,300,000,000
6	The Kroger Co.	United States	1	70,200,000,000
7	Schwarz Unternehmens Treuhand KG	Germany	24	69,350,000,000
8	Target Corporation	United States	1	63,400,000,000
9	Costco Wholesale Corp.	United States	8	63,100,000,000
10	ALDI Einkauf GmbH & Co. oHG	Germany	15	58,500,000,000

Source: "Deloitte/Stores 2009 Global Powers of Retailing: Top 250 Global Retailers," *Stores,* January 2009, G6–7.

Retailers that expand globally recognize that customers vary greatly and that different approaches are necessary. Some countries attract more international consumers online than others. For example only 45 percent of customers shopping on British Web sites are from the United Kingdom, whereas 95 percent of shoppers on German Web sites are German.[59]

Global concerns such as currency fluctuations, fuel oil supply and demand, terrorism, the balance of trade, wars, the economy, and consumer confidence are other factors that influence decisions made by retailers regarding global expansion. Retailers most likely to withstand the turmoil are those like Walmart and Costco that aggressively seek to expand their businesses internationally. In this way, operations and risks are spread over many different—although inexorably entwined—economies. The Top 10 Global Retailers, their home countries, annual sales, and level of international involvement are listed in Table 1.3. All are multichannel retailers.

> Emergence of China

The rise of China as an industrial entity has created a power shift that is affecting all world constituents politically, economically, socially, legally, environmentally, and competitively. No longer are the United States, Germany, Japan, and other fully industrialized nations the only leaders of commerce. A quick survey of your closet or kitchen will demonstrate that about 80 percent of all products used in the United States are now manufactured in China.

In 2007 and 2008, problems stemming from lax manufacturing and safety standards led to several product recalls and outbreaks of illnesses linked to tainted foods. Despite such safety concerns and reports of violations of human and intellectual property rights, and infringements of child labor laws, which seem commonplace, the Chinese economy continues to flourish.

Many global retailers have entered China and are prepared to wait until income levels and market demand within the country increase. The market for luxury goods such as designer apparel, cosmetics, and leather goods is expected to grow significantly.

> Multichannel Emphasis

The careful melding of channel initiatives evokes the greatest impact on sales and profitability, making multichannel retailing one of the key factors shaping business today. With its emphasis on integration, and consequent shift from push to pull, the power of multichannel as a retail strategy is mind-boggling.

> Organized Retail Crime

Major shifts in two negative trends affect retailers and customers alike. Internal and external theft has always been a problem for retailers, with unscrupulous individuals and employees the culprits when inventory shrinks. Presently it is more likely that organized retail crime is responsible for the majority of loss. **Organized retail crime** involves groups of people in multiple locations and jurisdictions that commit planned crimes against retailers, stealing merchandise with the intent to resell it.[60]

Using a variety of techniques, individuals, families, and other groups of people bilk retailers of merchandise, conduct illegal price changing, use refund scams, and commit credit card fraud to wreak havoc. Organized retail crime accounted for $40.5 billion in losses to retailers in 2007, up $3 billion from 2006.[61] Further information about the effects of organized retail crime on retailers and consumers is presented in Chapter 8.

Counterfeiting and violation of copyright laws are other crimes perpetrated against retailers that affect profitability worldwide. They also raise serious ethical issues that affect manufacturers, retailers, and customers. The sales of counterfeit goods online alone accounted for $87 billion in 2005.[62]

> Customer Privacy and Security

In the consumer sector, privacy issues concerning capture and use of personal data by retailers, and safeguards against fraud, data and identity theft, and unauthorized use of personal information are chief concerns. Data breaches such as the 2006 incident experienced by TJX Corporation, parent company of T.J. Maxx and other off-price stores, demonstrated the vulnerability of retailers to theft by hackers and the need to monitor and tighten the security of internal databases. TJX announced in early 2007 that more than 45 million customers' credit accounts were put at risk when perpetrators broke through security systems and accessed information.[63]

The Internet is prone to identity theft and to other forms of personal affronts. Phishing incidents cost online users $3.2 billion from scams in 2007. **Phishing** is an unscrupulous practice on the Internet performed by individuals who pose as authentic business people to lure people into disclosing sensitive personal information. For example, people impersonating bankers online try to solicit account numbers to use fraudulently.

> Sustainability

Ecology-oriented consumers and retailers are changing the way business is conducted and the ways in which products are sourced, manufactured, distributed, and sold. **Sustainability** refers to the maintenance and sustenance of our planet. Conserving energy, specifying ecologically friendly materials in the manufacturing of products, and reducing consumption of harmful materials are objectives of individuals and businesses that are concerned with sustainability. Retailers actively seek sustainable ways of constructing their stores; planning heating, ventilation, and air conditioning (HVAC) systems; and powering their electricity. Walmart's prototype store near Bentonville, Arkansas, has numerous skylights to take advantage of natural light in the daytime hours. After-hours photovoltaic panels provide energy for the store. The environmentally friendly store is featured in Figure 1.7.

Carbon-neutral emission is the objective for many high-energy users. Product developers are routinely selecting renewable fibers like flax for their apparel lines or specifying bamboo for home flooring and textile use. The footwear manufacturer and retailer Timberland includes information about chemical pollutants and car-

Sustainability is an earth-changing vision for concerned individuals and businesses. Walmart advocates many bio-friendly products and construction materials, and promotes energy efficiencies using natural light and photovoltaic cells to power electricity for its prototype superstore. [Source: Photograph provided by Lynda Poloian.]

bon emissions in data evaluated by designers before they specify materials for new products.[64] Expect more awareness of and commitment to environmental concerns as the issue of sustainability continues to gain prominence.

Multichannel retailing is a strategic imperative for retailers that expect to survive and thrive in the twenty-first century. A final note bolsters this sentiment: the NRF named online/multichannel retailing as the most important issue for retailers in 2008.[65]

Summary

Multichannel retailing is a concept that melds several business practices, forming a whole that is greater than the sum of its parts. The method uses a combination of options—brick-and-mortar stores, direct marketing, direct selling, and electronic retailing—to create better value and more options for customers. It is strategically a direction that no retailer can afford to ignore.

Key Terms

- Brick-and-mortar retailers
- Cannibalization
- Channels
- Dot-com
- Dual-channel retailers
- E-commerce
- Electronic spin-offs
- E-retailing
- Mobile commerce (m-commerce)
- Multichannel retailers
- Multichannel retailing
- Nontransactional sites
- Organized retail crime
- Overstored
- Penetration rate
- Phishing
- Pure-play retailers
- Radio frequency identification (RFID)
- Sustainability
- Triple-plays
- Vehicles

Companies opting for single or multiple ways to sell to their customers use several organizational structures. Pure-play retailers use only one channel. Dual, multichannel, and electronic spin-offs use more than one channel. Nontransactional Web sites of retail companies of various types and sizes provide information to customers but do not offer online selling.

The roots of multichannel retailing go back more than 100 years, but the contemporary model evolved in the 1990s. The advent of the Internet catapulted multichannel retailing to prominence.

Proponents of the strategy say that multichannel retailing helps retailers expand their customer base and customer service, thus helping a company to compete more effectively. Shareholders of publicly traded companies look for growth potential in the companies they choose to invest in, and multichannel retailing provides growth opportunities. Multichannel retailing offers companies large and small the potential to expand globally. By reaching the customer through more than one channel, retailers may reduce business risks. They also sell more goods to their customers than do retailers trading through only one channel.

The percentage of sales attributed to online selling is still in single digits, underscoring the growth potential for this channel. However, online sales growth is expected to slow and eventually plateau in the next decade.

Retailers continue to perfect their customer service outreach through stores, catalogs, and online—wherever the customer chooses to shop. The top multichannel retailers share several key characteristics including innovativeness, being adaptable to changes in the retail environment, constantly monitoring their product offerings, keeping in tune with and in touch with their customers, and maximizing technology to run their businesses efficiently.

Several agents of change affect all retailers and all channels. Among the most prominent factors being tracked by businesses are advances in technology, consumer behavior shifts, retail industry consolidation, merchandising polarity, supply chain initiatives, sustainability, global retail growth, the emergence of China as an economic power, and multichannel retailing itself. Negative aspects of change include increased problems with organized retail crime and consumers' growing concerns about privacy and security. Today multichannel retailers soar above their less aggressive counterparts.

> **Questions for Reflection and Discussion**

1. Explain bricks, slicks, and clicks. How do you prefer to shop? Why?
2. From a retailer's perspective, which of the organizational structures—pure-play, dual-channel, or multichannel—best suits a company that already has a significant brick-and-mortar presence?
3. What obstacles have faced multichannel retailing during its evolution as a current retail strategy?
4. Many reasons are given for the development of multichannel retailing. Which one do you believe is most significant for the long-term success of a company?
5. Select one of the leading retailers from the list of the Top 10 sales leaders. Define its organizational structure, and then discuss the attributes that make this company successful.
6. Drawing from the discussion of several factors in the changing retail environment that influence all retailers, choose the one factor that most affects the company you selected in question #5.

Notes >

1. National Retail Federation, "About NRF, Mission Statement." www.nrf.com.

2. "US Online Retail Sales Forecast, 2008–2013," *DM News*, "DataBANK: The Week in Stats," February 9, 2009. Statistical Source: Forrester Research US E-Commerce Forecast, 2008–2013 (February, 2009).

3. Allison Linn, "Online Shopping Growth to Slow in Next Decade," www.MSNBC.com. Statistical source: Forrester Research.

4. Coy Clement, "Five Questions: Coy Clement on Direct Marketing," www.dma.org.

5. Matthew Karnitschnig, "Discovery Plans to Buy Web Site," *Wall Street Journal*, October 15, 2007, A14.

6. Mary Ellen Lloyd, "Pier 1 Shows Signs of Revival," *Wall Street Journal*, October 31, 2007, B5.

7. Susanne Ault, "Virgin Megastores Launches New E-commerce Site," *Video Business*, November 13, 2007, www.videobusiness.com.

8. Ayinde O. Chase, "Rumblings About Wal-Mart Expanding into Online Shopping Growing Louder," October 29, 2007, www.allheadlinenews.com.

9. "Wal-Mart Expects 1,000-Plus Marketside Stores," *Convenience Store News*, www.csnews.com/csn/news/article_display.jsp?vnu_content_id=1003837463.

10. "Significant Number of Consumers Conducting Their Own Web Research," *Catalog Success*, (North American Publishing Company, 2007), www.catalogsuccess.com.

11. J.C. Williams Group, as published in *Wall Street Journal*, "Shoppers Who Blend Store, Catalog, and Web, Spend More," *Wall Street Journal*, September 4, 2004.

12. "Top 100 Web Retailers," *Internet Retailer 2008 Top 500 Guide*, 114.

Notes

13. Karen Kaplan, "Deal Divides a Fallen Compuserve; Telecom: The Industry Pioneer's Customer Base Will Go to Rival AOL, and Its Network Services to Worldcom in $1.27 Billion Accord," *Los Angeles Times*, September 9, 1997, D1.

14. Chantal Todé, "Big Books Make a Comeback," *DMNEWS*, October 15, 2007, 2.

15. Angus J. Kennedy, *The Internet, The Rough Guide 2000* (London: Rough Guides Limited, 1999) 433-437.

16. Associated Press, "AOL to End Support of Netscape Navigator," *New York Times*, December 29, 2007.

17. Robert Weisman, "Online, Off Target; Retailers Must Integrate Sales," *Boston Globe*, September 14, 2003, C2.

18. Chantal Todé, "Forrester Research Buys its Competitor for $23M," *DM News*, August 4, 2008, 1.

19. Kristi Ellis, "Shop.org Plans to Up Lobbying on E-tail Issues," *Women's Wear Daily*, August 16, 2007, 4.

20. Linda Hyde, PriceWaterhouseCoopers Presentation, AMS/ACRA Triennial Conference, Columbus, Ohio, November 5, 2000.

21. "Amazon Moves into Europe with its First E-commerce Services Deal," *Internet Retailer*, May, 2005, 11.

22. Computer Industry Almanac as cited in "Strike Up the Band Width," WWD Internet, *Women's Wear Daily*, May 2000, 8.

23. Ben Macklin, "500 Million Internet Users in Asia-Pacific," *eMarketer*, February 12, 2008, www.emarketer.com/Articles/Print.aspx?id=1005929. Source: eMarketer, January 2008.

24. David Barboza, "China Surpasses U.S. in Number of Internet Users," *New York Times*, July 26, 2008, www.nytimes.com.

25. InternetWorld Stats.com, "Top 20 Countries with the Highest Number of Internet Users." From data published by Nielsen//NetRatings, International Telecommunications Union, updated on June 30, 2007, http://www.internetworldstats.com/top20.htm.

26. Christopher Rhoads, "What's the Hindi Word for Dot-Com?" *Wall Street Journal*, October 11, 2007, B1.

27. Mark Brohan, "The Top 500 Guide Overview," *Internet Retailer 2008 Top 500 Guide*, 6.

28. Mark Brohan, "Harder Sell, Softer Landing," *Internet Retailer*, November 2007, 55.

29. Mylene Mangalindan, "New Marketing Style: Clicks and Mortar," *Wall Street Journal*, December 21, 2007, B5.

30. comScore press release, "Online Holiday Spending Through December Nears $28. Billion, Up 10 Percent versus Year Ago," December 30, 2007, www.comscore.com.

31. Various sources, *Internet Retailer 2007 Edition Top 500 Guide*, sales ranking and basic profile data. Other trade publication, periodical, and Web site resources are cited when appropriate.

32. Nick Wingfield, "Amazon Takes Page From Wal-Mart to Prosper on Web," *Wall Street Journal*, November 22, 2002, A1.

33. Catherine Rampell, "Web Retail's Higher-Fliers; Store's Shopping Advantages Are Adding Up in the Market," *Washington Post*, October 28, 2007, F1.

34. "Top 100 Web Retailers: #1 Amazon.com Inc.," *Internet Retailer 2008 Top 500 Guide*, 86.

35. "Top 100 E-Retailers: #2 Staples Inc.," *Internet Retailer 2007 Top 500 Guide*, 56.

36. "Top 100 Web Retailers: #2 Staples Inc.," *Internet Retailer 2008 Top 500 Guide*, 88.

37. Ibid. "#3 Office Depot Inc.," 90.

38. Diana Dilworth, "Dell to Sell Computers in Wal-Mart and Other Retail Stores," *DM News*, May 28, 2007, 2.

39. Bloomberg News, "Dell Agrees to Sell PCs at Retailer in China," *New York Times*, September 25, 2007.

40. "Top 100 Web Retailers: #48 Blue Nile Inc.," *Internet Retailer 2008 Top 500 Guide*, 169.

41. "Top 101-500 Web Retailers: #132 Red Envelope Inc.," *Internet Retailer 2008 Top 500 Guide*, 239.

42. Ibid., "#105 Lillian Vernon Corp.," 226.

43. "Lillian Vernon Downsizing Means Further Shift to Web," *Internet Retailer*, January 4, 2008, www.internetretailer.com.

44. Reuters, "Bankrupt Catalog Co. Lillian Vernon Finds Buyer," April 3, 2008, www.reuters.com/articlePrint?articleId=INNO347984520080404.

45. "Top 100 Web Retailers: #28 Macy's Inc.," *Internet Retailer 2008 Top 500 Guide*, 140.

46. Chantal Todé, "Retailers Commit to Integration," *DMNews*, February 20, 2006, 1, 38.

47. Ibid., 1.

48. "Sales at Restoration Hardware Shift From Stores to Catalogs," *Direct*, December 11, 2007, www.directmag.com.

49. Gary McWilliams, "Why Sears Must Engineer its Own Makeover," *Wall Street Journal*, January 15, 2008, B1-B2.

50. "Top 100 Web Retailers: #83 Restoration Hardware Inc.," *Internet Retailer 2008 Top 500 Guide,* 204.

51. Chantal Todé, "Kinset Takes Retailers Virtual," *DM News*, November 19, 2007, 4.

52. Shop.org Smartbrief Special Report, October 10, 2007. Newsclip citing Gartner Research from *Austin American-Statesman* (Texas), October 15, 2007, www.smartbrief.com.

53. Sarah Sulzberger Perpich, "New Site Storeadore's Shopping Community," *Women's Wear Daily*, December 12, 2007, 15.

54. Michael Grant and Jonathan Margulies, "Marketing Technology: The Bridge to Multichannel Success," *DM News*, February 26, 2007, www.dmnews.com.

55. Sophia Chabbott, "Bulgari Expands With Stores, E-commerce," *Women's Wear Daily*, December 19, 2007, 12.

56. Sharon Edelson, "Bluefly.com Opens Holiday Shop," *Women's Wear Daily*, December 17, 2007, 12.

57. Yahoo! Finance Press Release, "Bluefly.com Introduces 'The Tailor' Online: Men's Shop Channeling the Bespoke Suit Maker of Yesterday," May 14, 2008, http://biz.yahoo.com/bw/080514/20080514005944.html?.v=1&printer=1.

58. "World's Web Users Are Shopping Online," *eMarketer,* February 1, 2008, www.emarketer.com/Articles/Print.aspx?id=1005884.

59. Yahoo! Finance Press Release, "British E-commerce Very Different From Elsewhere in Europe," July 30, 2008, http://biz.yahoo.com/prnews/080730/ukw014.html?.v=101&printer=1. Statistical source: The Pago Report 2008, "Trends in E-commerce Purchasing and Payment Behaviour Based on Real Transactions."

60. National Retail Federation, *2008 Organized Retail Crime Survey Results*, May 2008.

61. Joe LaRocca, vice president of Loss Prevention, National Retail Federation, Washington, DC. Presentation at the New England Retail Crime Symposium, Worcester, MA, September 13, 2007.

62. Cate T. Corcoran, "Brands Fight Online Deluge of Counterfeit Goods," *Women's Wear Daily*, April 4, 2007, 10.

63. Denise Power, "More Data Safety Issues Expected in Year Ahead," *Women's Wear Daily*, January 3, 2008, 5.

64. Denise Power, "Timberland Has Designs on Green," *Women's Wear Daily*, October 10, 2007, 13.

65. Graeme Grant, "Time for Retailers to Up the Ante," statement from National Retail Federation as cited in *E-Commerce Times*, January 3, 2008, www.ecommercetimes.com.

Chapter 2

Components of Multichannel Retailing

Objectives

> To describe the components of multichannel retailing.
> To survey several types of brick-and-mortar retailers.
> To delineate direct-marketing and direct-selling methods.
> To introduce major aspects of online retailing.
> To present alternative forms of electronic retailing.
> To weigh the advantages and disadvantages of multichannel retail components.

>

Multichannel retailers reach customers in a variety of ways. This chapter highlights brick-and-mortar retailing, direct marketing, direct selling, and online and other electronic retailing methods. The characteristics, strengths, and weaknesses of each mode are presented, as is the competitive sphere in which retailers operate. Retailers operate through many different formats but the same business functions—merchandising, operations, finance, human resource management, promotion, and information technology—are performed in each. All multichannel retailers originate from one or more of the retailing channels described in this chapter.

Share of Web Sales by Type of Company* — Table 2.1

TYPE OF COMPANY	TOP 500 WEB SALES BY GROUP	2007 PERCENT SHARE	2006 PERCENT SHARE	2005 PERCENT SHARE
Retail Chain	$40,607,754,241	39.9	41.1	40.3
Catalog/Call Center	$15,695,911,589	15.5	14.4	14.3
Web Only	$31,419,481,972	30.9	30.8	30.2
Consumer Brand Manufacturer	$13,956,558,468	13.7	13.7	15.3
TOTAL	$101,679,706,269	100.0	100.0	100.0

* The type of company owning a Web site in the Top 500 is based on the definition of each company's historical merchandising channel or primary business.

Source: "The Top 500 Guide Overview," Internet Retailer 2008 Top 500 Guide and 2007 Top 500 Guide, 10. Share of Retail Web Sales by type of company. © 2008 Vertical Web Media LLC.

Brick-and-Mortar Retailing

Brick-and-mortar retailers are plentiful and are classified into a few major types. For the purposes of this discussion, coverage is limited to department stores, specialty stores, and discount retailers. **Department stores** are retail companies that occupy large facilities and carry broad assortments of goods organized by buy use, function, and brand. **Specialty stores** are retail outlets that present large selections of highly focused limited lines of merchandise in small or large facilities. **Discounters** are retailers that buy and sell at low prices and depend on high volume to be profitable.

In examining various types of brick-and-mortar retailers, characteristics such as size, target market, merchandise, image, pricing policy, turnover, gross margins, operational procedures, and location strategies are important. Strengths, weaknesses, challenges, and survival tactics are included in the discussion that follows.

Brick-and-mortar stores dominate sales across all channels used by retailers. In 2004 retail chains accounted for approximately 39 percent of sales of the top 400 retail Web sites. Pure-play sites accounted for approximately 27 percent. In 2007, based on sales of the top 500 retail Web sites, retail chains' share had increased slightly to 39.9 percent and pure-play sites increased to 30.9 percent. The increase in retail chain, Web-only, and catalog sales reflects declining sales of consumer brand manufacturers.[1] Over time retail companies have been encroaching on sales previously generated by their merchandise suppliers. The complete share breakdown for 2007 is shown in Table 2.1.

2.1

Saks Fifth Avenue is a limited-line department/specialty store targeting upper-income shoppers at lifestyle shopping centers like The Summit in Birmingham, Alabama. [Source: Photograph provided by Lynda Poloian.]

All retailers share common concerns regarding merchandising and operations. Brick-and-mortar stores are particularly concerned with location and layout, product display, and customer service.

> Department Stores

Although all department stores operate from large buildings—many in multi-stored facilities in major cities—there are distinctions between major types. Attributes based on merchandise carried, price points, target markets, and image help differentiate full-line and limited-line stores.

Full-Line versus Limited-Line Stores

From an organizational standpoint, each department in a department store is operated as a separate unit, and merchandise is grouped according to similarity. **Full-line department stores** carry both hard and soft lines of merchandise. Examples include Macy's, Bloomingdale's, Kohl's, and Belk stores. **Limited-line department stores** are retail companies that usually focus on upmarket soft lines. Stores such as Saks Fifth Avenue, Nordstrom, and Neiman Marcus share many merchandising and operating characteristics with full-line department stores. Also called department/specialty stores, these upmarket retailers carry nationally branded and designer merchandise as well as private-label brands in stores large enough to be shopping center anchors or freestanding stores. Saks Fifth Avenue's freestanding location at The Summit in Birmingham, Alabama—an outdoor lifestyle center—is illustrated in Figure 2.1.

38   Unit I > **The Road to Multichannel Retailing**

Both full-line and limited-line department stores have depth in most merchandise classifications and provide wide varieties of services.

Target Market and Pricing Strategies

Full-line department stores provide merchandise for all ages, but that is not the only determinant of target market. Lifestyle factors, brand preferences, and other demographics such as income and ethnic background are equally important.

J. C. Penney directs its merchandising efforts to the middle class. Customers want name brands and fashion as do their Bloomingdale's counterparts, but the average household income of the Penney shopper is significantly lower. Prices at J. C. Penney are lower and merchandise selections are geared to less urbane customers.

Target markets of limited-line stores are more narrowly defined and price levels typically are higher than in full-line department stores. Limited-line department stores that focus on apparel sell fashion-forward merchandise and operate on gross margins of about 50 percent.

Department Store Weaknesses

Department store market share has declined in the last two decades in the face of increased competition, lackluster merchandise, loss of focus, excessive promotions, industry consolidation, and inconsistent customer service. In the 1980s and 1990s department stores competed primarily against one another, perhaps becoming somewhat complacent. Aggressive specialty and discount stores challenged their lofty position in the marketplace. Competitive pressure intensified as off-price discounters, category killers, catalogs, and online retailers drew customers.

Traditional department stores are more conservative in their selection of merchandise than upmarket limited-line department stores and many specialty stores. Department store brands are perceived as ordinary and redundant when compared with the specialists. In recent years, innovation, once the lifeblood of department stores, lagged. Some of the apparent stagnation and reticence to take risks was due to pressure from shareholders to perform well financially. Merchants seemed unwilling to take chances on new vendors offering unproved merchandise. As a result, customers looking for fashion-forward merchandise preferred to shop elsewhere.

Industry consolidation also contributes to mundane merchandising. As companies make extensive acquisitions and become behemoth organizations, they adopt mass merchandising tactics. Larger organizations benefit from economies of scale

This Polo Ralph Lauren shop is well positioned in a department store for maximum exposure of the popular apparel brand. [Source: Photograph provided by Lynda Poloian.]

when they purchase large quantities of goods, but with this advantage comes the risk of more conservative merchandising and fewer exclusive products for customers.

In order to compete, department stores cut prices and promoted sales incessantly. Most analysts agree that the combination of these factors contributed to the loss of focus and market share experienced by department stores. Over time they were no longer perceived as leaders but, rather, as less competitive members of the retail pack.

Department Store Strengths

Department stores have attempted to win back market share in several ways. Some have combined the best aspects of specialty store retailing and branded merchandise by adding store-within-a-store formats featuring internationally known megabrand apparel lines like Polo Ralph Lauren and products by home furnishings guru Martha Stewart. A Polo Ralph Lauren in-store shop is shown in Figure 2.2.

Department stores achieve higher gross margins through private-label merchandise programs. **Private-label** goods are manufactured to store specifications and bear the retailer's name or other brand names created by the retailer. Examples include apparel brands INC or Alfani at Macy's, and Arizona and the newer American Living lines at J. C. Penney. The American Living lines of apparel and home furnishings are produced in partnership with Polo Ralph Lauren. Private labeling helps build brand awareness and consumer loyalty. One of the key indicators of change in a store is fresh brands and merchandise.

Department stores are also reaching out to underserved markets. Kohl's is bringing in new brands like Vera Wang to attract teenage shoppers. In other venues

2.3 Retailers are reinvigorating store services by adding nail-express counters. [Source: Photograph provided by Lynda Poloian.]

experimental kitchens and nail express bars have been added as retailers reconnect with shoppers. An example of an in-store specialty service is shown in Figure 2.3.

Traditional brick-and-mortar department stores have also moved into new markets by opening online stores. Online stores are a natural and necessary extension to business practices as department stores redefine their roles in the marketplace. All department stores now have them and occasionally have added independent Web sites for key brands as J. C. Penney did for Arizona. Although department stores continue to face intense competition, many are rising to the challenge admirably and are becoming recognized as truly exciting places to shop.

> Specialty Stores

Lauded for being on top of trends, delivering excellent customer service, and adapting to change more quickly than department stores, specialty stores may be single-unit sole proprietorships or huge domestic and international corporate chains. There are specialty stores for all merchandise categories—clothing, shoes, accessories, food, appliances, automotive supplies, home electronics equipment, furniture, toys, home furnishings, jewelry, health and beauty, books, and music, to name only a few. The service sector also has its share of retailers. Big-screen television installers, computer repair firms, photo finishers, and spas are all specialty retailers. Boutiques in department stores or stand-alone specialty stores that feature top-of-the-line merchandise collections by international designers such as Prada or Giorgio Armani also fall into this category.

Target Market and Pricing Strategies

Instead of trying to create broad appeal, specialty stores define narrower markets by age, interest, gender, income level, ethnic origin, lifestyle, and fashion orientation. Apparel collections by Prada are higher priced, more fashion-forward, and more exclusive than the mass-merchandised goods produced for the George line at Walmart. **Collections** are definitive, very expensive apparel lines produced by designers. Privé by Giorgio Armani and Prorsum by Burberry are examples.

To reach a broader market, some designers produce merchandise in two or more price categories that are sold in separate stores. **Diffusion lines** are merchandise that is produced and sold at lower prices than designer collections. Armani has collection as well as diffusion stores. Marc by Marc Jacobs is an example of a menswear diffusion line.

In their quest for global customers, many specialty retailers, such as apparel chain H&M, designer Donna Karan, and athletic outfitter Nike, have built flagship stores in major cities such as London, Paris, Tokyo, and New York. The opening of 20,000-square-foot monuments like these is an indication that power has shifted from department to specialty stores. This swing is evident from a sales growth perspective. From 2006 to 2007 apparel and accessories store sales grew 6.6 percent compared with department stores sales, which declined by 0.4 percent.[2]

Specialty Store Strengths

By concentrating on one kind of customer and one or a few types of products, specialty chains reduce risk. Several characteristics help these specialists to excel:

> Stores are easier to merchandise when targeted customers have the same tastes and buying power. Even if stores are geographically dispersed, this characteristic may remain true.
> High visibility accompanies intense saturation of the marketplace and is another reason for the success of apparel specialty stores. For retailers like Victoria's Secret, H&M, Zara, Arden B., Abercrombie & Fitch, and Forever 21, the store is the brand (Figure 2.4).
> Most specialty stores experience faster turnover of goods than department stores due to the nature of their business and to efficient sourcing and distribution systems.
> Apparel retailers that also sell online benefit from the growth trend experienced by online apparel retailers.

2.4 Specialty store chains like Abercrombie & Fitch have high visibility in the markets they serve. [Source: Najlah Feanny/Corbis.]

According to the International Council of Shopping Centers (ICSC), some specialty apparel retailers that are actively seeking new locations are J. Crew, Tommy Hilfiger, BCBG Max Azria, and Brooks Brothers.[3] Aggressive expansion plans indicate strength within a company and bode well for the specialty store sector. Retailers may revise expansion plans if downturns in the economy negatively affect sales.

Specialty Store Weaknesses

Downsides to specialty retailing are often the direct inverse of the positive aspects characterizing this type of retailer:

> Specialty stores are vulnerable to oversaturation. High visibility in the marketplace helps build a brand but it discourages exclusivity.
> With rapidly turning merchandise, every season has to be on-trend or sales suffer.
> Specialty retailers have to be especially cognizant of changes in customer preferences or of outgrowing a customer base on which they have become overly dependent.

With mixed results some specialty retailers have spun off new formats to combat shifts in their target markets and to grow their businesses. In 2005 Gap opened Forth & Towne, an apparel line intended to answer the needs of aging baby boomer women. Eighteen months later Gap closed the operation when sales did not meet the company's expectations. American Eagle Outfitters opened Martin + Osa in 2007 with much the same goal in mind. Early feedback indicated that Martin + Osa complimented other American Eagle chains. Other specialists that carefully monitor the retail environment for new opportunities may benefit from this strategy.

> Discount Stores

A product of the 1960s and 1970s, discount stores have increased in number, along with the income levels and sophistication of their customers. Fashion departments and electronic goods were added to meet changing demands as customers began to think of discount stores as places to buy more than cheap T-shirts and household necessities.

Key Characteristics

Attracting customers with low prices, discount stores are the top choice of many consumer groups in the United States. Prices in discount stores are almost always lower than those in department and specialty stores. It is difficult to pass up a 12-ounce package of Starbuck's coffee for $7.00 in Walmart when you know you will pay at least $9.49 in your local supermarket. Turnover is high and gross margins are lower than in department and specialty stores.

Types of Discount Retailers

General merchandise discounters, superstores, category killers, warehouse clubs, and deep discounters are highlighted in this section. These discounters are considered big-box retailers because they operate out of cavernous structures. **Big box retailers** are stores of 70,000 to 100,000 square feet or more that are usually operated by large discounters or mass merchants, although the term routinely is used to define any huge physical property. Off-price retailers and factory outlet stores—the specialists of discount retailing—also operate from large stores but not the big boxes described above.

General Merchandise Discounters Decor is minimal in Walmart superstores compared with Macy's department stores, but it is nonetheless effective for the discounter's purposes. **General merchandise discounters** are discount department stores that carry broad assortments of low-price merchandise in large storefronts with minimal decor. **Superstores** are huge retail stores, usually over 150,000 square feet, that combine general merchandise and food under one roof. Lighting in dis-

When Target added quick-food restaurants to its upscale discount stores, it created convenience for guests and co-branding opportunities with Pizza Hut. [Source: Photograph provided by Lynda Poloian.]

count stores tends to be bold rather than subtle, materials are more utilitarian than aesthetic, floor plans are more structured in appearance, and merchandise is displayed compactly. As the superstore format evolves, more discount department stores are raising their ceilings, widening aisles, adding numerous amenities for their customers, and looking for sustainability in their product and energy choices.

Discount stores such as Walmart and Target usually seek locations in community shopping centers or in freestanding locations on the periphery of cities. This tendency is changing as key players look to urban sites and anchor positions in regional malls. Discount department stores are becoming more like than unlike other retailers as new versions of these big box retailers emerge. Target went upscale, building its brand on a quasi-French "Targeé" image to reach its primarily young female market. In-store fast food restaurants like Pizza Hut add convenience for Target's customers, reinforcing brand and partnership recognition for both retailers as shown in Figure 2.5.

Category Killers Overgrown specialty stores with discount overtones are called category killers. **Category killers** are specialty superstores that focus on limited merchandise categories and great breadth and depth of assortments. Several examples illustrate the array of retailers that fit the description. The Sports Authority is strong in sales of sporting goods. Home Depot and Lowe's represent home centers and do-it-yourself (DIY) stores. Barnes & Noble dominates the book market, and Best Buy, the home electronics trade. Even household pets are not ignored and can shop with their families or attend obedience classes at PetSmart or Petco.

Off-Price Discounters The philosophy of off-price discounting is based on high volume gained through lower markup and faster inventory turnover—12 or 13 times a year. **Off-price retailers** are specialty discount stores that sell branded products at 20 to 60 percent less than traditional specialty or department stores. Fashion classifications sell well in this format, although off-price retailing is not limited strictly to apparel and accessories. Many traditional retailers, especially department stores, emulate off-price tactics by making advantageous buys from their vendors. Off-price companies include T.J. Maxx, Marshall's, and A.J. Wright, all owned by TJX Corporation, as well as Ross Stores, Loehman's, and Dress Barn.

Warehouse Clubs Bringing bulk quantities at competitive prices to their members is the objective of warehouse clubs. **Warehouse clubs** are large-format, bare-bones retail stores that sell diverse merchandise and services to business and individual members. They operate on very low gross margins and markups average 8 to 10 percent on most products. High volume on peak-demand product categories is the key to profitability as it is in all discount operations. Individuals and businesses pay nominal annual membership fees to shop at stores like Costco and Sam's Club. Costco has extended its reach through online stores and has taken calculated risks by moving into innovative product categories such as caskets. Sam's Club expanded its market to include high-income customers by offering expensive jewelry and items for the home. An outdoor grille that looks more like a kitchen counter and is priced at just under $1,000 exemplifies the company's initiative to reach more affluent customers (Figure 2.6).

Factory Outlet Stores Originally located on or near the manufacturing premises, factory outlet stores lend another dimension to discounting. **Factory outlets** are company-owned stores that sell a manufacturer's overruns, seconds, irregulars, or sample products.

Today most factory outlet stores are located in outlet malls that are destinations for countless shoppers. Prices on comparable merchandise initially were intended to be lower than those in department or specialty stores but gradually rose as the outlet industry matured. As a result, pricing in outlet stores has come under close scrutiny by consumers and retailers.

2.6 Sam's Club flouts its warehouse roots and brings luxury items like this elaborate $995 outdoor grill to its members. *[Source: Photograph provided by Lynda Poloian.]*

<u>Deep Discounters</u> Filling the needs of lower-income shoppers and bargain hunters are deep discounters like Big Lots, Family Dollar Stores, 99 Cent Stores, Tuesday Mornings, and others. **Deep discounters** are big box discount retailers that offer limited and changing product lines in no-frills environments at very low prices. They also may carry distressed merchandise including irregulars, seconds, and clearance goods from other retailers. **Distressed merchandise** includes goods sold by deep discounters that were purchased from retailers or manufacturers with surplus or slow-selling stock.

Mergers and acquisitions have changed the face of retailing in the discounting sector as they have in other brick-and-mortar sectors. The acquisition of Kmart by Edward Lampert in 2005 and the subsequent purchase of Sears and name change to Sears Holdings may be indicative of future changes for discount retailers.

> Brick-and-Mortar Retailers Encapsulated

Reflecting on the familiar retail examples mentioned in the previous section points up several important characteristics shared by brick-and-mortar retailers.

> > Stores with a physical presence convey three-dimensional excitement through their store layouts and designs.

> Visual merchandising is most effective when color, texture, lighting, and other sensory stimulation are evident.
> Customer service is extended on a one-on-one basis.
> Most brick-and-mortar retailers trade through two or more channels.
> Brick-and-mortar stores are particularly effective brand builders.

This discussion of brick-and-mortar retailers would be remiss if it did not include food retailers, including supermarkets, specialty food stores, convenience stores, and quick-serve and other restaurants. Though most are not triple-plays, many are dual-channel retailers with brick-and-mortar stores and transactional or nontransactional Web sites.

Tesco, the British supermarket and superstore retailer, was one of the first retailers to open a successful online grocery service. It has served as a model of success for other retailers. In addition, Tesco introduced a chain of convenience stores called Fresh & Easy in California in 2007. This was the company's first appearance in the United States although it has a strong presence in Europe and Asia. The new format is expected to compete directly with Walmart and many convenience store chains.

Brick-and-mortar stores are strong forces when used independently but grow exponentially when combined with other avenues of growth. Box 2.1 describes the startup of RobotGalaxy, an innovative specialty store that combines the best of brick-and-mortar retailing with an interactive Web presence. Direct marketing, direct selling, and e-retailing frequently are channels of choice when brick-and-mortar retailers become multichannel.

Direct Marketing and Direct Selling

This section examines the differences between direct marketing and direct selling, identifies key terms and techniques used by direct marketers, and surveys the major tools used to reach customers. The strengths and weaknesses for retailers of catalogs, direct mail, and telemarketing are highlighted. Distinguishing between direct marketing and direct selling is first on our agenda. Many multichannel retailers use both methods but each has its own attributes.

What's the Buzz? Box 2.1

> **Now Entering a New Galaxy**

When the movie *Robots* appeared on the big screen in 2005, its tagline was "You can shine no matter what you're made of." At RobotGalaxy, a new interactive store experience that caters to 5- to 12-year-olds, the chance to assemble their own robots, program them to say their names, and decorate them with an assortment of decals has kids beaming.

Modeled after specialty retailer Build-A-Bear, RobotGalaxy invites young explorers (primarily boys) to customize robots using various motorized parts, accessories, and decals, along with programmable features like sound, lights, and speech. Prices range from $27 to $70.

The universe's first RobotGalaxy stores are in Freehold, N.J., and West Nyack, N.Y. Kids who don't live near one of the two stores can get in on the action by visiting www.robotgalaxy.com, where they can build their own robot while interacting with other "explorers" via games, membership, and the like.

The concept is the brainchild of Oliver Mitchell, a Manhattan entrepreneur who credits his son with providing the inspiration; Mitchell approached the retail industry veteran Ken Pilot with the idea. Pilot, who was launching the Martin + Osa division of American Eagle Outfitters at the time, says, "I loved the concept, I loved his passion, loved his energy. And what I liked most was that it addressed a place in retail that wasn't being addressed."

Pilot, a former president of Gap brands, now goes by the title chief galaxy officer. He believes RobotGalaxy can reach 70 stores within five years.

Source: "Trends," compiled by Stores Editors, Stores, *January 2008, 16.*

> Direct Marketing versus Direct Selling

The Direct Marketing Association defines **direct marketing** as "an integrative process of addressable communication that uses one or more advertising media to effect at any location, a measurable sales, lead, retail purchase, or charitable donation, with this activity analyzed on a database for the development of ongoing mutually beneficial relationships between marketers and customer, prospects, or donors."[4]

Direct marketing has several attributes:

> Advertising pieces are characterized by the sense of immediacy that they convey to customers and prospects.
> Brand awareness is stressed across all direct marketing vehicles.

Trying out an array of products in an informal setting is one of the advantages of direct selling. *[Source: AP Photo/Mike Mergen.]*

> Contact methods are flexible.
> Direct marketers value channel integration. Many brick-and-mortar retailers use direct marketing techniques to reach their customers and online stores use direct marketing to drive customers to their Web sites.

Marketers in the United States spent $166.5 billion on direct marketing advertising in both business and nonprofit sectors in 2006. That investment generated $1.93 trillion in sales, which constitutes 10.3 percent of the U.S. gross domestic product (GDP).[5]

In contrast to direct marketing, **direct selling** is a personal form of selling that involves meeting with customers face-to-face. The Direct Selling Association provides this definition: "The sale of a consumer product or service, person-to-person, away from a fixed retail location."[6]

In direct selling, independent salespeople market products and services to customers. Depending on the company, the salespeople may be called distributors, representatives, consultants, or salespeople. Products are sold primarily through in-home product demonstrations, parties, and one-on-one selling.[7] Direct selling also takes place in the workplace as representatives set up displays during coffee or lunch breaks, or after work. Handing out samples is a big part of home parties for direct sellers as illustrated in Figure 2.7.

> ### Direct Marketing Terminology

Like all specialized business areas, direct marketing has its own vocabulary to describe standard operating practices. Most of these practices are used by multichannel retailers and are no longer the exclusive realm of direct marketers. They include:

> *Prospecting* Seeking qualified potential customers through screening and analysis of database information is called **prospecting**. Most direct marketers indicate that future customers are very much like present customers. Using customer profiling, probability models, and lifestyle analysis, direct marketers identify prospects.
> *Database Marketing* **Database marketing** is the process of capturing and using observable and quantifiable information about customer behavior and aspirations. Information is monitored, used, updated, and recombined to maximize efficiency and meet business objectives.
> *Mailing Lists* Collections of names and addresses of present or potential customers comprise **mailing lists**. Lists can be compiled in-house through use of retail transactions and online contact information or developed through secondary sources such as club memberships, census information, or list brokers.
> *Recency, Frequency, Monetary Value (RFM)* **Recency, frequency, and monetary value** comprise the set of measurements used by direct marketers to judge how recently customers placed an order, how often customers do business with the firm, and how much they spend per order.
> *Predictive Modeling* **Predictive modeling** is the practice of examining data concerning RFM of past sales to identify key prospects or future intentions of current customers.
> *Fulfillment* Using physical distribution systems efficiently to deliver products to consumers in a timely manner is called **fulfillment**.
> *Lifetime Value* The acknowledgment by direct marketers that the true worth of a customer to a company is not based on one large or a few occasional sales, but on sales generated over a long period of time, is reflected in **lifetime value.** In essence, this is the amount of money spent by a customer over time.
> *Customer Relationship Management (CRM)* The total company effort to satisfy the needs of all customers over time forms the core of CRM. **Customer relationship management** incorporates gathering and using database information to reach customers more effectively, identify their needs more specifically, and direct promotional and selling initiatives more precisely. This technique is discussed in more detail in Chapter 6.

> Direct Marketing Methods

Several vehicles are used to reach customers, including catalogs, direct mail, and telephone. Direct marketers have used catalogs and other direct mail pieces for some time. In the past these vehicles were used mainly by firms that concentrated on mail order, not in tandem with other marketing methods. Now that retailers are using multichannel strategies, they are synchronizing direct marketing activities with brick-and-mortar and online stores as they fulfill the needs of customers.

The strengths and weaknesses of each option for retailers are discussed next, along with comparisons to other channels where appropriate. The strengths and weaknesses to customers are covered in Chapter 3.

Catalogs

Never before have catalog shoppers had so many goods from which to choose. Catalog companies offer everything from expensive global positioning system (GPS) instruments and environmentally safe vacuum cleaners to apparel for tall men, petite women, and household pets. Catalogs can be a pure-play channel for a company or part of a multichannel initiative. Noncatalog companies such as entertainment businesses and airlines also use catalogs as a vehicle to reach their customers.

Catalog Selling versus Store Retailing Reviewing several differences between catalog and store retailing illuminates some of the key attributes of catalogs:

> Catalogs create mood through color, layout, photography, and paper quality, whereas retail stores rely on lighting, carpeting, music, and other design elements to create ambiance.
> Catalog retailers target a captive audience in their homes or offices for repeat sales whereas stores depend on foot traffic.
> Carry-over time is longer for catalogs than for item advertising or direct mail pieces distributed by stores. **Carry-over** is the period of time between the receipt of a catalog by a person and the sales actually generated by the catalog. Catalogs may remain in a home longer than other forms of direct marketing, and the pass-along rate to other individuals is higher.
> Catalogs present a significant percentage of repeat items whereas stores rely heavily on the continuous flow of new merchandise.

> Some catalog companies send the identical catalog under two different covers at close time intervals to different customers. This technique, which is used to test the strength of cover merchandise and to gain insight about customers, is impossible to replicate in a physical facility.
> Catalogs can vary the size and number of pages, but stores must work within the constraints of their existing square footage in most cases.
> When something is out of stock, direct marketers must back order or cancel the order. A brick-and-mortar store associate more easily can sell comparable items or suggest another option or brand.
> Catalog companies fulfill each item's projected demand whereas store inventory levels are planned in relation to overall sales and turnover expectations. However, the time it takes to move goods from producer to customer market is compressed as technology helps make multichannel planning decisions more efficient.
> To measure productivity, many catalog retailers use sales per square inch of catalog page whereas most stores use sales per square foot of floor space.
> Catalogs are accessible 24 hours a day whereas most department stores only maintain extended hours on special occasions. For example, it has become the norm for large department stores to extend their normal hours of operation in the weeks before Christmas. Macy's was open round-the-clock at its flagship store in Manhattan and in several other area branches for the last three days before Christmas in 2007.[8]

<u>Weaknesses of Catalog Selling</u> Many of the positive attributes of catalog retailing are identical or similar to those in the online sector. Some of the drawbacks of catalog retailing also apply to e-retailing:

> Fit, tactile, and quality assessment problems are major problems of catalog and online selling—especially for customers who intend to purchase soft goods and apparel. To help solve these problems, companies provide liberal return policies, fabric swatches, and often postage-paid return mailing labels.
> Costs of doing business increase when catalog production and paper costs and postage rates rise. Many catalog companies sell online concurrently with mailed printed versions to offset increases as they build sales in another channel with different cost parameters.

> The issue of consumer privacy is a touchy one for retailers. Reaching prospective customers is necessary in order to remain in business but becomes detrimental when customers find the contact intrusive or the arrival of scores of print catalogs excessive. The Direct Marketing Association (DMA) has taken a proactive stance on the consumer privacy issue. Direct marketing companies, by subscribing to the DMA Mailing Preference Service and maintaining in-house name removal lists, ensure that the public does not receive unwanted materials. Further discussion of this topic appears in Chapter 3.

> The issue of redundant merchandising, mentioned as a negative factor in the section on department store retailing, is also a problem in direct marketing. So is the "me-too" merchandising that is apparent in a competitive market. An observation by an executive at Millard Group, a leading catalog mailing list broker, noted that in one season several well-known catalog retailers, including Orvis, Home Depot, Lands' End, and Brookstone, featured similar wooden furniture on their covers.[9]

Retailers of all persuasions, including Target, Home Depot, and Pier 1, have experimented with catalogs as multichannel vehicles. For decades Neiman Marcus has had a world-famous catalog operation. Today virtually all catalog companies also operate on the Internet. Catalogs can be requested, and prices compared, online. FlipSeek.com is an online directory of catalogs. Hundreds of catalogs are included, and the directory features a price comparison tool so that customers can shop for the best prices on specific items across all catalogs featured on the Web site.[10]

Direct Mail

Consider the myriad offers that reach us through the mail. Coupons, sales letters, sweepstakes incentives, and invitations to try a new product or service—all try to entice us. Timeshare resorts in the Caribbean, financial services, book clubs, DVD sellers, and the U.S. Postal Service use this technique to reach old and new customers. **Direct mail** involves sending customers or prospects printed pieces through the mail that are designed to promote a special offer. Usually the offer is for one or more closely related products or services—a narrower focus than a catalog.

2.8

This direct mail piece featuring a pumpkin motif is an eye-catcher. *[Source: Service Credit Union, Portsmouth, NH; sample provided by Lynda Poloian.]*

The following examples show the positive, sometimes humorous, and ultimately effective uses of direct mail.

> During the Thanksgiving holiday period, a credit union sent a bulk mailing consisting of a standard size see-through plastic envelope that contained an attractive pumpkin card stating: "With 5.24% financing, Service Credit Union can turn a pumpkin . . ." Of course you had to open the card to see that the offer was for a car loan and the Cinderella-style pitch was: ". . . into the coach of your dreams" (Figure 2.8).
> A red, white, and blue envelope arrived from Sears with a bold statement addressed to me. It read: "Lynda Poloian, transform your kitchen into a dream kitchen." We have all experienced this type of personalization. When it coincides with the customer's needs at that moment in time, the direct-mail piece is doubly effective. Use of strong patriotic colors also intensifies the effectiveness of the offer.
> The U.S. Postal Service sent a multipiece direct mailing to small business owners alerting them to the benefits of direct mailing. Out popped a huge cardboard cutout of a Tyrannosaurus rex suggesting that, "without mail your marketing message might not withstand the test of time." In this case, sometimes bigger *is* better.

Chapter 2 > **Components of Multichannel Retailing**

Companies that exceed customer expectations and trigger awareness of a product or service may gain a deeper commitment from customers. Versatility is key as retailers seek the best direct marketing methods to fulfill their multichannel objectives.

Strengths of Direct Mail This method of direct marketing offers several advantages to retailers:

> Direct mail is very effective when targeting market segments. For example, a study showed that 85 percent of women aged 25 to 44 read direct-mail pieces compared with 53 percent who said they read e-mail advertisements.[11] This information is useful to companies that sell to women in that age bracket.
> Direct mail can be used in fresh ways to drive business. To increase traffic to its produce vendors at the famous Pike Place Market in Seattle one summer, the local development authority sent $5 coupons to local residents, households outside the regular market, and businesses for use as handouts to their customers. The initiative earned a 4 to 5 percent redemption rate and was considered an excellent promotion for the farmers' market.[12]
> Direct mail is used as a sales driver to encourage customers to visit brick-and-mortar stores and Web sites. It also is used for prospecting and for telemarketing follow-up.

Weaknesses of Direct Mail There are several challenges to companies that use direct mail:

> The mobility of the population is one factor that compromises the efficiency of direct marketing firms. Direct mail companies—and catalog retailers—constantly work to keep their mailing lists up-to-date. This is not an easy task when you consider that in the United States 39.8 million people moved their residence in 2005–2006.[13]
> Engaging customers is another challenge faced by companies that use direct mail. An engaging envelope, free offer, odd-size envelope, brilliant graphics, and personalization all help to entice customers to open their mail.
> Rising postal and printing cost affect direct mailers and catalog companies, yet the medium remains a creative and cost-effective way to reach customers.

Telemarketing

The telephone provides retailers with a cost-effective means of generating incremental revenue and expanding market penetration through telemarketing. **Telemarketing** is the practice of placing calls to customers for the purposes of generating sales or leads. **Call centers,** sometimes called "boiler rooms," are company telecommunication facilities from which telemarketers place calls. Historically about 60 percent of call centers have been located in rural areas.[14] Women, minorities, and second-jobbers comprise the majority of telemarketers. Today, many call centers are setting up in offshore locations and it has become common to be greeted by a voice from India, Sri Lanka, the Caribbean, or Mexico.

Location scouts are often used to select appropriate locations for call centers in foreign lands. A scout in Mexico finds it advantageous to research prospective workers at shopping malls. He informally studies the local culture, gauges customer service skills, and looks for evidence of good work ethics in the people he observes. Traits that indicate receptiveness to U.S. customers are highly valued because telemarketers call them regularly.[15]

Strengths of Telemarketing The telephone is a unique medium. A summary of the major advantages of telemarketing to retailers illustrates its effectiveness:

> *Person-to-Person Contact* Although not a face-to-face means of contact, telemarketing by well-trained representatives can achieve high sales rates and can recoup the missing personal touch through knowledgeable, friendly telephone service. Telephone representatives at Omaha Steaks consistently perform as well when handling reorder or customer service follow-up calls as they do when new customers phone in an order.

> *Immediate Response* Telemarketing, when properly structured and controlled, permits immediate statistical feedback as well as meaningful market information from customers. RFM statistics routinely are gathered, and well-trained and sensitive telemarketers also detect cues regarding product preferences that perhaps are learned from customers in no other way.

> *Incremental Method* The phone can be used alone, but when used in conjunction with other customer contact methods it increases the overall effectiveness of all media. Emphasizing Web sites or toll-free telephone numbers may enhance mail response. The immediacy of response is

attractive to many retailers as a means of order taking, encouraging multiple purchases, upgrading initial selections, cross-selling, and supporting online sales.
> *Cost Accountability* Like mail, the telephone is a totally cost accountable medium, enabling the user to track multiple performance variables such as cost per name, per call, per lead, and per order.
> *Careful Targeting* Prospective customers are selected on the basis of special interests, past sales behavior, and geography with relative ease via the telephone.
> *Inbound and Outbound Capabilities* Retailers utilizing telephone communications have flexibility. **Inbound telephone calls** are those that are initiated by customers or prospective customers. Inbound calls from customers primed to order are handled efficiently and provide customer service staff an opportunity to encourage multiple sales. **Outbound telephone calls** are those that are initiated by a company seeking sales, providing customer service, or prescreening prospective customers. Outbound calls allow the retailer to solicit new business, follow up on orders, provide caring customer service, and generate positive public relations.

Weaknesses of Telemarketing Like all other types of business, telemarketing poses its own challenges:

> *High Hang-up Rates* Many people monitor their calls and when they see an unfamiliar number either don't answer or hang up the phone as soon as they discern that a telemarketer has initiated the call.
> *Difficulty Reaching Customers* Due to heavy work schedules, many potential customers are not at home during the day to receive calls.
> *Invasion of Privacy* Some people feel affronted by telemarketers and do not want to be bothered by unsolicited phone calls.
> *Security Concerns* Customers may be reluctant to use credit cards over the telephone because they do not view the contact method as secure.

It may be difficult to gain the interest of customers via the telephone; however, retailers recognize that customers who often shop at their stores sometimes will want to shop by mail, electronically, and by telephone. Many retailers have gained respect for telemarketing and have integrated it into their multichannel plans because it works.

Direct mail, catalogs, and telephone once dominated direct marketing methods, but use of Internet marketing is increasing dramatically. Retailers recognize that changes are occurring across all contact methods and channels, and they are adapting to them.

> Direct Selling Methods

Despite the depersonalization of some electronic retailing options, many customers welcome the personal touch provided by direct selling. According to the Direct Selling Association, direct sales in the United States was $30.8 billion in 2007. In that year the industry employed 15.2 million salespeople—most of whom work part time.[16]

The two basic types of direct selling situations are face-to-face and remote selling. **Face-to face** selling takes place in homes or the workplace and accounts for 75.2 percent of all direct selling. Of the face-to-face portion, 67.1 percent is conducted one-on-one, 28.9 percent is done via party plan or group situations, and 3.4 percent is through customer-initiated direct order. **Remote selling** is done on the telephone or Internet and accounts for 24.8 percent of all direct sales.[17]

Face-to-Face Direct Selling

Many types of products are sold one-on-one or through home parties or other group situations. Clothing, accessories, and personal care products are the most popular category, accounting for about one-third of sales. Face-to-face selling may rely on individual or group contact methods.

Individual Contact When a salesperson calls on an individual customer personally at home or at the customer's place of business, contact is made by appointment or through random door-to-door contact. **Consultative selling** is a form of person-to-person selling that is set up by appointment and often done through a referral network. Cutco Cutlery is one of the premier direct selling companies and offers top-quality knives and utility products through a contact network set up by its sales associates. College students make up the bulk of the sales force and draw from friends and family initial contact and sales.

Although the salesperson still controls the direction of interaction when using consultative selling, the customer is put in a position of greater power than in many store environments. Consultative selling is done in-home or in-office by specialists whose expertise is valued by the customer. Home furnishing businesses, kitchen tool, and cosmetics companies frequently use this method.

Party Plan and Group Sales The party plan method encourages in-home or in-office selling to groups invited by the customer/host. Tupperware, Mary Kay, Party Lite, Sarah Coventry, and Arbonne are direct selling firms that use this method to reach customers, although most of these companies also use one-on-one or other contact methods as they seek competitive advantages.

Usually salespersons work from homes or offices giving demonstrations and selling the products. In fact homes are the most popular choice for parties, but because many people work, party plan dealers also bring their wares to places of business and many leave catalogs for future reference or ordering. The shop-at-home format is expected to persist because of its strong social interaction component.

Formerly, direct selling success seemed dependent on moderate to low price points for items that were geared primarily to middle-income families. This myth has been dispelled. In business since 1991, the Worth Collection features expensive apparel, including $1,800 cashmere wraps, at the top of its line. Its representatives sell to professional women and mothers not presently working outside the home. Another direct seller is Bill Blass New York, a division of the famous designer apparel company. Setting up distribution in 2006 and now employing 150 consultants in 30 states, it is considered the first designer direct selling firm.[18] As these examples show, consultative selling is also part of the home-party direct selling domain.

> Remote Selling

Many direct selling firms also sell and provide remote selling online and through telephone service. Mary Kay, the cosmetics company, reports that 90 percent of its orders are placed online.[19] Online selling gives a new dimension to the personal service for which Mary Kay has always been known.

Many original direct selling companies like Avon and Tupperware have become full-fledged multichannel companies. Avon—one of the first members to join the Direct Selling Association—sells through catalogs, brick-and-mortar, online stores, as well as through direct selling methods. Tupperware sells through home and office parties, online, and via marketplace carts in shopping malls (Figure 2.9).

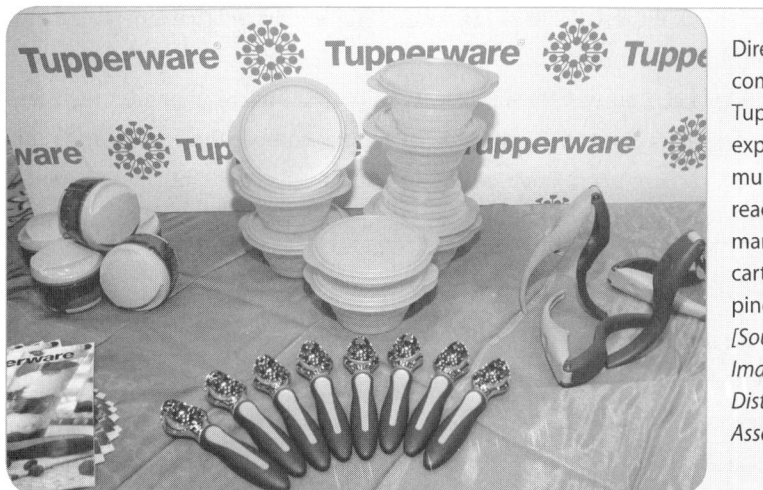

2.9 Direct selling company Tupperware expanded its multichannel reach through marketplace carts in shopping malls. [Source: Getty Images for Distinctive Assets.]

The Body Shop, originally a brick-and-mortar retailer, also operates The Body Shop at Home, its direct selling branch. Independent salespeople sell through face-to-face methods and use e-mail and telephone calling for reorders of the company's popular skin care products and cosmetics. These examples suggest that many direct sellers are confident in their ability to deal proactively with change.

Electronic Retailing

E-retailing is already an important marketing channel for retailers, but its full potential has yet to be realized. Television home shopping, in both broadcast and interactive forms, provides an alternative method of shopping for many people. Infomercials both entertain and educate, often softening the impact before a serious sales pitch occurs. **Infomercials** are television commercials that combine detailed product information, demonstration, and excitement with a sales pitch. Infomercials commonly run thirty minutes, providing ample time to fully engage a viewer.

Electronic kiosks supplement the marketing efforts of some retailers. **Electronic kiosks** are small display units in stores or other locations that use computer technology and often the Internet to generate sales or provide extended customer services. Kiosks provide valuable services for store retailers and busy shoppers. Locating merchandise on the floor, ordering out-of-stock items or sizes, or providing

Chapter 2 > **Components of Multichannel Retailing** 61

information when a sales associate is not available are services that now are being regularly sought by store shoppers.

It is difficult to keep abreast of all aspects of technological change, much less embrace them. Retailers must do both in order to stay competitive. Invariably multichannel retailers require a presence online in addition to doing business in more traditional formats. Electronic retailing also is one of the ways to create a global presence.

> Online Strategies: Reaching the Customer

We are well aware that the Internet has enhanced our professional and social lives, and at times taken over our waking hours and perhaps our sleepless nights. It has allowed us to catch up with friends with whom we had lost touch; research a term paper in record time, and submit it electronically; watch a favorite Hollywood or Bollywood film, or share one we made ourselves with the world. And lest we not forget—shop. It's becoming more difficult to remember a world without online capabilities. Not all people shop online, but the reach of the Web is staggering.

It is not surprising that many of the Top 500 online retailers in terms of sales are also highly rated in terms of customer satisfaction. Based on another study involving *Internet Retailer's* top online retailers done by the research company ForeSee Results, Netflix, QVC, Amazon, and Barnes & Noble were the top-ranking retailers based on customers' evaluations of company Web sites and their online shopping experiences.[20]

It is evident that high achievers perform well across many types of evaluation. Information on reaching online customers follows here and in Chapter 3.

Push and Pull Strategies

Initially Web retailing tended to push information onto the visitors rather than to let the customer pull information from the site. **Push strategies** are used when retailers initiate the selling process. For example, a retailer might send promotional messages to a broad spectrum of potential customers. **Pull strategies** are used when customers initiate the selling process. In this case a customer might contact a retailer for further information.

A push strategy is enlisted as retailers test new products on their Web sites. Retailers have discovered the benefits of pull strategies by letting customers extract information based on their specific interests and needs, and today most retailers use this technique. The shotgun approach that a push strategy implies is less effective than a pull strategy. The implications for merchandising, sales promotion, and customer service strategies are vast.

Most retailers offer gift directories. Using this service, a customer visiting the company's Web site can retrieve information on what a friend or family member wants for a wedding present. Cosmetic companies elicit detailed information regarding skin types and product preferences so that shoppers can benefit from specific product counseling. Bloomingdale's understands that most of its cosmetic business is from customers who are replacing favorite products. For their convenience, the company sells 70 percent of its store merchandise online.[21] Consumers make better product choices and perhaps purchase more products when a pull strategy is used rather than a push strategy.

Merchandise Preferences

In its early incarnations, online retailing worked best for certain types of retailers, including those that carried narrow and deep assortments, targeted highly defined specialty markets, and sold products that did not require close inspection or handling. Initially, it was believed that online sales of apparel would never generate a high percentage of total online sales. Times have changed and growth has been substantial. According to the *Internet Retailer,* 11.9 percent of online sales were attributed to apparel and accessories in 2006. For the first time apparel and accessories outpaced other merchandise categories, with 19.6 percent of total retailers garnering close to $10 billion in sales.[22] Table 2.2 shows 2007 data concerning merchandise categories for the Top 500 Online Retailers.

Shopping Options

The retail repertoire has expanded as online shopping malls, auction sites, and price comparison options add flavor and substance to the competitive online environment. In this environment, the choices customers make and why they make them are of great interest to retailers. Let's identify some of the many options.

Online Shopping Malls Online malls provide plenty of opportunity for dedicated shopping. Type in "online fashion mall" and you will get at least 150,000 hits on Google. They are not all appropriate to our search, but the volume alerts us to the want satisfaction that may be ours for a click. Many of the newer online malls combine social interaction with a wealth of popular brands and retailers. We depend

Table 2.2 Online Merchandise Category Performance for the Top 500 Web Retailers, 2007

CATEGORY	NUMBER OF RETAILERS	WEB SALES IN CATEGORY	2007 PERCENT OF TOTAL RETAILERS	2007 PERCENT OF TOTAL SALES
Apparel/Accessories	105	$12,359,338,597	21.0	12.2
Books/CDs/DVDs	27	4,142,811,147	5.4	4.1
Computers/Electronics	56	23,337,286,413	11.2	23.0
Flowers/Gifts	14	1,350,133,449	2.8	1.3
Food/Drug	21	2,372,420,854	4.2	2.3
Hardware/Home Improvement	30	1,366,388,492	6.0	1.3
Health/Beauty	24	2,453,699,146	4.8	2.4
Housewares/Home Furnishings	58	3,891,153,371	11.6	3.8
Jewelry	12	1,051,518,635	2.4	1.0
Mass Merchant/Department Store	29	29,309,294,731	5.8	28.8
Office Supplies	17	13,970,256,830	3.4	13.7
Specialty/Nonapparel	59	3,416,118,871	11.8	3.4
Sporting Goods	29	1,535,992,980	5.8	1.5
Toys/Hobbies	19	1,123,292,753	3.8	1.1
TOTAL	500	$101,679,706,269	100.0	100.0

Source: "Top 500 Guide Overview," *Internet Retailer 2008 Top 500 Guide,* 8. Comparing the Top 500 Categories. © 2008 Vertical Web Media LLC.

on our friends and other experts to guide us, so we appreciate the reviews of prior customers and hope their remarks make our shopping experience a superior one. For example, Yub.com (you're right, it's "buy" spelled backward) brings us almost 6 million individual products from popular retailers. We don't shop directly on Yub, but link to the retailer we selected where we place our order and receive up to a 25 percent discount for the privilege of going through Yub. How does Yub make money? From the commissions it receives from the companies it hosts.

International shopping experiences are cultivated by visiting a myriad of malls emanating from other countries. Luxury goods retailers find online homes at eluxury.com, a subsidiary of Louis Vuitton Moet Hennessy (LVMH), the French conglomerate. Designer fashions from Fendi, Dior, and Roberto Cavalli are readily available. Online shopping malls that emanate from the United Arab Emirates also are options.

Internet megastores like Buy.com are popular sites for one-stop shoppers. This Web retailer has evolved from an electronics and computer focus to include toys, books, and sporting goods. Jewelry was introduced for the 2007 holiday season.[23] From these examples it is easy to recognize that shopping centers are plentiful on the Web—the newest version of hanging out at the mall has arrived!

Online Auctions Electronic auctions are opportunities for customers to shop or become sellers themselves in an increasingly secure environment. Auction sites like eBay charge sellers a listing fee and percentage of the selling price. Whether you seek a ceramic aardvark or a zealously coveted pair of concert tickets you can probably find them. Online auctions face many problems such as bogus bids that drive up prices, product misrepresentation, negated deliveries, and other fraud. To ensure safe transactions, eBay.com has developed rules for online buyers and sellers. Sellers are prohibited from bidding on their own merchandise. Buyers are given free insurance against fraud or mislabeled goods. Finding hot *Hannah Montana* seats has never been easier for concertgoers who use eBay's service, StubHub, for ticket resellers.[24]

In an attempt to compete with eBay, Buy.com opened Garage Sale. This service, designed to work within social networking sites like Facebook, is featured in Box 2.2.

Comparison Shopping Sites Independent Web sites that encourage product comparisons are widely available to shoppers. By typing in pertinent information such as brand, price range, and delivery date, shoppers can evaluate multiple retailers as they search for the best value. Some will send you an e-mail when goods you are interested in are marked down. Glimpse.com and Shopstyle.com offer this service.

PriceGrabber.com has a special section on its site for companies that sell products made from sustainable materials to those who are ecologically conscious. Called *ShopGreen*, the area features goods from outdoor gear retailers like Patagonia and Backcountry.com.[25]

Many online retailers are incorporating their own price comparison tools for customers. This upgrade helps companies affirm their integrity and keep users on their Web sites.

Box 2.2 What's the Buzz?

> *Buy.com Hopes Garage Sale Lures eBayers*

Buy.com is looking to steal some customers from eBay with a new shopping service for online hangouts like Facebook. In 2007 it launched its Garage Sale service on the social networking Web site Facebook. It's intended to let users post and sell items on their profile pages.

Unlike eBay, which charges sellers a listing and final transaction fee, Buy.com is charging a flat 5 percent commission for items sold. Buy.com processes the transactions, which means consumers must use credit cards to pay for items. Sellers get their money via eBay Inc.'s PayPal or a check from Buy.com.

Garage Sale users can't auction items off to the highest bidder, but Buy.com is looking into allowing users to haggle with sellers and read buyers' comments within the profile page. Right now, any bartering would have to be done via e-mail.

With Garage Sale, buyers and sellers are more likely to know each other, setting it apart from other commercial avenues like Craigslist. Buy.com Chief Executive Neel Grover sees his service as different from the Marketplace section that Facebook offers for buying and selling items; there, users can list items that will show up on their profiles, but buyers won't always know sellers.

Garage Sale is not Buy.com's first foray into social networking—the company owns social shopping site Yub.com. Grover said it created Garage Sale with technology it acquired by purchasing online commerce technology company Shoperion.

The failure of many companies—including Yahoo Inc. and Amazon.com Inc.—to take on eBay is not lost on Grover. Still, assuming Buy.com eventually can implement Garage Sale across other social networks, he sees the company as competing with eBay. He said, "We're not going to create a site people are going to come to. We're going to where all the traffic is."

Source: Adapted from Rachel Metz, AP Business Writer, New York, August 7, 2007, posted on Boston.com. © 2007 The New York Times Company.

> Tactics and Concerns of Online Retailers

Like other retailing sectors, online retailing has its positive and negative aspects. Tactics used to overcome operational challenges and areas of concern to online retailers are listed here and covered in depth in successive chapters.

Online Tactics

Online retailers monitor several core areas, most of which are germane to the Internet. It is difficult for retailers to get customers to their sites and once they do, it is difficult to close the sale. Enticing customers to return and buy more is also challenging. In other words, "hits" are not the same as sales. The following tactics reflect online adaptations of two common retail issues—finding and satisfying customers.

Optimizing Search Engine Efficiency Driving sales to a Web site is one of the more crucial mechanics of online selling. The ability to locate retailers and products of our choice on the Internet depends on site search and navigation efficiencies. As consumers we rarely think about this until frustration cripples us when we cannot find an item that we covet. Search is also one of the areas in which retailers seek technical expertise. For retailers, the use of key words to spark the search process can greatly aid or encumber traffic to a site. Selection of key words is not an exact science and costs retailers money. For example, a hypothetical trendy jeans retailer called Bottoms Up might find that the company name as well as the words "jeans" and "denim" would be too generic to derive direct hits from people plugging these descriptors into their browsers. The mechanics of search are covered in Chapters 5 and 7.

Increasing Conversion Rates You, the retailer, have engaged a customer who is perusing your site. Turning the surfer into a shopper is the next step. The **conversion rate** is the metric used to identify the number of visitors to a site who have actually made a purchase. Women's apparel retailer Coldwater Creek has a 23.7 percent conversion rate—one of the highest online.[26] Recency and frequency of shopping are positively correlated to high conversion rates. The more a visitor shops, the more likely the visitor is to return to the Web site.

Reducing Shopping Cart Abandonment Despite their best efforts, many retailers do not bring potential sales to fruition because consumers ditch their merchandise before checking out. **Shopping cart abandonment** is the practice of shopping but discarding merchandise before completing an online transaction.

The reasons for shopping cart abandonment are varied. Some visitors to a site are simply surfing, others enjoying the fantasy of shopping without actually parting with cash, much like readers of a catalog "wish book." On other occasions a Web site may be difficult to navigate or boring to view. Other sites are not advanced and appealing enough for viewers accustomed to enhanced graphics and advanced interactive technologies.

Shopping cart abandonment rates run as high as 60 to 70 percent for some online retailers. The percentage varies greatly by individual retailer.

Increasing Frequency of Purchase Like other direct marketers, online sellers are concerned with repeat sales and go to great lengths to encourage loyal patronage. Online advertising, blogs, e-mails, incentives, contests, games, and social networking are only part of the retail repertoire at this level. All retailers recognize that that the majority of sales come from a minority of their customer base, but this group is deserving of extra incentives to purchase more frequently.

Online Concerns

Potentially negative aspects of doing business online include customer privacy issues, online fraud, and sales taxes on Internet purchases. These are concerns of retailers as is the ability to keep Web sites current and adapt to constant changes as the sector moves into maturity.

Customer Privacy Despite vast improvements in Web site development and online payment systems, customer privacy will continue to be a concern. Data collection policies sometimes offend customers—whether the methods are overt, like asking for a zip code, or covert, where information captured at the point-of-sale is used to compile data about customers' product preferences and purchasing history. Data storage procedures have come under close scrutiny by retailers and law enforcement agencies.

Sales Taxation Steps toward a country-wide Internet shopping tax thus far have been thwarted, but many individual states are collecting sales tax on goods purchased on the Web—whether or not the goods were purchased in the same state as the retail seller. Advocates expect to see a flat rate charged no matter where in the country a customer resides. Opponents envision a taxation system in which the percentage taxed varies according to the zip code in which one lives. More study and initiatives are anticipated in this area.

Updating Web Sites Today's customers are demanding, savvy, and constantly looking for the next big thing. Retailers need to be ahead of the curve when it comes to Web site design and enabling technologies for customers. The impact on conversion rates is apparent, but even more is at stake. Brick-and-mortar stores have tangible physical presences that help to promote their brands and merchandise. Online sellers must be more diligent and vigilant as they build their brands online.

Improving Customer Service This challenge is certainly not limited to the online sector because most retailers are cognizant of upgrading the level of customer service they provide. Online retailers must do this with a different set of tools. One-on-one customer interaction in stores is replaced by live chat and e-mail online. The use of e-mail as a contact method and promotional tool is expected to grow. According to JupiterResearch, between 2007 and 2012, e-mail marketing spending will increase from $1.2 billion to $2.1 billion.[27]

Extended services to customers might include free shipping and no-hassle return policies. The ability to order online and pick up bulky items at the store is a welcome option for many shoppers.

Today's sure thing may be tomorrow's folly. Despite the excitement and double-digit increases in online sales over the last decade or more, the high growth period may be over by the time you read this. Strategies of online companies change. Closures are not limited to outmoded retailers in the brick-and-mortar realm. Cutting-edge technologies are made obsolete rapidly and capital budgets for retailers are always limited. The pace of change in this sector will not slow, yet few retailers have budgets so ample they can acquire all the new technological gadgets or tools. Companies that cope with change, learn from their experiences, plan strategically, and keep abreast of trends are those that have a greater likelihood of being successful.

> Electronic Retailing Options

Placing an order with a retailer via cell phone is not a new concept. Magnify this approach with the addition of Internet accessibility and you have the newest wave in retailing: mobile commerce, or m-commerce. It has become so much more than simply buying a ring tone. If you have a spare moment while standing in line at the checkout, riding the subway, or killing time in the cafeteria, why not shop? M-commerce and other electronic options appeal most to consumers who are already comfortable with cell phone use—especially young people who do not remember life without utter connectedness. Electronic kiosks, Web-based interactive television, direct TV, and online video are other ways that retailers are reaching customers through technology.

Mobile Commerce

Early in the millennium it appeared that purchasing goods via a wireless device would not take off rapidly. By 2007, however, the pace had escalated. Hardware and

2.10

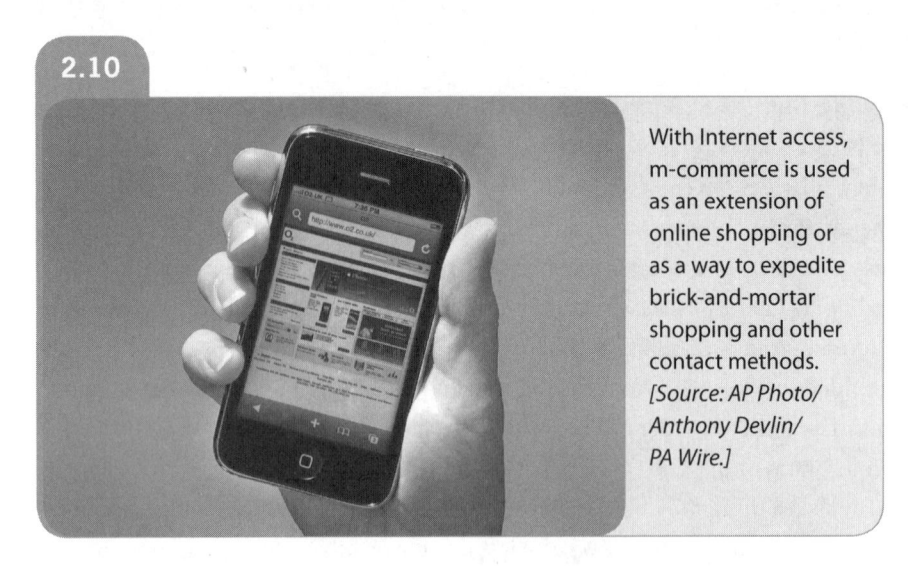

With Internet access, m-commerce is used as an extension of online shopping or as a way to expedite brick-and-mortar shopping and other contact methods. *[Source: AP Photo/ Anthony Devlin/ PA Wire.]*

software companies drove the market by introducing new technologies that would simplify the shopping experience. M-commerce was intensifying. Today more people have cell phones in the United States than landlines.

M-commerce is growing so rapidly that Web sites designed specifically for cell phone use are available and use the .mobi domain name instead of the conventional .com. So, will we call these dotmobi or what? An m-commerce transaction in progress is illustrated in Figure 2.10.

<u>Usage and Reach</u> We know we can do much more than talk on our cell phones. Paying bills or making money transfers is easy. Bank of America has extended its mobile banking service nationally. Ordering a new ring tune is amusing. The new Led Zeppelin collection released just before the 2007–2008 holidays will do, but may better suit the parents or grandparents of the heaviest users. Using GPS capabilities to locate a restaurant and get specific directions to the address saves time. Ordering takeout? Text it and pick it up on the way home. We can shop until we drop or simply hang up.

In 2007 mobile advertising reach in the United States was 171 million, and by 2011 that figure is expected to jump to 2.9 billion.[28] **Reach** is the number of viewers that are exposed to an advertising message in a specified period of time.

Mobile advertising spending worldwide was $3 billion in 2007 and is expected to hit $19 billion by 2011.[29] At this level of contact and advertising expenditure, it is evident that m-commerce offers untold opportunities to retailers who want to serve their customers with another shopping option.

Strengths of M-commerce Opportunities for m-commerce are far reaching for consumers and retailers:

> Easy to use, flexible, portable, and convenient for consumers.
> Offers choice of visual and auditory recipient preferences.
> Cell phone users can easily be reached by text messaging. Text messaging works well for retailers that are prepared to involve the customer with contests, rewards, humor, and buzz-creating interaction. Txts r up.
> M-commerce is experiencing high growth rates with enabling technologies keeping pace.
> Growth is not limited to the United States. Two of the fastest growing cell phone markets are China and India. The potential for selling is strong despite the fact that disposable income levels are lower than in fully developed countries because technology adoption rates are high.

Weaknesses of M-commerce Several aspects of cell phone use and telecommunication issues may impede the growth of mobile retailing:

> Cell phone use in public is often annoying to others and may curtail prolonged activity.
> The disadvantages of telemarketing, including hang up and privacy issues, also apply to m-commerce.
> Users may need protection from unscrupulous lotteries, sweepstakes offers, spam, and other potentially deceptive practices.
> As mobile phone services become more widespread and complex, full disclosure of mobile content service provider costs to consumers will increase in importance.
> Even with the rapid pace of technological change, it is difficult for retailers to keep up with customers' cell phone requirements such as bigger screens, more mobility, and better keyboards.

The Mobile Marketing Association (MMA) is a trade group that advocates for the growing industry and monitors many of these issues. The future of m-commerce parallels the other methods of customer contact. Integration of mobile phones, television, laptops, and GPS is the direction in which most large and small innovative retailers are heading. Early users of m-commerce include Amazon.com, Godiva Chocolatier, Overstock.com, and GameStop.[30]

Electronic Kiosks

Not a new innovation, kiosks have been in use for as long as ATMs. In fact, excluding ATMs there were 800,000 electronic kiosks in use in 2007 and 1.2 million are expected by 2009 in North America.[31]

Electronic units may sell or rent DVDs or serve as product preview or downloading stations. A survey done by *selfserviceworld* magazine ranked the Redbox DVD rental service as the best self-service kiosk in the market. Its kiosks are located in McDonald's restaurants and supermarkets in the United States and Redbox expected to reach 40 million rentals in 2007. The company's target market includes individuals aged 18 to 35 and parents of young children. Keeping new releases available is one of the merchandising objectives. Convenience and value for consumers makes Redbox an industry leader.[32]

Many electronic kiosks vend products without human intervention; information units provide store and local area highlights, and Internet access to customers.

Strengths of Kiosks for Retailers Some of the advantages to retailers include:

> - Kiosks take up little space and are located anywhere people are in transit, shopping, or seeking services at odd hours.
> - Interactive electronic kiosks are extensions to conventional businesses. Customers pay bills, update or redeem loyalty points, or shop when the conventional store is closed.
> - Retailers use the technology to provide faster checkout service. Self-service transactions at the point-of-sale reached $137 billion in 2006.[33]
> - Retailers use kiosks to extend their store inventories. North Face, the outdoor goods provider, uses kiosks to enhance its in-store inventory position. Although not yet available for online selling, the kiosk connection features the complete range of merchandise carried by the company as well as lifestyle-enhancing videos and interactive displays.[34]
> - Employment kiosks—on retail premises or off—help companies recruit, screen, and train new employees.

<u>Weaknesses of Kiosks for Retailers</u> As with all emerging technologies there are disadvantages of kiosks to retailers:

> Costs of implementation and maintenance can be high.
> Kiosks with too many options or unfriendly interfaces may deter customers.
> Customers who prefer human interaction may not be as amenable to interactive kiosks.
> Kiosks are an addition to, not a replacement of, retail sales promotion and customer service initiatives.

The diverse use of self-service kiosks is evident by the next examples. Due to the popularity of digital-photo kiosks, Walmart has lowered prices for prints to encourage customers to use the kiosks more often (Figure 2.11). Viking Range Corporation provides interactive kiosks for its dealers, retail accounts that they service, and top-of-the-line appliance shoppers. Customers can design their own kitchens and select the right appliance solutions while they are in the store. The informational aspects help sales associates perform their roles more effectively as well.[35]

The sales volume generated by interactive kiosks reached $968.9 billion in 2006.[36] It is expected to top $1 trillion by 2011.[37] These applications and figures suggest the great growth potential and creative options of kiosk retailing.

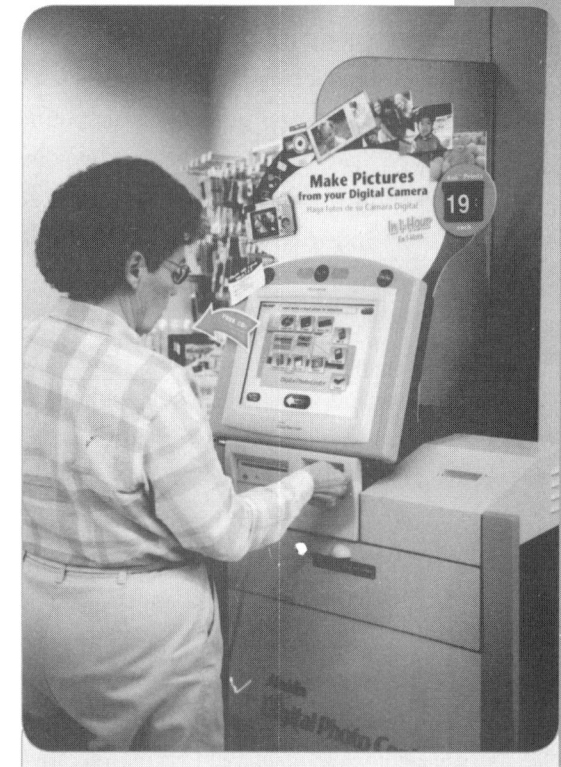

2.11 Photo processing kiosk at Walmart's Neighborhood Market is convenient and saves customers money. [Source: Photograph provided by Lynda Poloian.]

Chapter 2 > **Components of Multichannel Retailing**   73

Television Retailing

Experience a 30-minute infomercial on cable TV and you might think for a few minutes that you are immersed in a new reality show. The call to action is more likely to be, "Visit our Web site at www.buyme.com" or "Place a free call on your cell phone" than the older "Dial our 1-800 number" tactic. Zap that remote and see what the Home Shopping Network (HSN) and QVC have to offer. It might be jewelry, apparel, cosmetics, or camping gear. What could be better retail selling tools than HDTV presentation, surround-sound, compelling visuals, color, and action? In this section, home shopping channels, infomercials, direct and interactive TV are discussed.

Home Shopping Channels Once considered the principal pastime of senior citizens and collectors, home shopping channels reach markets that cross geographic, demographic, and psychographic boundaries. Two major channels compete in the United States. The first to enter the home shopping market was Florida's HSN, now owned by IAC/InterActiveCorp. To better serve its customers, the company formed a more integrative relationship between its shopping channel and Web site. HSN's strategic direction is the topic of Box 2.3.

The second home shopping channel was QVC, headquartered in West Chester, Pennsylvania. QVC operates globally and leads cable shopping channels in sales volume and viewers. Considered the more sophisticated of the two major shopping channels, QVC partners with fashion designers such as Michael Kors, Bradley Bayou, and Dooney & Burke. QVC's online store was launched in 1996. More information on this electronic retailer is presented in the Multichannel Retail Profile following Unit I.

Typical product classifications such as jewelry, dolls, and other collectibles have fared well on shopping channels. Apparel sales have not met expectations of television retailers because customers do not find that fashions are adequately portrayed on TV, and items cannot be touched or tried on. This point mimics complaints from online and print catalog shoppers. Shopping channels also have found that lower-ticket apparel sells well because of a lower perceived risk to consumers. Scheduling television segments in accord with audience preferences is another challenge.

Infomercials Extensive detail is given about a product and slick presenters are believable in thirty-minute messages that entertain as well as sell. Many of us do not realize we are watching an infomercial until well into the time slot. Production

What's the Buzz? Box 2.3

> *HSN Goes Interactive for Customers*

The Home Shopping Network is establishing itself as a beauty authority with its 360-degree lifestyle platform integrating television and the Internet. "We want to create a venue where people can watch, learn, be inspired, and gain confidence in the products that are right for them," said Mindy Grossman, chief executive officer of IAC Retailing at IAC/InteractiveCorp, which owns HSN. "Since we relaunched our Web site, we've changed our whole approach to creating both our live and creative content. The beauty category was already a big focus, but now we can create more assets and utilize our content."

With 75 brands in the assortment, the company plans to double its beauty business over the next two or three years, according to Grossman. "Beauty is one of our faster-growing businesses, and we want to see beauty outpace the growth of our overall business."

Before the push, HSN had viewed beauty as the most demonstrable category in terms of innovation, problem solution, efficacy, and emotion. But in order to grow the category, the company decided to incorporate television, Web, podcasts, and other multimedia content.

As part of the initiative, the company relaunched its Web site so that its editorial content and overall message was more cohesive with the television network. "If our whole strategy is to create a lifestyle, customers' experiences have to be consistent no matter where they interface with HSN," said Grossman. "Our mission on television and on the Web is to increase our active customer base and viewership. It's not about the products. It's about the actual innovators of the products telling you the how, what, and where."

The company's Web site includes "how-to" videos for every product designed specifically for the Web. As a result, the company has seen an increased session length and conversion rate on its site.

"In the past, we felt that television would bring our customers to the Web, but we believe that we can use the Web to drive customers to their televisions," said Grossman. "A multichannel customer is most valuable if they're engaged 365 days a year."

Other HSN initiatives include creating original content for podcasts as well as YouTube and on-demand television where consumers can browse through segments and shop by remote. The company plans to expand its "green" assortment by enlarging its beauty offerings with brands like Desert Essence Organics. HSN hopes to build its portfolio by offering more global brands that may not be accessible to the U.S. consumer, in addition to bringing in products and brands that appeal to a more ethnically diverse population.

Source: Excerpted and condensed from Michelle Edgar, Women's Wear Daily, *December 14, 2007, 14.*

and airtime costs can be prohibitive but companies that are able to reach their target markets during the nighttime hours when infomercials are usually aired find this approach worthwhile. Many infomercials are now presented using streaming video on the Web.

Interactive Television In 1998, Microsoft entered into an agreement with major cable company TCI to allow the marriage of cable and Internet technology to take place.[38] This direction has changed the face of retailing and will continue to do so. With Internet connection and a TV tuner card, viewers can watch regular TV, cable, or satellite broadcasts on their computer screens. Using TiVo, individuals can receive data from any of these sources twenty-four hours a day and store them for future use if desired.

The availability of broadband high-speed connections encourages more interactive programming. For example, by using a remote or other wireless device, students could access a special reading list while watching a program on a history channel or order merchandise seen on their favorite sitcom. Watching a sitcom is one thing; serious shopping is another.

The potential of interactive TV is compelling to retailers and has several benefits:

> Exclusive target markets are reached when people are more relaxed at home.
> It is a pull system—viewers initiate programming and ultimately product choices.
> E-mail can be used in conjunction with interactive TV viewing.

This chapter has explored many of the multichannel options available to retailers. A summary of the major advantages to retail consumers of each type of multichannel experience is presented in Table 2.3. As you read this, the technology sector is continuing to change the way we experience retailing; in fact, new avenues for commerce may already have appeared.

Advantages and Disadvantages of Major Channels to Retailers   Table 2.3

CHANNEL	ADVANTAGES	DISADVANTAGES
BRICK-AND-MORTAR STORES	> High visibility > Physical presence > Visual appeal of merchandise, layout, and design > Established brand builder > Generates highest proportion of sales if a multichannel retailer > Wealth of format options: specialty, department, discount, food and drug, etc.	> Oversaturated retail markets > Tired formats and mundane merchandising in some formats > Physical access for customers necessary > Less flexible business hours > Some formats in late maturity phase of retail life cycle
DIRECT MARKETING	> Variety of vehicles: catalogs, direct mail, telephone > Pioneers of RFM and CRM > Encourages immediate responses from customers > Convenience, receptiveness of customers > Creativity of promotional messages	> Customer mobility factor for mail and telephone lists > Some vehicles may loose share to online stores > Increased costs of printing and postage > Fit, quality, and tactile issues > Customer privacy issues > Hang-up and do-not-call-or-mail issues
DIRECT SELLING	> Personal connection with customers > Offers convenience of home or office shopping > One-on-one or group sales opportunities	> Dependent largely upon part-time workforce > Many sales shifting from home/office to Internet
ONLINE STORES	> Customer convenience 24/7/365 > Global reach > New revenue opportunities > Extension and support to original formats > Growing m-commerce possibilities > Excitement through advanced technology	> Fit, quality and tactile issues > Customer privacy, security, and sales tax issues > Customer conversion issues > Shopping cart abandonment > Web site maintenance

Note: CRM = customer relationship management; RFM = recency, frequency, monetary value.

Summary

The major components of multichannel retailing include brick-and-mortar stores, direct marketing, direct selling, online retailing, and many other electronic methods of customer contact. Each has its strengths and weaknesses that are evaluated as retailers make multichannel decisions.

For the sake of brevity and introduction, brick-and-mortar stores are classified as department stores, specialty stores, and discount stores. The retail industry is actually becoming broader and more all-encompassing as new formats develop. Many food retailers also are multichannel retailers.

Department stores are broken down into two general categories, full-line and limited-line operations. Full-line department store sales have declined in recent years but those retailers who have implemented new strategies for growth have shown they can survive. Limited-line department stores have fared better and continue to service their higher-income customers well. Specialty stores are much broader in scope and include apparel and accessory retailers; shoe stores; jewelry, food, drug, hardware, electronic, and toy stores; and a host of retail service businesses. Able to target their markets succinctly, specialty stores face much competition but also tend to move merchandise faster and are more focused on the customer than department stores. Discounters fall into several types, including general merchandisers, category killers, off-price stores, warehouse clubs, outlet centers, and deep discounters. Most share similar traits of lower prices, big box facilities, and more humble layouts and décor. Hybrids include upmarket discount department stores like Target and category killers like Staples that merge big box retailing with specialty overtones.

Direct marketing and direct selling sound the same but differ in the ways they reach customers. Direct marketers use catalogs, direct mail, telemarketing, and the Internet to draw customers. Direct selling relies on person-to-person selling efforts through home and office gatherings and consultative selling.

E-retailing includes online selling and several alternative electronic options. M-commerce, electronic kiosks, and interactive television are some of the other ways retailers reach potential customers. E-mail is expected to increase and facilitate these contact methods.

Integration of some or all of these methods typifies the multichannel approach. Retailers carefully weigh their options as they define their business models and strategies.

Key Terms

Big box retailers	Discounters	Outbound telephone calls
Call centers	Distressed merchandise	Predictive modeling
Carry-over	Electronic kiosks	Private-label goods
Category killers	Face-to-face selling	Prospecting
Collections	Factory outlets	Pull strategies
Consultative selling	Fulfillment	Push strategies
Conversion rate	Full-line department stores	Reach
Customer relationship management (CRM)	General merchandise discounters	Recency, frequency, and monetary value (RFM)
Database marketing	Inbound telephone calls	Remote selling
Deep discounters	Infomercials	Shopping cart abandonment
Department stores	Lifetime value	Specialty stores
Diffusion lines	Limited-line department stores	Superstores
Direct mail		Telemarketing
Direct marketing	Mailing lists	Warehouse clubs
Direct selling	Off-price retailers	

> Questions for Reflection and Discussion

1. In what ways is brick-and-mortar retailing crucial to multichannel retailing initiatives?
2. Compare the strengths of department and specialty stores. In your estimation, which retail format is most successful in today's marketplace?
3. How has discounting evolved, and which discount retail formats are most feasible in the present economy?
4. Why are retailers with a physical presence better brand builders? What techniques do non–brick-and-mortar retailers use to gain customer recognition and loyalty?
5. Distinguish between direct marketing and direct selling. How do multichannel retailers use each method?
6. "Lifetime value" and "customer relationship management" are terms that originated in the direct marketing field but have relevance to all types of retailers. How do both of these concepts extend to brick-and-mortar or online retailers?
7. What three tactics mentioned in this chapter do you believe are most relevant to the success of online retailers? Justify your choices.
8. M-commerce is one of the newer electronic retailing options. What techniques that support this concept are retailers using? To what market are most m-commerce initiatives directed?

Notes >

1. "Share of Retail Web Sales by Type of Company: 2005 Top 400 Guide and 2008, Top 500 Guide," *Internet Retailer,* 10.

2. Evan Clark, "Clothing Retailers' Sales Gain, Department Stores' Drop," *Women's Wear Daily*, December 14, 2007, 13.

3. Sharon Edelson, "Plenty of Activity at ICSC Conference," *Women's Wear Daily*, December 10, 2007, 19.

4. Direct Marketing Association, "What is the Direct Marketing Association?" "What is Direct Marketing?" from *The Power of Direct Marketing 2006-2007*, http://www.the-dma.org/aboutdma/whatisthedma.shtml.

5. Ibid., "Overview."

6. Direct Selling Association, Washington, DC, www.dsa.org/aboutselling.

7. Ibid., www.dsa.org/pubs/numbers/#sales.

8. David Moin, "Macy's Goes Round-the-Clock for Holiday," *Women's Wear Daily*, December 14, 2007, 2.

9. Chantal Todé, "More Retailers Flock to Catalogs," *DMNews*, May 8, 2006, 50.

10. Chantal Todé, "FlipSeekcom Catalogs Online Catalogs," *DM News*, November 20, 2006, .22.

11. Melissa Campanelli, "Vertis: Women 25-44 Prefer Direct Mail to E-mail " *DM News* January 22, 2007.

12. Chantal Todé, "Pike Place Market, Direct Mailer with Coupon Pulls 4%-5% Redemption Rate," *DM News*, November 5, 2007, 28.

13. United States Census Bureau, as published in Cara Wood, "Aim at Moving Targets," *DM News* October 22, 2007, 14.

14. Christa Heibel, "Let's Show Telemarketing's Good Side," *DM News*, October 10, 2005, 15.

15. John Lyons, "Siting a Call Center? Check Out the Mall First," *Wall Street Journal*, July 3, 2006, B1.

16. Direct Selling Association, Washington, DC, www.dsa.org/statistics.

17. Ibid.

18. Erin Skrypek, "One Home Shopping Network That's Really at Home," *Boston Globe*, Style & Arts, November 22, 2007, C1-C8.

19. Laura Klepacki, "Mary Kay: Human Touch Meets High Tech," *Women's Wear Daily*, March 1, 2004, 37.

20. Cecily Hall, "Netflix, QVC, Lead Online Satisfaction " *Women's Wear Daily* June 1, 2007, 13.

21. Bob Tedeschi, "When Beauty is More then a Click Deep," *New York Times,* October 1, 2007, 2, http://www.nytimes.com.

22. Ibid., 8.

23. Buy.com. Press Release, "Buy.com Launches New Store With Broad Selection of Jewelry and Watches," December 4, 2007, Yahoo! Finance, http:// biz.yahoo.com.

24. Ethan Smith, "Hannah Montana Battles the Bots," *Wall Street Journal,* Marketplace, October 5, 2007, B1-B2.

25. "Creating an Online Environment for Comparing 'Green' Products," *Internet Retailer*, June 15, 2007, www.internetretailer.com.

26. "Coldwater Creek Bubbles to the Top in Conversion Rates," *Internet Retailer*, December 31, 2007, www.internetretailer.com/printArticle.asp?id=24862.

27. "Strong Spending Ahead for E-mail Marketing," *eMarketer*, January 8, 2008, statistic from JupiterResearch's "U.S. E-mail Marketing Forecast, 2007 to 2012," www.emarketer.com.

28. Giselle Abramovich, "Marketers Optimistic on Future of Mobile Ads," statistic from Jupiter-Research as cited in *DM News*, July 20, 2007, http://www.dmnews.com.

29. "Mobile Ad Fans and Foes," *eMarketer,* April 19, 2007, statistic from ABI Research, http://www.eMarketer.com.

30. Bill Siwicki, "M-commerce: What's It, Where It's At, When Things May Happen and What Stands in the Way," *Internet Retailer*, May 2007, 14.

31. "Quick Stats and Facts," *selfserviceworld*, statistical source Summit Research Associates, November 2007, 6.

32. Patrick Avery, "Superstar Deployments," *selfserviceworld*, August 2007, 17-18.

33. "Quick Stats and Facts," *selfsercviceworld*, statistical source IHL Consulting Group, November 2007, 5, www.selfserviceworld.com/re2.php?cat_id=1.

34. Chantal Todé, "North Face Kiosk Improves In-store Inventory," *DM News*, March 26, 2007, 3.

35. Gary Wollenhaupt, "Range Roving," *selfserviceworld*, November 2007, 29.

36. "Trends: Revenues Generated by Interactive Kiosks Last Year," *Stores*, source Frost & Sullivan, December 2007, 20.

37. "Quick Stats and Facts," *selfserviceworld*, statistical source IHL Consulting Group, November 2007, 6, www.selfserviceworld.com/re2.php?cat_id=1.

38. Rob Fixmer, "Personal Computers; Windows 98 Feature Combines TV, Terminal and the Internet," *New York Times,* August 18, 1998, 5, http://web.lexis-nexis.com/univers.

Chapter 3

Multichannel Customer Behavior

Objectives

> To determine what constitutes value for customers across channels.
> To explore fundamental and contemporary customer behavior.
> To categorize bases for market segmentation.
> To identify positive and negative customer expectations of multichannel retailers.
> To recognize influences on and inhibitors of the shopping experience.
> To appreciate the relationship between multichannel customer behavior and retail performance.

>
The previous chapter presented many advantages and disadvantages of major channels to retailers. Here the focus is on customer behavior. Invariably it is the customer who determines the effectiveness of retail offerings—no matter what channel is used.

Retailers work to provide desirable products and an exemplary shopping experience and to sustain customer loyalty over time. In this chapter, the benefits of major channels are discussed from a customer perspective. Identifying how retailers maximize the customer experience through various customer service tactics is the focus of Chapter 8.

Ensuring Customer Value Through Multiple Channels

The question "What's in it for me?" may sound crass because it implies self-centeredness—not a trait most of us knowingly try to cultivate. Yet the customer is the center of the universe for retailers. For a selling method to be effective, true value must be evident to the customer. **Value** is the worth customers place on products and services. Worth may include merit, appeal, attraction, usefulness, status, as well as price. What value really means to the customer goes deeper than simply getting outstanding merchandise for a fair price. Retailing is more than a mechanical transaction of goods or services in exchange for money.

A precious and rare art object may be purchased for thousands of dollars on eBay or six pairs of socks bought at a low price from Walmart: each is perceived as being of value. Value is a relative thing and has different connotations to different people. The piece of art and the package of socks may be held in high esteem by the same person, adding further complexity to our attempts to understand customer behavior.

Each selling channel is more or less attractive to customers for a wealth of different reasons that are put forth in this chapter. Let's begin by looking at the values of consequence to customers who shop through brick-and-mortar, catalog, and online channels.

> Brick-and-Mortar Retailing

It is easier to evaluate the fabric of a cashmere sweater, the sample of Asiago cheese in a supermarket, and the alluring fragrance of a new celebrity scent in a brick-and-mortar store than through other channels. Customers interested in the sensory experience welcome store visits. If you love the look of the cashmere sweater but are unsure of your size and wonder how soft it will feel next to your skin, you can easily try it on in a fitting room. Color, sight, sound, and events compel customers to linger, and brick-and-mortar stores use all of these to entice and keep shoppers. Customers visiting Saks Fifth Avenue in Boston on their lunch hour may have wondered why crowds had gathered until they saw Victoria Beckham, also known as Posh Spice, promoting her new denim line, dVb. That is the kind of excitement one expects from brick-and-mortar stores.

Anyone who has gone into Lowe's on the weekend intending to purchase one gallon of paint to complete a do-it-yourself project and walked out with a new paper towel holder, a roll of insulation, three switch plates, and a new kitchen sink that he

Compelling brick-and-mortar stores are typified by an inviting store layout, vibrant visuals, and well-designed lighting. Saks Fifth Avenue's cosmetic department meets all three criteria. [Source: Photograph provided by Lynda Poloian.]

or she didn't expect to purchase, as well as the gallon of paint, has learned that the power of spontaneous shopping is strong. Brick-and-mortar has many advantages over other channels and brings value to customers in these ways:

> Visual inspection of products is inherent.
> Sensory stimulation through touch, smell, taste, hearing, and vision is possible and probable.
> Window and in-store displays present new merchandise and ideas.
> Emotions are triggered, and planned and spontaneous purchases are consummated.
> Communing with sales associates and fellow customers soothes the need for social interaction.
> The thrill of the hunt for a product provides a good dose of retail therapy.
> Gratification is immediate.
> Economic advantages occur when shipping costs are not necessary.

The brick-and-mortar retailer illustrated in Figure 3.1 conveys the essence of customer value. Compelling displays, lighting, merchandise selections, and the invitation to touch, try, and experience the merchandise all contribute to the attraction.

> Catalog Retailing

Take a break and browse the Cabela's catalog. If you cannot find the new camouflage gear you need for your hunting expedition in the bound copy of the Limited Edition containing over 1,500 pages of merchandise, chances are you would not elsewhere. Send in your order by mail, call the toll-free number, or for immediate gratification go to one of the company's stores. The Web site address is listed on the spine of the catalog for easy reference. Your choice of contact depends on your mood and when you need the merchandise.

The benefits to the customer of catalog shopping include:

> Customer convenience.
> Availability 24/7/365.
> Serving as wish books and idea generators.
> Color, glossy paper, and innovative formats that make shopping easy and upbeat.
> Sharp photography and appealing models that enhance customer's ability to visualize themselves with or wearing the product.
> Merchandise that is easily seen and interpreted without being overwhelming.
> Relaxing pastime.
> Economic advantages if orders are placed by telephone or online.

Cabela's includes a rich array of items in its online catalog that effectively represent store and print catalog merchandise. [Source: Cabelas.com.]

Cabela's Limited Edition mega catalogs present over 1,500 pages of products to customers in a bound-book format that begs to be kept in a bookcase and not discarded after you place your order. Fashion items from Cabela's online catalog are illustrated in Figure 3.2.

> Online Retailing

It's 2:00 a.m. You cannot sleep so you decide to search for the new iPod case you have been meaning to buy. You're not going out to an Apple store at that hour so

FIGURE 3.3 When shopping from home, "dress" is optional. [Source: Courtesy of Timothy Whyatt.]

you might as well go online. And even though casual is in, do you really want to be seen in a worn T-shirt and old shorts?

Most customers value the following aspects of online shopping:

> Stores are open 24/7/365.
> Access is provided to retailers worldwide.
> Shopping is convenient and saves time.
> Pricing comparisons are easy to make.
> Dressing is optional when you shop from home (Figure 3.3).
> Broader and deeper assortments of merchandise can be found.
> It's both efficient and economical.
> Reports from other online customers can be read.
> Merchandise selections can be shared with friends and their input considered before purchasing.
> Shipping is often free or reduced.

Despite the fact that many people now shop online, the desire for human contact has not diminished—even if contact has already been established via e-mail.

The IconNicholson electronic interactive mirror encourages friends to participate in the shopping experience from outside the shopping mall. [Source: Photographs provided by Lynda Poloian.]

3.4

According to JupiterResearch, customer service contacts begun online are expected to double from 2006 to 2012 but will still be only 14 percent of the total contacts made. Contact by e-mail or text messaging is preferred by some individuals, but most prefer to contact a company by telephone even though they do not like to use automated telephone systems.[1] Apparently punching #4 and listening to music is acceptable it if you really want to speak to a human about your online order.

At Amazon.com shoppers can preview a book before buying it, much like ruffling through the pages of a hot new release at Barnes & Noble while sipping an iced latte in midsummer. Does the online version approximate the in-store experience? Perhaps not, but many new technologies are making it easier to bridge the gap between on-site and online experience.

Technology that transfers value from one channel to another is now becoming available. An interactive mirror developed by IconNicholson is one example (Figure 3.4). Positioned outside a regular fitting room, it allows customers to evaluate

Table 3.1 Aspects of Customer Value Provided by Major Channels

STORES	CATALOGS	ONLINE
> Experience excitement through visual merchandising	> Experience convenience and time savings	> Experience convenience and time savings
> Touch, taste, smell, and sample products	> Serve as idea generators	> Access to many retailers globally
> Try on apparel and assess quality	> Focus on a wide range of specialty goods	> Available 24/7/365
> Engage in impulse purchasing	> Portable and easy to use	> Ease of e-mail customer service
> Satisfy social needs	> Available 24/7/365	> Options for online customer interaction
> Obtain immediate gratification	> Flawless execution of graphics and models may enhance self-image	> Vibrant multimedia Web sites
> Save money on shipping costs	> Relax while shopping	> Broader and deeper merchandise assortments
> Indulge in retail therapy	> Flexibility of ordering	> Easy to make price comparisons
> Access to trusted retail brands		> More economical to shop

different styles or change the color of a garment under consideration by using a touch screen on the magic mirror. As an added benefit, the experience is transmitted via a video feed so friends in the mall or at home can participate. When connected to the Internet, friends can voice their approval—or not—and suggest alternatives from a remote location.

Peer approval, ease of shopping, affinity for new media, degree of social interaction, and economic motives bring value to a purchase. Money is not the only indicator of worth of a product. Table 3.1 summarizes customer value in three channels—stores, catalogs, and online. More information on overcoming channel-specific limitations appears in Chapter 5.

A Primer on Customer Behavior

Probing the depths of the human psyche is not the purpose of this textbook. However, the fields of psychology and sociology provide valuable insight into the complexities of human behavior. Before examining customer behavior trends and market segmentation, a brief review of some basic concepts is helpful.

> Human Needs and Wants

Human wants and needs can be categorized in several ways. A **need** is the awareness of a discrepancy between the person's present and ideal states. In contrast, a want is anything used to satisfy a need. There are many interpretations of needs and wants when we apply them to retail customers.

Biogenic and Psychogenic Needs

Biogenic needs are physiological needs for food, warmth, shelter, and sex. **Psychogenic needs** stem from the socialization process and involve intangible aspects, such as status, acquisition, or love. Both have an impact on the individual and affect behavior. Dr. Abraham Maslow's classic **hierarchy of needs theory** suggests that people seek to satisfy needs in an ascending order of importance: biogenic, social, and psychogenic. Although not intended to predict shopping behavior, Maslow's theory helps retailers understand the buying motivations of customers.

Utilitarian and Hedonic Needs

Utilitarian needs serve simple human requirements such as comfort, body coverage, or maintenance. **Hedonic needs** are emotionally based and concerned with serving the ego. The feel-good response is anticipated when hedonic needs are met.

Aspirational Wants

The image of what individuals hope to become is closely allied with aspirational wants. **Aspirational wants** are those that relate to products and services that people perceive will help them achieve higher status in life. They also meld with hedonic values.

So great is their need to impress, aspirational customers may spend beyond their means even when there is a downturn in the economy.[2] Their generally positive nature leads them to believe that slowdowns will be short lived and reduced spending power or credit crunches will not affect them.

As you apply this material, think for a moment about your favorite vice—something that occasionally takes you over-the-top. It might be eating chocolate, smoking tobacco, or purchasing shoes indiscriminately. Do you want or need the product? If you like the sweetness of chocolate and are in the mood for a snack, you might say you *want* a chocolate bar (psychogenic or utilitarian). If you are a teacher with a stack of papers to correct or a student with a 25-page paper due the next day you might say you *need* a box of chocolates to help you reduce stress and finish the project (physiological). In this example, "want" implies a casual but often psychological connection with a product. "Need" implies a physiological craving for a product. Ah, those endorphins. If we take our chocolate quest further, we would see that some devotees satisfy their wants or needs with a generic candy bar whereas others believe that only a status brand like Godiva will satisfy their longing (hedonic). We can have lots of fun with this concept, but it's important to remember that although needs change, the quest for customer satisfaction does not.

Personality type, motivation level, and demographic variables also affect consumer behavior. Individual and group influences that help mold customer behavior are covered later in this chapter.

> Major Shifts in Customer Behavior

Who are today's customers? How are they different from those of previous decades? Why is it important for us to monitor changes in customer behavior? These are the questions asked by retailers. Several changes in our world today influence society and therefore retail business.

The Value/Price Equation

People have become more educated about the relationship between value and price. Customers are more knowledgeable about comparative pricing thanks to the Internet. Greater transparency across the supply chain and extensive media coverage have made customers more aware of manufacturing costs, import and export issues, distribution problems, and the economic impact of changes in these areas. Whatever their social class, household income level, or country of origin, customers worldwide look for the best product quality at an affordable price.

Unrestrained Choices

Individuals have more choices of products, services, and retailers than ever before. We may joke about the thousands of hits we get when we research a product online, but this experience reinforces the magnitude of options we have in all product categories imaginable and in some we rarely consider. Stumbling across a Web site that features hundreds of bicycle seat covers—even if we are not in the

> **What's the Buzz? Box 3.1**

> *Mobile Browsing and Text Messaging Are Giving Shoppers New Power in Stores*

After college students compile a list of textbooks they'll need for the coming semester, they head to the campus bookstore. Web-only retailer AbeBooks Inc. carries a wide range of textbooks and wanted to step into that mass migration to convince students it had better prices and persuade them to buy at AbeBooks.com.

AbeBooks decided to reach this youth market where it lives and breathes—text messaging. Late last summer it launched a test program that enabled college students browsing in bookstores to text-message the e-retailer with a textbook's International Standard Book Number (ISBN). Students received a reply text message containing AbeBooks lowest price for new copies of their textbook.

If a student decided to buy the book, he or she replied by typing "fwd" and his or her e-mail address. The e-retailer then replied to the e-mail address with a link to the AbeBooks.com page where the book is listed for sale. The student then could buy it later via a PC.

Although AbeBooks characterizes the program as a test and won't say what kind of response it achieved, it was a test that puts AbeBooks at the forefront of how customers shop. "As an online business, we have to watch the mobile channel," says Thomas Nicol, director of marketing. "The importance of this channel will increase."

(continued)

market for one at the time—alerts us to the vast possibilities online. However, a trip to Best Buy to shop in-store for a new printer or TV can also be overwhelming. The narrow and deep assortment offered by category killers is in the best interests of retailers because they purchase electronic goods less expensively from wholesalers and for customers who benefit from competitive retail pricing at every popular price point.

The Control Factor

The customer has always possessed the power to buy or not to buy; however, the nature of retail transactions has changed appreciably since the advent of the Internet. Customers have greater stature in the world of commerce. They control purchasing decisions, locus of sales, and customer service standards. They choose where and when they will do business. Box 3.1 discusses some of the ways in which shoppers gain control of their purchases using mobile browsing and text messaging.

> **Box 3.1 What's the Buzz?** *(continued)*
>
> M-commerce sites and services are popping up and many e-retailers and other e-commerce players such as comparison shopping sites are keeping a watchful eye. A new development among these sites and services bears particular scrutiny: A handful of companies are employing a strategy that encourages shoppers to access mobile offerings while the shoppers are in stores.
>
> This isn't mobile commerce where a husband orders flowers for his wife while commuting on a train or a film junkie adds a selection to his online DVD rental queue after receiving a recommendation from a pal at a party. This is a calculated move to drive shoppers from one merchant to another and it's focusing on price comparison.
>
> E-retailers like AbeBooks and BikeSomeWhere.com are urging shoppers to use their mobile offerings while in competitor's stores to judge which merchant has the better price. And Google Text, mShopper, PriceGrabber, ShopLocal, and Sifter offer mobile sites or services designed to help shoppers compare products and prices to decide whether they should buy at the store they're in at the moment or go to another store.
>
> AbeBooks recognizes the potential of m-commerce, which is why it conducted its experiment. To promote the test program, it sent employees to 30 college campuses to get students out of bookstores and onto AbeBooks.com. It also wrote about the text-based service in its e-newsletter for students on its Web site.
>
> "It's all about how close you can get to shoppers," Nicol of AbeBooks says. "For a Web site, shoppers have to go to the site. E-mail gets you closer because they check it on a regular basis. Mobile is another step closer to shoppers."
>
> *Source: Bill Siwicki,* Internet Retailer, *January 2008, p. 54.*

Perception of Time

The older we get the faster we seem to perceive the passage of time. Time also seems to pass more quickly when we are busier. This may be or may not be quantifiable, but the nature of modern-day life supports this supposition. We work harder, and longer, and experience more stress as a result. The element of speed transcends our very essence. Tapping feet are observed when someone is forced to wait a minute or less for service in a quick-serve restaurant, or pounding on a touch pad or mouse when Internet service is denied for a moment. Cumulative impatience is the standard by which we live and is acknowledged by retailers as a substantive consideration.

The Technology Revolution

Imagine living in a world where a cell phone is not part of your anatomy, texting a friend with news that requires an immediate response is not possible, or your media room lacks a 60-inch TV screen. The majority of people in the United States who are over 40 years of age remember a low-tech world, and as consumers they are plentiful. However, for today's young people, life without computers has never been an option. The adaptive changes brought by technology are unparalleled and will continue to affect customer behavior.

These are some of the agents of change that greatly influence retailers today. Other areas of change that have made customers more thoughtful and circumspect include heightened awareness of terrorism since 9/11, expansion of the global economy, and changes in political regimes. Events like these shape the nature of change and influence our lives. For instance, patriotic sentiment is often more pronounced during times of war, as shown in Figure 3.5. Economic and political influences on the retail environment are explored in more detail in Chapter 4.

Patriotism became stronger in the United States after 9/11 and continues to influence the retail sector as customers' viewpoints center on security and peace. Borders showed support for the troops in Iraq through these broadsheet posters. *[Source: Photograph provided by Lynda Poloian.]*

> Marketing Principles and Customer Behavior

Various aspects of marketing, including product life cycle, adopter categories, diffusion of innovation, shopping situations, and decision making, have an impact on customer behavior. A brief review of several marketing concepts follows.

Product Life Cycle

The **product life cycle** is a schematic that traces the life of a product in the marketplace. The product can be tangible or intangible; a physical good or a service; a store or brand, for example. The cycle consists of four stages: introduction, growth, maturity, and decline. Products and services pass through the product life cycle at different rates and may linger in one stage longer than in others. Knowledge of the life cycle helps retailers plan appropriate strategies to enhance a product's longevity or to make decisions about discontinuing a product. Retail stores, catalogs, online stores, and brands also experience life cycles.

In the fashion industry, the product life cycle is called the *fashion cycle*. Using descriptors such as "fads" and "classics," merchandisers trace the status of fashion products over time. Trend reports are crucial to forecasting retail sales and estimating customer demand.

Consumer Adoption Categories and the Diffusion of Innovation

All customers do not purchase items at the same stage of the product life cycle. Customers are categorized by the rate at which they adopt a particular product or trend. The groupings are called *adopter categories* and are part of the diffusion of innovation process. **Innovation** in this context implies being the first to develop a new product or service and bring it to market. To be the first to have a personal navigation device with voice, 3-D diagrams of buildings, and Web content is important to individuals who consider themselves innovators. Others are immune to peer pressure and retail sales promotion and will always rely on a printed map.

Adopter categories group customers into five major types: innovators, early adopters, early majority, late majority, and laggards. Most people fit into the two majority categories. As examples, shoppers identified as early adopters would be first to adopt the newest megapixel digital cameras. Laggards are still using a 35-millimeter camera.

Innovators most likely purchased satellite phones and items such as Amazon's Kindle electronic books when they were in the introduction stage of the product life cycle. These customers pay more at retail for cutting-edge products. High prices do not deter them because they want the fun and the social esteem attached to being technologically savvy. They do not like to defer gratification.

The majority of shoppers make purchases when prices go down, that is, during the maturity phase of the product life cycle. Their need for the newest technology is not as great as that of the early adopters. If and when the products move into the decline stage, customers known as laggards may purchase the items. The relationship between the product life cycle and customer adoption categories is illustrated in Figure 3.6.

3.6

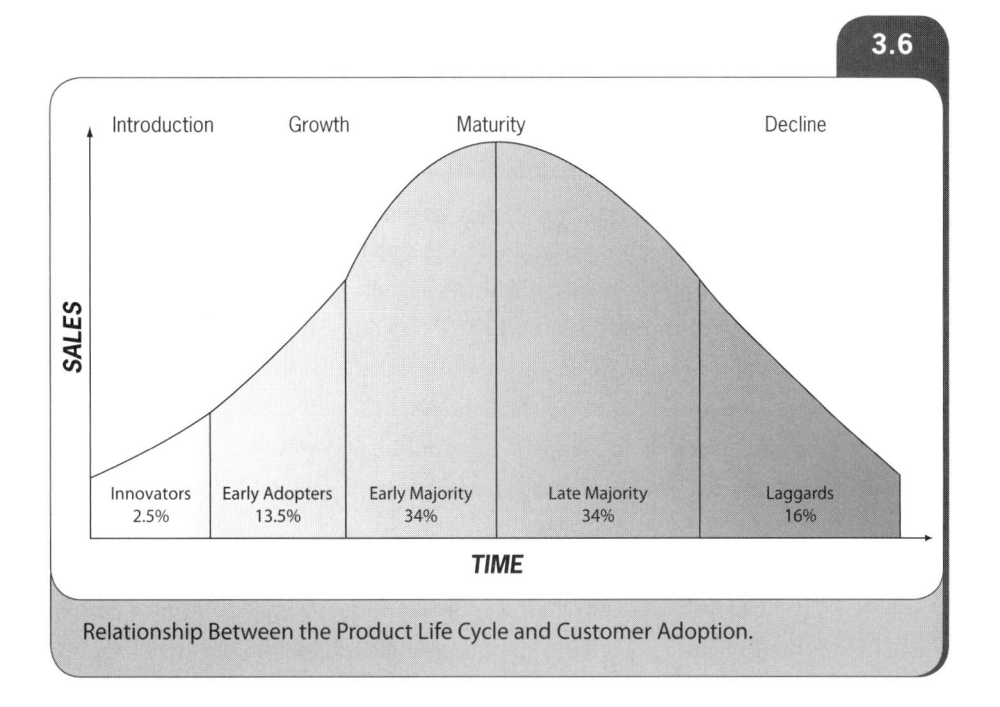

```
Introduction    Growth    Maturity         Decline

SALES

         Innovators  Early Adopters  Early Majority  Late Majority   Laggards
           2.5%         13.5%            34%             34%           16%
                                    TIME
```

Relationship Between the Product Life Cycle and Customer Adoption.

Classification of Purchasing Situations

The nature of products, buying circumstances, and price points affect customer behavior. Most goods and services are described by four types of purchasing situations based on the types of goods being considered. Occasionally one or more of the categories overlap.

Shopping Goods High-priced items purchased after considerable deliberation and consultation are called **shopping goods**. Important major personal and household purchases fall into this category. The decision to buy is premeditated, and most items under consideration are big ticket. People usually comparison shop online or in stores and speak with others before making final decisions. Furniture, automobiles, and diamond rings are shopping goods.

Specialty Goods Products bearing name brands or with special attributes buyers covet and go out of their way to purchase are called **specialty goods**. Customers are less likely to settle for substitutes, and possession is more important than price when shopping for specialty goods. For this reason this type of shopping also is

Chapter 3 > **Multichannel Customer Behavior**

called *destination shopping*. Doing without if you cannot get to a retailer that sells Christian Louboutin shoes is the mark of a true specialty fashion shopper. Although specialty products are not necessarily costly, often they are.

Convenience Goods Low-cost items that are purchased with minimum effort or time are called **convenience goods**. Products are purchased by habit with little preplanning. Picking up milk, gum, and the latest edition of *Elle* at On-the-Run constitutes a convenience purchase. Although traveling beyond a customary trading area to purchase convenience goods is sometimes necessary, being where the customer is present, such as in airports, near public access areas, or on commuting routes, is a characteristic of convenience shopping to which retailers have responded.

Impulse Goods Items that are purchased spontaneously are called **impulse goods**. Virtually no forethought goes into an impulse purchase, but impulse items are not necessarily low ticket. The availability of easy credit and understanding of hedonic needs makes it possible and plausible for expensive goods to be impulse purchases. The opportunity to purchase clothing on whim or escape to a romantic city for the weekend when funds are not in the budget creates stressful situations for customers and opportunities for retailers. In-store visual merchandising and easy online clicks encourage spur-of-the moment purchases.

Decision-Making Process and Time Frame

Your car quit—for the last time—on the way to school. When you acknowledge that you need a new vehicle, you put in motion a set of steps that may be simple or more complex but help guide you to your next purchase. By studying the decision-making process involved in consumer purchasing, retailers can develop strategies that lead to sales and diminish buyer's remorse. The steps in the decision-making process are identified in Table 3.2. People go through this process at different speeds and may skip some steps, depending on the price or importance of the product and the purchasing situation.

When making decisions customers use routine, limited, or extended time frames. Convenience goods are generally purchased routinely, but shopping goods require extended decision making. Specialty goods are often purchased with limited decision making, but the extended process is used when the product or service is

Steps in the Decision-Making Process Table 3.2

1. **STIMULUS** The decision to buy is not unprovoked. A signal comes from the external environment or from within oneself. The whiff of coffee emanating from Gloria Jean's could very well trigger the purchase of a pound of Colombian coffee beans. A visit to Best Buy for a printer cartridge may act as a reminder of the entertainment unit you need for your dorm room.

2. **PROBLEM AWARENESS** An unfulfilled need or want demands resolution. Your ancient microwave emitting a high-pitched noise and ceasing to function is an example of an obvious crisis requiring action.

3. **INFORMATION SEARCH** Customers seek facts and figures to expedite the decision-making process. Going online to search consumer reports or blogs, collecting brochures, seeking out advertising materials, and/or doing comparison shopping is initiated during this stage. Talking with knowledgeable friends or family before you move to the next stage is typical.

4. **EVALUATION OF ALTERNATIVES** Studying the information collected and ranking choices are part of the evaluation process. Product cost, shopping ease, delivery speed, service policies, brand preferences, and company reputation are a few factors that influence the purchasing decision.

5. **PURCHASE** One particular good or service is selected and the transaction is completed. Will that be cash, check, debit, credit, or electronic payment?

6. **POST-PURCHASE BEHAVIOR** Retailers try to make the shopping experience satisfying and pleasurable in many ways. Guarantees, warrantees, rebates, thank-you messages, and supportive e-mails should be part of the post-purchase experience. Follow-up is crucial because lifetime value is at stake; the transaction should not be a one-time event.

expensive or being bought for the first time. Because impulse goods are purchased spontaneously, it may appear the decision-making process is nonexistent. In fact it does occur, but responses to stimuli may be deep in the subconscious. Color, odors, and textures may conjure up past experiences and urge us to buy, even if we are not consciously aware of their influence. Even hunger may affect shopping habits as any starving college student who has gorged on a huge bag of chips while waiting at a checkout counter can attest.

Decision-making time frames are directly related to selling tactics, visual merchandising techniques, branding strategies, and price. To use these techniques effectively, retailers rely on target marketing. The next section explains how a universe of customers is broken down into manageable groups for the purposes of target marketing.

Bases for Market Segmentation

It is impossible to reach all people with one marketing message. Even if retailers could, the attempted execution would be wasteful, inefficient, and much too costly. All customers do not think or act alike. For these reasons groups within a larger population that meet carefully developed customer profile criteria are identified. **Market segmentation** is the process of breaking down a larger population to find identifiable, manageable, actionable target markets that are more likely to buy specific products or services.

In order to identify primary and secondary markets, retailers draw from many bases, including demographic, geographic, psychographic, and behavioral information about populations. A report attributed to the Direct Marketing Association noted that 83 percent of retailers responding to a survey use demographics, 70 percent use purchasing frequency, and 76 percent use products purchased as bases for customer segmentation.[3]

> Demographic Segmentation

Statistics on human populations, including age, gender, ethnic origin, education, income, occupation, type of housing, and other descriptors, are called **demographics**. Most businesses define their target markets by age but it is rarely the only characteristic used. Age more commonly is used in conjunction with other segmentation descriptors.

Age

Age groups respond differently to the workplace, leisure activities, shopping, and spending their money. Classic categories such as baby boomer, generation X, and generation Y designate age ranges as the basis for market information. To understand the significance of the newest age shifts in the United States, it is helpful to see them in relation to the baby boomers. This section considers key characteristics and values of different age groups in the United States from the oldest to the youngest. However, stereotyping is rampant and one must be vigilant when using general trends to describe markets.

Sterling Silver Seniors At the top end of the age spectrum are 37 million people in the United States who are over the age of 62. Contemporary senior citizens do not want to be treated like children nor do they want to be considered museum pieces. In fact they do not want to be categorized at all.[4] To be treated as individuals with all the rights and privileges that come with growing old gracefully is their goal.

Those with money want to travel, discover hobbies, or even start new businesses. Others are content to kick back and enjoy their homes after a long stretch in the workforce. Some who are not as well endowed financially look to save money in all phases of their lives, relying on discounts offered to members of the American Association of Retired Persons (AARP) whenever they can. A portion of the over-65 population is more concerned with health issues and finding ways to cope with life until their inevitable exit from the planet. Many become doting grandparents bestowing love, time, and birthday and holiday gifts of significant monetary value. Retailers would not want to treat all persons over 65 in the same way.

Also dubbed the "silver surfers," this age group is expected to grow significantly. Those older than 62 years are expected to comprise 12 percent of Internet users in 2011.[5] People in this age group are sometimes called "war babies" because many of the youngest were born during World War II. They share some characteristics of the oldest baby boomers, valuing achievement, respecting authority, and preferring structure in their lives.

Baby Boomers The 76 million people born between 1946 and 1964 are considered **baby boomers**. Baby boomers represent the broadest age range of any generational group. The youngest baby boomers may still have children living at home. The oldest—who are eligible for retirement—may have delayed retirement and still be in the workforce. The lives of many baby boomers are in transition, making it foolhardy to speculate on the behaviors of the group as a whole. More segmentation is needed to reach these markets successfully.

The oldest boomers have no children living in the household, and that may indicate that they have more discretionary income to spend on lifestyle maintenance and travel. *Road Scholar* is a travel program designed to appeal to older baby boomers and couples who want to see the world and be educated concurrently. In better health than previous generations, boomers are a viable retail market. These individuals grew up with rock-and-roll and conspicuous consumption. Some are on a quest for eternal youth, judging by the popularity of health and well-being products purchased by this group.

Justice targets 'tweens through a chain of experiential specialty stores. [Source: AP Photo/Jay LaPrete.]

Use of the Internet by baby boomers will increase over the next several years—countering the earlier estimates that young people would be the most significant online market. By 2011 *eMarketer* has predicted that 83.2 percent of the estimated 63.7 million baby boomers in the United States will use the Internet at least once per month. The boomers will account for 30.1 percent of all Internet users at that time.[6]

Generation X People born in the United States between 1965 and 1981 are identified as **generation X**. Children of early baby boomers, now in their thirties and forties, represent the first generation to grow up with great media influences. Other characteristics of this generational group include greater creativity and acceptance of diversity. Xers grew up in the era of AIDS and high divorce rates, and many represent the first generation born to dual-income parents. This combination of factors may underlie their often-stated desire to balance work and life effectively.

Generation Y and Millennials Persons born after 1981 in the United States are members of **generation Y**. These contemporary young adults and teens who came of age at the turn of this century also are called millennials. They are media and marketing savvy, love reality TV shows, and are the first generation to grow up with e-commerce. Members value social responsibility and prefer to work in environments that provide support as well as fun on the job. One-third of this group is African American or Hispanic.

'Tweens Neither small children nor old enough to be teenagers, youngsters between the ages of 8 and 12 years are called **'tweens**. They and their parents are viable markets to retailers. Justice, illustrated in Figure 3.7, is a specialty chain designed to enchant young girls in this age group. Through lively product presentation, demonstations, and affordable pricing, the company brings apparel, accessories, and fragrances to 'tweens and teens. Owner Tween Brands converted 560 former Limited Too stores to the Justice brand in early 2009.[7]

<u>Children as Consumers</u> The youngest individuals are defining a whole new generation of shoppers. According to one study, over 75 percent of children 8 to 14 years of age in the United States have completed an online shopping transaction. The children surveyed listed music, video games, movies, and MP3 players as top products and also voiced interest in celebrities.[8]

Some of the most popular gifts during the 2007 holiday period were cell phones, laptops, digital cameras, and MP3 players—for preschoolers! Recently, however, questions have been raised about this trend. Some child-rearing experts believe that such early exposure to these products may be detrimental to very young children because electronic devices do not allow their imaginations to develop as well as less technology dependent toys.[9]

Children are growing up faster, and Web sites designed for young surfers are abundant. Many activity sites are tied to toy manufactures such as Lego and Mattel. Webkinz, mentioned in Chapter 1, engages millions of young visitors each month. The Walt Disney Company launched Club Penguin, a virtual world where children can dress, groom, and play with penguin characters for $5.95 per month. It could be said that Club Penguin helps children learn to shop because users can accumulate points on the site that can be spent on virtual items for their penguins.[10]

<u>Gender</u>

Gender is used independently or with other bases for segmentation. When combined with income, for example, the discrepancy between male and female annual incomes is often cited because it may affect purchasing power. Other dimensions such as affinity for technology or product preferences may be influenced by gender. These and other gender issues are explored because knowledge of the relationships between shopping tendencies and gender may help retailers reach target markets more effectively.

<u>Gender Breakdown of Internet Users</u> Gender is used to segment markets—especially those involving products specifically desired by men or women. The gender breakdown of Internet users has shifted dramatically in this decade. Before

2000, more males than females in the United States had Internet access—one of the reasons more men shopped online. In early 2000, for the first time, the number of women online exceeded that of men. At that time an analyst at JupiterResearch noted, "It's no longer enough to think of women as the target audience. The sites that will be most successful in capturing future potential revenue from this market will target women through deeper segmentation."[11] The analyst successfully predicted that women should not be treated as a homogeneous market just because they shared the characteristic of having shopped online. As a segmentation strategy, gender was too broad and needed to be further differentiated.

Gender Differences in Shopping According to a *Time* magazine online poll, men and women differ significantly in their attitudes toward shopping. When asked if they shop only when they need something specific, 69 percent of men agreed compared with 42 percent of women. In response to the question, "Do you enjoy shopping even if you are browsing and not shopping for a specific item?" only 31 percent of men responded positively compared with 58 percent of women.[12] Despite earlier cautions, there is an element of truth in most stereotypes. Men do not like to shop as long or with the same intensity as women.

The term "metrosexual" blends gender and lifestyle to describe a discerning male market. A **metrosexual** is a young adult man who is attuned to a fast-paced urban lifestyle and who is a connoisseur of fine products and services. The connotation melds manliness with hedonic tastes, including a fashion emphasis usually attributed to gay men.

Gay and Lesbian Segments According to the 2000 U.S. Census, an estimated 3 million gay and lesbian people are living together as partners, but only 600,000 in families. Among the latter, there are 6 to 10 million children of gay, lesbian, and bisexual partners.[13]

Research has identified five demographic segments for gay and lesbian consumers:

> *Super Gays*—Highly educated, with high incomes; considered sophisticated, risk-takers, extroverted, and open about their sexual orientation; spend more time online than other segments.
> *Habitaters*—Tend to be older than Super Gays; consider themselves mature, traditional people; are in committed relationships and own homes.

> *Gay Mainstream*—Conservative middle Americans; equally represented regarding age, income, education, and gender; not as open about their sexual orientation.
> *Party People*—Youngest and least educated of segments; consider themselves cutting-edge, simple, and rebellious; comfortable with sexual orientation.
> *Closeted Respondents*—Are older and few are open about their sexual orientation; consider themselves serious, introverted, and mature; most are not in a committed relationship.[14]

Like other populations, gays and lesbians can be further segmented according to demographic, lifestyle, and behavioral dimensions. This is frequently the direction taken by retailers that value succinct and measurable market segmentation strategies over a mass-market or shotgun approach.

Differences between the sexes and changing viewpoints regarding target market strategies are covered throughout this text. The next section examines the discordant relationship between gender and income.

Household Income

Reviewing general income trends in the United States is illuminating in light of the assumed affluence of Americans. Although the United States has one of the highest standards of living in the world, the false perception of many people from other countries is that all Americans are wealthy. Data compiled by the Census Bureau show that in 2005 the median household income was $48,201.[15] This may not seem high by typical U.S. consumer standards, but in many countries, it would represent significant income.

Ramifications for Online Retailers Typically online shoppers are better educated, younger, technologically more sophisticated, and earn a higher income annually than those who shop only brick-and-mortar stores. Those who have researched products online and purchased them offline are more likely to earn more than their counterparts who are not cross-channel shoppers. They are also more likely to have a college degree.[16]

Internet Usage in Mainstream and Low-Income Families Computer use in the home for work or study tends to be greater in low-income families than in the general population. According to a study commissioned by the U.S. Department of Education, about 25 percent of households earning less than $25,000 per year have home access to the Internet. However, 70 percent of low-income households use their home computers for work-related activities compared with 55 percent of the general population. Regarding study-related online activities, 45 percent of low-income users versus 38 percent of the general population use home computers.[17] These statistics may defy the preconceptions of many readers.

<u>The Wage Gap</u> The difference in annual wages between men and women is significant. In 2006 women earned 76.6 percent as much as men earned, or seventy-seven cents to the dollar. Wage differentials are also reflected in ethnic origins. African-American women earned sixty-four cents to the dollar and Hispanic women fifty-two cents to the dollar compared with Caucasian women.[18] Income statistics are related to gender, education, geography, and ethnicity. All are significant when determining market segmentation strategies.

Ethnicity

Internet access is not proportionate across all ethnicities. For example, approximately 80 percent of Hispanics in the United States have Internet access compared with 71 percent of non-Hispanic whites and 60 percent of non-Hispanic blacks. More then twice as many English-dominant Latinos use the Internet compared with Spanish-dominant Hispanics. English-dominant Hispanics are also more likely to have cell phones. More than half of all Hispanics are English-dominant or bilingual.[19]

Asian households in the United States have the highest household income and savings rates across all ethnic groups and are better educated. This information is useful to retailers planning Web site content and advertising across all channels.

The number of Asian-Americans is growing and by 2009 was expected to reach over 14 million. The majority live in California, New York, New Jersey, Texas, and Hawaii. Studies have shown that Asian women spend more on apparel than their mainstream counterparts.[20]

Family Life Cycle

Family constellation refers to the makeup of a household, for example, single, married, or single with children. **Family life cycle** traces the progression of family groupings through their lifetimes. Because the buying power of family groups varies greatly depending on the type of family living arrangements, this information is useful in determining market segmentation. The composition of American families has not changed appreciably in this decade; however, several changes occurred between 1980 and 2004. Trends of significance in the United States include the following:

> More single parent families in both married (family) and co-habitating (nonfamily) households.
> More gay and lesbian households.
> A higher proportion of men living alone in nonfamily households (nearly doubling between 1980 and 2004); although women's numbers have increased, the change has not been as significant.
> A slight decline in the percentage of total family households from 2000 to 2004 (from 69 to 68 percent of households).[21]

Social Class Stratification

Social class theorists segment people into groups based on demographic data, including income, occupation, and education. Social class designators, including lower-lower, upper-lower, lower-middle, upper-middle, lower-upper, and upper-upper, provide a framework, but do not accurately or adequately predict all customer behavior. Social class categories for the United States are outlined in Table 3.3.

Retailers are interested in the purchasing tendencies and product preferences of people in the various categories. In practice what we call the middle class is the mass market used in other contexts.

> Geographic Segmentation

A host of other demographic data helps retailers diligently define their markets. A potpourri of geographic examples follows.

> Adding a geographic dimension to gender, a study showed that women living west of the Mississippi River were more likely to shop online. The top city in the United States for online shopping is Salt Lake City. One reason for the high numbers in the West may be attributed to fewer stores in close proximity to the survey participants.[22]
> A company selling books or international study tours appealing to highly educated individuals may want to direct its promotions to Arlington County, Virginia, where 35.9 percent of the population has an advanced degree.

Table 3.3 Social Class Stratification in the United States

SEGMENT DESCRIPTOR	CHARACTERISTICS	PERCENTAGE OF POPULATION
Upper-Upper	Inherited wealth; not ostentatious, value services; professionals; value philanthropy	1
Lower-Upper	First-or second-generation wealth; professionals and entrepreneurs; driven to succeed; more ostentatious consumption patterns	5 to 10
Upper-Middle	College educated, upwardly mobile; salaried managers and other professionals; child- and family-oriented expenditures; comfortable homes	30 to 35
Lower-Middle	Nonmanagerial, supervisory positions; high hourly wage earners; homeowners; want to educate children; own modest homes	30 to 35
Upper-Lower	Less skilled workers; try to make ends meet and enjoy life; apartment dwellers	9
Lower-Lower	Unemployed and unskilled workers; live below poverty level; many on public support	7

Source: Adapted from R.P. Coleman, "The Continuing Significance of Social Class to Marketing," *Journal of Consumer Research*, December 1983, 267.

> More single people reside in Clark County, Georgia, than anywhere else in the United States—55.6 percent of the men and 47.2 percent of women there have never been married. Dating services might find this information helpful.

> A company selling nutritious, quick-to-prepare meals to dual-income families might target Portage County, Wisconsin, where 83.8 percent of children under 6 have working parents.[23]

Geography, age, and gender are another combination used by marketers. Lifestyle and geography are used to determine store locations. For example, retailers selling bicycles may want to look to Seattle, Washington—one of the largest cycling markets in the country.

> Psychographic and Lifestyle Segmentation

Classifying people on the basis of their lifestyles, activities, interests, and opinions is called **psychographic segmentation**. In a customer behavior context, **lifestyle** describes the way people live, work, play, and spend their money. Society today is more ecologically enlightened than in the past; in tandem with this trend, media influences including the Internet have added new dimensions to shopping behavior. Fashion and ecological orientations are both examples of psychographic dimensions.

Fashion Orientation

Customers of fashion are described by their fashion orientation or direction. Fashion-forward, updated, and basic are three types that appear on a continuum. This concept is closely related to the consumer adoption categories introduced earlier in this chapter, but applies only to fashion attitudes. For example, a person considered fashion-forward is usually an innovator or early adopter of other product trends. Position on the scale depends on the degree of influence fashion has on an individual. The importance of fashion orientation to retailers is demonstrated by isolating traits of each type.

> **Fashion-forward customers** are trendsetters and purchase the newest apparel and accessories early in a fashion season. Fashion-forward customers are well-acquainted with designer merchandise and discriminate as to where they purchase fashion. They are brand conscious, expect personal service, and spend significant dollars annually with the retailers of their choice. Stores such as Neiman Marcus, Saks Fifth Avenue, Bergdorf Goodman, Fendi, and Louis Vuitton are favorite haunts. The Louis Vuitton in-store boutique illustrated in Figure 3.8 exemplifies the fashion focus of these customers. Fashion-forward customers comprise only about 5 percent of the population. Regarded as the prime market for luxury goods, these customers wield considerable influence on the fashion industry. They also shop online more frequently.

> **Updated customers** dress fashionably and purchase after a trend is introduced in the market. They are considered early adopters but purchase closer to the peak of the fashion curve. Typical retail choices include Bebe, Arden B., and Juicy Couture for young-thinking shoppers. Department stores such as Bloomingdale's and department/specialty stores such as Nordstrom are choices for older, updated customers. Updated customers shop diffusion rather than couture lines of merchandise. Price points on merchandise are lower than those in the fashion-forward category, but retail competition for customer dollars is fierce. Updated customers make up about 15 percent of the total fashion market. Box. 3.2 describes some popular online

3.8 High-end retailers like Louis Vuitton are magnets for fashion-forward customers. The company has freestanding stores as well as boutiques within department and specialty stores. [Source: Photograph provided by Lynda Poloian.]

> resources for contemporary apparel and lends insight into the affinity for Web shopping by fashion consumers.
> **Basic customers** are the majority of fashion consumers who shop in the maturity stage of the fashion cycle. This is the mass market for fashion goods, and members comprise nearly 80 percent of all customers. Basic customers look for lower price points, and shop more frequently when goods are on sale. They are more conservative in their apparel selections. Retailers of choice are Walmart, Kohls, and J. C. Penney.

Department and discount stores appear to be favorite destinations for women who are shopping for apparel. When women were surveyed about where they had shopped the top three choices were Walmart, Target, and J. C. Penney. To strengthen the point, 51 percent of women in the survey had shopped at Walmart.[24]

When gauging fashion appeal in terms of online searches, Coach topped the list of most-wanted clothing, accessories, and shoes on eBay in a measurement taken over a one-week period. Style director Constance White of eBay said, "Coach . . . cuts across all kinds of demographics. A 16-year old can receive this for her birthday as a special gift, but then again, it can be an affordable luxury for the accomplished baby boomer." Gucci and Prada followed Coach on the list of top searches.[25] Speculate on what fashion orientation most Coach customers have and you will conclude that they share the updated one.

What's the Buzz? Box 3.2

> *Shoppers Click on Contemporary*

More contemporary shoppers are buying on the Web, whether for a deal from Bluefly.com or the new young designer collection from Shopbop.com. Online sales of apparel, accessories, and footwear were expected to total $22.1 billion in 2007, according to a Shop.org report from Forrester Research. The study revealed that 10 percent of all apparel sales would be made online in 2007. The increase was attributed to more retailers launching Web sites.

Firms that produce contemporary apparel, especially those that want to remain on the cutting edge of the fashion industry, have discovered there is lots of business to be done on the Web. "People are more comfortable buying online," says Erin Crandall, head buyer at Shopbop. Citing her site, as well as Bergdorf Goodman and Barneys New York, Crandall said: "Customers trust the buyers and know they are going to get great quality and style. They can take that chance online."

"Newly launched collections have performed well," Crandall said. The site also features labels such as Diane von Furstenberg, Genera, and LaRok, among others. Overall, Crandall says that sales are up and she expects that trend to continue as more shoppers find it easier and more convenient to shop via computer.

In addition to Shopbop.com, Web sites such as Net-a-porter.com, Shopintuition.com, and Revolveclothing.com have become important players in multilane, contemporary online stores. Smaller retailers have also benefited from an online presence. Randi Evans Siegel owns three contemporary shops in Palm Beach, Florida, and her Web site shoprapunzels.com. She says her Web site brings in more volume than her freestanding stores combined. Her online customers shop at night more than ever before, a trend she attributes to increased broadband access. The brand Juicy Couture is a favorite with her customers and she stocks sizes that are not readily available at other retailers. Maternity fashions are available on her Web site because there is not sufficient room to carry them in her stores.

Many brands, including those from designers Betsy Johnson, Nanette Lapore, and Rebecca Taylor, also sell their lines on the Web. Jodi Arnold, founder of the lines Mint Jodi Arnold and the higher-end contemporary line Jodi Arnold collection, launched online and saw many positive results. Sales volume grew, she got more feedback from her retail customers, and her distribution spread worldwide. Arnold said, "Suddenly, we have a large amount of orders coming in from Australia." She concludes: "The Web really is the future of retail, so you just have to be in it and ahead of the game."

Source: Excerpted and condensed from Julee Greenberg Kaplan, Women's Wear Daily, December 6, 2007, 10.

"Green" Orientation

There is renewed zest for all things environmentally safe, sound, wearable, and consumable, from eco-fashion to organic food, sustainable building products, and green automobiles—and we do not mean green in color only. Many companies are concerned about reducing carbon emissions, minimizing packaging, maximizing recycling, and manufacturing ethically. A growing number of customers are mindful of the environment, and retailers are meeting the demands of the public.

Research shows that 38 percent of online teens are environmentally concerned. Of that group, 15 percent are considered "hard core" and therefore of special interest to marketers. Identifying other activities of teen consumers that may correlate with environmental interest, the study showed that environmentally attuned teens spend more time listening to music and more money purchasing music than teens in the general population.[26]

The company Gaiam sells a wide range of products from nontoxic cleaners to bamboo and organic cotton bed sheets, and it has been following the eco-friendly path since 1988. Using catalogs, a Web site, and television infomercials, the company also sells yoga mats and fitness videos through other retailers. In 2008 it tested a store-within-a-store concept in a Target fitness department.[27]

The green movement in apparel manufacturing and retailing extends worldwide as evidenced by the following examples. German retailer Karstadt and French department store Galeries Lafayette developed ethical apparel lines. Marks & Spencer opened a green store and Tesco lowered its carbon footprint by 60 percent in the United Kingdom.[28]

More than simply an option for socially and environmentally responsible customers, the green movement is gaining momentum in mass markets. Manufacturers are putting research, product development resources, and money into merchandise that is more in harmony with Mother Nature. Two e-commerce sites—eBay and Student/Advantage.com—have partnered to create evo.com, a Web site with a green theme.

> Behavioral Segmentation: New Parameters

The Choice™ Generation sounds like another generational group, but it is actually a behavioral category of young consumers. SmartReply, a company that provides voice and mobile marketing solutions, coined the term. **Choice™ Generation** members believe they have the right to choose and control what, when, and how they receive marketing messages. Eric Holman, president of SmartReply described the new group: "They are the polar opposite of the passive consumers of yesteryear who were receptive to one-directional marketing messages. Consumers of the Choice™ Generation require a two-way dialog where their input matters."[29] Although the group primarily represents younger consumers, the underlying philosophy regarding choice and control is important across most age and behavioral markets.

Other behavioral dimensions include time spent online and the proportion of that time spent shopping. Heavy users of a product or service frequently become the target of retailers looking to increase conversion rates. Knowledge of media habits is useful, as it alerts retailers to the types of promotional messages that reach customers most effectively.

Time Spent on Top Web Sites

According to a 2007 research study, the average time spent on the 15 largest retail Web sites was 9 minutes and 31 seconds. Visitors to Amazon.com, HPShopping.com, and Walmart.com spent more time than average. Customers stayed on QVC.com about 15 minutes and 32 seconds. Visitors did not stay as long as the average on sites in the top 15, including Staples.com, Dell.com, and JCPenney.com.[30]

Time spent on a site is not conclusive when evaluating performance, because it does not denote either a positive or negative experience with a company. A deeper look into the behavioral aspects of the customer's experience is required to fully understand the significance of time spent visiting an online store. Customers who arrive at well-designed, efficient Web sites that guide them to merchandise and help them complete transactions quickly have no need to spend much time on the site. Spending more time than average on a site may mean that the customer is totally engaged in product research or is probing the merchandise mix by breadth and depth. What is most important is the total customer experience, irrespective of whether the visit is long or short.

Online Purchase Decision Time Frame

From another time perspective, the total time spent online before an actual e-commerce purchase is made was 34 hours and 19 minutes in 2006—almost double the time invested in 2005. The researchers did not focus solely on retail sites; however, among the companies studied were Lillian Vernon, ShopNBC, PetSmart, and Vermont Teddy Bear.[31]

Extended shopping behavior is attributed to the plethora of sites that can be searched; the ease of comparison shopping, especially for big-ticket items; and the growing comfort level with the online shopping experience.

Segmentation helps retailers define their markets. Several bases for segmentation have been suggested in the preceding sections, but these are limited only by the creativity, expansion plans, and budgets of retailers. Methods may vary, but the constants remain the same. Market segments must be measurable and significant in size to be profitable. Reaching customers through appropriate contact methods and motivating them to purchase completes the picture.

Customer Expectations of Multichannel Retailers

The customer speaks: "I want to be able to order my new car online, pick it up at a dealership, download the users' manual when I feel like it, subscribe to the automobile manufacturer's lifestyle magazine, and blog with other drivers online. Is that too much to ask?"

The retailer responds: "No."

The customer responds: "Well, there are a few more things that I'd really like to have!"

> What Customers Want

To determine shoppers' expectations of multichannel retailers, let's look at general categories such as price and value, channel integration, operational and merchandising concerns, the human touch, and online-specific services.

Price and Value Commitment

When times get tough, the tough go shopping but not with the same intensity, frequency, or at the same price points as they do when the economy is more robust. Several studies have shown that price is the most important factor to online customers. One study found that 43 percent of online shoppers said price was the top priority when making a purchase. Next on their priority list was free shipping—also price related.[32] Pricing consistency is important to customers whether they shop primarily in stores, through catalogs, online, or using other vehicles.

3.9

The Customer Browse/Buy Relationship.

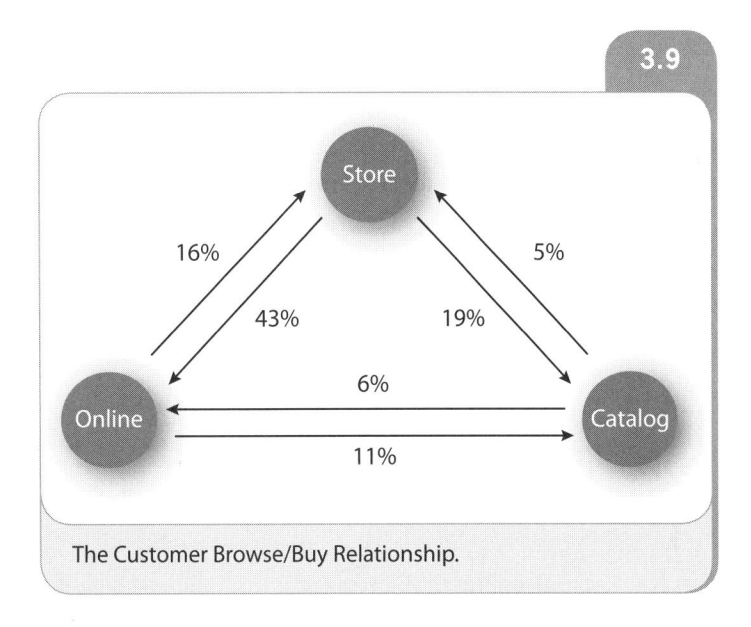

- Online → Store: 16%
- Store → Online: 43%
- Store → Catalog: 19%
- Catalog → Store: 5%
- Catalog → Online: 6%
- Online → Catalog: 11%

Integrated Services

Customers want flexibility when they conduct routine as well as unique retail transactions through any channel. Choosing the channel that is convenient at the time they need the service is most important to them. Customers and retailers recognize that needs are different today than they will be tomorrow. Channel preferences may shift due to personal schedules, availability of time, stress, family needs, and mood. Customers want purchasing and service options, promotions, communications, and gift card use to be available cross-channel.

Cross-Channel Shopping Every year the percentage of customers who research products online and buy them offline increases. A study showed that 64 percent of survey participants went online before making a purchase in the preceding three months. Of those who had incomes of $75,000 or more, 81 percent went online before shopping other channels.[33] The higher the income, the greater the likelihood that prepurchase research will be done.

Shoppers value options. Observing customer behavior across channels gives retailers an indication of the browse–buy relationship. Research results show that 16 percent of customers who browse online buy merchandise at a store. Conversely 43 percent of store browsers purchased goods online.[34] Browse–buy tendencies across channels are illustrated in Figure 3.9.

Promotions Customers are also looking for coupons, discounts, gift and wedding registries, and frequent-user incentives. They expect promotional pricing across all channels. Some retailers offer coupons in their catalogs that can be used in the catalog, online, or in their stores. Book-of-the-Month Club offers points for every dollar spent on books purchased online or through direct-mail pieces sent to members every three weeks. Points can be used toward future purchases and occasionally the book club offers free shipping.

Communication Even customers who usually shop at a favorite brick-and-mortar store may occasionally order from the company's print or online catalog. When they do cross-shop, they want their past-purchase history and product information from the retailer to be available, no matter which channel they choose.

It is the responsibility of the retailer to compile and sort information and maintain reliable databases. The systems should be up-to-date, responsive, and user-friendly while ensuring privacy for customers.

Gift Card Use Customers expect that their gift cards will be redeemable through store, catalog, and online channels. Although purchased for many occasions throughout the year, gift card redemption intensifies during the post-holiday period in the United States as customers treat themselves to merchandise and services.

Because customers do not have to visit a store or Web site to purchase gift cards, their use is more pronounced. Most customers are relieved when they can consolidate routine errands, and retailers have made it easier for them to purchase gift cards in other retail stores that they shop regularly. Retailers including Gap, Nordstrom, Appleby's, AMC Theaters, and Radio Shack sell their gift cards through supermarket or drugstores. Prepaid debit cards are also popular and are sold by major credit card companies. For the person who has everything, an American Express debit card makes a welcome gift.

The sales and subsequent redemption of gift cards has helped retail sales early in the year—traditionally a slow period. Retailers speculate that shoppers will cash in their gifts on new merchandise and spend beyond the card's face value while in the store or online.

Customer sentiment has changed regarding the social stigma once attached to giving a gift card rather than taking time to make a more personal gift selection. The fact that gift cards can now be linked to a favorite company, allowing them to be personalized to the individual recipient, and can be used at the convenience of the customer has helped change thoughts regarding gifting.

Operational and Merchandising Efficiencies

Customers have a shopping list of services that they require or view as desirable for retailers of the new millennium. Across all channels, shoppers expect that inventories will be monitored thoroughly to ensure full assortments when they are ready to shop. Many are looking for customization and personalization of products and services. Others value alternatives when purchasing or returning goods and arranging appropriate pick-up or delivery procedures.

Consistent In-Stock Position Having the right merchandise at the right time is not a new request of customers, but it is a legitimate need voiced by many. Customers expect that when they place an order or visit a store, their size, color, or model will be available. In the customer's eye, instant gratification is best; timely availability is second best.

Despite technologically advanced inventory replenishment systems, retailers are not always able to perform at a level consistent with customer expectations. Stock-outs equate to lost sales and erosion of brand equity.

Customization Although most retailers carefully segment their markets and bring thoughtful, targeted merchandise and messages to their customers, most individuals want more. Online retailers, especially, are tapping the depths of micromarketing to customize products for their clientele. Several sites have "design-your-own" options allowing the customer, for example, to personalize a pair of Steve Madden shoes, choose a favorite color combination at Nike, or customize a new pair of Oakley sunglasses.[35]

Personalized music for every occasion, monogrammed pet apparel, and made-to-measure jeans are other examples of customization that are readily available. Customization reflects the need for individual expression and is one of the key directions for retailers today.

Purchase and Return Options At one time it was impossible to purchase apparel from a Victoria's Secret catalog and return that merchandise to one of the company's stores. Granted Victoria's Secret stores sell lingerie and sleepwear, not jeans and other apparel, but customers become annoyed when they cannot return goods. That they are not aware of company policy or the nature of distribution does not assuage their discontent. Most multichannel companies now have sufficiently integrated inventory systems and customer databases to allow open purchase and return options across all channels.

To make returns easier many catalog and online companies include prepaid return shipping labels. Others offer hassle-free return policies between store, catalog, and online. Convenience for the customers is key.

<u>Pick-Up and Delivery Services</u> Retailers encourage customers to order online and pick up their purchases in-store if that is their method of choice. Customers diligently search for free shipping or discounted delivery charges if they are ordering from catalogs or online. Somewhere between retailer services and customer preferences is a compromise that meets the needs of both parties. For example, Amazon offers fixed-fee shipping that greatly benefits its heavy users. During holiday seasons many retailers offer free or reduced shipping charges but invoke a limited time period to control costs yet provide an incentive to customers.

During a slowdown in the economy, offers of free shipping are more apparent. Keeping customers in the loop is important to retailers. At some point, prices are increased or operating costs are reduced so that free shipping can continue to be offered.

Human Interaction

The personal touch is important to customers whether a transaction is made in stores, online, through catalogs, or using other vehicles. Personal shoppers and choices of customer contact are options customers request.

<u>Personal Shoppers</u> Once the domain of the rich and famous, personal shopping services now reach the masses. No longer is it necessary to shop in elite retail stores to obtain wardrobe planning or decorating advice. Personal service is all-encompassing. Macy's offers a personal shopping service, and most large furniture retailers offer interior design assistance. Home Depot will do a plot plan for your new kitchen cabinets either in the store or online, illustrating that personal service has reached even do-it-yourself retailers.

Quintessential retail services are stipulated in upmarket retail stores. Saks Fifth Avenue employs personal shoppers who serve all customers if requested. A core group of specialists works exclusively with long-time preferred customers. Clients who spend five-figure dollar amounts annually make appointments with their personal shoppers, who work closely with them to satisfy every need. Merchandise is selected in advance of their arrival using intensive customer profiling, including information about product and brand preferences. Customers are escorted to large, well-appointed dressing rooms where refreshments and other amenities are available. Relationships are built over time, and the focus always is on the customer.

Telephone and Internet Options Land line, mobile phone, texting, online instant messaging, or e-mail—what will it be? Chances are, all of the above. Once again, the customer leads the way as multiple contact options are delivered to customers when, where, and how they want customer service or product information.

Irrespective of whether face-to-face contact is requested or efficient telephone or Internet services will suffice, there is one truth. Customers value human interaction.

Online-Specific Amenities

E-retailing has spawned many new methods of customer contact. E-mail, live chat, and social networking options abound. Secure Internet transactions and payment options are other services sought by customers.

E-mail Alerts and Follow-Up Many customers view personalized e-mails as an important part of the relationship-building process between retailer and customer. In a study charting the effectiveness of e-mail product recommendations, 80 percent of survey participants said they had purchased a product after receiving a product recommendation from a retailer. In the same study, 65 percent said they would like to receive e-mail alerts from online retailers with which they had registered preferences.

Click-to-Chat Services Being able to communicate instantly with a customer service representative is for some customers a step above e-mail contact. The element of instant response also binds some customers to this extension of live chat. **Click-to-chat services** allow online customers to click on an icon, add their telephone number, and receive an immediate callback.

Liveperson and Estara are instant connection services used by retailers such as Sears and Macy's. About 15 to 20 percent of customers who are offered click-to-chat service accept.[36]

The need for immediate contact with a company representative was not possible earlier in online history, and customers occasionally had to wait days to receive responses to their e-mail inquiries from customer service representatives. This has changed for the better since the inception of live chat options.

Social Networking Availability Increasing numbers of customers are requesting blogs, vlogs, podcasts, and social media sites to help them make shopping decisions. **Blogs** are written narratives that convey opinions and solicit reader feedback on the Web. Retailers are setting up their own blogs to elicit customer responses and generate discussion with other customers. Researchers are looking at the impact of blogs on customers. A study shows that 29 percent of women have used information read on blogs to make a purchase and 28 percent have used blog information to not make a purchase.[37]

Vlogs are blogs with a video component. **Podcasts** use audio files to lend credence, opinion, or detail to Web-based content. Most podcasts are used through personal computers, although mobile applications are under development.

According to one study, the opinions of others were most important to those aged 18 to 44 years. YouTube videos, blogs, and MySpace product profiles were cited as important influences.[38]

Electronic Kiosks Customers appreciate the option of accessing an electronic kiosk on or off the premises of a brick-and-mortar store. Kiosks offer greater product depth or breadth to merchandise selections when used as an extension of store inventories.

Secure Systems and Payment Options Despite data breaches, identification theft, and PayPal malfunctions, most online customers are willing to share personal and credit card data with retailers that they respect. The better the branding, the stronger the retailer–customer bond. If a customer already has a good relationship with a retail store, most likely that positive image will transfer to the company's catalog operation or online store. Customers demand secure sites, password protection, immediate deletion of credit card numbers after use, and "no sell"/"no tell" policies involving data sharing with other companies.

The "want list" conveys only the surface of customer expectations. Customers in general have become more cognizant of their rights as customers, more discerning in the retailers and brands they prefer and support, and more engaged by the multichannel experience—smarter and more demanding, perhaps, but customers' needs will be satisfied. Factors that influence customers to return to online stores are graphed in Figure 3.10.

3.10 Factors that Influence Customers to Return to an Online Store.

Factor	%
Free or conditional free shipping	92%
Online order tracking	88%
Discounts or exclusive offers for members	85%
Guarantee and privacy policies	84%
Rebates/coupons	76%
Online outlet/clearance areas	75%
Customer ratings/reviews from other shoppers	74%
Product comparisons	72%
Coupons sent frequently for percent of product	67%
E-Mail alerts of price-drop or in-stock status	63%
View/redeem rewards offline as well as online	63%
In-store returns	58%
Broad network of participating merchants	58%
Live help available	57%
One click shopping/express checkout	52%
Guides or how-to content	51%
Internet-only specials or limited-hours sales/specials	50%
Special offers other than on products sold	49%
Exclusives	48%
Wish lists or stored shopping lists	48%
Recently viewed	46%
In-store pick-up	37%
Invitations to events	34%
Personalized communication via e-mail	30%
Replenishment programs	22%

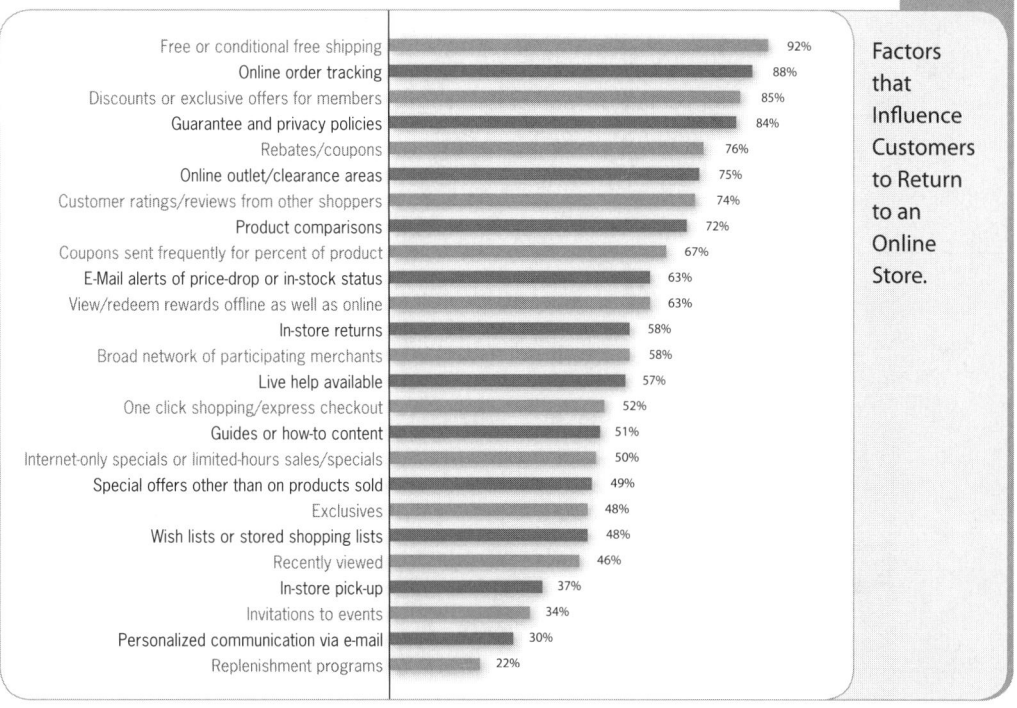

> What Customers Do Not Want

The downside of multichannel retailing reflects the converse of many customer expectations. The following lists highlight negative aspects of the retail experience across channels.

Brick-and-Mortar Stores
> Over-eager or too few sales associates
> Out-of-stock merchandise
> Inconsistent pricing policies
> Mundane merchandising
> Unclean restrooms; sparse rest areas
> High transportation costs to get to store

Catalog Retailers
> Discord between quality, color, and styles of merchandise as conveyed in catalog and experienced upon delivery
> Late, lost, or incomplete shipments

- > Long waits when attempting to contact company for customer service
- > Out-of-stock merchandise
- > Incomplete detail in catalog descriptions
- > Inability to try on apparel
- > Concerns about data privacy and payment security

<u>Online Stores</u>
- > Discord between quality, color, and styles of merchandise as conveyed on the Web site and experienced upon delivery
- > Inability to try on apparel
- > Confusing navigation; too many clicks
- > Slow-loading pages
- > The need to download extra software in order to use site features
- > Log-on pages that restrict use
- > Ineffective site search tools
- > Incomplete product information
- > Out-of-stock merchandise
- > Slow checkouts
- > Concerns about data privacy and payment security

The Multichannel Customer Experience: Influencers and Inhibitors

Although humans possess formidable mental capacity and moral acuity and are capable of making small shopping and monumental life-changing decisions independently, chances are they do not. Attitudes are not shaped and decisions are rarely made in a vacuum. They are molded, refined, and sometimes even changed by our interactions with friends, family, peers, and professional associates. A discussion of influencers and inhibitors in the multichannel customer experience follows.

> **Influencers of the Multichannel Customer Experience**

People use inner resources such as experience, habits, preferences, and other factors to help them make decisions. They consult family, friends, classmates, Facebook buddies, and favorite blogs for input as well. Although influencers such as these play a significant role in all types of retail transactions, never before has knowledge of influencers of the shopping experience been more relevant. Integrated technologies, new media, and greater expectations of multichannel customers and retailers require a fresh viewpoint. Understanding classic concepts of customer behavior and adapting them to the contemporary multichannel marketplace is essential.

Groups and Individuals

Two types of groups and individuals that have a significant impact on retail decisions are reference groups and opinion leaders.

Reference Groups People depend on reference groups for affirmation of their shopping prowess. **Reference groups** are social or professional associations with which a person identifies and to which he or she looks when forming opinions. Fraternities and sororities, business affiliations, sports team membership, and church congregations are examples of formal reference groups. Roommates, class members, and even spectators at a soccer game form informal reference groups.

Opinion Leaders Certain individuals are perceived as being trendier and more persuasive and are charismatic leaders within a reference group. **Opinion leaders** are individuals who shape decisions due to their knowledge of or experience with a product. Film and television actors, celebrities, and sports heroes also are opinion leaders through their product endorsements and high media visibility. All wield power over shopping decisions made by people who hold them in high esteem. Other influencers of human behavior include word-of-mouth and related marketing communication techniques.

Marketing and Communication Tools

Several marketing tactics show the importance of persuasive contact made by individuals or groups that know their target customers well. Personal communication methods ring true in the ears of people who place their faith and loyalty in voices that sound like theirs.

Word-of-Mouth (WOM) The old lament about word-of-mouth applies to retailing as to all other facets of life—if you've had a great experience, you tell a couple of friends; if you've had a dreadful experience, you tell a dozen friends. **Word-of-mouth** is the passing of positive or negative information from one person to another.

It is a powerful form of communication because we trust the input of friends, family, and opinion leaders. The negative side of word-of-mouth can be debilitating, because many customers will never again do business with retailers with which they have had a bad experience.

One study showed that 60 percent of customers shared product advice with others. Forty percent of customers in the study indicated that they neither gave nor received advice on products.[39] Word-of-mouth has an impact on purchasing decisions regarding all types of products and services.

Viral Marketing   Using the power of word-of-mouth, creative marketers have devised ways to reach mass audiences. **Viral marketing** uses customers to generate excitement called "buzz" to help sell a product. By adapting word-of-mouth techniques to reach mass markets through online discussion groups, consumer panels, video sharing, and social networks, companies spread advertising messages that are believable and trustworthy. Though not toxic, viral is what it sounds like—something that is spread from person to person. It is contagious in a positive sense.

Charmin bathroom tissue used this technique when it staged a promotional extravaganza in Times Square in New York City in 2006. A storefront was outfitted with spotlessly clean bathrooms for public use during the campaign. YouTube provided a platform for viral marketing and visitors to the Charmin facility were encouraged to post their own videos to share with the world. In early 2008, Gigunda, the experiential marketing agency that produced the Charmin event, turned the same location into an indoor dog park and adoption center for the Pedigree pet food brand.

Guerilla Marketing   More intense than viral marketing, guerilla marketing is very well organized despite its spontaneous appearance. **Guerilla marketing** uses creative street promotions and online events implemented by hired groups of outgoing people to raise brand awareness. It can be quite outrageous. Many new music releases have been promoted using guerilla marketing.

Social Networking   The realm of MySpace and Facebook is only the tip of the marketing iceberg. Many newer sites depend on like-minded individuals to use their services and patronize their advertisers. Shop until you drop is ever so much more fun if you have friends to do it with online. Box 3.3 looks at the benefits of social shopping sites.

What's the Buzz? Box 3.3

> *Social Shopping*

Cyberspace can be a lonely space for shoppers. Although retail therapy in the physical world is often used as a way to connect with friends, "that social aspect of shopping has been absent online," says John C. Jackson, president and CEO of DecisionStep. The company is trying to change that with a new solution called ShopTogether.

The Internet has proven to be a "powerful social force," says Jackson, who believes ShopTogether offers a way for retailers to tap into that force. It is being used in pilot format by NetShops, an online retailer that operates several specialty stores such as Hammocks.com and WorldGlobes.com.

ShopTogether allows visitors to NetsShops.com to invite a friend to shop with them. By using an assigned code, a shopper then sees one window featuring what they are looking at and a second window that allows them to view items that their friend is admiring. A third window is for shared favorites, and message bars allow for a text exchange.

"We wanted to help our customers buy products where multiple people had an influence on the decision but were not at the same place at the same time," says Jay Gordman, director of e-commerce for NetShops. Although still in its early stages, initial customer feedback is positive, he says.

Netshops' customer service agents who field questions from those customers looking for something specific are also using ShopTogether. This keeps agents from having to walk a particular customer through multiple steps while wondering if that customer is keeping up.

ShopTogether works particularly well for shoppers at the "What should I get for Mom—I have no idea" stage of the game, according to Jackson. "The tool disappears very quickly and it literally becomes a conversation between two people . . . where products are what matters."

DecisionStep gets numerous requests for the capability to bring more than two people together to shop and it is in the works, says Jackson, who is in discussions with retailers of all sizes about adding the ShopTogether feature to their e-commerce sites.

DecisionStep is also pursuing the possibility of making ShopTogether a choice for retailers looking to promote specific sales or events. For instance, a group of friends scattered across the country might be able to pick one night a week and "meet" to shop.

Source: Excerpted and condensed from Rebecca Logan, Stores, *January 2008, 48.*

Media

Media influences—online and offline—shape consumer attitudes regarding branding, educate us about new products, reinforce our past behaviors, and persuade us to buy. What viewer was left emotionally untouched by the Budweiser commercial featuring the Clydesdale horse in training that aired during the 42nd Super Bowl? (If you missed it, you can view it on YouTube.)

Media habits speak to the impact of word-of-mouth and other marketing tactics. Not only are people watching and listening to traditional and contemporary media, they are creating it themselves.

According to a study by Deloitte & Touche, 45 percent of American consumers are creating online content such as Web sites, music, videos, and blogs. Fifty-four percent of respondents use social networking sites, and 45 percent have posted their own profiles. Television advertising appears to have the most influence on consumer buying habits, with 85 percent reporting this preference.[40]

Retailers are making great strides to enhance the customer experience across all channels. Several research groups report standards of online customer service. At a minimum most companies surveyed include company Web site addresses on in-store material. Almost half of all respondents said customers could redeem gift cards online and in stores.[41] Additional information about customer services provided by retailers appears in Chapter 8.

New communication tools reverberate in a socially compelling way, bringing challenges and opportunities to marketers. Customer needs are being met in proactive, creative, and cost-effective ways.

> Inhibitors of the Multichannel Customer Experience

Potential threats or small glimpses of distrust endanger the multichannel experience for customers. Some customers find it difficult to transcend the comfort of traditional stores to shop the less-familiar realm of the Net. Others find it impossible to purchase anything without touching, trying on, smelling, or listening to products. Still others are worried about loss or misuse of personal information or payment schemes that go amiss. Many surf but few are called into action by the Web sites they visit. Shopping carts are abandoned when customers do not discover the full measure of customer satisfaction online.

Intangibility and Perceived Risks of Online Shopping

Despite its many values to customers, online shopping has some attributes that deter customers from making a purchase. Customers are understandably worried about the quality of goods that cannot be fully examined or touched because they are intangible. Shoppers are unsure that their needs will be satisfied and find it difficult to take the leap of faith necessary when dealing with the unknown. Academic researchers have explored the nature of intangibility and the perceived risk it holds for customers. Here are some of their conclusions and recommendations:

> Customers tend to depend on experiential cues to make a choice, indicating that customer recommendations (blogs, social networking, endorsements) might help customers reduce their concerns about products they cannot examine.
> Despite the general acceptance of the Internet, many people perceive that online purchases are riskier than offline purchases.
> Web sites that provide difficult-to-obtain products, low-cost information access, and efficient product- and price-screening agents can reduce feelings of unease.[42]

Another study suggested that use of pictures in the search process, customer control over information presentation, and the use of third-party reviews reduced uncertainty about intangibility when people were shopping online.[43]

Privacy and Security Concerns

Giving out an e-mail address or telephone number to an online retailer or a catalog retailer is becoming less likely for many customers who do not want their personal lives, including finances, divulged. Catalog retailers, telemarketing firms, and online retailers all have their own versions of screening programs that are used to protect customers' wishes regarding contact. Credit card use and electronic payment options are other areas of concern. The threat of identity theft puts shoppers in a less receptive state as they explore multichannel shopping options.

Preference Services Opt-in or opt-out is the choice customers make when they weigh the decision of whether they should or should not divulge personal information to retailers. **Opt-in** means to accept offers from a company to receive its communications. **Opt-out** means to decline offers from a company to receive its communications. Offers include incentives, promotions, and other materials sent by retailers through various modes of contact.

Payment Problems The need for security when paying online or via the telephone is palpable. Customers are rightly afraid to part with credit card numbers unless they are dealing with a well-established company—not possible if one is dealing with a new online business.

A study by the Office of Fair Trading found that 79 percent of Web users were "very concerned" about the security of online payment systems. The report also showed that many customers would give up potential savings from shopping online for the comfort of purchasing goods through other channels.[44]

Identity Theft Having a credit card stolen is bad enough, but when a written or electronic record of your entire life, including financial data, is usurped it is a more threatening matter. The number of adult victims of identity fraud in the United States reached 9.9 million in 2008, and the average fraud amount per victim was $4,849.[45] Consumers can protect their identities by:

> Checking their credit reports regularly, and reporting and correcting errors
> Refusing to divulge credit card or social security numbers to all but the most trusted businesses and organizations
> Investing in a shredder to destroy sensitive personal documents
> Enrolling in fraud-protection services

Retailers and credit card companies work in tandem to ensure security for their customers. New technologies help in the quest to prevent identity theft.

Shopping Cart Abandonment

Frustration ensues when customers' needs are not met online. The ensuing angst sometimes manifests itself in shopping cart abandonment, the equivalent of a store walkout after browsing for an extended period and not consummating the purchase.

Shopping cart abandonment not only concerns shoppers, it is the major source of lost sales to retailers. To some degree, communication between retailers and customers is not open regarding this issue. The e-tailing group's Sixth Annual Merchant Survey showed that 75 percent of the companies surveyed did not communicate with customers who abandoned their carts while visiting online stores. Some merchants were not aware of their shopping cart abandonment rates.[46] Strategies for improving abandonment rates are discussed in Chapter 5.

Technological Malfunctions

Emerging mobile technologies provide challenges to retailers. Customers waiting to access the Internet or make a video call while riding—preferably as a passenger—in an automobile can do so but not yet at the speed of broadband services. As with cell phone service, moving out of range puts the caller in a dead zone that prohibits contact where and when a customer wants service.

Other types of imperfections will persist as the nascent technologies develop. When the cry of "server's down" is no longer heard, we will know we have finally reached nirvana.

Economic Impact of Customer Behavior on Retailers

Customer behavior has an impact on the bottom line of multichannel retailers. Customers who shop more than one channel spend more with that retailer and customers respond positively to brand building across channels.

Macy's store customers who also shop online spend approximately 18 percent more than those who shop only in Macy's brick-and-mortar stores.[47] The company uses e-mails to alert online customers to sales promotions in stores. When the company sends out new credit cards to customers, a special discount coupon helps convert store shoppers to multichannel shoppers.

Borders has partnered with a social networking forum that is in tune with the company's target market. Gather.com solicits customer comments on store services and merchandising initiatives. Feedback is used to improve customer services.[48]

Neiman Marcus has found that multichannel shoppers spend 3.5 times more than a single channel shopper. Members of the luxury retailer's InCircle loyalty program account for almost half of all sales.[49]

These practices are repeated again and again by all high performance retailers. Multichannel retailers respond to customers needs and wants with compelling merchandise, customer service, and promotional incentives across channels. Chapters 4 and 5 examine the strategic planning process and identify the specific techniques that bring customers satisfaction while increasing revenue streams for retailers.

Summary

The customer is central to the retailing process—no matter what channel is used. Shoppers derive value from the channels they select and most use more than one. Major options, including brick-and-mortar, catalog, and online channels, bring their unique attributes to customers. Brick-and-mortar stores offer tactile and sensory stimulation, physical inspection of products, and the ability to try on apparel. Catalogs and online stores do not have these advantages, but make up for them by offering customers more conveniences such as saving time and shopping from home.

Multichannel retailers use a body of knowledge that brings deeper understanding of the wants and needs of the customers. Linking psychological and sociological knowledge with contemporary marketing practices helps retailers develop methods to communicate with customers and satisfy their needs.

To efficiently identify consumers who have the means and intention to buy, retailers use market segmentation. There are many ways of segmenting markets, including the use of demographic, geographic, psychographic, and behavioral characteristics. Usually a combination of these is used to select market targets.

Customers have high expectations of what they want from multichannel retailers. Key areas include pricing and value dimensions, cross-channel services, merchandise availability, and operational flexibility. Many services are germane to online retailers and include e-mail, click-to-chat, and social networking options. Customers want secure transactions online or offline.

Just as adamant about negative aspects of shopping, multichannel customers are frustrated by out-of-stock merchandise. They do not like inconsistent pricing policies and are concerned with security breaches and payment scams. They voice complaints when merchandise is presented well in catalogs or online, but fails to live up to expectations once the goods are received and examined.

Several groups and individuals act to influence the multichannel experience. The people and organizations with which we live, work, and play affect our attitudes and purchasing behaviors. Opinion leaders in whom we place our trust offer judgment on products based upon their expertise, knowledge, or status as an influential person or celebrity.

Key Terms

Aspirational wants	Hedonic needs	Psychographic segmentation
Baby boomers	Hierarchy of needs theory	Reference groups
Basic customers	Impulse goods	Shopping goods
Biogenic needs	Innovation	Specialty goods
Blogs	Lifestyle	'Tweens
Choice™ Generation	Market segmentation	Updated customers
Click-to-chat services	Metrosexual	Utilitarian needs
Convenience goods	Need	Value
Demographics	Opinion leaders	Viral marketing
Family life cycle	Opt-in	Vlogs
Fashion-forward customers	Opt-out	Want
Generation X	Podcasts	Word-of-mouth (WOM)
Generation Y	Product life cycle	
Guerrilla marketing	Psychogenic needs	

Several marketing and communication tools are used to influence customers. Word-of-mouth is the umbrella term for one-on-one conversations involving good and bad shopping experiences. Viral and guerilla marketing are used to influence larger markets. Social networking achieves some of the same benefits of word-of-mouth through online customer contacts and product promotions. The media, in all of its manifestations, continue to influence customers' shopping habits and destinations.

Several inhibitors of the multichannel experience remain to be resolved. Researchers are studying product intangibility and the perceived risk to customers shopping online. Privacy concerns center on controlling customer contact by retailers through opt-in and opt-out programs. Payment and identity theft issues are other inhibiting factors. The collective dissatisfaction that makes customers abandon their online shopping carts before completing purchases is another problem. Technological issues also create customer discontent.

Multichannel retailing brings many advantages to customers. Despite some negative attributes that haunt retailers, the economic force of multichannel retailing is impressive. Retailers that are committed to probing the depths of customer behavior and providing service across all channels are those that will continue to prosper.

> ## Questions for Reflection and Discussion

1. Multichannel retailers reach and satisfy customers through major channels, including brick-and-mortar stores, catalogs, and online. Using each channel, what two attributes do you believe are most valued by customers? Which channel brings you the most value?
2. Several major shifts in customer behavior bring challenges and opportunities to multichannel retailers. Using examples from the text and your own experience, how is the technology revolution affecting retailers and customers?
3. Let's say you consider yourself an expert on Xbox games and usually purchase the newest versions at regular price when they first hit the shelves. To what stage of the product life cycle do the games most likely belong? What type of a product adopter are you? Justify your answers.
4. You have spotted a pair of Lucky jeans for $120 at the mall. Your debit card balance is low but you just have to have them. What purchasing situation do you find yourself in? Consider all four situations before you make your choice and justify your answer.
5. Using the retail product of your choice, how can the demographics of age and gender be used together to segment a market for that product?
6. Discuss the impact of fashion orientation on apparel purchases. Do you consider yourself a fashion-forward, updated, or basic customer? Justify your choice.
7. Behavioral dimensions of market segmentation involving time are particularly important to online retailers. Does the fact that customers spend little time on a retail Web site indicate that the company is doing well or poorly? What factors did you consider in your decision?
8. What kinds of integrated services do multichannel customers want? What techniques are retailers using to encourage cross-channel shopping?
9. Is human interaction with customers more or less important since the advent of the Internet? What are retailers doing to encourage contact with their customers?
10. The power of influencers and inhibitors of the multichannel experience is significant. Selecting one from each category, which do you think are of most consequence to retailers? Justify your choices.

Notes >

1. Phyllis Korkki, "Still that Need for a Human on the Line," *New York Times*, October 7, 2007, www.nytimes.com.
2. Scott Patterson, "Glum Consumer Adds to Concern Over Fate of '08," *Wall Street Journal*, January 8, 2008, C1.
3. Jack Loechner, "Two Out of Five Retailers Don't Have a Store," research brief, The Center for Media Research, January 29, 2008, http://blogs.mediapost.com/research_brief/?p=1628. Statistical source: "Channel Integration and Benchmarks in the Retail Industry," Direct Marketing Association, New York.
4. Charles Duhigg, Six Decades at the Center of Attention, and Counting," *New York Times*, January 6, 2008, www.nytimes.com/2008/01/06/weekinreview/06duhigg.html.

5. "Don't You Dare Call Them 'Old,'" *eMarketer*, source: eMarketer study using International Communications Union and U.S. Census Bureau data, December 6, 2007, www.emarketer.com.

6. Ibid.

7. Marla Matzer Rose, "Ready, Set, Cut Prices; Tween Brands Hopes Justice Scores with Strapped Customers. *Columbus Dispatch,* February 12, 2009 www.columbusdispatch.com

8. "Children Shopping Online," *eMarketer,* July 20, 2007, www.emarketer.com. Data source: Stars for Kidz.

9. Matt Richtel and Brad Stone, "For Toddlers, Toy of Choice is Tech Device," *New York Times*, November 29, 2007, www.nytimes.com.

10. Brooks Barnes, "Web Playgrounds of the Very Young," *New York Times*, December 31, 2007, www.nytimes.com.

11. "Women Outpace Men Online," *Internet Retailer*, August 9, 2000, www.internetretailer.com. Statistical source: Media Metrix and Jupiter Communications.

12. "Shopping Trends: Battle of the Sexes," *Time Style & Design*, Spring 2006, 63.

13. David Bancroft Avrick, "Redefining U.S. Households," *DM News*, February 6, 2006. Statistical source: U.S. Census Bureau.

14. Karlene Lukovitz, "Consumer Preferences Vary Among Gay/Lesbian Segments," *Media Post Publications*, October 24, 2007, http://publications.mediapost.com. Data source: New American Dimensions and asterixGROUP.

15. Infoplease.com, "Median Income of Households by Selected Characteristics, 2006," www.infoplease.com/ipa/A01046688.html. Source: U.S. Bureau of the Census, "Income, Poverty, and Health Insurance Coverage in the U.S. 2006."

16. Jenn Abelson, "Buy in the Store or Online? Retailers Hope It's Both," *Boston Globe*, November 20, 2006, E1.

17. "Digital Divide Narrows," *eMarketer*, October 25, 2007, www.emarketer.com. Source: U.S. Department of Education, study conducted by the Michael Cohen Group.

18. "The Wage Gap," infoplease.com, 2006, www.infoplease.com/ipa/A0763170.html. Source: National Women's Law Center.

19. Melissa Campanelli, "32 Percent of Spanish-Dominant Latinos Go Online," *DM News*, March 19, 2007, 2. Source: Pew Hispanic Center and the Pew Internet & American Life Project, *Latinos Online*, 2006.

20. Valerie Seckler, "Marketers Focus on Asian-Americans," *Women's Wear Daily*, September 7, 2005, 21. Trend source: Cotton Inc. *Lifestyle Monitor*.

21. U.S. Census Bureau, Households by Type, 1980-2004, www.infoplease.com/ipa/A0880690.html.

22. "Women Out West Shop on Web More," *eMarketer*, January 8, 2008, www.emarketer.com.

23. Erika Lovley, "America, Up Close and Personal," *Wall Street Journal*, October 26, 2006, D1. Statistical source, U.S. Census Bureau.

24. "The WWD List: Updating Their Wardrobes," *Women's Wear Daily*, April 26, 2007, 12.

25. "The WWD List: Online Treasure Hunt," *Women's Wear Daily*, January 17, 2008, 12.

26. "Green Teens Are Avid Web Buyers, Sweepstakes: Survey," *Promo Magazine,* www.promomagazine.com/news/green_teens_avid_web_buyers_sweepstakes_080207/index.html.

27. "Retailers Sells Yoga Mats, Organic Sheets to the Ecologically Aware," *Investor's Business Daily,* January 15, 2008, www.money.cnn.com/news.

28. Ellen Groves, "Leading the Way," *Women's Wear Daily*, October 30, 2007, 18.

29. "Holiday Marketing in the Age of the Choice Generation™," *SmartReply*, Special Report, 2007, 4, www.smartreply.com/bts05.html.

Notes

30. "Average Session Times Grow for Most Big Retailers," *Internet Retailer*, September 5, 2007, www.internetretailer. Statistical source: Hitwise, Inc.

31. Evan Schuman, "E-Commerce Customers Today Taking Longer to Buy," July 5, 2007, www.storefrontbacktalk.com. Statistical source: ScanAlert.

32. Sarah Mahoney, "Study: To Online Shoppers, Price is Everything," *Media Post Publications*, December 14, 2007, http://publications.mediapost.com. Statistical source: Guidance, Marina del Rey, CA.

33. "High-value Consumers Routinely Channel Hop," *Internet Retailer*, February 5, 2008, www.internetetailer.com. Statistical source: Sterling Commerce.

34. Balaji Yellavalli, Michael Grandinetti, and Dawn Holt, "Delivering a Uniform Customer Fulfillment Experience in a Multi-Channel Retailing World," Yantra and Infosys white paper, 2004, 2. Statistical source: the *Multi-Channel Shopping Study-Holiday 2003* by doubleclick.net.

35. Lan N. Nguyen, "Designs to Set Us Apart from the Crowd," *Wall Street Journal*, February 7, 2008, D2.

36. Michele Chandler, "Browse, Click, Talk," October 2, 2006, www.mercurynews.com.

37. "57% of Women Who Read Blogs Say Blogs Influenced Purchasing Decisions," *Internet Retailer*, May 13, 2008., www.internetretailer.com/printarticle.asp?id=26377. Source: "BlogHer/Compass Partners 2008 Social Media Study."

38. Jane Larson, "Survey: Online Shoppers Turning Younger," *The Arizona Republic*, September 24, 2007, www.azcentral.com/business/consumer/articles/0924biz-icrossing0925.html. Statistical source: iCrossing, Inc.

39. "Word of Mouth for the Masses," *eMarketer*, December 5, 2007, www.emarketer.com/Articles/Print.aspx?id=1005671. Source: Forrester Research "NACTAS Benchmark Survey."

40. "Americans More Wired: Survey," *New York Times*, Reuters/Hollywood Reporter, December 28, 2007, www.nytimes.com/reuters/technology/tech-media-survey.html. Statistical source: Deloitte & Touche.

41. Shop.org/Forrester, 2005.

42. Michel Laroche, Zhiyong Yang, Gordon H. G. McDougall, and Jasmin Bergeron, "Internet versus Bricks-and-Mortar Retailers: an Investigation into Tangiblity and Intangibility and its Consequences," *Journal of Retailing* 81, no. 4 (2005): 251-67.

43. Danny Weathers, Subhash Sharma, and Stacy L. Wood, "Effects of Online Communication Practices on Consumer Perceptions of Performance Uncertainty for Search and Experience Goods," *Journal of Retailing* 83, no. 4 (2007): 393-401.

44. Natasha Lomas, "Online Shoppers Still Getting Security Sweats: Who's Afraid of the World Wide Web?" June 19, 2007, www.silicon.com. Statistical source: Office of Fair Trading.

45. Jonathan Stempel, "Identity Fraud Up in Total Dollars, Victims," February 9, 2009, www.reuters.com/articlePrint?articleID=USTRE51831G20090209. Statistical source: surveys by Javelin Strategy & Research.

46. Michelle Megna, "Rescuing Sales from Abandoned Shopping Carts," Jupitermedia Corporation, November 9, 2007, www.ecommerce-guide.com/news/research/print/php/3710206.

47. Jenn Abelson, "Buy in the Store or Online? Retailers Hope it's Both," *Boston Globe*, November 20, 2006, E4.

48. "How Customers Helped Two Online Retailers Fine-tune New Site Features," *Internet Retailer*, February 1, 2008, www.internetretailer.com/print.asp?id=25252.

49. "Neiman Marcus Profile Summary," *TNS Retail Forward*, www.rfkb.retailforward.com/CompanyProfile.aspx?cid=494.

> Overview

Visiting QVC Headquarters in West Chester, Pennsylvania, and experiencing the vast production staging areas where product spokespersons—including many celebrities—tout their wares 24 hours a day, 365 days a year, gives tour participants a glimpse into the amazing inner workings of the world's largest home shopping TV network. QVC generated close to $7.4 billion in revenue in 2007,[1] a figure twice that of its closest competitor, the Home Shopping Network (HSN). Liberty Media Corp. has owned QVC as part of its Liberty Interactive Group since 2003. QVC was founded in 1987 and went online in 1996.

Evolving into a multichannel retailer, QVC is now ranked #11 in the *Internet Retailer 2008 Top 500 Guide*. The company scored second in the categories of both customer satisfaction and purchase intent behind Netflix.com and Amazon.com, which hold first place in these respective areas.[2]

In addition to its TV network and Web site, QVC dabbled in catalog selling at various points in its history and maintains a retail store at its headquarters. The Studio Store draws employees and visitors and also serves as a product test market for the company. Adjacent to the store are Internet-enabled kiosks for easy access to QVC.com and marketplace carts displaying promotional items.

> Merchandising

Product categories include jewelry, home furnishings and decorative items, cooking and dining wares, electronics, and sports and leisure lines. The fashion division houses apparel, accessories, and beauty products. Fashion accounts for about 25 percent of all sales. In spirit QVC considers itself more a department store than a specialty store and that is evident by its merchandising assortment.

The company uses a mixed branding strategy, merging national and international brands with private-label and emerging designer brands. Famous names include Dooney and Bourke, Stila, L'Occitane, Sony, Dell, Bosch, Timberland, and Steve Madden. Private-label brands are always under development and have included Multiplicity, Velocity, Fresh, Larkspur, and Sunberry. Diamonique jewelry is a key private-label line. The attractive stones look like real gems but have a much lower, cubic zirconia-like price tag. Products are sourced internationally and standard practice for product development teams is to identify upmarket items and then redesign them to be sold at lower price points. The company also identifies and launches its own trends.[3]

> QVC Marketing and Metrics

QVC customers are 95 percent female, with household incomes of $50,000 to $75,000 and substantial discretionary income. Important geographic markets for QVC include the eastern seaboard and southern California—especially the Los Angeles metropolitan area.[4] Baby boomers and seniors comprise the primary target market.

Multichannel Retail Profile > QVC

Promotions run the gamut from studio tours to pointed mailers advertising "Gem-Week" and "Mother's Day Gift Special." Regular customers look forward to "Today's Special Values" and listings of their favorite hosts' shows.

QVC sold out of a $49.75 yellow polka-dot silk shirt by Chloe Dao, a winner on the popular TV show, *Project Runway*, in less than one minute.[5] This example illustrates QVC's ability to attract and engage younger customers. The company also provides an arena in which smaller companies can thrive under the QVC banner, although it is difficult for new vendors to pass the close scrutiny of brand managers.

Unlike other television retailers that sell airtime to vendors, QVC partners earn their time on air. Productivity is measured in terms of dollars per hour. If a product does not meet QVC standards, it does not remain on the air. Customer responsiveness ultimately determines vendor selection.

Very metric oriented, QVC uses state-of-the-art communications systems that provide constant performance updates to its employees. (For more information about performance metrics, see Chapter 10.) Orders and inventory information are revised every 6 seconds. Orders-per-hour range from 5,000 to 15,000, and viewers-per-hour from 500,000 to 1.5 million. Approximately 93 percent of sales are from repeat customers. The company communicates with customers from its in-house call center.[6]

> Keys to Success

QVC lists several factors that contribute to its ongoing appeal to customers and strong sales growth:

> Under-promise, over-deliver
> No artificial promotional stimulants
> Positive corporate culture
> Solid quality assurance
> High believability on air

One practice that contributes to the high level of credence is the intensive screening process for new hosts. Potential candidates must be telegenic and deliver an outstanding 2-minute sales presentation. The company hires approximately 1 out of 1,000 hopefuls.[7]

The future of QVC looks bright, with growth emanating from global expansion and its online store. The company has shopping networks in Germany, Japan, and the United Kingdom. QVC serves 22 million U.K. households, operating there since 1993. In 2007 sales in the United Kingdom were about $700 million.[8] The company expects to launch programming in Italy in 2010.[9]

The company believes that its television channel location is the equivalent of a physical store. QVC tries to locate near major networks on cable provider stations.

> QVC.com

When QVC went online, it drew from a wealth of experience and existing fulfillment infrastructure. The Web site has sustained several major transformations in its 12-year history.

Expanding daily specials to the Web and adding more interactive opportunities for customers such as blogs, customer reviews, polls, forums, and live chats with QVC hosts and celebrities are examples of online store developments. Video capabilities have also improved and as a result sales generated by this medium grew 56 percent. For the first time in the company's history an advertising campaign was launched in cities coast-to-coast for the 2007–2008 season. The phrase, "iQdoU?" served as the theme of the multimedia push.[10]

In 2007, QVC generated $1.881 billion in Internet sales. HSN's online revenue was $871.2 million.[11] QVC stands for quality, value, and convenience, fitting attributes for this multi-channel retailer.

> Points to Ponder

1. Visit QVC.com and HSN.com. Compare and contrast Web site features and customer services. Look for differences and similarities in target market, merchandise mix, brand focus, pricing, and promotional activities.
2. Visit QVC and HSN television shopping networks. How do branding tactics on television differ from each company's online presence?
3. If QVC considers its retail format similar to that of a department store, how would you classify HSN's approach?
4. What is QVC doing to expand its reach to new demographic and geographic markets?
5. What advantages does QVC gain by selling national, international, designer, and private-label merchandise?

> Notes

1. "Top 100 Retailers," *Stores,* July 2008, T9, www.stores.org.
2. Larry Freed, "The Value of Customer Satisfaction: Satisfaction and Purchase Intent Scores for the Top 100," *Internet Retailer 2008 Top 500 Guide,* 20.
3. Douglas Rose, vice president of Merchandise Brand Development, QVC, "Changing Channels: An Introduction to QVC," presentation to American Collegiate Retailing Association, West Chester, PA, April 15, 2005.
4. Ibid.
5. Laura Petrecca, "QVC Shops for Ideas for Future Sales," *USA Today*, May 4, 2008, www.usatoday.com/money/media/2008-05-04-qvc-home-shopping_N.htm.

Multichannel Retail Profile > QVC

6. Rose, QVC.
7. Rose, QVC.
8. Kamcity.com, "UK: QVC Reports Good Sales Growth," *Namnews*, March 5, 2008, www.kamcity.com/namnews/asp/newsarticle.asp?newsid=39562.
9. Press Release, "QVC Extends Global Reach to Italy," *Yahoo! Finance*, September 26, 2008, http://biz.yahoo.com/prnews/080926/nef005a.html.
10. "Top 100 Web Retailers: 11. QVC Inc. (Liberty Interactive Group), *Internet Retailer 2008 Top 500 Guide,* 106.
11. Ibid., "Top 100 Web Retailers, 25. HSN," 134.

Multichannel Retail Profile > J. C. Penney

> Overview

Number 15 in the *Internet Retailer 2008 Top 500 Guide*, J. C. Penney had online sales of 1.5 billion in 2007.[1] On the cusp of innovation, J. C. Penney has steadily broken down barriers to selling apparel and other soft goods online. J. C. Penney is well on its way to achieving the $2 billion sales goal it set for its online store several years ago.[2] Total revenue for the company was just under $20 billion for 2007.[3]

The company's long and rich history dates to the turn of the twentieth century when founder James Cash Penney opened The Golden Rule in Kemmerer, Wyoming. His humble general store featured provisions for miners and sheep ranchers and their families—a stretch from the mass-merchandised stores so well known today. The company runs department stores, furniture and home furnishings stores, catalogs, and its online division.[4] In the 1990s, J. C. Penney acquired Eckert Drug Stores as it experimented with diversification but sold that company in 2004 to concentrate on its department store business.[5] Penney's headquarters is in Plano, Texas.

Considered a mid-market, moderate price department store, J. C. Penney's merchandise mix features 55 percent national brands and 45 percent private-label brands. Half of the company's 1,100 stores are located in malls and the remainder in freestanding and other sites.[6]

> Branding Strategies

J. C. Penney is brand conscious, having developed many private labels that have withstood the test of time. In the face of industry-wide retrenchment, Penney escalated brand development as a way to fuel growth. The company's foray into exclusive celebrity brands, such as those developed for specialty chain H & M, department store Kohl's, and discount retailer Target, is indicative of this direction. Its Fabulosity line features hip-hop-inspired sportswear for young women women by Kimora Lee Simmons, a former model and partner in the Phat Farm and Baby Phat businesses. Penney released Fabulosity in 2008 in time for the back-to-school season.[7]

Other moderately priced lines launched prior to Fabulosity included a casual apparel line for teens called Decree, the men's apparel label WhiteTag, and furniture and home décor items under the name Linden Street. These brands are in contrast to the earlier release of the more expensive brand of apparel and home furnishings called American Living, a joint venture between Penney and Polo Ralph Lauren.[8] Additionally, in response to the economic slowdown of 2008, which affected sales of the American Living brand, the company revisited its strategy and announced plans to lower prices on some merchandise for the Spring 2009 lines.[9]

Another noteworthy initiative is the partnership with cosmetics retailer Sephora. In late 2006, Penney launched Sephora boutiques in selected stores across the country.[10]

The move added excitement to Penney's stores and more visibility for Sephora. The 1,500- to 3,000-square-foot Sephora ministores are usually located near main entrances to the J. C. Penney store. For Sephora the partnership significantly increased the company's presence in the United States. Perhaps it is no coincidence that CEO Myron "Mike" Ullman III was once directeur general of Louis Vuitton Moet Hennessy LVMH, the owner of Sephora.[11]

> J. C. Penney Online

The company's experience as a catalog retailer facilitated online selling because Penney already had astute merchants, management, and fulfillment practices in place. Its Web site, added in 1994, now features an interactive online catalog, color swatching, product recommendations, and useful widgets.

J. C. Penney encourages its customers to shop online first—not only to research product availability and check prices, but also to see the weekly promotions—before visiting a store. The company boasts 23,622,000 monthly visits to its Web site, a conversion rate of 3.35 percent, and an average purchase of $160. Search engine traffic drives 26 percent of all shoppers to its site and predominantly comes from natural rather than paid search.[12]

The company runs several specialty Web sites, including its seasonal gift site JCPgifts.com and Baby Solution. It also has partnered with Condé Nast Bridal Media. Visitors to the site can click on "Click It. Pick It" to access J. C. Penney's gift registry.[13]

In 2006, J. C. Penney connected point-of-sale systems to the Web in all of its stores, giving sales associates access to stock availability information. This practice enables sales staff to provide superior customer service. Associates can also place catalog or online orders for customers while they are in the store. Customers who are offered the service regard J. C. Penney more favorably than those who are not offered the service. The company believes that customer loyalty increases as a result.[14]

Multichannel Retail Profile > J. C. Penney

> Outlook

Although the company has operated stores separately from its catalog and online businesses, Ullman stated in a 2008 interview that Penney would fully integrate merchandising between its store and direct marketing divisions. This tactic was intended to reduce costs and give customers better service, but was expected to involve reallocation or loss of 100 to 200 jobs. A test of the concept showed that when all divisions are synchronized, Penney would generate more sales.[15]

The severity of the economic downturn in 2008 made many retailers more cautious in their expansion plans. Ullman indicated that in his 39 years in retail business he had never seen an environment as unpredictable. The company cut back store expansion plans for 2009 from 50 to 36 new stores, and adjusted the number of store renovations from 65 to 20. Other openings and refurbishing were curtailed through 2011.[16] In contrast, the in-store Sephora cosmetic shops will continue on a growth trajectory, adding 20 units in 2008 and 50 to 70 in 2009.[17]

A visionary leader, strong branding, high visibility, and a strong multichannel viewpoint help J. C. Penney compete with stores like Macy's, Kohl's, and Target. During a trade association presentation, Ullman had this to say about Penney's expansive multichannel approach: "We are channel agnostic. We don't care which way the customers come in as long as they come in."[18]

> Points to Ponder

1. Integration of store, catalog, and online channels is a business practice in use or being considered by most multichannel retailers. What is Penney's position on this tactic?
2. How are J. C. Penney's branding practices similar or dissimilar to those of other retailers with which you are familiar? Consider the ratio between national and private-label brands in your evaluation.
3. If possible visit a J. C. Penney store and compare the merchandise with one of the company's print catalogs or its online merchandise assortment. What are your conclusions?
4. Faced with an economic downturn, what strategies is J. C. Penney implementing in order to stabilize its business?

> Notes

1. "Top 100 Web Sites, 15. J. C. Penney Co. Inc.," *Internet Retailer 2008 Top 500 Guide,* 114.
2. Rusty Williamson, "Penney's Aims for $2B Internet Revenues," *Women's Wear Daily,* April 17, 2006, 3.
3. "Top 100 Retailers," *Stores,* July 2008, T5, www.stores.org.
4. "Company History," J. C. Penney Company Brochure, undated.
5. Kortney Stringer and Ann Zimmerman, "Polishing Penney's Image," *Wall Street Journal,* May 7, 2004, B1.

6. Rusty Williamson, "J. C. Penney Building on Strengths," *Women's Wear Daily,* April 18, 2007, 4.
7. Nicole Maestri, "J. C. Penney Celebrates Latest Brand Launch," Reuters, July 16, 2008, www.reuters.com/articlePrint?articleId=INN1538715620080716.
8. Vicki M. Young, "Penney's Scales Back Expansion Plans," *Women's Wear Daily,* June 26, 2008, 3.
9. Maria Halkias, "Penney's American Living Brand Getting a Redo," *Dallas Morning News,* August 15, 2008, www.dallasnews.com/sharedcontent/dws/bus/indistries/retail/stories/081508dmbus.
10. Pete Born, "The Happy Couple: A Strong Start for Penney's-Sephora Venture," *Women's Wear Daily,* January 19, 2007, 1, 4.
11. Ibid.
12. *Internet Retailer 2008 Top 500 Guide,* 114.
13. Lauren Bell, "Condé Nast and J. C. Penney Target Brides-to-Be," *DM News,* August 27, 2007, 2.
14. "Store Customers Like Having Access to JCP.com at J. C. Penney Stores," *Internet Retailer,* July 1, 2008, www.internetretailer.com/printArticle.asp?id=26961.
15. Cheryl Lu-Lien Tan, "CEO Pinching Penney In a Slow Economy," *Wall Street Journal,* January 31, 2008, B1, B2.
16. Cheryl Lu-Lien Tan, "J. C. Penney Curbs Expansion, Pushes Private Labels," *Wall Street Journal,* April 17, 2008, B9.
17. Vicki M. Young, "Penney's Scales Back Expansion Plans," *Women's Wear Daily,* June 26, 2008, 3.
18. Dianna Dillworth, "J. C. Penney is Channel Agnostic: CEO at Shop.org's First-Look," *DM News,* February 2, 2007, www.dmnews.com/cms/dm-news/catalog-retail/39870.html.

Unit II

STRATEGIC IMPERATIVES

Chapter 4

The Strategic Planning Process

Objectives

> To identify the steps of the strategic planning process.
> To survey forces in the retail environment that affect strategic decision-making.
> To review strategic planning tools and market strategies.

> Multichannel objectives are achieved with less risk if thoughtful plans are made and executed. The history, present status, and future direction of a company is considered in the strategic planning process. **Strategic planning** is the process of gathering and analyzing information from internal and external sources to identify concrete tactics that will reduce risk as business plans are executed. This process, which is relevant to all businesses, is addressed here in the context of specific considerations for multichannel retailers.

Steps of the Strategic Planning Process

Strategic planning requires assembling information that is crucial to decision making. Perpetual assessment of assets and liabilities is necessary, and doing this in a constantly changing world is not easy. Planning is done by individuals, teams, or company-wide and is practiced by businesses that are concerned with growth. Planning needs leadership, but input should come from all levels of the organization and not be a top-down directive. Strategic planning involves fundamental steps including:

1. Conducting a situation analysis.
2. Determining a differential advantage.
3. Preparing a vision statement.
4. Developing goals and objectives.
5. Identifying specific strategies.

> Conducting a Situation Analysis

By completing a situation analysis, core competencies of a company are assessed. A **situation analysis** determines the current strengths and weaknesses of a company by looking at business practices internally and externally. Internally a company might look at operations, management structure, merchandise practices, and advertising effectiveness as examples. External environmental scanning is part of a retailer's ongoing research activities. **Environmental scanning** is the practice by which retailers detect opportunities and threats outside the company. Sources of external data from which retailers draw information include trade association conferences, periodicals, and Web sites; market research and annual company reports; media and advertising sources; and government records and reports. Information on the competition is collected by personal visits to stores or by employing professional shoppers or consulting firms. Monitoring Web sites, catalogs, and other direct marketing materials is also commonplace.

Many retailers find that SWOT analysis is a useful tool. **SWOT analysis** involves listing **s**trengths, **w**eaknesses, **o**pportunities, and **t**hreats in matrix form and using the information to determine future direction. SWOT analysis is a flexible tool that helps retailers brainstorm a company, division, the corporate culture, the competition, the customer, and other areas where cogent details are needed.

Table 4.1 Sample SWOT Analysis for Pier 1

STRENGTHS	WEAKNESSES
> Highly focused furniture and decorative products > Mid-market prices > Appealing in-store visual merchandising > Broad international product sourcing base > New CEO may bring fresh ideas and leadership	> Highly stylized wicker and ethnic decorative products may have limited appeal > Scaled back online and catalog businesses; Web site nontransactional > Diminishing sales reflected lost leadership of casual, trendy imported furniture market > Shift to modern/retro designs in 2005–2006 not successful > TV advertising ineffective
OPPORTUNITIES	**THREATS**
> Lower prices may make business more recession-proof and help regain market share > Develop more unique products drawing on international sourcing expertise > Re-branding initiatives > Possible sale of company	> Competition from companies like HomeGoods, Marshall's, Target, Crate & Barrel, Pottery Barn, IKEA, other specialty retailers offline and online > Downturn in economy negatively affects home-related sales > Declining sales over several years

Pier 1, the trendy but affordable importer of items for the home, once operated over 1,200 stores, a catalog business, and a transactional Web site. The Texas-based company reached a peak sales volume of over $1 billion in 1999, but has been on a downward spiral with little relief since 2004. At one time Pier 1 operated in several countries and also ran a chain of Pier 1 Kids stores.[1] The company has been closing more stores than it has been opening in an attempt to strengthen its position. It retrenched its catalog business, and stopped selling online in 2007. A hypothetical SWOT analysis of Pier 1 is shown in Table 4.1.

> Determining a Differential Advantage

Competition is intense for all retailers across all channels. Developing characteristics to set one apart from other players is essential. **Differential advantage** describes the unique attributes of a business that may give it a superior position in the marketplace.

Differential advantage is closely related to positioning. **Positioning** is the perception a customer has of a company, store, or product in relation to others. Strategic planning cannot go forth without careful consideration of both aspects. For example, Nordstrom's is positioned as an extremely customer service–oriented store. Walmart is known for its everyday low pricing policies. These qualities constitute a differential advantage when they distinguish a seller or product as better than the competition. Customers have a clear image and can easily identify the intentions of each retailer.

> Developing a Vision Statement

Next, planners are ready to write vision and mission statements. The vision statement is succinct and future directed. Building a **vision statement** involves articulating a company's core business and its differential advantage, usually in a brief sentence or paragraph.

A **mission statement** is part of a vision statement that speaks to how a company will reveal its vision, its roadmap for performance. A mission statement may be short and concise or longer, integrating a company's role in society, its ethical stance, and the principles by which it intends to operate. It may be more inclusive of values the company holds and how it intends to run its business in accord with those principles.

What business are we in? What customers do we want to serve? What image do we want to portray? What is our company culture? Retailers consider questions like these as they draft their vision and mission statements.

> Preparing Goals and Objectives

Company goals are usually general, stated with a clear focus, and may take several forms. **Goals** are statements that indicate company aims or end results. An established discount store may be most concerned with achieving a high sales volume. A specialty retailer selling only high-definition DVDs and players using the new Blu-ray format may be more interested in establishing itself as an expert in cutting-edge technology. Goals relate to long-term efforts to build a business.

A goal for a fashion apparel retailer might be "To speed up the private-label product development cycle." Objectives to meet that goal should be written so that end results are actionable and easy to measure. **Objectives** are specific intentions stated by a company. For example, the apparel retailer involved in private-label product development might state this objective: "To increase speed to market by 30 percent."

This is a measurable objective, but too broad. It would be better to state it this way: "To increase speed to market by 30 percent in the next product development cycle by implementing new software tools." Once objectives are carefully constructed, the next step is to devise operational procedures that will bring the objectives to fruition. One task could be: "To interview three software vendors in the next month to identify the best product management solution for the company." Tying the objective to a concrete plan of action—by outlining specific strategies—is more meaningful.

> Planning Detailed Strategies

Developing strategies involves seeing the big picture. Action plans that prescribe tactics used by a company to reach common goals and objectives are called **strategies**. Retailers make decisions in many areas including but not limited to channel selection, global expansion, store location, management hierarchy, operations, pricing policies, merchandising, service offerings, distribution, store image, human resources, and promotion. These areas are considered controllable elements because they emanate from within the organization. Retailers have little or no control over competition, government laws, customers, or technology. Equally uncontrollable are economic, political, social, and environmental conditions as well as unplanned events worldwide. These factors are considered during the strategic planning process and are discussed in the next section.

Monitoring the Retail Environment

Retailers are attuned to events and trends outside their organizations. The cumulative effects of change may affect retailers more deeply than change in any one sector of the retail environment. Retailers follow current world, national, regional, and local news in order to plan appropriate strategies and to sustain momentum in an uncertain economy. As this text was being written the United States was experiencing an economic crisis with worldwide repercussions. The country was in a recession. Rising wholesale and retail prices threatened inflation. Inability to secure loans or capital for expansion, wavering consumer credit markets, and deterioration of major financial firms compounded the issue. The unemployment rate was rising and consumer confidence was at its lowest level in decades. Specific issues change; change within the economy remains constant. This is the world in which our discussion of the retail environment begins.

> Economic Impact

Recession, inflation, war, peace, and prosperity are all reflected in our wallets and at the point-of-sale. Retail sales and strategies change in response to events such as increases in the price of crude oil, problems in the credit and lending markets, tax increases or reductions, stock market fluctuations, or currency crises. Layoffs in major industries or openings of new businesses also affect retail planning.

Monetary Dynamics

Knowledge of how recession, inflation, currency devaluation, and interest rates affect business is important to retailers.

<u>Recession</u> A **recession** is a period in which there is less money in the economy than previously. Consumers spend less on goods and services during a recession than in prosperous times. In the manufacturing sector, recession is anticipated when wholesale orders for products slow down appreciably. This hurts retailers, because sales may be down but the basic costs of doing business (wages, energy, credit) remain at prerecession levels or may increase as the price of oil did during the 2008 recession. The last recession experienced by the United States occurred in 2000–2001 when many e-commerce companies failed. The terrorist attacks and subsequent turmoil in financial markets exacerbated this situation. In periods of recession, retailers generate low or no business growth, and bankruptcies increase. The recession in 2008 saw diverse retailers including Mervyn's and Boscov's (department stores), Linens 'n Things (home goods), Steve & Barry's (apparel), and Sharper Image (unique gifts and electronic gadgets) file for Chapter 11 bankruptcy protection.

Recession also affects human resources. Layoffs may occur as retailers cut payroll costs. If retailers attempt to keep employees working while sales are sluggish, eventually profits are affected. Early in 2008 several retailers announced plans to lay off employees; several others announced plans to economize. Executive perspectives on recession are conveyed in Box 4.1.

<u>Inflation</u> Currency inflation is another economic phenomenon that is watched and addressed. **Inflation** is the abnormal increase in the volume of money and credit, resulting in a substantial and continuing rise in price levels. The rate of inflation is affected by other economic factors.

> Box 4.1 What's the Buzz?

> ### > Remember Recession?
> ### Industry Vets Prescribe Ways to Cope With Blahs
>
> As New York Fashion Week kicks into high gear, everyone from the designers to the retail executives and perhaps even the models on the runways has one word on their minds beginning with the letter "r"—and it isn't the color red. It's "recession."
>
> Suddenly consumers, that engine of the American economy, think it's unfashionable to spend money. The credit markets are tight; the stock market is dyspeptic; major U.S. financial institutions are turning to China and the Middle East for financial lifelines; oil prices continue to flirt with $100 a barrel, and the once-mighty dollar now looks like a 90-pound weakling against the euro and the pound. No wonder retailers and industry executives are nervous. And because it's a presidential election year, many are questioning where America is heading.
>
> Because the last major recession was 20 years ago—*Women's Wear Daily* decided to do an informal survey of leading executives who have weathered prior downturns for their tips on how to get through the tough times ahead. Here are two of their strategies and suggestions:
>
> #### Leonard Lauder, chairman of the Estée Lauder Companies
> "This is the fourth recession I've been through—and each previous recession was unique in its own way. I think this is as much a recession of economics as it is a recession of confidence. The root cause is that people saw the value of their homes decrease and in many cases evaporate. They still have money, but they don't have the house money to fall back on and give them confidence in the future. The only advice I can give is be confident, and follow Mrs. Estée Lauder's advice, which she gave at the end of the Great Depression: 'There is no such thing as bad business. Business is there if you go after it.'"
>
> *(continued)*

Inflation affects the importation of goods and consumer spending. Without imports coming into a country from foreign markets, there is no incentive for domestic firms to moderate prices. If there are no imports, prices are set at what the market will bear, which is generally higher than in a competitive marketplace.

Retail profit declines because the basic costs of doing business increase along with vendors' prices. To cover their costs, retailers increase prices and customers pay more for some products, perhaps more than they are intrinsically worth. Because many retailers depend on imports as a large percentage of their inventories, the rate of inflation also is considered during the merchandise planning process.

Customers often change their expenditure patterns during periods of inflation. People eat at home more, selecting mid-range family restaurants rather than

> **What's the Buzz?** *(continued)* **Box 4.1**

Michael Gould, chairman and chief executive officer of Bloomingdale's

"Bloomingdale's will continue to take prudent risks, continue to explore new merchandise, new resources, and continue to ratchet up its desire to have new receipts on a regular basis. What this climate says to us is that there is a ton of business to be done. We have many new programs rolling out—new loyalty programs, intensified clienteling. In this climate you cannot win by playing a defensive game. You may not treat all of your children (businesses) equally, but treat them all fairly. We will stay the course with our brand strategy—to be more upscale, less promotional, and provide a better in-store experience and more Bloomingdale's DNA for excitement."

Several tips for surviving a recession summarize those given by executives who participated:

> Stay the course, but consider taking marketing chances.
> Focus on customer service, and offer compelling merchandise.
> Cultivate brand loyalty.
> Control inventory and costs. Reduce costs where needed.
> Get used to fluctuating stock prices.

Source: Excerpted and condensed from WWD Staff, Women's Wear Daily, *February 4, 2008, 1, 40–41.*

gourmet eating establishments when they do dine out. They shop discount retailers more frequently than pricey specialty retailers. Luxury goods retailers are less affected by inflation because they target people with high incomes whose spending habits are less influenced by downturns in the economy. Online stores are somewhat less disturbed by inflation since they operate on different overhead, distribution, and profit models. Customers psychologically see the online shopping experience in an economically positive light when they believe they are saving money by not driving to the mall.

<u>Currency Volatility</u> Most world currencies are linked to the U.S. dollar. Historically, this valuation came about because of the size of America's economy, the stability of its currency, and the solid performance of its stock and financial markets over time. At least until recently, the dollar had been considered less volatile than many foreign currencies. During 2007–2008, the value of the dollar declined substantially against several world currencies—most notably the British pound sterling and the European Union euro. When the worth of a currency decreases, devaluation has occurred. **Devaluation** is a reduction in the international exchange value of a currency. This occurs for many reasons

4.1

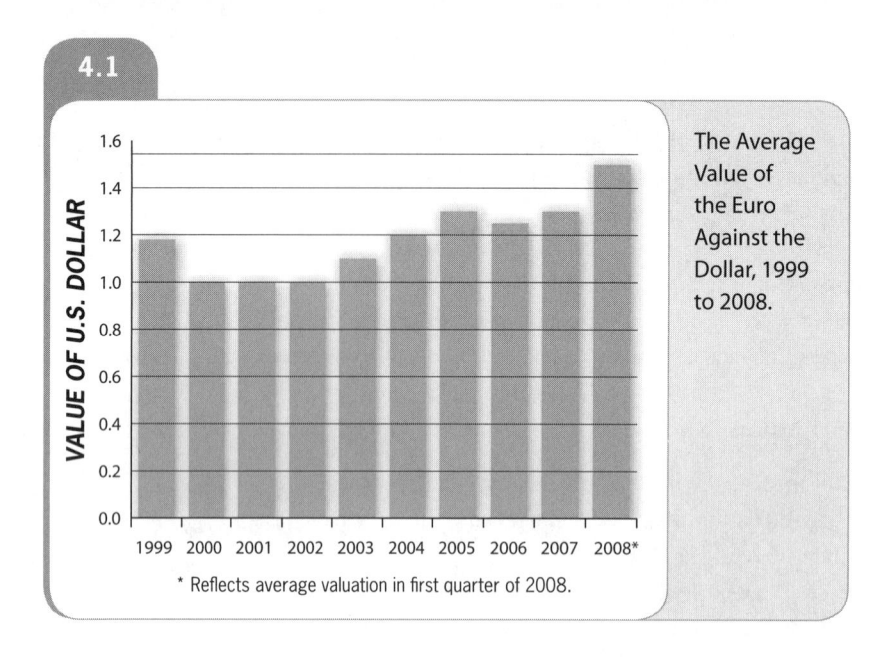

The Average Value of the Euro Against the Dollar, 1999 to 2008.

* Reflects average valuation in first quarter of 2008.

including bank failures, stock market crashes, unrestricted foreign investments, poor financial management, and panic. When a currency declines, consumer buying power is diminished, retail sales decline, expansion is put on hold, and importing becomes more costly.

On the other hand, weakening of the dollar makes it more advantageous for foreign tourists to shop in the United States. Multinational companies may also perform well. Levi Strauss & Co. conducts much of its business overseas and benefited from the decline in the value of the dollar against the euro in 2007. In fact had it not been for the strong euro, the company would have seen a decline in total sales over the previous year.[2] Figure 4.1 graphs the value of the euro against the dollar over time. Reverberations from currency instability are felt worldwide.

<u>Interest Rate Fluctuations</u> Carefully watched in the United States by the Federal Reserve, interest rates affect retail sales and development. Fluctuations in the prime rate affect many sectors of the economy. The *prime rate* is the interest rate charged by the Federal Reserve Bank to commercial lending institutions. During a recession interest rates usually decline, but under certain circumstances they may increase when inflation is also present. (This is called stagflation.) Using furniture as an example, changes in the prime rate coupled with other economic factors may

ultimately affect consumer lending practices and interest rates, credit card use, and retail home mortgage loans in the following ways:

> Lower mortgage interest rates usually precede a rise in new home construction.
> Lower prime interest rates along with inflation may increase consumer loan rates, thus lowering the probability that new home seekers will purchase homes or current homeowners will refinance mortgages.
> More housing sales may mean that homeowners will purchase more furniture.
> Furniture purchases may be charged, because lack of cash is frequently the plight of new homeowners.
> If credit card interest rates are high, homeowners may put off purchases and make do with what they already have.
> If interest rates are low, customers may use credit cards and not defer their purchases.
> If credit is hard to get, customers may forgo furniture purchases.
> If the economy suffers a mortgage loan crisis, some householders may loose their homes if their adjustable rate mortgages skyrocket, necessitating the need to sell not buy furniture.
> Some individuals curtail spending irrespective of the interest rates and choose either to pay cash or not purchase at all.

The furniture market experienced declining sales during the economic downturn in 2008, as did electronic, book, and sporting goods retailers, and restaurants. Furniture sales fell for six straight months, the longest period in recent history.[3]

Economic Indicators

Buying power, gross domestic product, consumer confidence levels, unemployment trends, and consumer prices are some of the indices and statistics watched by retailers.

> *Buying power* is the amount of money a family has available for purchases after taxes. It indicates ability and inclination to spend at retail. Many teenagers are notorious for spending their money unwisely; they, too, are affected by sticker shock in retail stores and at the gas pump. According to a

consumer panel study, young people have begun spending more on essentials like filling up their gas tanks than they do on apparel and accessories.[4]

> *Gross domestic product (GDP)* measures the total value of goods and services produced in a country annually. Retail companies that are considering global expansion use this information to help them determine the viability of their overseas ventures.

> *Consumer price index (CPI)* is an economic indicator that measures changes in the cost of living due to inflation. The figure is released monthly by the U.S. government and is based on price fluctuations in a group of retail products tracked over time. When the index increases, individuals are able to purchase less for their money. Inflation causes wholesale prices to increase as well. Retailers must pass along price increases to their customers or expect lower profits.

> *Employment rates* are a general indicator of the health of the economy. During the 2008 downturn, unemployment was rising well over the 4.5 to 5 percent level at which it had remained for several years, and reached 8.5 percent in 2009.

The financial community in the United States releases key statistics monthly. Scores of data on all sectors of the economy are available to assist retailers with their planning.

Implications for Multichannel Retailers

During 2008, oil topped $140 per barrel, unemployment crept up, and sub-prime mortgages were called in by lenders as homeowners could not meet increased payments on their adjustable-rate or interest-only loans. How these events affected retailers and consumers is a topic worth reviewing. Usually one negative factor in an otherwise robust economy is cause to pause and reflect; the convergence of multiple factors brings much greater discontent to retailers and customers.

The significance of powerful and complex economic change has driven retailers to take corrective action and occasionally drastic measures. The weak economy was not the only factor involved in cutbacks implemented by retailers. In response to declining sales some companies closed stores or catalog divisions, others reduced the number of regional offices or distribution centers. Many made human resource cuts at executive and support staff levels. Some filed for Chapter 11 bankruptcy protection as they attempted to reorganize and recapitalize their businesses. **Chapter 11** is the federal bankruptcy protection statute that allows companies to stay in business while they reorganize under the supervision of the court.

Although few companies file Chapter 11, many refine their business models and reduce expenses during difficult economic periods. The coping strategies of several retailers in early 2008 provide useful insights:

> **Eddie Bauer**—The apparel company cut staff at its corporate headquarters by 16 percent.[5] The company had been plagued by declining sales and had been closing stores prior to the 2008 slowdown.
> **J. C. Penney**—The company closed one call center that services catalog orders affecting 275 employees of the facility. It combined some merchandising and marketing functions to create efficiencies and cost savings for its store and direct businesses (including catalog and online operations). The department store company eliminated 150 staff positions.[6]
> **Home Depot**—The giant do-it-yourself home building supplier eliminated 500 employees representing 10 percent of staff at its Atlanta headquarters.[7] Earlier it had eliminated some of its catalogs and was struggling to meet sales objectives in the face of competition and executive changes.
> **Macy's**—The largest department store group, Macy's said it would shrink the company by 2,550 positions and reduce the number of regional offices from seven to four. Although the downturn in the economy and resulting housing slump played a role, they were not the only reasons for the decisions. Internal problems relating to the acquisition of May Department stores in 2005 were also cited.[8] Re-branding issues played a role as well, but it is evident that complex internal and external factors were involved in the downsizing.
> **Lillian Vernon**—The gift and gadget catalog and online company filed for Chapter 11 protection shortly after laying off about half of its remaining staff in February 2008.[9] The company had previously cut 25 percent of its employees and reduced its catalog circulation, citing declining sales and postal increases as reasons.
> **Sharper Image**—In filing for Chapter 11 protection, the company cited a significant drop in sales over a two-year period and announced it would close 90 of its 184 stores in 2008. Its product mix featured unique gifts and

must-haves for technophiles.[10] The company eventually was acquired by two retail liquidators that will attempt to reincarnate Sharper Image as a wholesale brand and will sell to Web sites, catalogs, and via infomercials.[11]

> **Starbucks**—As part of a restructuring plan, the upscale coffee merchant dispensed with 600 field positions that were considered café support staff. In addition, it doubled its number of regional divisions, now totaling four, and was expected to close low-performing stores. Howard Schultz, chairman and chief executive, said this regarding the changes: "We have to step up to the challenge of being strategic as well as nimble as our business evolves."[12]

Tax refunds and the government stimulus package of 2008 were believed to be too little, too late, to reverse the downward spiral of some retailers. Those that were experiencing poor performance due to the economy took drastic but strategically appropriate measures to curb the ebb tide of retail sales. Borders countered declining sales by reclaiming its online operations from Amazon.com and adding services to its new independent Web site. Read more about Borders' strategies in Box 4.2.

> Political Influences

Political events often bring about governmental policy changes that affect businesses. During a presidential election year, hopes are high that a new administration will revitalize economic policies and initiate legislation that will benefit retailers and customers. Volatile political regimes and trade agreements influence the retail environment. Because most multichannel retailers are also global retailers, world events profoundly affect business strategies. Offshore product sourcing and retail expansion plans are particularly influenced.

Trade Agreements

Political motivations frequently are the basis for establishing trade alliances between countries. Many such partnerships exist throughout the world, including the **North American Free Trade Agreement (NAFTA)**, a trade alliance to promote trade among the United States, Canada, and Mexico. Supporters of the agreement believe that certain areas of the United States—particularly cities and towns close to the Mexican border—have benefited from trade and increased job opportunities. Detractors believe that NAFTA has not met expectations and that American jobs have been lost, making the residual effects of the agreement a topic of continuing debate.

> **What's the Buzz? Box 4.2**

> ### *Borders Hopes Web Site Helps Turnaround*

> Borders Group, Inc., views the launch of its new Web site as a chance to control its own destiny and help spur a turnaround at the book retailer, executives said. Borders has been running its site in an alliance with Amazon.com, but that will change early in 2008 when Borders' agreement with Amazon is no longer in effect.
>
> "We're literally starting with a blank page," says Rob Gruen, executive vice president of merchandising and marketing at Borders, regarding its efforts to build its own Web site. Although the retailers may be late in the game, executives said that developing a site from scratch has allowed it to closely integrate its online efforts with its store operations and try to mimic an in-store experience online.
>
> On the test version of the site that Borders launched in 2007, it developed a "magic shelf," which is a virtual bookcase that displays recommended books, movies, and music. Another function that was popular with users involved in the test was the ability to check to see if an item shown online was in stock at a local store. If it was, customers could then reserve the item online and pick it up at their nearest store. Borders hopes customers will then spend more money in stores when they pick up their reserved books.
>
> Borders is taking on the responsibility of its Web site as part of a larger turnaround plan, which it began in 2007. It is closing its underperforming Waldenbooks stores, weighing options for its international units, and refocusing on its core U.S. store operations. The retailer is trying to fend off competition not only from Barnes & Noble, but also from online retailers, to which consumers have been turning for cheaper books, CDs, and DVDs. Borders may also offer MP3 music downloads on its Web site as CD sales wane.
>
> To take advantage of the 23.5 million customers enrolled in its "Borders Rewards" loyalty program, it will let customers earn rewards for shopping online on the new site, something they could not do when affiliated with Amazon. Borders has not disclosed how many customers visited its test site, but executives concur that the new site will be an important part of future growth.
>
> *Source: Reuters, January 15, 2008. Copyright 2008 Reuters.*

Trade Restrictions

Another issue involves manufacturer- and retailer-sponsored programs that support domestic manufacturing. The term **protectionism** describes government policies that support domestic manufacturers by placing restrictions on foreign producers of the same goods. Despite their patriotic feelings, most customers realize that the best prices and values are obtained by purchasing goods produced in countries with low labor rates. Protectionist policies are expected to decline as retailers and manufacturers become more committed to international partnerships, free trade agreements, and the resulting cost savings.

Certain impediments limit the movement of goods and the selection of trading partners. A **trade embargo** is a restriction placed on the importation of goods by a government. Some trade embargoes are politically motivated. The United States does not trade with Cuba because the government is a communist one and in direct opposition to our capitalistic way of doing business. Because of the ill health of Fidel Castro and his brother's succession as leader of the country, speculators wonder if trade relations between the United States and Cuba eventually will resume. Although the dollar is not officially sanctioned, ironically it has always been popular in Cuba despite the country's communist ideologies.

Impact of Globalization

Globalization has created sources of power that are influenced by political and governmental interests. Consequently, huge companies that operate on many continents wield great influence on political platforms and legislation. Many multichannel retailers do business in foreign countries and, conversely, foreign companies do business in the United States. The amount of foreign investment in U.S. retail companies escalated early in this decade but by early 2008 had slowed.[13] Although acquisition of U.S. companies by foreign buyers declined 50 percent for the first two months of 2008 compared with the same period in the previous year, the trend did not appear to affect luxury retailers. For instance, in early 2008 the Icelandic company Baugur, which owns 8.5 percent of Saks, Inc., was rumored to be considering acquisition of the entire company or a part thereof.[14] However, continued turbulence in the global economy, tight credit markets, and strengthening of the U.S. dollar later that year made it unlikely that the transaction would go forward, and in early 2009 Baugur filed for the equivalent of bankruptcy protection in London.[15]

Retailers also are concerned with taxation, escalating health care costs for their employees, and other issues. Consumer and human rights activists, industry trade associations, and retailers themselves have influenced current federal laws affecting retailers. These legal issues and requirements are considered next.

> Multichannel Retailing and the Law

Evidence of the impact of the law is seen in informative labels, advertising that warns people of potential health hazards, and increased product safety standards.

Privacy, especially as it affects Internet commerce, is growing in importance. How credit is extended, how customers pay, taxation of goods purchased on the Internet, and how sales are conducted are key issues. Lobbying groups seek to influence lawmakers to pass legislation that supports retail business and international trade.

Legislative Lobbying Practices

When retailers make decisions, they pay close attention to changes in the legal sphere. The National Retail Federation (NRF) and its state affiliates employ lobbyists to monitor legislation at the federal and state levels. One objective of the NRF is to keep Congress informed of the impact laws have on retailing and to be aware of retailers' positions on key issues. Wholesaling, importing and exporting, hiring employees, advertising practices, privacy regulations, and credit policies are regulated by government agencies. Many consumers are knowledgeable about retail law and are quick to identify their rights.

Legal and Ethical Issues

Most retailers recognize that doing business legally and ethically is best. Sweatshop and fair wage issues have dominated the discussions of ethical issues for decades. Several companies were cited for underpaying factory workers, illegally withholding wages, physically abusing workers, employing children, and running unsafe operations. These occurrences were noted in China, other global manufacturing bases, and occasionally in the United States.

Care should be taken to avoid being judgmental and to have all the facts before taking a stance in conflicts relating to business practices in countries other than one's own. Cultural values, choice of trading partners, presence of laws, degree of punishment for violating laws, and ethical orientations of participants are only some of the topics to consider when legal and ethical issues arise.

Regulatory Laws Affecting Retailers

The legal environment is not immune to change. The law affects strategic planning and the implementation of new tactics for multichannel retailers. Following are examples of laws that influence retail growth and market dominance, data privacy, and product safety standards.

Antitrust Laws Several laws enacted in the United States regulate merger and trade activity, including the Sherman, Clayton, and Antimerger Acts. Occasionally the Federal Trade Commission (FTC) invokes antitrust laws in order to disallow monopolies from forming. For example, a U.S. Federal Court order required Staples to cease and desist from its merger plans with Office Depot, another office supply chain.[16] The court determined that the proposed merger would result in unfair competition in certain markets. Staples is a multichannel and global retailer.

Federal antitrust legislation that would prohibit hidden MasterCard and Visa fees was introduced in Congress. The Credit Card Fair Fee Act of 2008 was designed to standardize the amount credit card companies could charge retailers every time a credit card is used. The average fee paid to credit card companies is 2 percent, totaling an estimated $48 billion in fees in 2008.[17] The NRF supports this bill and sees lower product price benefits to customers if it is passed.[18]

Data Privacy Laws The need to assimilate vast amounts of legal information is intensifying as retailers expand globally. However, attitudes regarding the use of customer data vary greatly by country. The European Union, for example, has more restrictive attitudes toward the collection and sharing of data than does the United States.[19] Enforcement of the European Commission's Directive on Data Privacy began in early 2002 and could negatively affect U.S. retailers doing catalog and online business in Europe.

Product Safety Laws A rash of recalled products, including toys, food, and pharmaceuticals, led to initiatives to improve U.S. safety laws in 2008. The U.S. Senate voted to strengthen product safety laws, and the Consumer Product Safety Commission was also scheduled for review. Fines for infractions of the new product safety law were increased from $1.25 million to $20 million. Among several provisions intended to protect consumers were the creation of a database of safety complaints and a requirement that independent laboratories test children's products for safety.[20]

These represent only a fraction of the laws enacted or pending at state and federal levels that affect consumers and retailers. Other areas of special interest include Internet taxation, identity theft, and video surveillance.

Pier 1's competition comes from retailers like Target that present similar merchandise in temporary merchandise displays like *Global Bazaar*. [Source: Photograph provided by Lynda Poloian.]

> Population Dynamics

Several demographic factors were discussed in Chapter 3 in the context of market segmentation. These aspects are equally important when monitoring the retail environment. Other demographic information pertinent to the strategic planning process is population growth, decline, and density.

Large populations alone do not indicate a viable retail market; growth rates and population density are equally important measures. **Population density** is the number of people per square mile or kilometer living in a specific geographic area. Retailers depend on present and future population data to plan for and sustain business through multiple channels.

Factors such as birth and death dynamics, immigration figures, health standards, and marriage and divorce rates also help retailers understand a population. Other significant statistics include the number of households in the retailer's market, percentage of owners and renters, and income per capita. Internet usage data lend new dimension to population trends.

> Internal and External Competition

All retailers are determined to increase sales, and few hesitate to invade another's domain. Competition is multifaceted because it is both horizontal and vertical. **Horizontal competition** pits retailer against retailer. Pier 1, discussed in the SWOT analysis section, competes horizontally with Target as illustrated in Figure 4.2.

Chapter 4 > **The Strategic Planning Process**

Vertical competition places a retailer against a wholesaler or manufacturer that also engages in retailing. Vertical competition has become more apparent since the birth of online shopping. It is not unusual for manufacturers of consumer products also to sell online to retail customers.

In addition competition comes from outside the industry, as people decide how to spend their annual bonuses, tax refunds, or government stimulus rebates. Will the money go toward new stainless steel appliances and glass tiles for their kitchen or will it be deposited into their retirement account? Will it be used to pay fuel bills or purchase costly but needed medications? Those are the questions that concern retailers and families.

Finding a differential advantage is an important part of the strategic planning process. Retailers have different perspectives depending on whether internal or external competitive tactics are required.

Internal Tactics

Internally, retailers use many techniques including selling private-label or other unique merchandise, infusing unexpected goods into their outlets, providing incomparable service, or using innovative promotional techniques. Trading from an architecturally interesting building or building an impressive architecture to run their Web site are other potentially competitive advantages. Several examples illustrate internal techniques.

Scrambled Merchandising Carrying products unrelated to a customary or predictable retail merchandise assortment is called **scrambled merchandising**. For example, if a supermarket adds a walk-in medical clinic adjacent to the produce section or if a coffee shop decides to sell DVDs, the retailers are practicing scrambled merchandising.

Loblaw's, a Canadian retailer, introduced a line of men's and women's apparel called Joe Fresh Style in its supermarkets. Competitively priced goods are manufactured in China and India; a women's trench coat retailed for $34.[21] Soft goods are rarely found in a traditional supermarket so the psychological impact of finding a great deal when shopping for groceries is appealing to customers and profitable for the retailer. A Joe Fresh Style department at Loblaw's is illustrated in Figure 4.3.

When customers do not expect to find unique products, initially they may pay more attention to the merchandise. Retailers' goals are to gain or maintain a competitive edge and to increase sales.

> **4.3**
>
> The Joe Fresh Style apparel department in Loblaw's supermarket comes as a pleasant surprise to customers who are not yet familiar with the scrambled merchandising technique used by the company. [Source: Courtesy of Fairchild Publications, Inc.]

<u>Advantageous Locations</u> Seeking a competitive advantage by locating where throngs of people gather at an historic landmark or in an airport gives some retailers an opportunity to stand out in a crowd.

Heathrow Airport outside London recently completed its expansion of Terminal 5. Upscale retail tenants include Coach, Tiffany & Co., Prada, Thomas Pink, and Harrods.[22] In addition to 333 posters or billboards and 206 flat-screen TVs to tantalize the senses, the complex also has Krispy Kreme doughnuts. Of the 27 million people expected to use Terminal 5 in its first year, an estimated 30 percent have incomes of more than $100,000.[23]

Of the 200,000 square feet allocated for retail space, 20 percent is devoted to beauty products and services. Watches, sunglasses, and British food are other categories planned for the arcade, as well as a central bar for white-knuckle flyers. One of the challenges airport retailers face is attracting business since it is estimated that only 20 percent of airline passengers shop in airports.[24]

Other than the expected food and beverage retailers, companies such as Borders, Hudson News, Golf Pro Shops, Landau Jewelery, Brookstone, The Body Shop, and the Metropolitan Museum of Art are often tenants in U.S. airport malls. Going where customers congregate or catching them on the fly involves making optimal site selection decisions.

Product Differentiation Retailers add name brands, private labels, or new departments in order to enhance their merchandising strategies and create new revenue streams. As examples, Kmart sells moderately priced sheets designed by Martha Stewart and Macy's sells a higher priced line of Martha Stewart kitchen products. Of course customers can purchase Martha's products online and access the company's how-to and product information services.

Let's look at how one small multichannel retailer departed from a traditional treatment focus and added private-label product lines, a transactional Web site, and a promotional twist to gain a differential advantage. Kriss Cosmetics, a single-unit makeup studio and retail store in Manchester, New Hampshire, gained national exposure when the company's private-label makeup line was used on presidential candidates in preparation for a series of nationally televised debates in 2008. Kriss Soterion, the owner and operator of Kriss Cosmetics and a veteran makeup artist under contract to CNN, had been in the business for almost 20 years but it took a female contender for president to bring makeup and image into the forefront of campaign strategies. After the first debate, the media called Soterion "Hillary's secret weapon." By several accounts the senator had never looked as good on TV until Soterion worked her magic. Initial press, TV, and Internet coverage led to appearances by Soterion on *Inside Edition* and *Access Hollywood*. The day after the *Inside Edition* piece, Soterion received 1,400 orders on her Web site, far more than normal. Many were for her custom lipstick color called, appropriately, "Debate." Seizing the opportunity to advance her products, Kriss Soterion exemplifies how even small business owners can benefit from private-label merchandising, creative promotion, and a multichannel approach. The Kriss Cosmetics store, product lines, and unique outreach are illustrated in Figures 4.4a, 4.4b, and 4.4c.

External Tactics

Aggressive acquisitions, mergers, and divestitures are some of the ways retailers compete. Because these actions take place outside of the store, they are considered external techniques. Such techniques are also used to implement strategies for market share growth.

Acquisitions and Divestitures Retailers may attempt to control competition by purchasing rival firms, believing that if they own their competition, profits can be

4.4a Kriss Cosmetics private-label makeup lines on display in her studio. *[Source: Courtesy of Kriss Cosmetics.]*

4.4b Working her magic with Pat Buchanan. *[Source: Courtesy of Kriss Cosmetics.]*

funneled into one corporate pocket. Many turn their attention offshore to markets that may be less saturated and receptive to foreign retailers.

Several recent acquisitions and sell-offs give credence to these practices and lend insight regarding the strategic direction of the companies involved:

> The owner of Lord & Taylor, NRDC Partners, purchased the Fortunoff jewelry and houseware retailer. Fortunoff had filed for bankruptcy protection before the acquisition. NRDC perceived synergies between the merchandise quality and target customers in both companies and announced that it expected to keep Fortunoff's 20 stores while adding in-store boutiques to enhance Lord & Taylor's jewelry presentation.[25] Lord & Taylor was a unit of May Company until it was purchased by Federated Department Stores in 2005.

> After selling Lord & Taylor, Macy's (then known as Federated Department Stores) made a strategic decision to focus on its core department stores and sold its two bridal divisions, David's Bridal and Priscilla of Boston, to Leonard Green & Partners in 2006. It also sold its tuxedo business to Men's Wearhouse. Despite the divestiture, the affiliation with David's continues as that company named Macy's its exclusive department store wedding gift registry partner.[26]

4.4c

Façade of Kriss Cosmetics' brick-and-mortar store in Manchester, New Hampshire. *[Source: Courtesy of Kriss Cosmetics.]*

> Godiva Chocolatier was sold by Campbell Soup Company to Turkish company Ulker Group, a division of Yildiz Holding AS. A multichannel retailer, Godiva sells through company-owned and franchised retail specialty stores, an online store, and via wholesaling to department and other specialty stores. Campbell Soup divested Godiva to concentrate on its food businesses. Ulker is a confection, food and beverage company, perhaps a better fit for Godiva.[27]
> Borders sold its bookstores in the United Kingdom and the Republic of Ireland to Risk Capital Partners in 2007.[28] In this case the divestiture allowed Borders to concentrate more fully on its domestic business. Bringing cash into the company to offset sluggish sales in the United States was another benefit.

It is evident that the reasons for acquisitions and divestitures are varied. Some sales are precipitated by poor performance or fit within the holding company. Other sales, and many acquisitions, are determined by aggressive expansion plans, changing focus, the opportunity to gain prime real estate, and occasionally personal reasons of key shareholders and executives. Several sales have been to foreign companies or to private equity firms, two trends of note in retailing today.

<u>Market Share Growth</u> Seeking dominance by gaining market share at the expense of fellow retailers is a strategy used by some retailers. **Market share** is the percentage of industry-wide product sales earned by one company. Earlier this decade, Hollywood Video gave Blockbuster serious competition by boldly

opening stores very near Blockbuster—sometimes directly across the street. At one time Blockbuster had more than 5,000 stores and held a 25 percent market share for video and DVD rentals. Hollywood Video's market share was approximately 5 percent. Location might have been the key to success if customers did not care from which video store they rented. To the customer, brand name might have not been as important as convenience. In actuality, neither of these factors was important; rather, a shift in direction due to changing technology and new competition drove the market elsewhere.

By 2008, Netflix.com had taken share from the entire video rental business. Several video rental retailers have since gone out of business and Blockbuster continues to counter competitive tactics. When Blockbuster learned of Netflix's policy to charge a flat monthly rate and not penalize customers for late returns, Blockbuster followed suit in its company-owned stores. The decision cost Blockbuster between $250 and $300 million per year in late-fee payments.[29]

Competitive battles will escalate as changes in customer preference, the advent of new methods of distribution, and more online retailers enter the fray. Competition will come from distant shores and from within our own countries. Retailers that practice constant environmental monitoring, develop coping strategies, and study the competition will win. They must also adapt to transformations in the retail environment, have high ethical standards, and deal with unexpected events.

> Unpredictable Events

In addition to economic, political, legal, population, and social changes and knowledge of competition, unexpected events affect customers and retailers. Wars, raging storms, tsunamis, earthquakes, disease, terrorism, tainted foods, and unsafe products—these and other uncontrollable aspects of the environment greatly affect planning and implementation of multichannel strategies and have had a tangible effect on retailers over the past decade. Even the deaths of celebrities influence retail trade. For example, interest in Diana, Princess of Wales, has resurfaced every time a new retrospective of her life is published and featured in bookstores around the world.

Natural disasters influence retailing in positive and negative ways.

Hurricane Katrina wreaked havoc on New Orleans and the Gulf Coast of the United States in September 2005 and has had lasting repercussions on retailers and customers in the area. During and immediately after the storm, travel services were deluged with calls and e-mails from people attempting to exit New Orleans or those canceling Labor Day reservations and seeking refunds for what they had hoped would be a holiday break.

Because so many people were left homeless, scheduled deliveries from catalog and online retailers could not be made. Web traffic was down considerably. Amazon.com could not deliver a significant number of packages scheduled for customers in New Orleans.

Catalog and online orders for Orvis, the fishing supply retailer, were down 10 percent during Katrina. The company attributed 80 percent of the decline to the hurricane and believed that the rest was due to customers elsewhere in the country who were shocked by the events and had no desire to shop. Orvis had 50,000 catalogs ready to be mailed that never reached New Orleans.[30]

The negative impact on individuals and businesses was severe, but the outpouring of aid was intense. The International Council of Shopping Centers (ICSC) worked with the Federal Emergency Management Agency (FEMA) to help direct hurricane victims to temporary housing in unused retail properties in the area. The ICSC and its members donated heavily to the Red Cross as local residents tried to piece their lives together.[31]

In early 2008, fearing that beef from sick animals could have been used in the processing of several products destined for U.S. supermarkets and specialty food stores as well as institutional users, several grocery supply chain members were forced to recall products, including more than 200,000 cans of soup manufactured by General Mills. The company placed telephone calls, e-mails, and faxes to retailers recalling the products. Recalls not only affect retail sales, they strongly affect customers' perceptions of products, brands, and the retailers themselves. The recall also had legal implications. Since the events of 9/11, anti-bioterrorism laws have made it necessary for all manufacturers of food products to trace their production one step forward and one step back in the supply chain.[32]

The most profoundly unsettling event in many decades was the terrorist attack on the United States carried out on September 11, 2001. The events that occurred on that day and in successive months in the United States and other countries have affected and will continue to influence our lives and business practices.

All elements of the retail environment are of considerable importance to retailers, but no other aspect is having as significant an effect on business as the technological revolution. It has given retailers the means for instant sales and inventory updates, accurate and speedy credit and check approvals, video conferencing and online training capabilities, radio frequency identification (RFID), the Internet, and countless other tools that help retailers make better decisions and operate more efficiently.

Decision-Making Tools and Market Strategies

Multichannel retailers use various tools, applications, and techniques to identify and refine their strategic planning. Examining some of the most common planning tools in detail can illuminate how they provide a framework for decision making.

The Boston Consulting Group's classic growth-share matrix, the product/market expansion grid, and market segmentation strategies let multichannel retailers brainstorm and identify the status and capabilities of their companies or products. Articulating and organizing information is sometimes the most difficult task when planning strategically.

> Growth-Share Matrix

Developed by the Boston Consulting Group (BCG) to provide a planning tool for a company's entire business portfolio, the concept of the growth-share matrix works well in a narrower vein such as retailing. The matrix looks at the possible relationships between market growth and relative market share through four types of strategic business units (SBUs), illustrated in Figure 4.5. A **strategic business unit** is one part or division of a company that is treated as a separate entity in terms of its mission and strategic plan. Four possibilities are identified:

> *Star*—High market share and high market growth indicate a stellar position for the SBU. This sounds very positive, but stars are vulnerable to competition and market pressures over time. Stars often evolve into cash cows.
> *Cash Cow*—With high market share in a low growth market, the cash cow is a consistent performer. Companies strive to keep their cash cows productive over time.

4.5

Boston Consulting Group Growth-Share Matrix uses animal analogies and other symbols to describe possible outcomes and facilitate strategic business unit analysis.

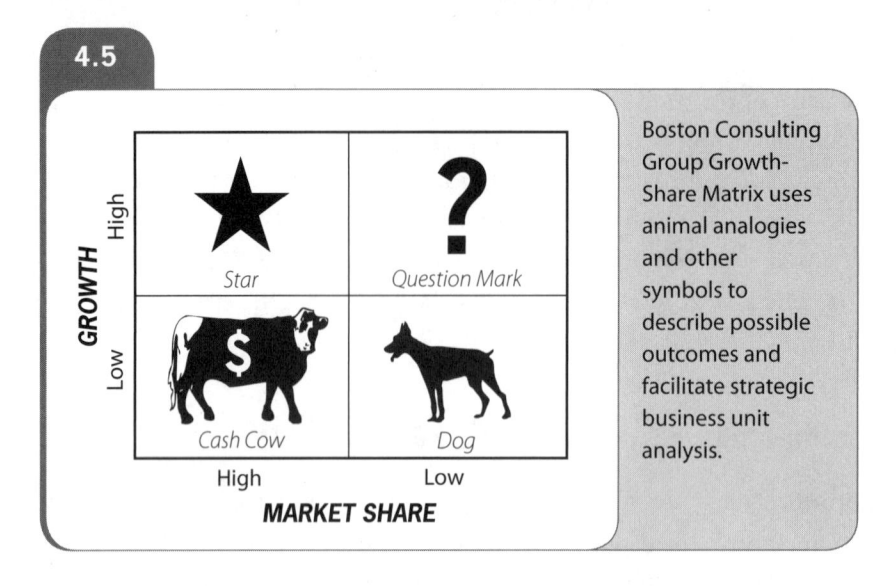

> *Question Mark*—With low market share in a high-growth market, the question mark is in a delicate position. The company may pump more money into the venture to keep generating sales and possibly become a star—or not.
> *Dog*—Low market growth and low market share businesses are problems. Even though they may generate sales, revenues are not significant enough to keep the SBU afloat for long. Many dogs are eventually divested or closed.

> **Product/Market Expansion Grid**

The product/market expansion grid is used to help identify strategic options. The four categories on the grid depict the interplay between existing and new products and markets. Often the product is the store, catalog, or Web site.

Understanding the Grid

Four possible combinations are described:

> *Market Penetration*—When a retailer has an existing product in an existing market, the objective is to sell more products to current customers.
> *Market Development*—If a retail product is a proven one, the company expands into new markets. Markets can be geographic, demographic, lifestyle, behavioral, or another identified segment.

Product / Market Expansion Grid Table 4.2

	EXISTING PRODUCTS	NEW PRODUCTS
EXISTING MARKETS	Market Penetration	Product Development
NEW MARKETS	Market Development	Diversification

Source: H. Igor Ansoff, "Strategies for Diversification," *Harvard Business Review* (September-October 1957), 113-24. See also Armstrong & Kotler, *Marketing: An Introduction*, 8th ed. (Upper Saddle River, NJ: Pearson Prentice Hall, 2007), 44-45.

> *Product Development*—When a retailer has a well-established market, it may elect to develop a new product for that market. Because retailers know their customers well, they are aware of unmet needs and new opportunities.
> *Diversification*—When a retailer develops a new concept for a market it has not yet served it is using diversification as a strategy. Companies turn to diversification to provide a buffer against possible economic downturns or changes in customer sentiment. Often a company does not want to be overinvested in one core business.

The product/market expansion grid is illustrated in Table 4.2.

Using the Grid to Formulate Strategies

Several examples illustrate how information gleaned from the product/market expansion grid is used by retailers.

Market Penetration Encouraging current Internet users to access a Web site more often and using the Web to direct customers to catalogs and stores are logical extensions of market penetration.

Wireless shoppers are enticed to use mobile coupons toward the purchase of products and services. For example, Supercuts uses mobile coupons to draw customers to its chain of hair salons. The service retailer has over 2,000 locations in the United States and tested the program in 75 of its New England stores. The company Cellfire provides the coupon service via an opt-in customer database for Supercuts' selected area of coverage. Customers can sign up for Cellfire's mobile coupon service by texting a five-digit number or accessing the Web site in order to receive the $2 discount for a haircut or $5 off a color treatment.

4.6

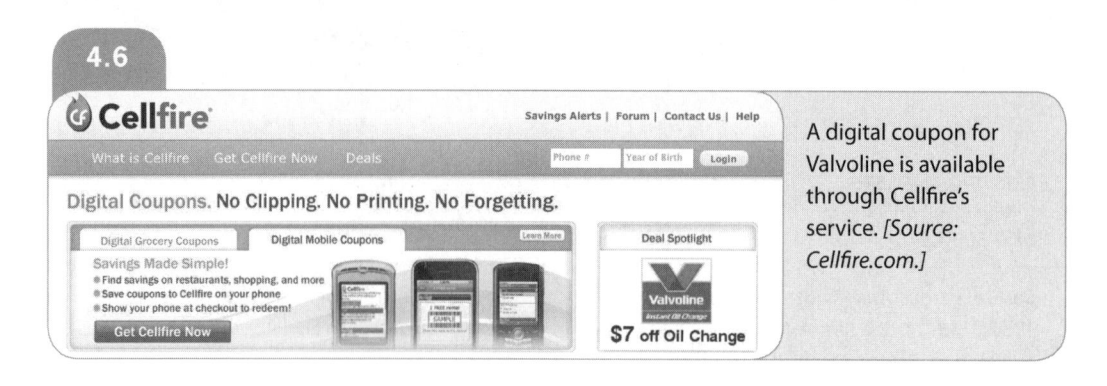

A digital coupon for Valvoline is available through Cellfire's service. *[Source: Cellfire.com.]*

Other retailers using the service include 1-800-Flowers.com, Hollywood Video, and Hardee's, the fast-food chain.[33] Even coupons for oil changes are available, as illustrated in Figure 4.6.

Turning more Web surfers into shoppers and more store and catalog browsers into customers is tantamount to market penetration. Converting average customers into top-tier customers is another aim.

Market Development Using geographics or demographics—or both—retailers can develop new markets. Aeropostale, the casual apparel retailer, chose foreign expansion to extend its market base. The company's plans call for opening 80 to 100 stores in Canada starting in 2007. Targeting more fashion-forward customers, Aeropostale's newest stores are more contemporary in design and hip in customer orientation.[34]

REI, the outdoor equipment and apparel retail cooperative, recognized that many shoppers in Japan were ordering through its catalogs. Responding to these data, the company opened stores in Japan. Similarly, after closely examining its customer database, and cognizant of changes in the economy, the company opened REI-Outlet.com to satisfy the needs of bargain-hunting Web shoppers. Approximately 20 percent of sales come from REI's Web sites. In 2008, the company celebrated its 70th year in business.[35]

Web-enabled kiosks are other devices that can be used to employ market development strategies. Several shoe retailers have turned to kiosks to extend their reach by offering sizes beyond the normal range in their brick-and-mortar stores. In this way customers who wear unusually small or large, narrow or wide footwear become a whole new market for the retailers.

Target targets teens with its "Bullseye Advice" section on its Web site. The company's primary market is young married women, but in order to venture into new markets the company has added fresh merchandising concepts and services geared to engage younger customers.

Product Development Innovation regarding new merchandise or extensions of services highlight product development strategies. Best Buy and Circuit City compete head-to-head in the consumer electronics market. In seeking to gain market advantage, Best Buy added Geek Squad as its computer service provider. The company also opened a music download site, Rioport.com/bestbuy to gain another differential advantage. Illustrating the highly competitive nature of this market, Circuit City used e-mail to run online sweepstakes, and provided live product demonstrations on weekends. But Circuit City could not keep pace and closed its doors in early 2009.

Photoworks, originally a mail-order film developing service, added digital printing services, design-your-own books, archiving capabilities, and electronic picture frames as it eased from 35-millimeter processing to digital technology. Product development tactics allow the company to compete in an industry in transition.

Diversification Departing from the norm or the expected works well when a company deems it necessary to expand its interests. Before Eddie Bauer launched Eddie Bauer Kids stores it first tested the apparel online—a novel tactic at the time.

When Giorgio Armani unveiled 144 private residences in a Dubai high-rise in 2007, it was practicing a new breed of brand extension and diversification by the standards of most designers, manufacturers, and retailers. The company also launched a Web site for the new division and announced that it would open a resort in Morocco in 2009.[36]

These applications show that there are few limits to the creative use of the product/market expansion grid. Its importance as a framework for decision making is evident.

Market Segmentation Strategies

In Chapter 3, several bases for market segmentation were presented, including age, gender, income, lifestyle, ethnicity, class, geographic location, and behavior. Segmentation strategies that pertain to type and degree of market coverage are covered here. Four basic strategies are identified: undifferentiated, differentiated, concentrated, and micromarketing.

The choice of market coverage depends on retail objectives, budget, and the nature of the products or services carried. The degree to which a company narrows the field determines the type of marketing segmentation selected.

The purpose is to select a viable target market that is reachable with a well-designed marketing mix. **Marketing mix** is the unique arrangement of product, pricing, distribution, and promotion tactics selected to appeal to target customers. Depending on the type of segmentation, if more than one segment is selected, two or more marketing mixes may be developed.

Each of the four strategies listed below represents a different approach to segmentation:

> *Undifferentiated*—This is a mass marketing approach by which a retailer offers one marketing mix to an entire market. Undifferentiated means there is no segmentation, and all possible customers are treated the same. In practice, this is a less popular choice for retailers.
> *Differentiated*—Often called multisegment marketing, the differentiated approach is used when retailers identify more than one viable target market. Using differentiated segmentation the task is to create separate marketing mixes for each market. This is a popular approach to segmentation.
> *Concentrated*—Also called niche marketing, a concentrated approach is used when the retailer selects only one segment and creates one or more marketing mixes to reach that group. If the segment is a strong one, the approach is beneficial to the retailer. However, should the target market no longer desire the company's merchandise, loss of significant sales could result unless other options are in the works. A bridal shop targeting only Hispanic brides-to-be exemplifies a concentrated market segment.
> *Micromarketing*—Customization, mentioned as a customer preference in Chapter 3, is at the crux of micromarketing. **Micromarketing** is the creation of a tailored marketing mix that is delivered to a small group or to even one individual. Also called individualized targeting, this technique is used frequently by online retailers. Sophisticated databases have helped make this possible. Target, Tommy Hilfiger, Lands' End, J. C. Penney, Timberland, and Nike are some of the companies that offer customization options.

Multichannel retailers who are at the top of their game have reduced risk by planning carefully and thoroughly, and leaving their minds open to changes in the environment. Retailers draw from as many tools as they can assemble to guide the choices they make when making strategic decisions. Chapter 5 looks specifically at strategies used by multichannel retailers and those considered industry best practices.

Summary

The strategic planning process helps retailers assess their status, delineate competitive advantages, articulate direction, and develop realistic goals and objectives. These steps bring retailers to the ultimate step of defining and implementing succinct strategies. Compulsion to conduct this procedure is high because expansion, growth, and profitability depend upon strategic planning and proficient execution. Planning is done for entire companies, divisions, stores, merchandise units, and products.

Without knowledge of dynamics outside the company retailers cannot cultivate or effectively bring their plans to fruition. The economy is one of the most forceful aspects that impinge on decision making. The need to monitor political and legal sectors, population dynamics, and social and ecological changes is also necessary. Keeping aware of competition is an ongoing activity for most retailers and several internal and external tactics are used to counter contenders for sales and market share.

The best plans need modification when the unexpected occurs. Maintaining flexibility to alter strategies is necessary when cataclysmic weather events, wars, terrorist attacks, blights, or disease threaten the world or local regions.

Many tools are available for retailers that plan strategically. The growth-share matrix helps planners allocate resources for expansion or retrenchment; profile divisions, stores, or products; gauge productivity; and seek new directions. The product/market expansion grid encourages retailers to look at current products or future innovations in the light of their companies' current and potential markets. Market segmentation strategies also guide retailers regarding the scope and direction of market selection and customer targeting.

Strategic planning is not a luxury. It is a necessity for retailers of all sizes and channel capabilities.

Key Terms

Chapter 11
Devaluation
Differential advantage
Environmental scanning
Goals
Horizontal competition
Inflation
Market share
Marketing mix
Micromarketing
Mission statement
North American Free Trade Agreement (NAFTA)
Objectives
Population density
Positioning
Prime rate
Protectionism
Recession
Scrambled merchandising
Situation analysis
Strategic business unit
Strategic planning
Strategies
SWOT analysis
Trade embargo
Vertical competition
Vision statement

> Questions for Discussion and Reflection

1. The strategic planning process is made up of several steps. Where do you start and why?
2. What is the difference between a vision statement and a mission statement when developing a strategic plan?
3. If one of your company's goals is to increase sales by 5 percent over the next four quarters, what two objectives might help you reach that goal?
4. What aspect of the retail environment is most challenging and multifaceted to retailers today? Why is this so?
5. Why do we say that the aspects of the retail environment are external to the company, and therefore uncontrollable? Give an example of one aspect of the environment and suggest ways in which retailers can develop strategies to deal with changes in the area you have chosen.
6. As retailers organize data and make sense of the dynamics within their organizations in preparation for strategic planning, several tools are used. How does the Boston Consulting Group's growth-share matrix help companies determine where they should place their time and financial resources?
7. The product/market expansion grid presents four strategic options to retailers. If you are selling private-label orange juice from Florida through multiple channels and your goal is to sell more of your product to new customers, which strategy will you choose? Justify your choice.
8. Give an example from the text or your experience of a retailer that has successfully used product development as a strategy. Could the retailer have considered any of the other three options? Why or why not?
9. What is the difference between the concentrated approach to market segmentation and the micromarketing segmentation strategy? Use specific multichannel examples in your answer.
10. Why do multichannel companies plan strategically?

Notes >

1. Kris Hudson and Joann S. Lublin, "As Pier 1 Continues Its Redecorating, Some Think It's Time for a New CEO," *Wall Street Journal*, June 22, 2006, C1, C5.
2. Ross Tucker, "Currency Rates, Tax Benefit Buoy Levi's," *Women's Wear Daily*, February 8, 2008, 2.
3. Kelly Evans, "Sales in January Rose, Aided by Gas Prices; Big-Ticket Items Lagged," *Wall Street Journal*, February 14, 2008, A4.
4. Jeanine Poggi, "Teen Panel Reflects Shifting Spending Habits," *Women's Wear Daily*, June 11, 2007, 23.
5. Chantal Todé, "Retailers Beset by Cutbacks," *DM News*, February 4, 2008, www.dmnews.com/Retailers-beset-by-cutbacks/PrintArticle/104876.
6. Ibid.
7. Ibid.
8. David Moin, "Macy's to Cut 2,550 Jobs in Restructuring," *Women's Wear Daily*, February 2, 2008, 3, 25.
9. Jim Tierney and Tim Parry, "Chapter 11 for Sharper Image and Lillian Vernon," *Multichannel Merchant*, February 20, 2008, www.multichannelmerchant.com/news/Chapter 11-sharper-Lillian.

10. "2 Retailers Bankrupt After Sales Declines," Associated Press report, *Boston Globe*, February 21, 2008, E2.

11. Jeffrey McCracken and Peter Lattman, "Sharper Image Lives—as a Brand," *Wall Street Journal*, June 26, 2008, B1.

12. Janet Adamy, "Starbucks Eliminates 600 Jobs in Overhaul," *Wall Street Journal*, February 22, 2008, B6.

13. Stephen Grocer, "Foreign Shoppers: Just Looking?" *Wall Street Journal*, March 4, 2008, C3.

14. Vicki M. Young, "The Bidding for Saks: Baugur Said Still Keen but in Holding Pattern," *Women's Wear Daily*, February 11, 2008, 1, 22.

15. Samantha Conti, "Baugur May Beat a Retreat From Saks," *Women's Wear Daily*, September 8, 2008, 36. James Davey, "Update 4—Baugur's Demise Puts UK Retail Assets in Play," February 4, 2009, www.retuers.com/articlePrint?articleId=1NL 470083120090204.

16. John R. Wilke and Joseph Pereira, "Office Depot, Staples Deal is Blocked," *Wall Street Journal*, July 1, 1997, 1, A3.

17. Cara Wood, "Fair Fee Act Could Help Small Retailers," *DM News*, September 15, 2008, www.dmnews.com/Fair-Fee-Act-could-help-small-retailers/PrintArticle/116588.

18. National Retail Federation, Press Release, "NRF Welcomes Antitrust Legislation Addressing $40 Billion in Hidden Credit Card Fees," March 6, 2008, www.nrf.com.

19. Tony Seideman, "Threat of Sanctions Heats Up Debate Over European Privacy Rules," *Stores*, June, 2001, 92.

20. Stephen Labaton, "Senate Votes to Strengthen Product Safety Laws," *New York Times*, March 7, 2008, 1-2, www.nytimes.com/2008/03/07/business/07consumer.html.

21. Dan Alaimo, "Supermarkets Try Some New Wares," *Women's Wear Daily*, May 8, 2006, 17.

22. Lucie Greene, "Retail cleared for Takeoff at Heathrow's Terminal 5," *Women's Wear Daily*, December 27, 2007, 11.

23. Aaron O. Patrick, "Mass of Messages Lands at Heathrow," *Wall Street Journal*, February 15, 2008, B3.

24. Pete Born and Jennifer Weil, "Countdown to Terminal 5," *Women's Wear Daily*, October 26, 2007, 7.

25. David Moin, "NRDC to Acquire Fortunoff," *Women's Wear Daily*, February 4, 2008, 2.

26. "Federated Sells Bridal Group for $850 Million," *SCT Extra*, November 20, 2006. Newsletter published by *Shopping Centers Today*, International Council of Shopping Centers, New York.

27. Julie Jargon and John R. Wilke, "Chocolate Makers Face Probe Over Pricing," *Wall Street Journal*, December 21, 2007, A4.

28. "Borders Sells Its UK Book Stores," *BBC News*, September 21, 2007, http://newsvote.bbc.co.uk.

29. Karen Richardson, "Blockbuster's Backbreaker: No-Late-Fee Policy," *Wall Street Journal*, January 5, 2006, C1.

30. Bob Tedeschi, "Not Even Web Retailers Will Be Exempt from the Aftereffects of Katrina," *New York Times*, September 5, 2005, www.nytimes.com.

31. "ICSC, FEMA Catalog Empty Retail Space to House Hurricane Katrina Refugees," *SCT Extra*, September 6, 2005. Newsletter published by *Shopping Centers Today*, International Council of Shopping Centers.

32. Julie Jargon, "Retracing the Beef-Supply Trail," *Wall Street Journal*, March 4, 2008, A12.

33. Mickey Alam Kahn, "Supercuts Tests Mobile Coupons for Haircut Discounts," *Mobile Marketer*, February 22, 2008, www.mobilemarketer.com/cms/news/commerce/574.print.

34. Debra Hazel, "Aeropostale Targets Canada," *GSR*, ALM Properties, Inc., February 13, 2007, www.globest.com.

35. "REI Web Sales Climb Nicely in 2007," *Internet Retailer*, February 27, 2008, www.internetretailer.com/printArticle.asp?id=25508.

36. Luisa Zargani, "Armani's Hotel Milestones," *Women's Wear Daily*, WWD/Global, October 2007, 2.

Chapter 5

Implementing Multichannel Strategies

Objectives

> To identify key impact areas for strategic decision making.
> To delineate how multichannel retailers develop and execute strategies to overcome channel limitations.
> To exemplify industry best practices in strategy development.

> The nexus of decision making encompasses several sectors for multichannel retailers. Chapter 4 pointed out that retailers must be cognizant of uncontrollable factors in the retail environment as they plan for future growth and development of their companies. Likewise they must be aware of unintended consequences that may occur in multiple areas under their responsibility.

Impact Areas for Strategic Decision Making

Topics to consider in the planning process include but are not limited to enabling technologies, retail expansion, branding and product development, marketing and communications, and distribution and fulfillment.

> Enabling Technologies

Multichannel retailers demand new technologies, and what is cutting-edge today is archaic tomorrow. Adding to or updating computer systems is a priority, but necessary changes can be costly. Many examples given in this section are channel-specific. Others are used across one or more channels.

Whether you want to electronically measure traffic that enters your store, count the number of hits on your Web site, or monitor the database of your catalog customers, technology can achieve these objectives. You met the "magic mirror" that lets customers experiment with fashion in Chapter 3. There is much more electronic and Web-based wizardry to tantalize customers.

Store-Centered

Many innovations are designed to enhance the in-store shopping experience. Huge plasma screen TV monitors with streaming video or advertisements are almost compulsory in retail stores. "Smart" manikins and mood-evoking displays provide visual appeal and atmosphere.

Touch-screens built into manikins allow customers to access product information directly from the display. Availability of sizes and preferred colors is easily checked. The company EuroTouch Kiosks markets the touch-screen manikins illustrated in Figure 5.1.

If you have an opportunity to walk into a store and feel as though you are walking through a cloud, do so. It's fun and undeniably draws attention to retailers. FogScreen is an interactive vapor panel that combines the intangibility of a cloud with visual imagery. This amazing technology uses digital images that are projected directly on a vapor stream. The stream serves as a screen for brand-enhancing photos or video. Positioned near a store entrance, it enables customers to walk through the cloud into the store—a memorable experience.

Less esoteric but just as valuable, ShopperTrak makes pedestrian-counting tools that allow retailers to monitor traffic flow continuously. Web-based technologies

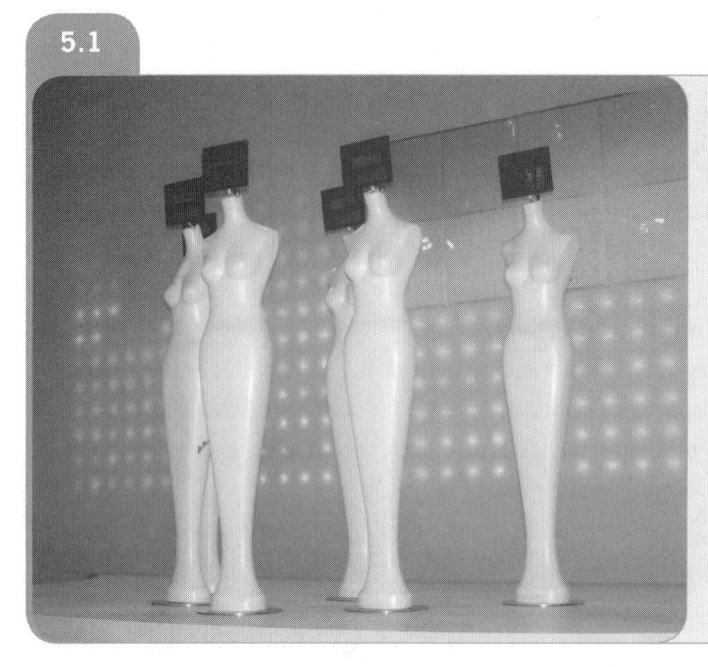

5.1 Touch-screen manikins provide more than tempting visual merchandising since customers can also access product information such as size range, color, and product availability. *[Source: Photograph provided by Lynda Poloian.]*

ensure data in real-time for access by all appropriate managers. Information is used to plan sales associate coverage for peak periods, identify weak times for further analysis, reconfigure displays, and compare against previous periods.

Catalog-Oriented

Catalog retailers are dependent on customer databases and facilitating software that helps them prospect, build mailing lists, coordinate e-mail requests and personal and shopping data from customers, and then mine the collective data for marketing purposes. And that is just the beginning. The underpinning of what are now multichannel solutions derives from the pioneering efforts of catalog companies. As you learned in Chapter 2, recency, frequency, and monetary value (RFM) form the core of information used by catalog houses to chart performance, measure productivity, and plan for the future.

Internet-Centered

Increasing erudition of online customers is being matched by sophisticated advances in Web technologies. The same powerful tools that fuel commercial, entertainment, and social networking sites have increased the demand for parallel technologies in the e-retailing area. Collectively called **Web 2.0 e-commerce,** these tools are advanced technologies that enable high-level user interaction and offer rich media, heightened graphics, and three-dimensional (3-D) capabilities.

The opportunity to see store layouts and construction plans in 3-D has been possible for some time; in fact, even the old 3-D movies popular in the 1950s have staged a comeback as production houses revamp the technology for contemporary film viewing. Three-dimensional technology lets us view products from every angle and is becoming a feature of choice for more online retailers, including automobile dealerships. The full 360-degree treatment online is more pleasurable for some customers than a grueling car shopping experience in a showroom. When combined with design-your-own products like clothing, 3-D technology is indispensable. However, 3-D can be expensive because the cost of digitizing one piece of apparel is about $1,000.[1]

Developing proprietary software is another option for enterprising online retailers. Health-conscious individuals will find Peapod's virtual nutritionist service useful, and food retailers will envy the competitive advantage. Peapod.com is the leading online grocer in the United States, operating in eight states and the District of Columbia. The company was founded in 1989 and presently is owned by Royal Ahold of The Netherlands.[2] Read more about Peapod's technology and customer interface in Box 5.1.

No functional area in retailing is left untouched by technology. Although currently the standard by which e-commerce sites are judged, Web 2.0 technologies are being supplanted by Web 3.0 as part of an ever-evolving process of advancing capabilities. Details on Web infrastructure, Web site development, and technologies that facilitate the online experience are covered in Chapter 7.

> Retail Expansion

Always on the lookout for opportunities, retailers build on strategies designed to reach new markets. They tailor stores to specific market areas and devise original concepts that vibrate on a different marketing level. Many companies look beyond their national borders to generate new revenue sources.

New Concept Development

Brick-and-mortar retailers, catalogs, and some online stores are creating fresh formats to reach new target markets. If the new concept is a brick-and-mortar store, once it is built and tested, usually it is rolled out simultaneously to the Web.

Box 5.1 What's the Buzz?

> *Peapod Offers First Ever Virtual Nutritionist*

Peapod has developed and created its own software program that essentially reads the labels for its customers. Like a virtual nutritionist, NutriFilter sifts through all the products available online and highlights the ones that meet customers' unique nutritional needs, whether it's for gluten-free, peanut-free, or low-fat foods, or foods that meet other requirements, such as being kosher, organic, high-or-low fiber, or even as specific as high in vitamin A or calcium.

Customers have the option of using five pre-set plans—with more to be added in the future—or they can create as many of their own custom plans as they'd like. One can create a sort of dream label, specifying maximum calories, grams of fat, milligrams of potassium, and so on, and then activate that special filter before hitting the aisles to shop in the most customized way possible.

NutriFilter includes the U.S. Department of Agriculture guidelines for each nutritional component providing more information than a cereal box ever would. For example, you've heard that eating lots of fiber can help you lose weight—but how many grams of fiber should you eat in a day? For the answer click on your virtual label, and then specify how many grams of fiber you'd like the items in your own customized "High-Fiber Plan" to contain. When you shop, these high-fiber items will automatically jump to the top of the "shelf."

Aside from the obvious convenience, NutriFilter offers to people with dietary restrictions, it is also an excellent resource for any health-conscious person, from a nutritionist helping his or her client plan the next shopping trip to a mom who wants to choose the healthiest foods for her family. The service is available to anyone who logs on to Peapod.

Source: Excerpted from Peapod LLC press release, March 18, 2008.

Abercrombie & Fitch has spun-off several new retail formats, including Hollister Co. and Ruehl No. 925, to reach different style, age, and income markets. When the company announced its newest strategic direction many were pleasantly surprised. Gilly Hicks sells young women's underwear in an Australian-themed store evoking the spirit of adventure. It is meant to be a counterpart to Hollister in terms of target market and price points. The first store opened at the Natick Collection in Massachusetts in 2008. More units are planned for the United States and international expansion is possible.[3] Gilly Hicks new concept store is shown in Figure 5.2.

Catalogs retailers also develop spin-offs to reach out to new markets. The Territory Ahead, a catalog geared to rugged male and female travelers, brought forth its Isabella Bird catalog, which appeals to sophisticated women who prefer updated casual wear with more urban appeal. An Isabella Bird catalog cover is featured in Figure 5.3. Note the customer directive to visit the Web site for more options.

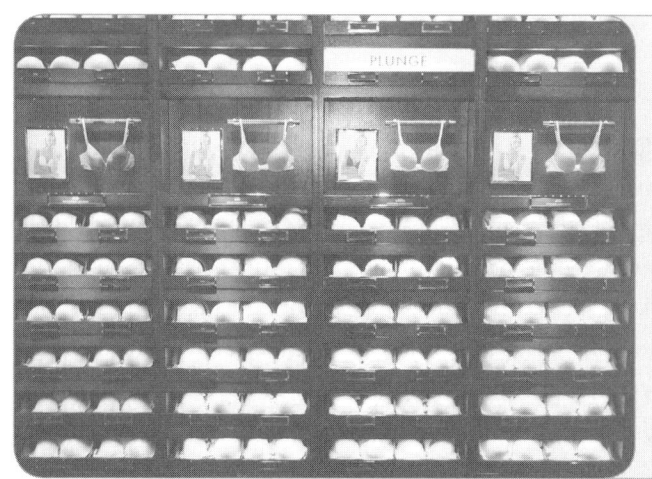

5.2 Departing from its focus on casual apparel for young men and women, the latest spin-off for Abercrombie & Fitch is Gilly Hicks, a lingerie store. *[Source: Courtesy of Fairchild Publications, Inc.]*

Zappos.com, the shoe retailer, acquired 6pm.com, an online handbag shop. In this case the strategy involved acquisition rather than growth from within. The compatibility of products was probably one of the deciding factors when executives weighed the pros and cons of the purchase.

Global Expansion

Large retailers are well aware of the issues they will face when they take their operations global. Differences in culture, management philosophy, government regulation, merchandising, and customer service standards all shape strategic direction. International outreach online also brings associated benefits and disadvantages. With online usage on the rise in many parts of the globe, retailers carefully weigh the risks of online expansion. The stakes are high regarding increased revenue, customer base, and branding potential. Three

5.3 Isabella Bird urges customers to shop on its Web site by printing a few words of encouragement on the catalog cover. *[Source: Isabella Bird 2008 catalog cover; sample provided by Lynda Poloian.]*

Chapter 5 > **Implementing Multichannel Strategies**   181

examples suggest areas that are ripe for planning consideration by online and other retailers.

Cultural Differences Consumer sentiment toward product quality levels and customer convenience varies greatly in international online markets. For example, Swedish consumers are more stringent about quality and convenience than their German counterparts. Seventy-nine percent of Swedish people, as opposed to 55 percent of German people, indicate that they will pay more for quality and convenience online.[4] Information like this is not always apparent as retailers contemplate online customer behavior across cultures, yet it is crucial to strategy development. The best research in the global multichannel sector goes well beyond the superficial.

Online Payment Preferences Customers in some countries other than the United States are more reluctant to pay by credit card. The online company eBags.com discovered that the online payment service PayPal, owned by eBay, is an acceptable alternative for European customers who prefer not to use credit cards online. Customers accustomed to stores that are closed for long lunch hours or on Sundays find the extended hours available when they shop online most beneficial. That is why eBags chose Europe for online store expansion.[5]

PayPal operates in 15 languages—at the same time. Using "polylingual simultaneous shipping" also called "SimShip," the software allows the company to refresh information needed to better manage its operations in all geographic areas. International business is 44 percent of PayPal's revenues.[6]

International Shipping Issues Retailers in the United States have been reluctant to ship goods to customers from other countries due to the currency exchange and shipment hassles. In the face of economic recession, however, some retailers are initiating customer contact abroad. Both Neiman Marcus and Bergdorf Goodman now ship to Canada and expect to ship to other global markets in 2009. The online jewelry retailer Blue Nile already ships internationally and expects to expand its base from 3 to 15 international locations in 2008.[7]

Most global retailers find global expansion a thoughtful but enriching strategy. Advocates of this approach cite revenue growth, income balancing, and customer acquisition as central factors in their decision. Ongoing market research for use in future expansion plans is another benefit gained from operating in international markets.

Brand Building and Product Development

Retailers spend considerable effort in building and maintaining their brands. "The store is the brand," is a statement often heard in retailing. The words reinforce the importance of taking a broad view of marketing. Branding may be the single most important factor in determining longevity in the marketplace for a retailer. **Branding** is the integrative process of building, maintaining, and refining strategies that present the total retail concept to the public. It is the epitome of image building. Multichannel retailers have the additional responsibility of ensuring that the brand travels well across all channels. It is important to create a consistent brand image across all channels of operation. **Brand image** is the perception that customers have of a brand.

Product development extends the brand to actual merchandise. **Product development** is the process that merges the buying function in a retail organization with product sourcing and technology. The contemporary view of product development emerged as retailers sought competitive advantages. The definition also embraces the broader concept of new department and product line development and is not confined to the development of one specific item. The next section explores the importance of branding and product development through several examples.

Brand Positioning Talbots, the women's apparel retailer known for dressing professional women well, is in a period of transition. The Hingham, Massachusetts-based company brought in a new CEO in 2007, replacing a 20-year veteran who retired. J. Jill, a multichannel women's apparel retailer with a distinctly different target market, was acquired in 2006. The acquisition put the company in a financial bind that was exacerbated by the recession in 2008. One of the directives of the new leadership is to revisit its brand positioning. Details on this and other company strategies are presented in Box 5.2.

Customizing Retail Locations As a branding strategy Home Depot uses signs that are customized to the geographic location on its store façades. Town or area names are featured prominently under the company logo on store as well as access-road signs. By personalizing its brand Home Depot gains the loyalty of customers. Customers experience warmer feelings toward retailers that identify with their communities. A Home Depot sign in one of Maine's seacoast communities is shown in Figure 5.4.

Box 5.2 What's the Buzz?

> **Talbots to Review Brand Positioning**

Talbots has retained a business consulting firm to assist in a strategic review of the company's brand positioning. A strategic review of the company, which includes catalog, online, and retail stores, has been a part of the plan since Trudy Sullivan took over as president and CEO. "The consulting firm will be assisting Ms. Sullivan and the management with the review, with a particular focus on brand positioning, operational effectiveness, and growth opportunities," a company spokeswoman said.

The goal of any strategic plan will be to drive sustainable profitable growth and enhance performance, according to Talbots. The results of the review by the consulting firm coupled with the merchant's internal assessments will be used to bring about changes in the way the company does business.

In addition to the positioning and expansion opportunities of the Talbots and J. Jill brands, the consulting engagement will address store growth, productivity, non-core concepts, and distribution channels. Ms. Sullivan said, "The decision to evaluate the positioning of our brands in the marketplace is one of the most important initiatives that our team is undertaking."

Source: Excerpted and condensed from Chantal Todé, DM News, *October 15, 2007, 3.*

5.4 A branding technique used by Home Depot is personalized signage like this one in Ellsworth, the gateway to the Acadian region in Maine. *[Source: Photograph provided by Lynda Poloian.]*

Private Labeling Through the creation of store brands and other private-label merchandise, retailers use differential advantage to gain customer loyalty, increase sales, and improve return on investment. Many retailers find that private-label business is more lucrative than dealing in national brands because the margins and pricing are less restrictive. Product development plays an important role in private labeling, and it is through internal discourse that proprietary brands are best established.

Walgreens, the largest drugstore retailer in the United States, planned to launch a private-label clothing line in most of its 6,000 stores in 2008. Not over-the-counter medications, not greeting cards, or cotton balls, but fashion apparel. Called Casual Gear, the selections will include Capri pants, sweats, vests, and T-shirts for men and women. Private label accounts for about 20 percent of general merchandise sales for Walgreens.[8] Introduce an element of scrambled merchandising and it becomes apparent that there are no limits to the quest for a competitive advantage.

Product Development at Amazon.com The path to online superstore for Amazon began simply with books and music but became more complex due to the calculated growth of online stores, partnerships, and affiliate programs. A brief chronology of product and service development at Amazon illustrates several manifestations of the company's strategic planning:

> 2003—Apparel and gourmet food departments were added.
> 2004—Beauty products were added from a variety of resources in a wide range of price points. Merchants joining early included Sephora, Avon, Crabtree & Evelyn, N. V. Perricone, and MensEssentials.
> 2005—Custom diamond jewelry service was added; online customers could now design the diamond ring of their dreams.
> 2006—Accessories were added to the online store mix.[9]
> 2007—E-book reader Kindle was added.[10]
> 2008—Two new services, Amazon Giver and Amazon Grapevine, were added, enabling Facebook users to share "wish lists" and product reviews.[11]

That many of the company's new offerings were added just prior to the holiday selling period is noteworthy. Timing is critical to the successful implementation of strategies. Amazon is featured in the Multichannel Retail Profile at the end of Unit III.

Marketing and Communications

How best to reach customers is a never-ending quest. Although many new marketing and communication avenues are opening, matching customers with the appropriate vehicles is still challenging. Customer interface occurs through conventional media such as newspapers, magazines, television, radio, and billboards, but the newest media incarnations have changed the rules of engagement.

Magazines are putting their content on mobile devices. Newspapers print standard and online editions. Direct mail still works but so does e-mail. TV can be had on any size screen when and where you want it—and not necessarily in the family living room. The blog-vlog-pod social networking world is ours for the taking and the retail industry knows this. It also knows that the customer controls the choice of medium and degree of interaction.

E-mail Contact We love it; we hate it; we use it. Retailers find it a cost-effective way to deliver service with a personal touch. It is also a reliable source of customer data that is easy to track. The following guidelines aid in designing effective e-mails:

> For best response, recipients should be segmented according to specific demographic or other traits sought by the retailer.
> Opt-in e-mail programs work best.
> The key point of the message should be apparent *before* the reader opens the e-mail; the subject line should be relevant, personalized, and accurate.
> Branding should be visible up front and key points positioned near the top of the message.
> Short messages work best.
> If links are used, they should be workable.
> As with any effective advertising piece, white space brings attention to the e-mail; excessive variation in font styles should be avoided; if illustration is used it should not dominate the e-mail, but rather enhance the message.
> Avoid using words, phrases, or symbols that may activate sensitive spam filters: the word "free," "you have been chosen," dollar signs in the subject line, and sexual innuendo are examples.
> Privacy of the recipient should be respected; excessive contact defeats the purpose.

> The call to action should be clear and ethically conceived. In other words, ask customers nicely for their business and always thank them!

According to the Direct Marketing Association e-mail accounts for more than $16 billion in sales and influences another $100 billion.[12]

<u>Blogging</u> Today's customers expect top Web sites to provide feedback, reporting, comparative viewpoints, and engaging Web technology. Brick-and-mortar retailers seeking customer input use Internet innovation equally. The use of company-sponsored and independent blogs is growing. Progressive retailers must overcome fear of criticism if blogs are to be fully utilized. An open forum is not unbiased, and some comments from customers may be more useful than others. Open-mindedness dictates the usability of responses for retailers. Customers enjoy the opportunity to let off steam and like it even better if their positive comment or complaint is noticed by other bloggers. As with all methods of communication, it's not all good or bad.

<u>Digital Shopping Malls</u> Cable networks are adding digital marketplaces to their offerings. The Scripps networks, known for its shows on HGTV, including "Designed to Sell" and other home-oriented shows, created an online shopping mall called Marketplace. Merchants pay slotting fees rather than pay-to-click to place products in the shopping center. A **slotting fee** is money paid by the retailer to a host for the privilege of displaying a product. Slotting fees are used in other circumstances such as when a manufacturer pays a supermarket to place products on prime shelf or display areas. Scripps does not handle selling and fulfillment functions for the hundreds of merchants on the site and relies on third-party service providers to facilitate customer transactions.[13]

It is natural to tie products to viewers' interests, which is why sites like the HGTV Marketplace offer primarily house- and garden-related products. Targeting customers with high interest levels proves to be more effective for most retailers than mass marketing strategies.

Distribution and Fulfillment

How would a customer feel and behave if the living room sofa ordered from a catalog was not delivered in time for her housewarming party? If poor fulfillment

Table 5.1 Fulfillment: Who Ships How Many?

	ORDERS SHIPPED	PERCENTAGE OF ALL RESPONSES	PERCENTAGE OF STORE-BASED RETAILERS	PERCENTAGE OF CATALOGS	PERCENTAGE OF VIRTUAL MERCHANTS	PERCENTAGE OF CONSUMER BRAND MANUFACTURER
A	25,000 or less	46.1	47.9	23.1	53.1	38.2
B	25,001 to 50,000	12.3	8.3	7.7	16.0	5.9
C	50,001 to 75,000	6.0	2.1	5.1	8.0	2.9
D	75,001 to 100,000	5.6	4.2	7.7	6.2	2.9
E	100,001 to 250,000	9.2	4.2	12.8	8.6	14.7
F	250,001 to 500,000	5.3	4.2	7.7	4.9	5.9
G	500,001 to 750,000	3.5	8.3	10.3	1.2	0.0
H	750,001 to 1 million	2.1	2.1	5.1	0.0	8.8
I	More than 1 million	9.9	18.7	20.5	2.0	20.7

Source: Mark Brohan, "Time & Money," *Internet Retailer*, Survey results, February 2008, 38, www.internetretailer.com.

practices were the cause of her problem, she might be very irritated and do no further business with the furniture retailer.

Satisfying customers' needs through an efficient back-end distribution system is vital for multichannel retailers. Although not the glamorous side of retailing from the customer's perspective, physical distribution of goods is one of the most significant areas when it comes to cost savings and bottom line management from the retailer's perspective.

Retailers have made great strides in improving physical distribution through upgraded distribution facilities, technologies, and innovative services. The goals of fulfillment strategists are to keep inventories low while avoiding out-of-stock positions, provide speedy customer service, and ensure customer satisfaction. The majority of retailers fulfill orders within one or two business days. The percentage of annual shipping volume attributed to key channels is presented in Table 5.1.

Most multichannel retailers synchronize their information technology systems to serve all channels efficiently while providing 360-degree access to customer data. Fully utilizing Web-based technologies in a collaborative way is significantly more effective than fueling turf wars, as was the practice in the earlier days of multichannel retailing.

Efficient distribution centers use advanced technology to meet fulfillment goals and contribute to profits for retailers. [Source: Photograph provided by Lynda Poloian.]

Distribution Center Synergy The goal of modern distribution centers is to move merchandise as quickly as possible and to have as few hands as possible touch the goods. Everything is automated. Some facilities feature robotics, and others photo imaging or radio frequency identification receptors—although these technologies have not been embraced as rapidly as originally anticipated.

Through cross-docking, the use of automated advance shipping notices (ASN), and sortation systems, retailers improve their distribution practices. **Cross-docking** is the practice of receiving goods and then rapidly preparing them for shipment from the distribution center. **Advance shipping notices** are invoices for products scheduled for imminent shipment from a manufacturer to a retailer or distribution center. Most are now delivered electronically. The southern regional distribution center for the Saks Department Store Group in Alabama was considered state-of-the-art when it opened in 2001. Visitors to the center were surprised to see little merchandise in storage. The company's objective was not to warehouse goods but to move products in and out of the facility rapidly. The distribution center features an advanced RapidSort™ system by Catalyst that enables cross-docking in 15 minutes; it is illustrated in Figure 5.5.

Conflicting Outcomes Distribution centers occasionally find it difficult to meet the shipping demands of online retailers. In fact the characteristics that make e-retailing successful and desired—flexibility, speed, and low cost—are the same characteristics that challenge distribution centers. As they expedite goods to retailers and ultimately customers, these factors must be weighed. The end results differ by retailer.

Webvan, one of the first retailers to sell groceries and other products online, failed to provide quick delivery at low cost to the company and so ultimately ceased operations.[14] In comparison Tesco, the top supermarket in the United Kingdom and the fifth largest retailer in the world, pioneered online grocery shopping and from a fulfillment perspective is rated one of the most efficient sites.

The reasons for the success of Tesco and the demise of Webvan may lie in the vast experience built up over time for Tesco. The fledgling Webvan could not match the branding equity, buying efficiencies, and economies of scale practiced by Tesco.

Based on understanding of the dynamics in each of these impact areas, a retailer's strategic direction is fine-honed. Needs are determined and research is completed. Plans are written and strategies are executed and eventually evaluated. If retailers know what the problems are, they will be able to fix them.

Overcoming Channel-Specific Limitations

In Chapters 2 and 3 we identified many advantages and disadvantages of the popular channels for both retailers and customers. Finding new strategic direction offsets specific channel limitations. Multichannel retailers look internally and externally as they devise strategies to grow their businesses.

> Brick-and-Mortar Strategies

Traditional storefronts contend with several potential revenue-threatening issues. Possible solutions to limited store space, market saturation, evolving formats, and changing customer expectations are worth exploring.

Supplementing Limited Store Space

The obvious physical confines of brick-and-mortar stores, the inflexibility of existing retail space, and the inability of floor space to keep pace with inventory expansion contribute to the lack of adequate selling space. Increasing inventory online and extending merchandise access through in-store kiosks are two ways retailers are overcoming the problem of limited store space. Several examples in previous chapters have illustrated the benefits of retailers' broadening and deepening the merchandise assortments on their Web sites. Similarly, Williams-Sonoma and Pottery Barn add products to their catalogs and on the Web that are not available in their stores.

Coping with Market Saturation

Marketplaces brimming with retailers and customers sound like a retailer's dream and often they are, but oversaturation disperses market share—a common complaint for retailers in many cities and shopping centers. Consumers have more choices, but retailers have more competition, making it difficult to execute strategies and make money. By shifting business to other channels, retailers can deal with saturated markets. Some fine-tune their Web sites to counter intensely competitive markets. Others look to global expansion. When experiencing market saturation, retailers find new ways to redefine their businesses.

> Catalog Strategies

The high costs of producing catalogs, pricing inertia, and wasted circulation are problems for catalog retailers. Many catalog companies diminish the impact of rising postal and printing costs by shifting emphasis to their online stores. Catalogs include percentage-off coupons for use online. Sales incentives like this are part of the catalog's master plan to encourage customers to save online while shifting the operational expense of catalog production and mailing to their less costly e-retailing business.

Catalogs can overcome problems that arise when dealing with fixed prices once they are committed to print. Prices are raised or lowered as the market and retailer dictates. By encouraging customers to shop more often in their brick-and-mortar and online stores, retailers leverage their ability to adjust price points.

Some catalogs are adapting their marketing strategies and graphic techniques to reach fashion-savvy customers. Designer Christian Lacroix unveiled lines of apparel and home furnishings in the French catalog, La Redoute. Prices range from 15 euros for a key chain to 985 euros for a chair and ottoman set. The companion Web site is e-commerce ready with expanded merchandise selections, including decorative items. La Redoute along with Gucci group and a host of other catalogs is owned by Pineault Printemps Redoute (PPR), the luxury retail group.[15]

To gain customers' attention, catalogs are selecting cover models from popular TV shows. Redcat USA's Metrostyle catalog featured one of the winners of the show *America's Next Top Model* on its cover. To overcome the inability to touch fabrics on its catalog pages, L.L. Bean experimented with an actual piece of fleece on page 3 of its catalog, using a cut-out portion of the cover so customers could feel the texture.[16] Stimulation visually and in a tactile way continues the level of excitement to which today's customers have become accustomed.

> Online Strategies

Web retailers have a whole new vocabulary of tactics that transcend the limitations of online storefronts. Strategic directions revolve around pushing and pulling customers to their Web sites, countering the lack of tactile sensations and fit problems, encouraging customers to make purchases, and keeping them coming back for more. All are major tasks, yet many retailers are meeting their online objectives. Blockbuster's use of the Web in its transition from video rental store to multichannel retailer is chronicled in Box 5.3.

Optimizing Search

Many pure-play Web sites have turned to catalogs to overcome lack of visibility on the Web. Alloy, Red Envelope, and Wine.com all started catalogs after opening online stores. Some have been successful in their attempts to attract customers and build sales, others have not. The use of search has become one of the more compelling means of ensuring success online. **Search** is the process of using information technology to identify pertinent Internet resources on a topic of interest. This could be information for a research project on Terpsichore or the location of the nearest Forever 21 store. The obscure and the commonplace are encountered during the search process.

Mechanics of Search A **search engine** is a computer program used to seek, find, and index all the information that is available on the Web. Google—so famous it has become part of the vernacular and is not only a company name but also a verb—commands about 60 percent of all search activity on the Web.[17] For a listing of other search engines and their share of market, see Figure 5.6.

Search engine optimization (SEO) is the industry term for harnessing ways to increase the number of visitors to a site by increasing the site's ranking within the

What's the Buzz? Box 5.3

> **Blockbuster Sees the Web as the Key That Unlocks More Multichannel Sales**

The Internet and e-commerce will play a big role in helping Blockbuster Inc. make the transition from a DVD rental company into a multichannel retailer, CEO Jim Keyes told retail analysts. Customers will be able to log onto Blockbuster.com and purchase movie downloads. Blockbuster also plans to incorporate digital download technology into a pilot test of interactive store kiosks.

"We launched a new and improved Blockbuster.com that sets the stage for multichannel offerings," Keyes said. "We added an important new dimension with our acquisition of Movie Link in 2007, allowing Blockbuster to provide customers with digitally delivered content to their personal computers, portable device, and eventually their television at home."

Blockbuster, No. 51 in the *Internet Retailer Top 500 Guide*, is also using the Web and a marketing deal with Yahoo! to generate more sales online and in stores and will partner with Paramount Pictures and MTV Networks on exclusive digital content deals. "All of these initiatives underscore our determination to position Blockbuster as the only provider of media content across all platforms—in-store, by mail, and by digital download," according to Keyes.

In 2008, Blockbuster also expected to spend about $130 million on capital projects, including about $40 million on information technology and Web infrastructure. Keyes said, "As new entertainment technologies emerge, consumer options multiply. All of this means new opportunities for Blockbuster."

Source: Excerpted and condensed from Internet Retailer, *March 12, 2008, www.internetretailer.com. Copyright © 2008 Vertical Web Media.*

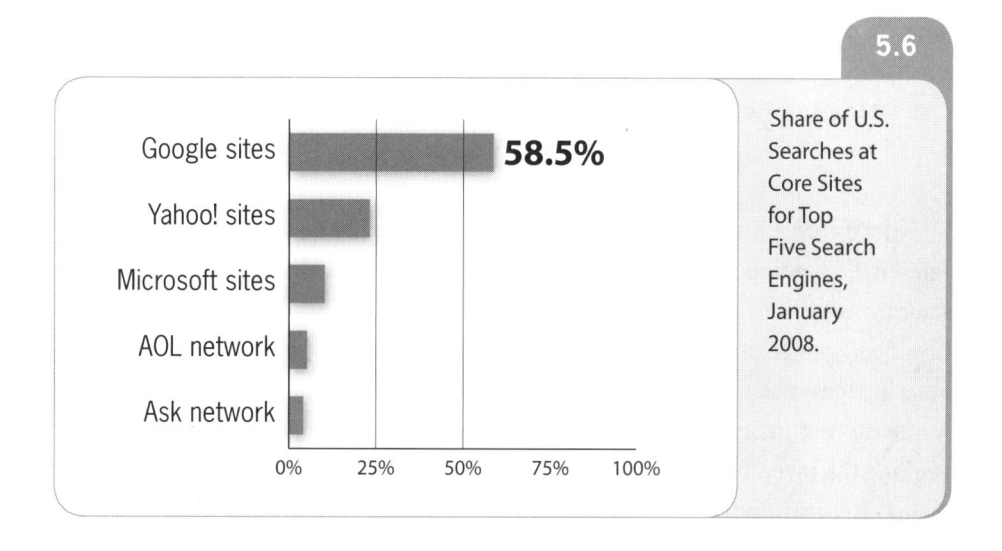

5.6

Search Engine	Share
Google sites	58.5%
Yahoo! sites	
Microsoft sites	
AOL network	
Ask network	

Share of U.S. Searches at Core Sites for Top Five Search Engines, January 2008.

search engine. SEO is one of the principal bases for strategy development for online stores today. Search engines have made search easier for customers and more efficient for retailers. The results usually are positive, bringing more potential customers to a Web site. However search does not compensate for implementation problems.

The difference between natural search and paid search is of consequence to commercial sites, although the distinctions blur in practice. **Natural search** describes the general search results that appear when you look up a general topic of interest or do research. **Paid search** involves the advertisements that appear in the sponsored links boxes at the very top of the page when you look up a topic. Paid search is also called **search engine marketing (SEM)**. There's one catch: even though natural search is supposedly free, specialists and companies trained to keep a company's name and Web content on the top of the search results list charge for their services, and companies pay for the service to ensure visibility.

The selection of keywords is crucial to the success of the search process as is the choice of search engines. **Keywords** are names, places, words, or phrases that are used by a search engine to seek out pertinent information on the Web. Pay-per-click (discussed later) is the industry standard for search engine compensation. Companies that use SEM pay more for keywords that are clicked frequently.

Search works well because it is self-selecting. That is, customers are interested in a product or company or they would not have searched in the first place. Search, used in this way, is a type of advertising that works in opposition to that of conventional mass media, such as newspapers or television. Through conventional media, a message is put forth; many people see it, some ignore it, but fewer act on the message when compared with the response to self-initiated search advertising. The following examples lend insight to search strategies.

<u>Visual Search Engines</u> Launched in 2006, Like.com has experimented with strategies that encourage fashionistas to shop for items like those worn by their favorite actors, models, or friends. By using a highly specialized visual search engine called Riya that can detect small parts on a photo of a must-have accessory and then find other images that have similar characteristics, the site allows users to use "visual search" to zero in on an attractive handbag, favorite designer, or color and then start working the inventory of the same or similar products until they find one that suits them.[18] Imagine finding the identical bracelet worn by Paris Hilton in her latest TV appearance or an Ed Hardy T-shirt.

Expanding Search The case of Red Envelope.com shows that even sound strategies do not always work. Red Envelope carries gifts for discerning customers through its catalogs and Web site (Figure 5.7). Its pure-play business went online in 2000 followed closely by the company's first print catalog. Soon Red Envelope developed strategic objectives that included increasing the number of customers and frequency of purchase. To grow its business, it determined that it needed to expand its keyword base from 250 to 3,000. In 2002, customer search yielded 12 percent of Red Envelope's online sales and by 2004, accounted for 35 percent of those sales.[19] Despite sound strategy and marketing tactics, however, the company had not achieved sustained profitability.[20] More about Red Envelope's strategic direction and performance appears in the Multichannel Retail Profile following Unit II.

Red Envelope's home page shows the strong brand identity of this multichannel gift retailer. [Source: Redenvelope.com.]

The combined advantages of high traffic, customers who are in the mood to shop, and the increased brand exposure magnify the power of search advertising. It is a major piece of online strategy building.

Enhancing Apparel Sales and Services

Online retailers have a bevy of tools and technologies to choose from as they plan to increase sales, market share, and brand visibility. Several new technologies work to overcome customers' problems with apparel fit and color selection at retail and other supply chain levels.

Overcoming Fit Problems According to a major research group, 84 percent of women have problems with fit.[21] Difficulties in finding apparel that fits well stem from the wide variety of body types and the standard fit measurements used by many manufacturers. However in some cases a women's size 8 from one manufacturer is the equivalent of a 10 in another. Individual interpretation of a physical ideal also plays a role when assessing good fit. The use of virtual surrogates and body-scanning software is helping to diminish fit quandaries and bridge the gap between physical dressing rooms and online apparel shopping.

Lands' End was one of the first online retailers to use My Virtual Model technology. The service encourages customers to create their own electronic image scaled to their dimensions. Users can add their own hair color and other pertinent details. The models are viewed wearing various styles and colors and informed choices are made because the worries of fit are diminished. Dressing room anxiety is kept to a minimum because customers can try on outfits in the comfort of their laptops or PCs. Customers also benefit from online personal shopper applications that recommend merchandise based on customers' preferences. The responsibility is on customers to give accurate measurements—not always a pleasant task to complete. Retailers see increased sales and profits, fewer returns, and more customer loyalty as positive aspects of My Virtual Model technology.[22]

By using software with 3-D full body scanning capabilities, designers and technicians create flat patterns that are used in apparel construction. Body scanning technology helps get a more reliable, better fit in mass-produced fashion, but also has custom design capabilities. It can be used in conjunction with virtual fit models by online stores offering this customer service.

Color Management One of the great challenges in apparel manufacturing is matching colors specified by designers and product developers with what overseas dye houses and contractors have available. Using spectrophotometers, designers and suppliers can collaborate on color decisions over the Internet. **Spectrophotometers** are color-measuring devices that aid the color-matching process. Dillard's, the department store chain, and Liz Claiborne, a manufacturer and retailer, use such facilitating software, which greatly speeds the product development process and reduces time to market.[23] The same concept has applications at retail as customers attempt to color-match items already in their wardrobes when shopping in-store or online.

Online Trunk Shows The practice of designers taking their new lines on the road to a few select department stores for private showing to their preferred customers has now expanded to online shows. Online trunk shows are more encompassing because virtual shows are available to anyone. Retailers that have used this technique have also used e-mail to alert customers to an upcoming online show. The experience is less personal but with soundtracks and video interviews with the designer, some of the traditional in-store atmosphere can be captured. Major retailers are using this virtual sales promotion tool. Neiman Marcus did a Dior show, Saksfifthavenue.com focused on Ralph Lauren and other designers, and Nordstrom featured Juicy Couture.[24]

Improving Customer Conversion Rates

The overriding tactic of capturing customers upon arrival at a shopping site is important to online strategy development. Retailers implement various techniques to boost conversion rates by increasing click-through, encouraging repeat purchases, personalizing contact, and offering shopping incentives. These techniques are implemented with the common goal of reducing shopping cart abandonment.

<u>Increasing Click-Through</u> When visitors to a Web site select one of the embedded hyperlinks in an advertisement, this increases traffic to the landing page at the other end of the link—often a retailer. Often the hyperlink is located within a banner ad or other area on the Web page. **Click-through** measures the number of times Web site visitors use a link. **Pay-per-click** denotes the remuneration earned by the search engine every time a link is used. This is the most popular method of online advertising and is predicated on appropriate keyword selection and use.

<u>Encouraging Repeat Purchases</u> Loyalty programs have the distinction of increasing sales for retailers and bringing rewards to customers. Win-win programs like Neiman Marcus's InCircle program keep their best customers fully engaged. As a special incentive, the company has a members-only Web site where customers can redeem points they have earned for making purchases. To keep customers interested, Neiman Marcus uses extra point bonuses and high-to-low redemption criteria that encourage both immediate gratification and long-term participation in the program.[25]

<u>Personalizing Contact</u> Increasing human interaction on retail Web sites is a precursor to delivering quality customer service. Among the ways in which online retailers customize content and contact with their online customers are the following:

> Use the customer's name in greetings: "Hi, Leanne, what are you shopping for today?"
> Follow up contact with personalized e-mail messages for which the customer has opted-in.
> Use the personal touch consistently across all channels. Encouraging customers to shop more channels does not mean that there is a shift in allegiance to the original channel used or that cannibalization will result.
> Personalize contact by flagging customers demographically or geographically—similar to the way in which a home page can be set up to feature local weather updates.

<u>Offering Meaningful Incentives</u> Most customers consider free shipping a significant incentive when they shop online. Some retailers used free shipping as part of their customer service strategies long before opening their online stores. L.L. Bean is well known for its liberal merchandise return policies and also for free shipping during holiday periods. However, even L.L. Bean has had to tighten its policies when shipping large heavy goods like beds or canoes. Others promote free shipments on select merchandise as an extra incentive to buy.

> **Alternative Multichannel Strategies**

When examining innovative ways to maximize shopping channels, some companies give new twists to age-old tactics. Adaptive strategies include online franchising and reseller formats.

<u>Online Franchising</u>

A popular ownership option for business expansion is franchising. A **franchise** is a contract by which an individual or group (the franchisee) agrees to operate a time-tested business format for which the owner (the franchisor) charges a fee and percentage of business over time. We understand the impact of the McDonald's business model but may wonder about the feasibility of taking the franchise system to the Web.

Virtual franchising is an online business ownership format that uses Web pages in place of physical stores and clicks rather than visits. The GroceryGame.com is an online service that tracks the best deals for people who like to clip supermarket coupons. The company has franchises in 50 states. There are advantages of online franchising over conventional franchising. When dealing online, it is easier to set up a Web site rather then spend countless hours and money searching for the perfect commercial land location. Owners of online franchise systems find it easier to monitor the quality of their franchisees.[26] Increasing numbers of support services to the retail industry, including marketing firms and advertising agencies, are setting up online.

Online Resellers

Individuals who choose to sell items on established auctions sites like eBay are numerous, but online entrepreneurs have taken the practice to new levels. More than a million people generate incomes—much of it unreported—by selling goods online through various suppliers.

The sources from which resellers purchase their products create problems for some conventional retailers. There appears to be a fine line between being a customer who purchases large quantities of merchandise and a reseller who confounds the marketplace. To protect inventories and brand equity, some retailers have put limits on purchases made by individuals.

Certain retailers including Coach, Gymboree, Abercrombie & Fitch, and Target are favorites of resellers. One report noted that a woman's silk top by designer brand Proenza Schouler that originally sold at Target for $34.99 was later spotted on eBay for $255.[27] Target is celebrated for its special apparel collections offered at reasonable prices by designer standards. A Proenza Schouler display at Target is featured in Figure 5.8.

Brand Resurrection

When all else fails, try it again. In the early days of Sears, Roebuck and Co. and J. C. Penney, another contender competed successfully for a share of the general merchandise market: Montgomery Ward. Many older consumers remember this department store and catalog retailer, which was founded in 1872. Succumbing to the pressures of competition, Montgomery Ward stores and catalogs ceased operation in 2001.

Direct Marketing Services acquired the brand in 2004 and is in the process of bringing the buzz back. The company runs several Web sites, including Home Visions.com, CharlesKeath.com, and WardKids.com, but its new venture will revive

5.8 Proenza Schouler is considered a prime fashion label for resellers who find the designer's merchandise at Target. *[Source: Photograph provided by Lynda Poloian.]*

Montgomery Ward's catalog business by featuring general merchandise for the home. It will also launch a Web site. The company intends to use a viral promotion called "Tell a Friend About Wards and Win" that involves using the Internet to spread the news. Customers can vie for gift cards by registering online and then entering friends' contact information along with personal messages to them at the Ward's site.[28] In this case, the phrase "I'll be back" seems made to order.

Evaluating Multichannel Best Practices

As retailers evaluate strategies and make choices between approaches, they must address the following considerations:

> Calculate costs of implementation and return on investment.
> Acknowledge that there is now less distance between communication channels and sales channels; indeed a merging of customer and retail interests has occurred.

> Provide more personalized contact and content, which are expected by customers no matter what strategy is employed: the greater the individualization, the higher the click-through rate.
> Evaluate new technologies—which are plentiful—based on customer needs and knowledge of the marketplace.
> Explore and invest in SEM.

Some retailers are closing stores and concentrating on the Web; others are closing down transactional Web sites and focusing on stores. Citing concern for the environment, the company Eluxury.com made a "green" decision and is discontinuing its print catalogs to focus on its online version.[29] Whether these actions represent discordance or recognition that this is the natural progression of multichannel retailing is open to discussion. Perhaps some of both extremes exist. More coverage of this topic appears in Chapter 6.

Summary

In Chapter 4, you learned the steps of the strategic planning process. Here you have seen that no two retailers follow exactly the same path and that rules are malleable.

Several key functional areas of retailing are scrutinized as business intelligence is gathered and decisions are made. Facilitating technologies are plentiful and are selected to smooth the process of running multichannel organizations. Others are designed to serve the needs of individual channels, including brick-and-mortar, catalog, and online stores.

Expansion of some kind is in the forefront of retail planning. Some retailers acquire or spin off new formats to attract new markets, as Gap has done with Banana Republic and Old Navy. Others are starting new operations in the global marketplace.

Branding is the most succinct way retailers can create a meaningful, recognizable, and highly desired retail concept. Discussions of brand go much further than a single product or line. The sum total of what the retailer presents to the market must be in accord with customer expectations or the brand positioning strategy will not succeed. Product development is a way retailers personalize their brands and sometimes reach markets not previously served. Private-label brands

Key Terms

Advance shipping notices (ASN)
Brand image
Branding
Brand positioning
Click-through
Cross-docking
Franchise
Keywords
Natural search
Paid search
Pay-per-click
Product development
Search
Search engine
Search engine marketing (SEM)
Search engine optimization (SEO)
Slotting fee
Spectrophotometers
Virtual franchising
Web 2.0 e-commerce

are usually more profitable to sell than national brands and help build image for retailers.

Fulfillment is a back-end procedure with a bottom-line focus. The movement of goods from producer to ultimate consumer must be smooth, fast, and accurate to meet the demands of the customer. Distribution centers are state-of-the-art technological palaces designed to increase the flow of goods through modern technologies.

Communication with customers, whether through major or new media, online or offline, or on a mass or personal basis, must be carefully evaluated, otherwise the best merchandise in the universe will not meet its mark. Newer electronic media are already fully integrated into most markets but are still in the early stages of high-technology evolution.

Many of the disadvantages of the various channels that were discussed in Chapter 2 are overturned as retail objections are met and strategies are developed. Tactics vary to a greater or lesser extent depending on goals and objectives of each company, budgets, and degree of integration of channels. Numerous online strategies emphasize the need to attract interest, acquire customers, coax them to buy, and satisfy their cravings forever after. And retailers must make the experience easy, fun, and fast for them.

Strategy development is as creative as the level of dynamism present in a retail organization. Growth, return of investment, profitability, and shareholder value are the prizes, but the game is risky.

> Questions for Discussion and Reflection

1. How are technological advancements used to help multichannel retailers formulate strategies? Give an example of a revenue-building tactic in your answer.
2. Compare and contrast impact area characteristics for brick-and-mortar stores and online stores. Where do you see commonalty in the approach to ensuring customer satisfaction?
3. Explain brand positioning in the context of image and focus. What brands do you believe are well positioned in the markets they serve? Justify your example.
4. Fulfillment is considered a back-end function, yet it is as important as other more visible retail aspects such as merchandise presentation when effective operations and sales growth are considered. Why is this so?
5. How are retailers using blogs and other online avenues (vlogs, pods) to drive business to their multiple channels and enhance the customer experience?
6. Brick-and-mortar stores such as Lowe's and Home Depot consider market saturation as they devise combative strategies. What does market saturation mean to retailers, and how are they coping with this situation?
7. Which channel has the most capacity for changing prices if necessary during the time that a product is in the market? Justify your decision.
8. Several Internet-based tools are helping apparel companies with problems of fit or other issues stemming from the inability to fully examine products. Choose one that you believe is effective and discuss the reasons why.
9. What should be done about online resellers? Are they a threat to established retailers? Why or why not?

Notes >

1. Paul Korzeniowski, "Around the E-Commerce Corner: More 3-D, Avatars," *E-Commerce Times*, March 11, 2008, www.ecommercetimes.com.

2. "Peapod Offers First Ever Virtual Nutritionist," Peapod press release, March 18, 2008, http://biz.yahoo.com/prnews/080318/aqtu018.html.

3. Molly Knight, "Abercrombie's New Idea: Down Underwear," *Shopping Centers Today*, International Council of Shopping Centers publication, March 2008, 28, 30.

4. "Opportunity and Obstacles Face U.S. E-retailers Expanding Abroad," *Internet Retailer*, January 29, 2008, www.internetretailer.com/printArticle.asp?id=25184.

5. Ibid.

6. Laurianne McLaughlin, "How PayPal Keeps E-commerce Humming in 15 Languages," March 14, 2008, www.cxo.com/article/print/197151.

7. Vanessa O'Connell, Rachel Dodes, and Mylene Mangalindan, "Going Online to Lure Foreign Shoppers," *Wall Street Journal*, February 8, 2009, B1, B2.

8. Sandra Jones, "Walgreens Shifts Self-Promotion," March 17, 2008, www.chicagotribune.com/business/chi-mon-walgreen-wag-clothes-mar17.0.7012689.story.

9. www.amazon.com and various trade publications.

10. Mylene Mangalindan and Jeffrey A. Trachtenberg, "Ipod of E-Book Readers? Amazon Taps Apple Strategy," *Wall Street Journal*, November 20, 2007, B1, B2.

11. Jonathan Birchall, "Amazon Pushes Social Shopping," *Financial Times*, March 13, 2008, www.ft.com/cms/s/bc5487dc-f129-11dc-a91a-0000779fd2ac,dwp_uuid=8083b5e3.

12. Bob Hale, "3 Reasons for Smart Retailers to Use Multichannel Tactics," *DM News*, May 21, 2007, 14.

13. Abbey Klaassen, "Scripps Taps a New Digital Revenue Source," *Advertising Age*, September 18, 2006, http://adage.com/Print?article_id-111915.

14. Mick Mountz, "Fulfillment: The Unexpected Key to Successful E-commerce," *E-Commerce Times*, February 11, 2008, www.ecommercetimes.com.

15. Miles Socha, "Lacroix Unveils New Lines for La Redoute," *Women's Wear Daily*, May 24, 2007, 15.

16. Chantal Todé, "Uncovering the Catalog Cover's New Role," *DM News*, April 9, 2007, 1, 30.

Notes

17. Mike Shields, "Google Nears 60%, Nielsen Says," *Adweek*, December 27, 2007, www.adweek.com/aw/national/article_display.jsp?vnu_content_id=1003689497.

18. Walter S. Mossberg and Katherine Boehret, "Where to Find a Famous Look: The Mossberg Solution," *Wall Street Journal*, November 8, 2006, D3.

19. Brian Morrissey, "Red Envelope Looking for Holiday Success," *iMarketing News/DM News*, October 25, 2004, 1, 18.

20. Jim Tierney, "Red Flag for Red Envelope?" *Multichannel Merchant*, February 15, 2008, www.multichannelmerchant.com/news/RedEnvelope-red-flag-0215.

21. NPD Group, quoted in Ann Zimmerman, "Cricket Lee Takes on the Fashion Industry," *Wall Street Journal*, March 17, 2008, R1, R4.

22. "My Virtual Model Inc. and Quickdog Inc. Join forces to Provide Unique Personalized Shopping Experience," My Virtual Model™ press release, Montreal, Canada, January 2001, updated www.myvirtualmodel.com.

23. Cate T. Corcoran, "Future Tech: More Connected," *Women's Wear Daily*, September 7, 2005.

24. Ann Zimmerman, "Why Trunk Shows are Going Virtual," *Wall Street Journal*, August 11-12, 2007, 1, P3.

25. Bill Brohaugh, "Neiman Marcus Sweet Rewards Target Loyalty," *DM News*, March 19, 2007, 15.

26. Colleen DeBaise, "Virtual Copies," *Wall Street Journal*, October 1, 2007, R8.

27. Elaine Hughes, "Online Resales Worry Retailers," *USA Today*, July 31, 2007, www.usatoday.com/tech/products/services/2007-07-31-resale-ebay_N.htm.

28. "A 19th Century Brand Launches a 21st Century Promotion," *Internet Retailer*, March 14, 2008, www.internetretailer.com/printArticle.asp?id=25705.

29. Lauren Bell, "Eluxury Ditches Catalog, Citing Green Intentions," *DM News*, March 13, 2008, www.dmnews.com/Eluxury-ditches-catalog-citing-green-intentions/PrintArticle.107.

Chapter 6

Cross-Channel Collaboration

Objectives

> To identify the components of cross-channel planning and design.
> To acknowledge the need for synchronization of business functions across channels.
> To investigate solutions to common cross-channel problems.
> To address marketing initiatives from a cross-channel perspective.
> To examine the role of organizational leadership in implementing cross-channel strategies.

> Integration, not isolation, is the goal of multichannel retailers. Customer-centric retailers provide a consistent shopping experience in any and all channels through which they reach their customers. By capturing valuable information on their clientele, they build useful and valuable company databases. About 50 percent of all multichannel retailers have fully centralized customer data; the other half are storing customer data separately by channel.[1] Using centralized systems, retailers tap into their databases and discern shopping patterns, product preferences, as well as demographic, psychographic, and geographic information. Through this process they are able to provide more services and better customer experiences through their online and offline stores, catalogs, electronic kiosks, mobile commerce systems, or any other wireless device they use to reach customers efficiently. We begin with the essential components of cross-channel collaboration.

Elements of Cross-Channel Collaboration

According to Forrester Research, 55 percent of customers are using cross-shopping.[2] Contemporary shoppers seek convenience above all and are utilizing options not available a decade ago. Successful retailers are those that not only make multiple selling channels available, but also encourage customers to shop all of them.

> Cross-Channel Organizational Design

Several elements need to converge for superior multichannel performance to occur. Retailers should:

> - Develop strategies inclusive of all channels and not treat selling formats individually.
> - Cultivate loyal customers by adopting a customer-centric attitude.
> - Select technologies that keep pace with all cross-channel activities.
> - Use cross-channel performance measurement tools.
> - Cultivate executives who buy into the multichannel philosophy.
> - Develop sales associates who embrace online sales as opportunities for customer service and sales.[3]

Organizational formats for multichannel retailers were introduced in Chapter 1. For maximum effectiveness, companies also look at internal operational structures that mandate teamwork and collaboration. Communications between the core business and other participating channels should be open, well organized, and accessible by all participants.

In a benchmark study for Shop.org done by the J.C. Williams Group, three structural models were described. They are semi-integrated, fully integrated, and independent formats. **Semi-integrated structures** share some but not all operational and informational tools across channels. Researchers found that most of the retailers surveyed used a semi-integrated team structure. For example, merchandising and pricing in a core brick-and-mortar business could be different from the company's online store or some divisions might be run separately or partially integrated.

Rarely are multichannel companies fully integrated and when they are, they are often large global retailers. **Fully integrated structures** are those in which all key business functions and information are shared across channels.

6.1

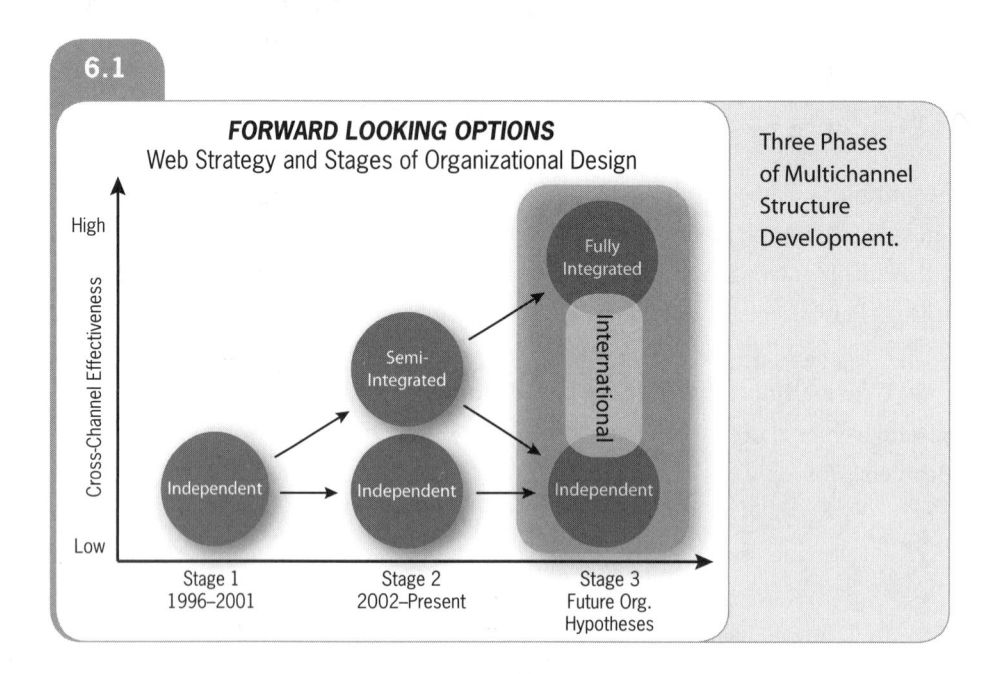

FORWARD LOOKING OPTIONS
Web Strategy and Stages of Organizational Design

Three Phases of Multichannel Structure Development.

Independent structures are those in which all operating channels are run separately and information is not shared across channels. Smaller retail companies tend to use this format.

There are benefits and disadvantages to each approach. For example, decision making and response times may be faster in independent organizations than in fully integrated larger companies. Consistency of branding across channels is probably more effective in fully integrated companies than in those with independent structures.

From a historical perspective, independent structures were common in the early days of online selling, 1996 to 2001. Semi-integration took place between 2002 and 2006, and fully integrated teams emerged after that time period. All versions are present in the marketplace, but it is expected that in the future more robust organizations will utilize global, fully integrated team structures.[4] A chart of the evolution of multichannel team structures including a view of the future is shown in Figure 6.1.

> Significance of Channel Synchronization

Achieving the pinnacle of multichannel service requires careful planning and management. Branding must be consistent across channels. Appropriate technology is selected to operate complex merchandising and distribution systems. Communications networks must embrace all dimensions: inter-company, inter-channel, and throughout the supply chain.

Cross-channel collaboration is important because it affects brand equity, sales, and profits. Online shopping today is what window shopping was to past generations. Both experiences serve the purpose of bringing customers to the point-of-sale, yet the path to fruition is changing. Cross-channel customers spend on average 30 percent more than individuals who shop only one channel, yet many retailers have not yet reached optimal operating conditions through which they can maximize revenue growth while satisfying their customers. Today's customers are changing the essence of retailing. Their expectations are high that they will receive consistent merchandise choices and customer service across channels.

In a study done by Aberdeen Group, retailers identified as best-in-class cited three pressures on multichannel retailers as they approach channel integration. Seventy-five percent of respondents cited "expectations of seamless process across channels" as a driving factor for retailers. Next in importance was "cross-channel research and shopping patterns" with 69 percent, and third was "hypersensitive-competitive multichannel selling environment" with 31 percent of retailers responding that these factors were foremost as they evaluated external challenges.[5] A look at several challenges faced by retailers sets the tone for the discussion of obstacles to cross-channel collaboration and their solutions that follows.

> Solutions to Cross-Channel Collaboration Problems

Several potentially detrimental factors emerge as retailers explore cross-channel options. For companies, finding ways to draw from existing strengths as they add to their customer contact and service repertoires is not easy, quick, or without vast human intervention and monetary expenditures. Technological infrastructures and costs of implementation play key roles, as do several operational and facilitation issues. The following discussion highlights six key areas of concern and suggested solutions to common cross-channel tribulations.

Synchronizing Information Technology

Facilitating technologies are readily available for retailers that manage their business across channels. There is more new development in this business sector than any other, judging by the plethora of companies that exhibit their wares and expertise at retail trade shows. In fact the abundance of resources may be one reason why retailers find it difficult to find the solutions that are appropriate to their needs.

Integrative software is available for retailers of all sizes and types, but some retailers find it difficult to elucidate their requirements.

Planning calendars are not always synchronous with the merchandising efforts of multichannel retailers. For example, catalog and online retailers selling wool sweaters might have difficulty determining inventories for their online stores if many of their customers reside in Australia where the winters are directly opposite those in the northern hemisphere. Global climate variation is factored into the selection of appropriate inventory planning software.

Some companies have successfully met the integration challenge. One candy company reaped sweet rewards when it implemented a new platform that centralizes core functions across three channels. Ghirardelli Chocolate Company is the focus of Box 6.1.

Sharing Customer Data

Retailers have been capturing information on their customers for decades. Most have a wealth of data—not all of it useful to the directive at hand. Collecting information is easy; using it appropriately is more difficult. Retailers that maintain databases and use them to their advantage have the upper hand. We are aware that privacy issues and laws limit the ability of retailers to gather certain types of sensitive data or capture information without the permission of the customer. Herein lies the key to data collection and use. The best databases comprise information that has been created through opt-in methods. When customers share personal information with retailers, they expect something good in return.

Implementing Customer Service Procedures

Procedures for cultivating new customers that worked well before the advent of the Internet may no longer generate interest and responsiveness when applied to new sales channels. Antiquated guidelines for order fulfillment or returns do not work in an era where the customer controls the process and competition is vigorous. Often support systems are realigned as retailers embrace new channels or try to deliver customer service through vehicles not previously used.

Training and development of human resources needs to keep pace with cross-collaborative efforts. Sales associates in particular need to be fluent not only in the new information technologies but also in the kind of customer interface that encourages cross-channel shopping and interactive service. The established practice of teaching

What's the Buzz? Box 6.1

> Channel Integration Tastes Sweet to Ghirardelli

There's a lot of talk about the need for retailers to integrate customer channels to improve the shopping experience and achieve operating efficiencies, but few companies have done it yet. Multichannel merchant Ghirardelli Chocolate Co. blazed the trail and integrated its catalog, 10-store retail, and e-commerce channels using a Web-based system from CORESense. Previously, the company outsourced its e-commerce solution and managed the catalog and telephone businesses through various systems that had been cobbled together in-house.

"We were looking to realize savings on fulfillment and marketing costs by combining the different channels into one business unit," said Jason Zdanowicz, Ghirardelli's business development manager for restaurant and retail. The company also wanted better control of its e-commerce business as it has matured.

Many multichannel merchants haven't integrated because they've invested a lot of time and money in their legacy systems and are reluctant to start over from scratch, or some top executives still aren't convinced of the merits of direct retailing. However, the benefits that Ghirardelli realized are significant.

The San Leandro, California–based candy company is using CORESense for its centralized product catalog, order fulfillment, inventory management, and customer relationship management. One highly visible change is the customer service experience. There is now one system where all of a customer's information is available, regardless of the channel in which an order has been placed. The integration "allowed us to concentrate our efforts where we could have one dedicated customer service staff for all channels," Mr. Zdanowicz said. When customers are speaking with a customer service representative, that person is knowledgeable about the merchandise and that customer's history.

The biggest cost savings so far have come from centralizing the fulfillment needs of its catalog, telephone, and Web businesses, which were previously in four locations. Bringing the Web business in-house let Ghirardelli make it more dynamic.

The company previously was locked into merchandise forecasts for the entire holiday season. Now it can put more emphasis on a specific item that was performing well or make changes to an item that wasn't selling well. For example, the company realized that the fastest-moving gift baskets offered online during the holidays were at the higher price points. The company put together a $149.95 gift basket—the highest-priced gift basket had been $99.95 at the start of the season—and got it on the Web two weeks before Christmas. "During those two weeks, it was one of our best-selling baskets, and we would have lost that opportunity in the past," Mr. Zdanowicz said. These adjustments in holiday marketing let Ghirardelli realize a full return on investment of its new integrated system before the end of the year.

Source: Excerpted and condensed from Chantal Todé, DM News, February 5, 2007, 1, 34.

new hires multiple selling techniques will be supplemented with cross-channel suggestion selling tactics. It is a challenging new role for the typical sales associate who is a part-time employee or using the position as a stepping-stone for promotion. Working schedules may differ radically if online sales assistance is required at any time of day or night.

To encourage full participation, new compensation policies are needed. Innovative retailers, with the help of cross-channel business technology systems, give sales associates commissions on items that were shopped at length in-store even though the transaction may have been completed online. Similarly a transaction initiated online but completed in the store may be credited to either division, equally or in part.

Best Buy does not pay commissions to sales associates, but the company credits its stores for sales that customers complete online and have shipped to their homes. Previously stores were only given credit if a customer used an in-store kiosk to make a purchase or if customers picked up a purchase in-store after ordering it on the Internet. By using this technique stores do not feel as though the online channel cannibalizes sales.[6] Decisions appropriate to retailer's goals, operational methods, and accounting practices are expected to vacillate as new policies are developed.

Technology-savvy customers have no problem finding information or customer service assistance online. However not all customers fall into this category. Although many individuals are comfortable initiating product searches or accessing inventory information online, others are not confident in a self-help environment. Still others are perfectly able to extract information online but prefer not to do it themselves and avail themselves of the luxury option of customer assistance.

Countering Limited Financial Resources

Inadequate capital can paralyze the efforts of retailers to invest in technological improvements in the best of times, and more so in a poor economy. Despite the likelihood that investment in systems will intensify the retailer's ability to generate revenue growth, allocation of funds for new technology is not always possible or paramount.

Despite elusive budgets and internal battles for resources, retailers get creative when it comes to deriving cost-saving measures or developing low-cost answers to problems. For example, catalog retailers can increase sales economically by using e-mail—a low-cost vehicle—to alert customers to anticipated catalog delivery.

Although sales must ultimately drive planning, they are not the only focus when developing viable cross-channel agendas. Appropriate metrics are used in tandem with tactics to identify cost-saving and revenue-driving actions. Integration with a continued customer-centric focus should be the primary goal. Revenue will follow.

Developing Internal Expertise

Earlier discussions mentioned the trend toward developing online stores in-house rather than farming them out to third parties, as was done in the early stages of multichannel retailing. Several factors are reversing the need to outsource:

> Online stores now have a history! During the last 15 years an abundance of expertise has emerged.
> New recruits are available—particularly from the ranks of young, fast-track workers.
> Despite the rapid pace of change in new technologies, new areas of expertise have surfaced and individuals who are amply qualified in fields as arcane as Web analytics or m-commerce customer behavior are in demand.

However, for companies that are attempting to build a sound in-house team, the supply of human resource talent is barely keeping pace with demand. When asked, in a survey conducted by *Internet Retailer,* to describe the market for attracting employees with e-commerce experience, 55 percent of Web retailers said the market was "difficult." In the same survey the top two priorities for new hires were Web developers and search engine specialists.[7]

Proactive retail companies maintain organizational hierarchies in which the directors of e-retailing are part of the senior executive team. Another study determined that 42 percent of retailers have a top person in charge of e-commerce who "ensures that online operations are synchronized with brick-and-mortar and call center operations."[8] Acknowledging the importance to strategic planning and organizational leadership, most heads report directly to the chief executive officer (CEO) or president of the company. A complete e-commerce executive reporting breakdown is listed in Table 6.1.

Embracing Change

Changing established mindsets is one of the most challenging aspects of implementing a new strategy. Some corporate cultures are resistant to change; others are

Table 6.1 E-commerce Executive Reporting Breakdown

WHO DOES YOUR TOP E-COMMERCE EXECUTIVE REPORT TO?	PERCENTAGE OF RESPONSES
Chief executive officer (CEO)	30.0
President	28.3
Chief information officer (CIO)	3.0
Chief financial officer (CFO)	3.4
Chief operations officer (COO)	3.4
Chief marketing officer (CMO) or executive vice president (EVP)/senior vice president (SVP) of marketing	20.7
EVP/SVP business development	8.0
Our chief e-commerce officer is the company's top executive	3.2

Source: "Help Wanted: Internet Retailer Survey, Salaries and Personnel Management," *Internet Retailer*, April 2008, 53–55.

more open to innovation. Thinking beyond the status quo and finding new solutions outside the boundaries of common thought is essential.

Technology solutions help retailers integrate data and merchandising and delivery functions, but these advances are only part of the solution. Ideally, retailers leverage the best resources from one channel and use these to facilitate operations in others. The goal ultimately is to increase total sales and profitability. To use an old adage, the whole may be worth more than the sum if its parts.

DeliVision kiosks installed in Stop & Shop Supermarkets reinforce this point. Rather than endure a long wait in line at the deli counter, customers who prefer can use convenient electronic kiosks to place their orders. Smart kiosks are programmed to let shoppers know what they purchased from the deli on prior visits. Printed tickets inform them when their orders are expected to be ready for pick up and the store's public address system also alerts them to their order's availability. Stop & Shop expects that customers will use the wait-time to complete other grocery shopping and perhaps pick up a few extra items, thus increasing overall sales for the retailer and saving precious moments for the customer.[9]

Retailers that succeed in multichannel retailing plan proactively and look for changes in the retail environment that present opportunities for expansion, redesign, or outreach. Search engines for exclusive use on mobile networks, a wireless mouse that perfectly fits a traveler's hand, and neuromarketing are examples of new technologies, products, and methods of customer behavior assessment that are indicative of creative adaptation to change.

Neuromarketing uses brain wave function to measure customer response to products or concepts online and offline. Using real-time brain imaging, researchers determine responses to advertisements well in advance of their public release and in time to tailor pitches to select customer segments—or individuals. Neuromarketing sounds like the science of tomorrow, but it is in use today. Preparing to launch an ecological campaign, Sam's Club used the technique to help the warehouse club assess customer reaction to its proposed "green" logo.[10]

Physical businesses and online stores are no longer viewed as independent of each other. Cross-channel integration is one of the top priorities in retailers' growth plans. The quality of the total multichannel experience is dependent on the careful selection of appropriate marketing strategies. Building customer loyalty that is sustainable over time and across all channels is the end result.

Integrated Marketing Strategies

The classic components of marketing—product, price, place, and promotion—are recognized and embellished as retailers find effective ways to conduct multichannel business. Branding, merchandise selling and pricing, fulfillment optimization, effective sales promotions, and winning customer service programs are considered when developing integrated marketing strategies.

> Building Brand Equity Across Channels

The significance of the store as brand, and branding in the sense of building a recognizable and sustainable image over time, has been emphasized in previous chapters. Here we discuss ways that multichannel retailers are extending their brands across channels.

It is easy to identify retailers that recognize the benefits of brand management. Victoria's Secret implements a common theme right down to color, type font, style, model selection, and merchandising across stores, Web, and catalog channels. Customers need go no further than to their cell phones to access a known commodity

Brand building across channels comes naturally to Victoria's Secret as evidenced by image consistency in stores, catalogs, and Web site. *[Source: Jeff Greenberg/Alamy (below); Victoriassecret.com (left).]*

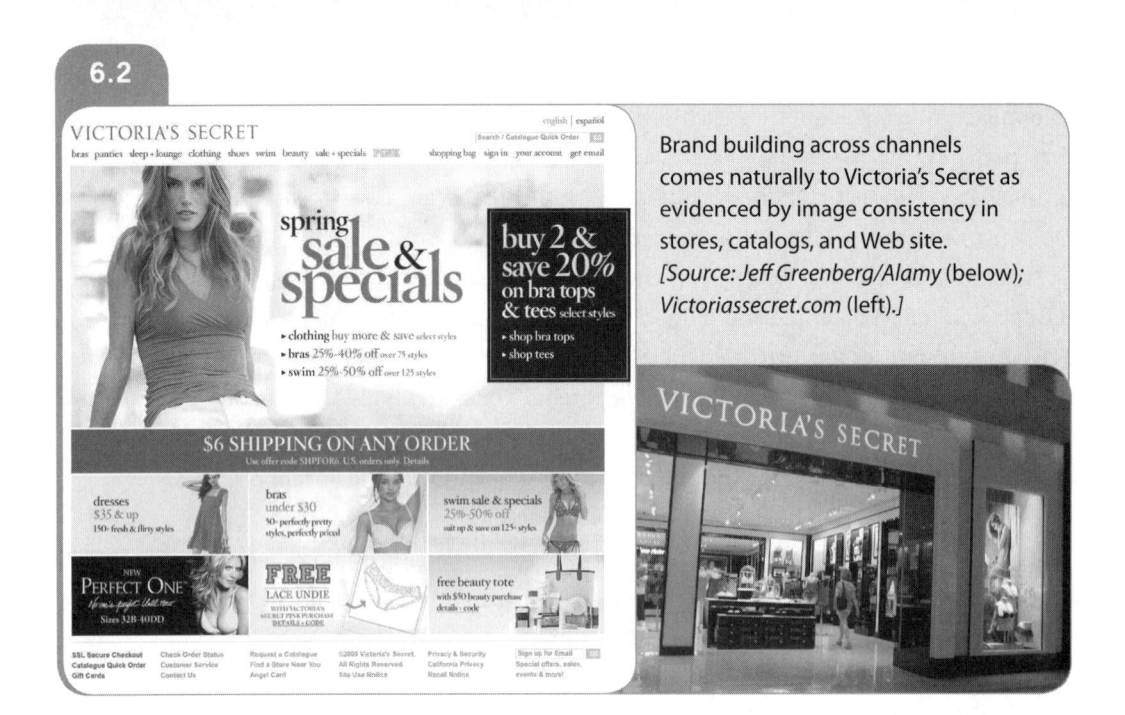

and an unswerving image. It was by chance that Victoria's Secret learned about the power of e-commerce. In 1999 when it launched its Web site, traffic on the Internet was paralyzed as hordes of people attempted to watch one of its now famous online fashion shows. Now it is common practice to support an event like a fashion show with common theme merchandise, catalog covers, in-store displays and graphics, online video, and e-mail advertisements. Viewers know they are at Victoria's Secret and not at Fredericks of Hollywood. That is the power of brand image and diversification. Look for many brand presentation consistencies across Victoria's Secret store and home page in Figure 6.2.

Using other types of brand strategy, retailers link with other retailers to meld the best of both companies into winning situations. Some affiliations have been successful whereas others have not. For example, Amazon turned to many retailers to enhance its limited merchandise mix. In 2000 Amazon teamed up with Toys "R" Us. The category killer toy retailer provided needed specialty products, and received sales that were welcome in that era. The partnership did not meet expectations and Toys "R" Us had left the Amazon online superstore by 2005.

Retailers around the globe acknowledge the importance of branding. The House of Fraser, a major department store group in the United Kingdom, launched its first transactional online store in late 2007. Peter Callaway, director of e-commerce, said this regarding the importance of brand: "The strength of House of Fraser is its brand. . . . The whole ethos behind the website is to push the brand messaging and customer communication across all channels."[11]

> Merchandise Selling and Pricing Tactics

The merchandising function is said by many to be the heart of the retailing organization. Having the right goods at the right place, at the right price, at the right time is a useful conception of marketing objectives. Merchandising involves the selection and buying of goods, product development of new items, assortment planning, and allocation to chain stores and divisions. Selling the merchandise cannot occur unless sufficient buying power and expertise are present and systems compatible with the complex needs of multichannel merchants are in place. Pricing tactics vary greatly by type of business and channels used.

Cross-Channel Selling

To refine its cross-channel sales initiative, California-chic apparel retailer The Territory Ahead implemented a Java-based retail management system. It helps the company provide order management, fulfillment, and customer service through store, catalog, and online channels. The software program developed by Commercial/Ware Inc. has the capacity to manage warehousing, inventory control, merchandising, marketing, and finance.[12] Full-spectrum systems like this are the backbone of multichannel retailers.

Selling Luxury Goods

The market for luxury goods usually remains strong despite downturns in the economy. Luxury Web sites lend a fresh perspective to the sale of fine merchandise. Initially, it was considered unlikely that apparel would do well on the Web, much less luxury goods, but the predictions have been proven false. Mavericks such as Natalie Massenet are market movers and are responsible in part for the growth of the category.

Massenet, founder of the Web site Net-a-porter, believes that the increasing popularity of online apparel shopping and the rising comfort level of customers contribute to the success of her company. The average order is about $1,000 and the company's gross profit margin is 48.4 percent. Based in the United Kingdom, the company's goal is to ship globally to as many luxury shoppers as possible and to expand distribution to the Middle East and Australia. When the Internet retailer

Girlshop ceased operations in 2007, Net-a-porter bought 100,000 names from the company that aided its expansion in the United States.[13]

Net-a-porter features merchandise from famous designers such as Christian Louboutin, Miu Miu, Burberry Prosum, and Vera Wang. Luxury sites depend on a steady stream of customers with a penchant for fine fashion and deep pocketbooks to match. Massenet's office is in the Whiteley Shopping Center building, a venerable brick-and-mortar establishment in London. Founder William Whiteley operated a department store there in the mid-1800s. One would expect that in spirit he approves of Massenet's tenancy and the ironic touch it lends retail history.

Retailers are unified in their quest to increase performance of their online stores, whether or not they sell luxury goods. A study showed that the top priority for increasing conversion rates online was through improved merchandising.[14]

Pricing Techniques

Customers have become accustomed to the continuous dependence on sales to move merchandise in traditional retail department and specialty stores. This is not the case with many online stores that tend to do less promotional pricing. Although discount sites abound, the pricing practices appear to be more consistent and less dependent on seasonal and clearance sales. Net-a-porter, mentioned in the previous example, depends on consistent year-round sales and is less dependent on holiday and seasonal business than most brick-and-mortar businesses. Markdowns are taken less frequently as well, contributing to higher gross margins.

Comparison shopping online has made people more confident about their ability to discern top value at the lowest prices. This characteristic has fueled changes in price negotiations in brick-and-mortar stores and other venues. Once the domain of automobile dealerships, flea markets, and occasionally jewelry stores, price negotiations are now carried out by customers who use their new skills and confidence across channels. The sluggish economy in 2008 also helped propel the practice of haggling. Having gained momentum, many customers are taking the initiative to negotiate prices in retail stores that were previously off limits. By using online prices as leverage, people are asking for and receiving discounts in specialty apparel, electronics, and furniture stores.

Pricing is a critical element for all retailers—a science but also an art. Awareness of several price setting variables helps retailers set and maintain prices across all channels in which they operate. Here are some considerations on which to reflect:

> Customers are part of the pricing equation. Their behavior tells a retailer whether or not an item is priced right. They vote with their wallets at the point-of-sale.
> Branded goods usually are priced higher than generic goods or staple merchandise.
> Private-label goods are often priced lower than nationally branded or designer goods but are more profitable to retailers.
> Doing research on competitors' pricing tactics is necessary, but meeting or bettering competitors' prices should not be done in panic or haste. First consider company goals, pricing objectives, and customer expectations of the quality–price relationship.
> High quality of materials or construction should but does not always command the highest prices. Quality and price are sometimes inversely proportional.
> Resist the temptation to raise prices even when the economy is rosy and business is good.
> Reduce prices some when history tells you that by doing so you will improve the flow of goods and therefore benefit in the long run by making way for fresh merchandise.

Balancing the merchandise mix and managing pricing go hand-in-hand. When retailers add channels most try to maintain pricing consistency across all channels. As we know the majority of customers are cross-channel shoppers. Making price changes is a lot easier on the Web than it is in stores and, especially, in catalogs. The ability to act fast gives retailers the power to profit. However, retailers should not disenfranchise their loyal customers by frequent or confusing manipulation of prices. Lifetime value should not be disregarded for the sake of a quick pricing fix.

> **Effective Distribution Practices**

Fulfillment solutions lead the way when it comes to providing renowned customer service. Often answers to complex distribution problems emanate from the acquisition of new technologies.

Customer Expectations

Customers expect some or all of the following fulfillment options:

> - Purchase goods online and pick up at a store; this practice is often called site-to-store.
> - Select goods through a catalog and purchase online or in a store.
> - Anticipate fully cross-channel merchandise return policies.
> - Receive and use promotions and incentives through any channel.
> - Have basic customer profile, buying history, and other information available through any channel.
> - Supply fully cross-functional customer relationship management data to retailers if individuals select to opt-in.
> - Have access to all merchandise from any location or channel at any time.

Fulfillment Strategies

To address customer expectations, retailers use several strategies involving technologies that make distribution more efficient and customer-friendly. Examples of these strategies follow. Recreational Equipment Inc. (better known as REI), Anthropologie, and Walmart are distinctly different types of retailers but all are leaders in cross-channel fulfillment.

In 2003 the outdoor product and apparel supplier REI initiated an automated system that lets customers order online and have the merchandise shipped free from company distribution centers to an REI store. As an extension of that service, customers can use in-store kiosks to order merchandise that is shipped from warehouses directly to their homes or to an REI store. Customers determine estimated delivery time from distribution center to store by using a convenient link on the Web site. Throughout the process customers receive e-mail updates. Approximately 40 percent of REI's online orders are picked up in-store.[15] An REI retail store is illustrated in Figure 6.3.

The apparel company Anthropologie had mixed results when it refined its integration systems. Initially the company found that maintaining separate systems for its stores and direct business helped the company grow rapidly. For Anthropologie, the direct business includes catalogs and online stores. Separate information technology systems use stock-keeping unit (SKU) numbers with varying amounts of digits, making channel monitoring difficult for employees. Thus, a sales associate might not know what a customer—who had spotted a dress online—is asking for because the SKUs and product descriptions differ on each system. Anthropologie would like a tighter interface between divisions and is seeking a common technology platform. The company expects the move to total integration to take about five years.[16]

It is no surprise that the world's largest retailer, Walmart, was the first to offer online purchase and store pick-up options nationally. The company tested the concept for two years before implementing the service regionally and eventually in all of its stores. Walmart states that 75 percent of its customers shop online. To publicize the service, Walmart sent e-mails to its entire customer database and placed icons next to products on its Web pages that featured merchandise for which the service could be used. The company also placed advertisements on its in-store TV network, and in sales circulars and direct mail pieces. Customers are able to purchase products online that are not routinely available in Walmart stores.[17]

Using REI's automated ordering system, customers can order online and have merchandise shipped free from company distribution centers to an REI store, or use in-store kiosks to order merchandise that is shipped from warehouses directly to their homes or to an REI store. [Source: Courtesy of Fairchild Publications, Inc.]

Obviously the technologies that enable automated, cross-channel options are highly developed. Full-blown systems like this do not appear overnight but are the result of trial and error over time. The Direct Marketing Association reported that only 33 percent of retail respondents provide cross-channel order fulfillment.[18] This indicates that implementation of services and new technologies in this vital sector is still in the planning or testing stages for many retailers.

> Promotion in Perspective

Retail sales promotion specialists have typically deployed a multitude of advertising media, sales promotion tactics, and direct marketing methods to reach customers. The Internet juxtaposes new media laced with layers of visual excitement with traditional customer contact methods. Internet advertising has affected customers' perceptions of promotion and the way retailers buy advertising. Customers' media habits have changed as well. Social networking sites like MySpace and Facebook affect the way users relate to advertising and the role influencers play as they make purchasing decisions. It is indeed a brave new world for promotional activities.

For the first time in 2007, online advertising captured a greater market share than radio advertising. Internet display ad revenue was approximately $11.3 billion compared with $10.7 billion for radio.[19] Similar changes have occurred in the use of other traditional advertising media. Although newspaper readership has slowly declined throughout the last decade, this advertising medium remains a choice of many store retailers, especially supermarkets, discounters, and department stores. Television advertising is also losing share.

Sales promotion tools that are popular across channels are coupons and sweepstakes. Brick-and-mortar stores find sales associate referral promotions effective. Often called friends-and-family sales, these promotions, involving a 20 percent off coupon or other incentive, are welcome especially when recommended by someone you know.

Economic factors precipitate media shifts. For example, Williams-Sonoma adapted its advertising strategies during an economic decline. The gourmet gadget retailer was spending 90 percent of its advertising budget on catalogs but shifted its print emphasis to Internet search advertising to counter the plummeting market conditions in 2008. By analyzing the ways in which catalogs influence sales in its stores and online channel, the company discovered that customers in Texas were more likely to be driven to stores by the catalog than customers in other states. Although it may cut back catalog distribution in other geographic areas, Williams-Sonoma planned to intensify distribution with smaller catalogs but more frequent mailings in Texas.[20]

6.4

Year	Spending
2001	$7.1
2002	$6.0
2003	$7.3
2004	$9.6
2005	$12.5
2006	$16.9
2007	$21.4
2008	$27.5
2009	$32.5
2010	$37.5
2011	$42.0

Note: eMarketer benchmarks its U.S. online advertising spending projects against the Interactive Advertising Bureau/PricewaterhouseCoopers data, for which the last full year measured was 2006; excludes mobile ad spending.

U.S. Online Advertising Spending, 2001–2011.

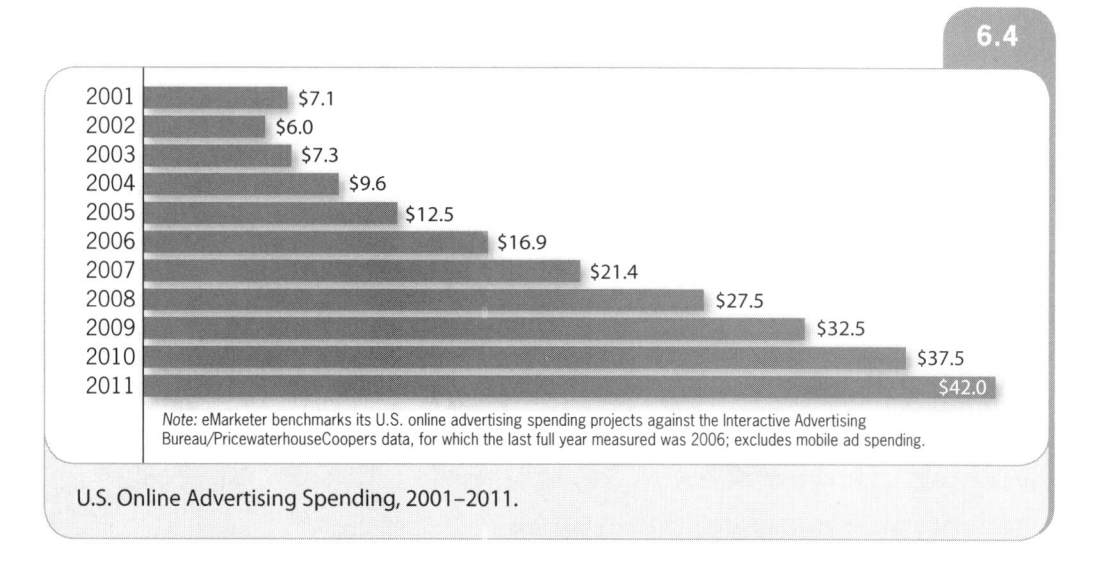

Online advertising is expected to command a greater share of advertising budgets in the future. Expenditures for online advertising from 2001 forward, including projections to 2011, are graphed in Figure 6.4.

Consistent Cross-Channel Exposure

When a retailer advertises the latest, greatest electronic gadget online, that item had better be available on the brick-and-mortar selling floor concurrently. Coordinating merchandising and promotion is as important as synchronizing the entire cross-channel experience. Although this may appear to be a given, all too frequently the execution misses the mark of seamless availability. As retailers add channels, the need to coordinate extensive inventory information grows.

The launch of Finish Line's spin-off, Paiva, exemplifies a well-timed retail introduction, making full use of cross-channel synergies. The women's athletic fashion business opened in April 2006 in this manner:

> The first store opened in Austin, Texas, on April 14.
> The online store opened on April 17.
> A 50-page catalog was received in area homes by April 21.
> The catalog and online store were designed to echo the merchandising and branding in the brick-and-mortar store.

Chapter 6 > **Cross-Channel Collaboration**

Paiva, the women's athletic fashion retailer, uses cross-channel marketing strategies when it opens new stores.
[Source: Courtesy of Fairchild Publications, Inc.]

> The catalog served as a brand introduction and was also promoted in-store.[21]

Integration and timing of marketing initiatives is crucial to the success of multi-channel retail operations. Store openings are often the first view shoppers have of a new concept. The triple-whammy produced by Paiva may well be indicative of what has become an established practice as the multichannel concept grows. The Paiva store and home page are shown in Figures 6.5a and 6.5b.

Modern Media Trends

Alternative marketing methods place pressure on traditional media and are an experimental position for many retailers. Whether it is a small banner ad for a department store, a large pop-up for a financial service, or a prominently placed search-sponsored listing for a specialty store, retailers are clambering for visibility and customer access on the Web. Media that are accustomed to tailoring communications directly to customers and special interest groups dominate contemporary advertising. The personal touch is apparent. Social networking sites provide innovative ways for retailers and designers to reach new markets and

6.6

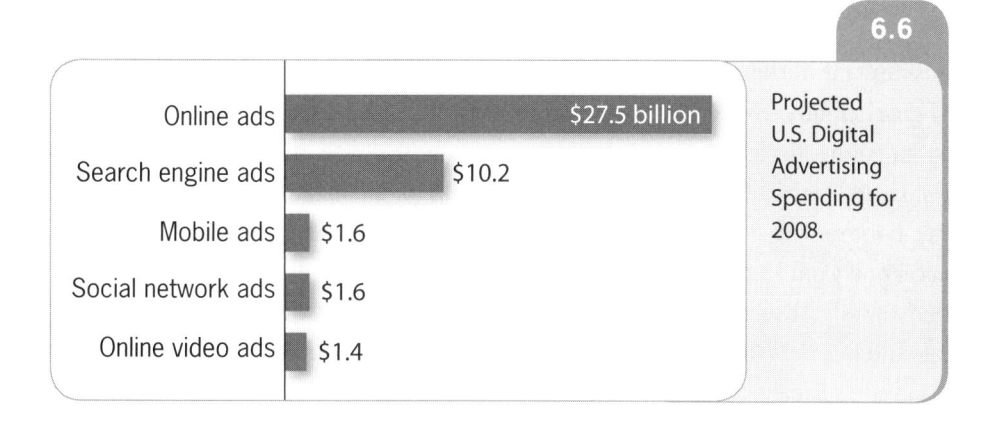

Online ads	$27.5 billion
Search engine ads	$10.2
Mobile ads	$1.6
Social network ads	$1.6
Online video ads	$1.4

Projected U.S. Digital Advertising Spending for 2008.

expand their relationships with current customers. E-mail use is rapidly growing and is an inexpensive way to reach customers worldwide. As retailers recognize the need for a strong Web presence, many are reconsidering how search and inter-channel advertising dollars will be spent. Projected digital advertising spending for 2008 is shown in Figure 6.6.

Personalization Retailers use personalization in its many guises to reach customers online. **Personalization** is any relationship-building tool used by online retailers that tailors a message, using a customer's name or demographic characteristics, to make an advertising message unique. Studies have shown that the more elements of personalization used on the Web, the greater the click-through rate.

Nike connects with customers by offering a small device imbedded in running shoes that tracks the progress of the runner who wears them. Called Nike+, the sensor is capable of recording the person's progress on an Apple iPod carried by the runner. The report is posted on a special Nike Web site where other runners converge and swap running stats and stories. By shifting to personal forms of advertising, Nike has cut back its TV and other media placement by 55 percent compared with a decade ago.[22]

Social Network Advertising Social networking sites like MySpace and Facebook have expanded their reach from students to a broader audience. Initially young people were the target audience for meeting and greeting their friends and meeting new ones, but eventually the market expanded to adults who might set up a page for

Chapter 6 > **Cross-Channel Collaboration** 225

business networking, résumé enhancement, or sharing photos with their children or grandchildren. Facebook began experimenting with friend-to-friend advertising by attaching advertisements to user messages on the site in 2007. Then it began testing its Beacon feature, which allowed Facebook to track users' activities off the site. For example if a Facebook user made an apparel purchase at a specific Web site, Facebook would let the user's friends know—often without the user's permission. In this way advertisers could get a foothold on new markets and contact them by interests and in a personal way. Soon the obvious privacy invasion issues were raised and resolved as Facebook continued the service on an opt-in basis.

MySpace created a fashion social networking component on its site to lure the shop-until-you-drop market consisting of mostly young fashionistas. Retailers and designers responded by running contests, posting videos, and buying banner ads on MySpace and other sites. MySpace has about 70,000 users of its fashion page. According to Forrester Research, marketers spent $600 million on social networking and related sites in 2007 and expected that figure to increase to $6.9 billion by 2012.[23]

Not all users are enamored over the inundation of advertisements on social networking sites. Some users would rather pay a monthly fee for services on a Web site that is promotion free. Although advertising on social networking sites is up, the time spent by users is down and the growth rate of users may be slowing. Advertising effectiveness trackers say that the click-through-rate for individuals who see ads on social networking sites is 4 in 10,000 compared to 20 in 10,000 generally across the Web.[24]

The believability of advertising on a social networking or other site is another issue that has surfaced. There is a fine line between editorial content and advertising on many sites and searches. For example, a shopping site that uses a graphic and description of a branded fashion item in its online "hot pick" section may be a paid advertisement for the designer or manufacturer. Or it could be an independent customer panel or credible source such as an industry expert who has determined the "hot pick." This tactic also is used in magazines but appears more difficult to discern on the Web. Information on the ranking of credible sources of company information is presented in Table. 6.2.

<u>E-mail Customer Contact and Advertising</u> The many uses of e-mail make it a useful, powerful, personal, and cost-effective tool for retailers. The most common kind of e-mail used by retailers is a transactional message. **Transactional messages**

Credible Sources of Company Information Table 6.2

SOURCE OF INFORMATION	PERCENTAGE OF RESPONSES
Person like themselves	60
Financial industry analyst	56
Academic	54
Doctor/healthcare specialist	53
Nonprofit/NGO representative	50
Regular employee of company	43
CEO of company	23
Blogger	12

Source: "Credible Sources of Information about a Company According to U.S. Opinion-Elite Consumers, October-November 2007," *2008 Edelman Trust Barometer*, January 22, 2008, as reported in "The Growing Influence of Social Shoppers," *eMarketer*, April 7, 2008, www.emarketer.com.

are e-mails that confirm or check the status of an online order or convey pertinent delivery information. There are other reasons for e-mail contact:

> To deliver product and service information, including rebates and warrantees.
> To thank customers for their purchases.
> To alert customers to product recalls, extended service programs, or product safety information.
> To alert customers to new products related to previous purchases that are now offered by the company.
> To introduce loyalty programs or update information.
> To send a newsletter.

The use of e-mail is cost-effective. According to Shop.org, e-mail delivers sales at about $7.00 per order compared with $71.89 for banner ads, and $26.75 for paid search.[25]

Banner Advertising Grows Up Banner advertisements are a staple in Internet marketing but now seem outmoded by many Web aficionados' standards. A **banner**

Chapter 6 > **Cross-Channel Collaboration** 227

advertisement is a paid electronic message that appears on a landing page, home page, or elsewhere promoting a product, service, or other Web site. Shopping.com is one of the largest shopping comparison sites on the Web and has departed from the conventional rectangular banner ad format. The site uses a technology that scans a Web page and selects a product that has been determined to be of interest to a reader. It then displays small shopping comparison pages that are dressed up as miniature banner ads. The ads come complete with prices, product reviews, and links to merchants. Merchants pay about $1.00 per click for the service. Called eMiniMall, the new tool may revolutionize the function of banner advertising.[26]

Some early banner ad devotees have found that other methods of promotion are more effective. Sephora, the beauty products retailer, uses viral marketing to attract new customers. Using a customer panel format called *In Girl*, members chosen through a peer nomination process try out new products and review them for the company. Catching the viral bug, successful panel members spread the Sephora word through their own blogs and pages on social networking sites. Sephora found that the panels produced a significantly higher response rate than banner ads or e-mail campaigns.[27] All forms of customer reporting, referrals, and interaction are more believable to shoppers and therefore valuable promotional tools for cross-channel retailers.

Widget advertising may also supplant traditional banner advertising. **Widgets** are embedded code in an HTML page that users can insert into Web sites, blogs, or social networking pages to provide information, interactive activities, and items for sale. They are also called gadgets, plug-ins, snippets, minis, and other techno terms. Widgets can deliver online quizzes, photos and videos, preference rankings, and services. PayPal, for example, offers a widget that inserts into a Web page to expedite payment for goods bought online.

Retailers are using this feature in several ways. Facebook offers its users scores of fashion-related widgets that provide trend information, personal style quizzes, and other options. Users of the widget Mintbox are able to select their favorite retailers from lists provided and use the service to plan shopping expeditions with their friends. Topshop, the United Kingdom–based fashion retailer, provides one of the most popular fashion widgets with over 1,300 daily users compared to about 100 users of other widgets. Other retailers involved include Lucky Brand, Diesel, Miss Sixty, Louis Vuitton, and The North Face, to name only a few.[28] Fashion widgets on a Facebook page and a Lucky Brand store are illustrated in Figures 6.7a and 6.7b.

6.7a

6.7b

Fashion widgets used on Facebook. *[Source: Courtesy of Fairchild Publications, Inc.]*

Lucky Brand draws new customers to its online and brick-and-mortar stores through the use of widgets, activated by Web users interested in interactive experiences and online fashion action. *[Source: Photograph provided by Lynda Poloian.]*

Traditional banner ads are paid for on the basis of CPMs. **CPM** is the cost per thousand (cost per mille) advertising impressions. This system is used to price conventional advertising media such as print and broadcast as well. This is in contrast to pay-per-click (PPC), which is used for paid search advertising. Widget applications are paid for using either PPC or CPM.

Many consider widget advertising the wave of the future. Advanced applications, including the use of widgets to guide customers to sales, provide "tickets" to special events, and implement more direct participation in sales transactions, are rapidly being developed.

Search Drives Sales Helping customers find what they are looking for quickly when they access a Web site is one of the objectives of retailers that seek to maximize sales effectiveness. We have all experienced frustration when we receive a "cannot locate" message. Retailers would prefer to circumvent this costly inability to make contact with a prospective customer. Updating search keywords and systems never stops for online retailers.

Apparel retailer J. Crew determined that customers who use the advanced search function on its Web site make a purchase seven times more often than customers who do not use the tool. The company also found that allowing customers to narrow their search internally provided them with fewer but more appropriate product selections.[29]

Search and e-mail are widely used advertising techniques, according to a study by Shop.org that was conducted by Forrester Research. Of the 125 online retailers surveyed, 90 percent use paid search and 92 percent use e-mail.[30]

<u>Interchannel Promotion</u> Several suggestions for maximizing customer service and traffic flow summarize the breadth of thinking required when planning strategically across channels. Multichannel retailers have adjusted their promotional mindsets accordingly.

> Use a catalog to reference the company Web site.
> Use a Web site to reinforce an in-store sale.
> Use a Web site or e-mail to announce that a catalog is in the mail.
> Use m-commerce to announce a new store opening.
> Use text messaging or e-mail to alert cell phone users to a special mobile-commerce-only sale.
> Be sure gift registries can be created, shared, and used across all channels.
> Use in-store kiosks to supplement in-store merchandising and to provide extended services and product information.
> Use direct mail—even a simple postcard—to remind customers about your Web site.
> Use new media to direct online customers to all channels.

Channel usage is greatly influenced by promotion: 37 percent of all e-commerce dollars come from catalog shoppers and 41 percent of Americans shop both catalogs and online. Direct-mail and Internet communications work best when used in tandem.[31] New methods of contact will enhance the already inventive options.

Other venues that are being tapped for advertising placement are video game sites. YouTube is blending video and e-commerce to create another vehicle for promotion. Video podcasts, introduced in Chapter 3, are being used for product demonstrations, providing valuable information for customers. Product demonstrations also work well in video podcast format, as do human resource training modules.

Amazon's *TextbuyIt* service lets mobile shoppers compare prices and order merchandise with a minimum number of keyboard strokes. Picture this: You are in a bookstore and see a title you like. Flip on your cell phone, punch in the ISBN identification number and send it to 262966—that is Amazon. Amazon will respond with an in-stock notification and price. Then you punch one number, and if previously registered with Amazon, order the book and have it shipped. Somewhere along the way, you will find a small but cool piece of advertising.

> Customer Relationship Management

Customer relationship management (CRM) was introduced in Chapter 2. Successful CRM requires a fusion of customer data, the ability to mine that data, and actionable strategies designed to satisfy the customer. A customer-centric orientation is not sufficient; infrastructure and talent must be in place to fully integrate CRM. The trend toward fully operational inter-channel communications systems is evident among many retailers. For retailers, establishing loyalty programs that run cross-channel helps cement brand image and company resourcefulness in the minds of their customers.

Database Development and Use

One of the leaders in cross-channel data gathering and use is the women's apparel retailer Coldwater Creek. This multichannel retailer was a frontrunner in the race to develop systems that allow it to share customer information across all sales channels. Online sales accounted for about 28 percent; catalog sales, approximately 34 percent; and stores, 38 percent of total revenue in 2004.[32] Although this sales distribution appears to be well balanced, the company accelerated store openings to create more brand visibility in underserved geographic markets. By 2008, the company's Internet and phone sales accounted for approximately 25 percent of sales; its full-price stores, outlet stores, and spas about 75 percent.[33] Coldwater Creek's cross-channel program is illustrated in Figure 6.8.

6.8

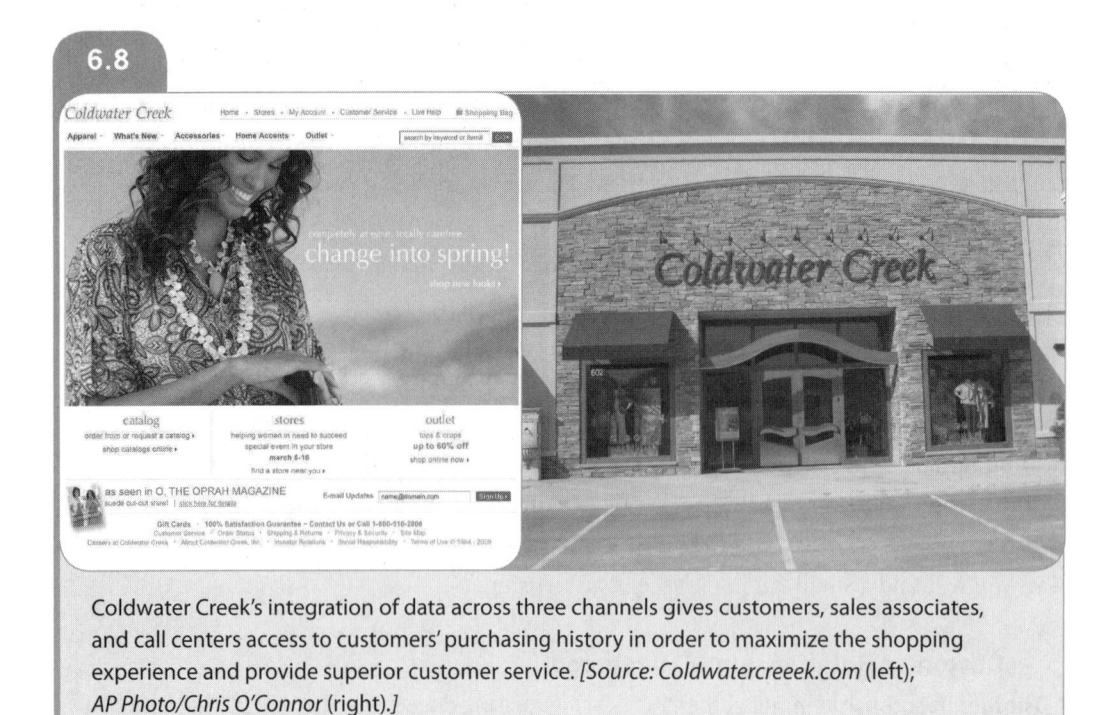

Coldwater Creek's integration of data across three channels gives customers, sales associates, and call centers access to customers' purchasing history in order to maximize the shopping experience and provide superior customer service. *[Source: Coldwatercreeek.com (left); AP Photo/Chris O'Connor (right).]*

Title Nine is a multichannel seller of women's sports apparel that has successfully consolidated its database. Read how the company better serves its customers as a result in Box 6.2.

Data Mining to Facilitate Advertising

The company Acxiom builds databases through its own surveys and public records, which are used to identify likely prospects for promotional pitches. Acxiom developed lifestyle clusters structured around a database of 133 million households broken down into 70 demographic/lifestyle groups.

Acxiom's clusters are similar to geodemographic tools created by Prizm and Acorn. All facilitate market segmentation. Acxiom uses catchy descriptors to encapsulate key characteristics of its clusters. For example, "Cartoons and Carpools" describes community-minded middle-income married couples with children, and "Urban Scramble" includes young professionals and students who live in major—and expensive—cities.[34]

Retailers use database information, gathered with the help of cookies placed on computers, to generate advertising placement recommendations.[35] **Cookies** are

> **What's the Buzz?   Box 6.2**

> *How a Multichannel Retailer Benefits from Cross-Channel Data*

Title Nine sells women's sports apparel online, in stores, and through a catalog, and two years ago had three separate systems for collecting customer data. Now that data is collected in a single database, which allows the retailer to better serve its customers, however they shop, says Renee Thomas-Jacobs, chief financial officer and executive sponsor of the data-integration project. Title Nine integrated its customer and inventory data in a single location, with technology from Commercial/Ware, part of Micros-Retail.

Knowing how customers shop also makes it possible for Title Nine to segment them for marketing purposes, Thomas-Jacobs says. For instance, customers who live close to one of the chain's nine stores have three options: they can shop the catalog and place the order by phone or mail, go to the Web, or visit a store. In fact, 30 percent of transactions from customers who live near stores are still completed online, she says. This information makes it possible for Title Nine to begin substituting e-mail for catalogs for those customers, because they are comfortable shopping online. "We're aggressively trying to send fewer catalogs," says Thomas-Jacobs. "Spending money on e-mail is more efficient than spending money on catalogs." But the retailer first makes sure its e-mails are opened by the customer, something its e-mail service provider tracks.

Customers checking out of a store are asked for their name and zip code, which brings up the record of customers who are in the retailer's database. If they are new customers, they are asked for their full addresses. Title Nine captures the addresses of 70 percent of its customers in stores, and is capturing customer data on 94 percent of all transactions, including Web and phone. For 75 percent of the transactions captured in 2007, the retailer also obtained the customer's e-mail address, allowing for follow-up marketing.

The company-wide view of inventory available also makes it possible to save sales that might have been lost. If a store is out of a style or size, an associate can check the Web inventory from the point-of-sale (POS) system and place the order for delivery to the customer's home. If the distribution center that services the Web and catalog orders is out of stock, an agent can have the item shipped from a store that has it in stock. In one month, 2 percent of orders were filled through a different channel than the one with which the customer started. To Thomas-Jacobs this represents a significant amount of sales. "Having an integrated system is not just part of marketing," she says, "It's part of our brand."

Source: Adapted from Internet Retailer, *March 6, 2008, www.internetretailer.com, © 2008 Vertical Web Media.*

small files that are placed on users' browsers by Web site servers for the purpose of identifying prospective customers and delivering targeted messages. Individuals usually opt-in by answering a survey, quiz, or subscribing to a newsletter, for example. Retailers use cookies to capture demographic information and personalize communications with customers. Yahoo!, Microsoft, and AOL use databases like these to refine and expedite the media plans of companies that advertise on their respective sites.

One way of reaching markets is through behavioral targeting. **Behavioral targeting** is the use of database information based on affinity to identify prospective customers. Web advertising is directed to selected market segments, and retailers are cognizant of the fact that past behavior is a predictor of future behavior. Previous search behavior or other actions observed in the virtual world are valuable to retailers as they seek new, or refine existing, markets.

Cross-Channel Loyalty Programs

Loyalty programs are designed to provide incentive for customers to shop more frequently and spend more money in an atmosphere that generates trust in the retailer. Well-targeted promotions and exclusive merchandise gifts increase the inclination of preferred customers to shop. Building up points to eventually convert to merchandise, services, or discounts increases customers' motivation to shop. Loyal shoppers usually jump at the opportunity to save 20 percent during the preseason special opening for "club" members. Feeling special is an emotion most of us like to experience on a regular basis.

Retailers such as J. Jill send coupons to charge account holders to use cross-channel. Often there is an extra incentive to make a store visit at the beginning of a season. The gift of a flowing plant and offer of refreshments go a long way to encourage customers to come into the store to see the new spring fashions—before they get picked over. The social engagement aspects are a lure for many customers, and sales associates are trained to perpetuate the welcoming store environment. An extra coupon tucked in the catalog helps, too.

The Gap sends coupons to customers when their online and offline purchases exceed a certain amount. Costco e-mails offers on select items to preferred in-store customers. Technologies are readily available to ensure the cross-channel administration of loyalty programs for any retail format.

> Organizational Leadership

The importance of attracting executives and staff who buy into a company's culture are well documented. To recruit individuals who have an affinity for the multichannel message is another aspect of cross-channel operations. Building a strong talent pool, training and developing managers and staff, and imparting appropriate benefits and reward systems is crucial.

An example from Facebook underscores the importance of organizational leadership, company growth, and the need to stay on the cusp of change yet adapt when necessary. Mark Zuckerberg, the CEO of Facebook, is in his early twenties. He has kept his humility while building and growing the organization, facing choices and challenges that many people would find daunting. In 2008 he recognized that in order to continue to grow and keep pace with competition, power within the company had to shift. He brought in a well-versed chief operating officer (COO) to develop a new business model. Hailing from Google and several other notable stints, Sheryl Sandberg was very well qualified to take over.

These are some of Sandberg's tasks as she implements new management and operational procedures:

> Build a management team.
> Set guidelines for employee performance reviews.
> Develop new processes for identifying and recruiting new employees.
> Set up management training programs.
> Develop better communications between sales and engineering.
> Expand internationally.

Early in her tenure she discovered that some employees were apprehensive that the corporate culture would change as the company grew. She expressed her understanding of their feelings and then told them that growth would be worth the discomfort as the company shifts from small to giant.[36]

Recognizing that there will be glitches and that not everyone will buy into a new direction is an important part of organizational leadership. The ability to handle such issues adroitly and compassionately is a rare skill.

Human Resource Management

We may not yet be ready to send our avatar to a job interview that we have scheduled, but rest assured, technology has already made that inevitability possible. An **avatar** is a digital representation of a human figure or other character. Avatars are used for a number of virtual reality applications. Individuals can create avatars of themselves or interact with cartoon-like interpretations of celebrities, sports heros, or designers. Some avatars equate to media spokespersons, although many are totally fictional images. There are even animal avatars with human attributes! More information on avatars and their use on Web sites and in product development is included in Chapter 7.

Drawn from the premise of Second Life, the Web community where users can create fantasy images and lives for themselves, some businesses are experimenting with interviewing in absentia through the online virtual community. Human resource personnel are using Second Life as a screening device to help pare down a pool of applicants, not as a replacement for an in-person interview. That is probably a good thing as there is a tendency to glorify one's physical attributes when designing an avatar.[37]

Some companies have tapped Facebook, MySpace, and YouTube as recruitment grounds, setting up information pages and advertisements on these sites. Most companies use Monster.com and Careerbuilder.com and other specialized online recruitment firms, but the importance of networking and personal referral should not be underestimated.

Several training methods used by companies involve classroom, online, and on-the-job learning. Both synchronous and asynchronous learning are popular. **Synchronous learning** occurs when trainees participate in online leaning activities at the same time. **Asynchronous learning** takes place at different times, usually at the convenience of the learner. Asynchronous learning is used when trainees are not able to meet concurrently or are in different geographic areas or time zones. Online tutoring, testing, and mentoring have also become part of training and ongoing professional development.

Retailers take a proactive view of technology and the needs of a multichannel marketplace when implementing new recruitment, placement, and training programs. Multichannel "cheerleaders" are required at all levels, and retailers search for new talent that complements their management teams and brings enthusiasm and passion to the workplace.

Profitability and Productivity

Leaders of the multichannel pack recognize that new ways to measure profit and loss are necessary when companies work through more than one channel. Now decisions are made as to where income should be recorded, whether or not it should be handled independently through each channel, recorded as belonging to one entity, or a combination of the two methods. Allocation of expenses is quite different when

Table 6.3 Sample Multichannel Merchandise Profit and Loss Comparisons between Catalog and Online Channels

FINANCIAL DATA	CATALOG	ONLINE	TOTAL
Net Sales	$2 million	$5 million	$7 million
Gross Margin (35%)	$700,000	$1,750,000	$2,450,000
Catalog Expense	$500,000	$1,750,000	$2,450,000
Online Marketing Expense	$0	$250,000	$250,000
E-mail Marketing Expense	$0	$50,000	$50,000
Home Page/Non-Shop Expense	$0	$50,000	$50,000
Department Landing Page Expense	$0	$100,000	$100,000
Merchandise Page View Expense	$0	$100,000	$100,000
Pick, Pack, and Ship Expense	$200,000	$500,000	$700,000
General and Administrative Expense	$143,000	$357,000	$500,000
Earnings Before Taxes (EBT)	-$143,000	$343,000	$200,000
+EBT as a Percent of Net Sales	-7.2%	+6.9%	+2.9%

Source: Kevin Hillstrom, "Multichannel Merchandise Profit and Loss," *DM News*, August 14, 2006, 28.

you are working through online as compared to traditional channels. The hypothetical example in Table 6.3 compares catalog and online profit and loss statements. Notice how the picture changes as companies embrace new revenue centers.

Reporting of income poses a dilemma for some retailers. For companies that began as stores and added online sales later, sales growth of online sales is customarily much higher than for brick-and-mortar stores. However, the proportion of sales attributed to brick-and-mortar sales is significantly higher than that attributed to the online sector. Some retailers find that it is difficult to resist the temptation to report growth rates company-wide. The averaging technique obviously skews the results when reporting same-store sales if online store growth rates are included in the average. **Same-store sales** reflect sales growth in stores that have been operating for at least a year. This method of calculating sales factors out growth generated by the opening of new stores from the sales growth measurement.

As retailers become savvier about cross-channel marketing, measures of productivity are changing from the number of hits using search engines to the relevancy of the contacts that are made. The level of interaction with customers and the increased knowledge that comes from practicing behavioral targeting are more important than the sheer number of contacts. Charting customer behaviors that convert to sales transactions are a truer measure of success.

For retailers, an operational system that makes it possible to complete all business functions in real-time across all channels profitably is not an unreasonable expectation. The quality of the total retail experience offered customers is the goal and also the root of many challenges retailers face as they adapt to change. The technology that will allow multichannel retailers to soar exists and is being perfected as you read this.

Summary

Physical store, online, catalog, and other direct marketing divisions no longer are independent of each other in progressive retail organizations. Cross-channel collaboration is a major initiative of all multichannel retailers.

Multichannel structures bring distinctive advantages to retailers that embrace one or more channels of delivery. Three common structures are semi-integrated, fully integrated, and independent. The trend is toward fully integrated organizations that also operate internationally.

Obstacles that are overcome by retailers as they implement cross-channel actions include synchronizing information technology, sharing customer data, providing appropriate customer service policies, dealing with limited financial resources, attracting competent employees, and above all—adapting to change.

Integrated marketing strategies accompany changes in business structure and supporting technologies. Branding across channels, merchandise management, pricing tactics, and distribution procedures all are addressed in the context of cross-channel image building and needs fulfillment. Remarkable changes are occurring in promotion. Reallocating promotional budgets is common as new media jockey for position with traditional methods. Search, social networking, and constantly emerging Web-based formats and technologies link together to play important roles in the changing face of advertising.

Key Terms

Asynchronous learning
Avatar
Banner advertisement
Behavioral targeting
Cookies
CPM
Fully integrated structure
Independent structure
Neuromarketing
Personalization
Same-store sales
Semi-integrated structure
Synchronous learning
Transactional messages
Widgets

Cross-channel shoppers make up the majority of shoppers. They are discerning and reflective of today's customers. They seek convenience above all and are comfortable shopping online or in any other channel—as long as it is at their own discretion and within their own boundaries.

Effective organizational leadership is needed to design and manage multichannel organizations that meet or exceed customer expectations.

To justify cross-channel collaboration and the technological infrastructure through which it runs, one need only look at the figures: retailers who practice their craft across channels increase revenues, profits, and return on investment, and reap the benefits of dealing with customers who spend more with their companies and feel more loyal toward them.

> ## Questions for Discussion and Reflection

1. Since the inception of e-commerce, organizational structures have evolved from independent, pure-play sites to more complex fully integrated structures. What structure will command the majority of multichannel retailers in the future? Justify your choice of structure.
2. Of the six obstacles to cross-channel collaboration, which one do you believe is the most pressing issue for retailers? State and elaborate on two solutions to the problem you have selected.
3. The impact of brand building has been emphasized in this chapter and in earlier chapters. Give two examples of ways that retailers can extend their brands effectively across channels.
4. Customers have high expectations when it comes to cross-channel shopping and service options. What fulfillment solutions are needed to make the online order and in-store pick up option a viable one? Use examples from the text and your own experience in your answer.
5. The use of alternative media is growing as new technologies emerge. What is the status of advertising on social networking sites? Support the advantages and disadvantages of this new advertising medium in your answer.
6. If online banner advertising is becoming mundane, what is replacing the tactic? Discuss two options or possibilities in your answer.
7. Customer relationship management (CRM) is an integral part of all marketing plans. How are multichannel retailers using CRM to enhance the multichannel customer experience?
8. How are recruitment, placement, and training practices changing in the light of advances technologies? What aspects of the hiring process are unlikely to change completely?
9. What key components affect the profit and loss of online stores compared with catalog retailers? Should retailers treat each channel as a separate profit center or consider the company's performance as a whole?

Notes

1. Don Davis, "Do you Know Me?" *Internet Retailer*, April 2008, 43. Statistic attributed to Retail Systems Research.

2. Andrew Halley, "Online and Offline Marketing: More then the Sum of the Parts," *DM News*, August 6, 2007, www.dmnews com/cms/dm-opinion/columns/42015,html.

3. J.C. Williams Group, excerpted from *Organizing for Cross-Channel Retailing*, a Shop.org study, January 2008, 4-6.

4. Ibid.

5. Aberdeen Group, Boston, MA, "Managing Customers, Merchandise, and Data," *The 21st Century Benchmark Report*, January 2007, 1.

6. Desiree Hanford, "Best Buy Follows Industry Lead in Crediting Web Sales to Stores," *Wall Street Journal*, June 22, 2005, B2B.

7. Mark Brohan, "Help Wanted," *Internet Retailer*, April 2008, 54. Statistics from "Salaries and Personnel Management."

8. "Merchants Improving on Cross-Channel Retailing," *Internet Retailer*, March 25, 2008, www.internetretailer.com/printArticle.asp?id=25809. Statistical source: AMR Research.

9. Len Lewis, "Following Orders," *Stores*, April 2008, 68-69, www.stores.com.

10. Susan Reda, "Marketing's Next (Brain) Wave," *Stores*, April 2008, 55, www.stores.org.

11. "Major Upscale Retailer in the U.K. Launches E-commerce Site," *Internet Retailer*, February 8, 2008, www.internetretailer.com.

12. Dianna Dilworth, "Territory Ahead Sails on Cross-Channel Waters," *DM News*, January 29, 2007, 6.

13. Cate T. Corcoran, "Net-a-porter Revenue Up 74.6%," *Women's Wear Daily*, May 31, 2007, 10.

14. "Catering to Multichannel Customers," *eMarketer*, September 8, 2008, www.emarketer.com/Articles/Print.aspx?id=1006516. Source: Retail Systems Research (RSR), sponsored by Gomez and Microsoft, August 2008.

15. Mary Wagner, "Blending Systems, Technology and Process Powers Seamless Service for Order Online/Pick-up in Store," *Internet Retailer*, March 2008, 66, 68-69.

16. Cate T. Corcoran, "Retailers Mix and Match Systems," *Women's Wear Daily*, June 13, 2007, 8.

17. Chantal Todé, "Wal-Mart Touts Site-to-Store," *DM News*, July 24, 2007, www.dmnews.com/cms/dm-news/catalog-retail/41877.html.

18. Jack Loechner, 'Two out of Five Retailers Don't Have a Store," Research Brief, Center for Media Research, posted January 29, 2008, http://blogs.mediapost.com/research_brief?p=1628.

19. Erik Sass, "Internet Ad Revenues Topped Radio in 2007: TNS," *Media Post Publications*, March 28, 2008, http://publications.mediapost.com. Statistical source, TNS Media Intelligence.

20. Chantal Todé, "In Lean Times, Williams-Sonoma Puts on Thinking Cap," *DM News*, March 13, 2008, www.dmnews.com.

Notes

21. Chantal Todé, "Finish Line Starts Paiva Fashion Brand Across Three Channels," *DM News,* April 17, 2006, 1, 34.

22. Louise Story, "The New Advertising Outlet: Your Life," *New York Times*, October 14, 2007, www.nytimes.com/2007/10/14/business/media/14ad.html.

23. Cate T. Corcoran, "What's Next for Fashion Networks?" *Women's Wear Daily*, November 14, 2007, 8.

24. Spencer E. Ante and Catherine Holahan, "Generation MySpace Is Getting Fed Up," www.businessweek.com/print/magazine/content/08_07/b4071054390809.htm.

25. National Retail Federation, "Multichannel Retailing, Part I; E-mail Marketing," SmartBrief Special Report, October 30, 2007, www.smartbrief.com. Statistics from Shop.org., *State of Retailing Online 2007*.

26. Bob Tedeschi, "Internet Banner Ads to Get More Interesting (and Thus Less Easy to Ignore)," *New York Times*, July 11, 2005, www.nytimes.com/2005/07/11/technology/11ecom.html.

27. "For Consumer Response, Sephora Finds Viral Networking Better than Banner Ads," Internet Retailer, February 2008, www.internetretailer.com.

28. Cate T. Corcoran, "Facebook Users Pick Favorite Fashion Retailers," *Women's Wear Daily*, February 6, 2008, 16.

29. Denise Power, "Guess Refines Site Search," *Women's Wear Daily*, September 6, 2006, 19.

30. Natalie Zmuda, "Online Retailers Try New Approaches," *Advertising Age*, April 8, 2008, http://adage,com/print?article_id=126253.

31. United States Postal Service®. " Mail and the Internet: One Smart Media Pair," *Value of Mail*, research report, 2006, Usps.com/dminfo.

32. Glenn Kalinoski, "Coldwater Creek's Stock Price is Running Hot," *DM News*, June 7, 2004, 8.

33. http://coldwatercreek.mediaroom.com/index.php?s=43&item=159.

34. Emily Steel, "Mistaken Identity," *Wall Street Journal*, September 20-21, 2008, W5.

35. Kevin J. Delaney and Emily Steel, "Firm Mines Offline Data to Target Online Ads," *Wall Street Journal*, October 17, 2007, B1-B2.

36. Carol Hymowitz, "New Face at Facebook Hopes to Map Out a Road to Growth," *Wall Street Journal*, April 14, 2008, B1, B5.

37. Anjali Athavaley, "A Job Interview You Don't Have to Show Up For," *Wall Street Journal*, June 20, 2007, D1, D8.

Multichannel Retail Profile > Red Envelope

> Overview

RedEnvelope, the gift specialist, has had a dynamic if not smooth evolution from pure-play to multichannel retailer. The company is #132 in the *Internet Retailer 2008 Top 500 Guide*. Despite strong branding and an innovative spirit, RedEnvelope's identity as an upmarket online gift specialist has been challenged by the highly competitive marketplace and economic downturn.

Located in San Francisco, the company has a mission statement that speaks to the spirit of gifting: "RedEnvelope is dedicated to inspiring people to celebrate their relationships through giving."[1] A gift presented in a RedEnvelope is a symbol of good luck and affection according to an Asian tradition. This sentiment inspired the company name.[2]

Competition comes from brick-and-mortar gift shops; gift departments in department, discount, and off-price stores; home furnishing and decor stores like HomeGoods; and online retailers like 1-800-Flowers.com and other Web specialists.

> Strategic Dimensions

The company was founded in 1997 and opened RedEnvelope.com in 1999 after doing business online under other names. This initiative was followed by a rapid release of its first catalog in 2000—a milestone for a pure-play retailer.

In 2007 RedEnvelope's total revenues were $88.5 million, but Web sales had slowed to $66.7 million, from $77.5 million the previous year. Despite new online tactics, customers did not respond as well as expected during the fall and holiday 2007–2008 seasons.[3] Order shipments for that period declined by 20 percent. Not only were sales down, but profits also lagged substantially.

One retail investment analyst suggested that RedEnvelope's troubles stemmed from the inability to turn a profit. Stuart Rose, managing director for Tully & Holland said: "Eventually companies need to make money. RedEnvelope is in deep trouble and has been for a while. It never built a profitable business model."[4]

In April 2008 the company filed for Chapter 11 bankruptcy protection, and in May 2008 it was sold at auction to the company Provide Commerce. In addition to RedEnvelope, that company owns several other online stores specializing in flowers, fruits, and sweets.[5] Strategically the acquisition is expected to buoy RedEnvelope.com's presence since Provide Commerce has strengths in product sourcing, supply chain management, and technology.

> Marketing Strategies

For a unique gift of good quality, RedEnvelope.com has positioned itself as the place to shop. Fresh hydrangea plants in contemporary zinc containers, Murano-like beaded bracelets, an eco nap pet lounger, and fancy bars of soap were representative of RedEnvelope.com's merchandise assortment for summer 2008.

A branding technique that appears throughout the Web site is a red gift box with white ribbon, reminiscent of Tiffany's famous branding strategy using its signature blue packaging with white trims. Used more extensively in some of its first Web site incarnations, the gift box symbol now seems secondary to bold merchandise and promotional messages.

Leading up to the change of ownership, RedEnvelope.com had used several types of promotion. Full-page magazine advertisements conveyed a warm, family-oriented approach promoting its Web site and catalogs for holiday shopping.

The company experimented with customer loyalty programs, at one point offering a $20 rewards certificate for every $200 spent. E-mails were sent to customers announcing the program and offering an opportunity to sign up using a convenient link in the e-mail. The goal was to increase repeat business from existing customers and gain the attention of new shoppers.[6]

> Web Site Tactics and Performance Metrics

Simply designed to focus attention on the wide array of well-photographed merchandise in an attractive format, RedEnvelope.com presents choice gifts to its shoppers. Although graphically intensive, the site loads quickly and is easy to navigate. Gift categories are arranged by occasion, recipients, and merchandise categories. A special section moves users quickly to categories such as business or last-minute gifts. By using another quick link customers can order seasonal print catalogs. Customers have the choice of using live chat, and the company's toll-free number is prominently displayed on key shopping- and customer service-oriented pages.

In 2007, 33 percent of all traffic on its Web site came from search engines. Monthly visits averaged 2,621,000, the sales conversion rate was 3.2 percent, and the average sales ticket was $93.[7]

When one company acquires another, the expectation is that positive attributes of each will make the whole stronger. RedEnvelope brings an established brand concept and customer base, and new product categories, to Provide Commerce. In turn, the acquirer provides a financial footing as well as sourcing and management capabilities. Time will tell if the merging of resources will be profitable.

> Points to Ponder

1. Visit RedEnvelope.com and compare the site to other online and offline stores. Assess the competition of this specialty gift retailer.
2. What factors contributed to the need for RedEnvelope to file for Chapter 11 bankruptcy protection?
3. Assess the strengths and weaknesses of RedEnvelope. What key attributes will Provide Commerce bring to its newest acquisition?

Multichannel Retail Profile > Red Envelope

Review the marketing strategies used by RedEnvelope and determine if they create differentiation of the brand. Suggest other marketing tactics to strengthen RedEnvelope's position in the marketplace.

> Notes

1. "Frequently Asked Questions," RedEnvelope.com, http://investor.shareholder.com/redenvelope/faq.cfm.
2. "About Us," RedEnvelope.com, www.redenvelope.com/re/gifts/customer_service/customer_service.jspnc=3366&ref.
3. "Top 101-500 Web Retailers, #132 RedEnvelope, Inc.," *Internet Retailer 2008 Top 500 Guide*, 239.
4. Jim Tierney, "Red Flag for RedEnvelope?" *Multichannel Merchant*, February 15, 2008, www.multichannelmerchant.com/news/RedEnvelope-red-flag-0215.
5. Provide Commerce Press Release, "Provide Commerce, Parent of ProFlowers, Adds RedEnvelope to Its Portfolio of Brands," San Diego, CA, May 27, 2008. www.prvd.com/PressRoom_Release20080527.aspx.
6. Melissa Campanelli, "RedEnvelope Tests Loyalty Program," *DM News*, September 19, 2005, 6.
7. *Internet Retailer*, 239.

Multichannel Retail Profile > L.L. Bean

> Overview

In business for close to a century, L.L. Bean is a landmark in its hometown of Freeport, Maine, and a familiar brand worldwide. Much of L.L. Bean's popularity comes from its rich history as a provider of products for outdoor enthusiasts, its strong commitment to quality, and its generous return policy. From "Bean boots" to apparel lines for men, women, and children, home furnishings to gourmet goodies, and fishing lures to canoes, L.L. Bean stands out as a provider of expert, friendly customer service. Its evolution from a single-line manufacturer of the Maine hunting shoe to catalogs, stores, and eventually online retailing makes it a significant triple-play company. The company has successfully extended its brand, bevy of product information experts, and noteworthy customer service skills across channels.

Ranked #23 in the *Internet Retailer 2008 Top 500 Guide*, L.L. Bean generated just under $1 billion in online sales in 2007.[1] Total company revenues are about twice that. The company operates L.L. Bean Outlet stores and a few larger lifestyle stores. It did not begin to expand its outdoor lifestyle stores until 2000.

Competition comes from other outdoor goods retailers such as Cabela's, EMS, and Orvis. Cabela's opened its first store in Maine in spring 2008, challenging L.L. Bean on its home turf for the first time. L.L. Bean does twice the Web business of Cabela's, although both companies are on growth trajectories.

> Strategic Initiatives

Several marketing and expansion initiatives were announced after the company named a new advertising agency of record in 2008. One objective is to increase the customer base by drawing from younger and more geographically diverse customers. Another is to entice customers to shop more, year round.[2]

Store expansion is another avenue of growth and strategic planning as L.L. Bean strives for national exposure. The company intends to increase its store count to 32 by 2012. South Barrington, Illinois, a suburb of Chicago, is the site of L.L. Bean's first Midwest store. Considered a signature lifestyle concept store, it features participatory experiences for customers, including fishing, kayaking, and snowshoeing lessons and clinics through its L.L. Bean Outdoor Discovery School. Other lifestyle stores are located in New York State, Massachusetts, and Connecticut.[3]

The company also expanded its flagship hunting and fishing store in Freeport. A 2,400-square-foot addition was added to the freestanding building, located on the periphery of a parking lot near the main store. Some of the wood used in the construction came from an old L.L. Bean factory store, keeping the tradition of this environmentally conscious retailer. Other plans for the Freeport location include a theme park incorporating a hotel and restaurants as well as many outdoor recreational activities for visitors.[4]

The first of five stores in China opened in Beijing in 2008, featuring décor similar to the flagship store in Freeport. L.L. Bean partnered with Youngone Corp. of Korea for this inaugural venture in China.[5]

> Online Metrics and Methods

At a time when other retailers were beginning to feel the pinch of an economic downturn, L.L. Bean boasted significant increases online for the 2007–2008 holiday season. During its busiest day in December, the company processed 97,000 online orders, an increase of 20 percent from the prior year. In 2007, it hosted more than 6 million average monthly visitors, and it is estimated that the company has an 8.8 percent conversion rate and an average ticket of $139. L.L. Bean also scores well in customer satisfaction and consistency of Web performance. The company expected to add an e-commerce site for Canadian customers in 2008.[6]

L.L. Bean fully integrates customer information across all channels of operation. Even customer participation in outdoor sports clinics is included in the database. This information is used to help the company target catalogs and other marketing messages of interest to its customers.

Multichannel Retail Profile > L.L. Bean

Steve Fuller, senior vice president of corporate marketing, makes it clear that L.L. Bean values shoppers in all channels equally. He says: "A customer who makes one purchase online and a couple of purchases in a store [is not necessarily] more valuable than a customer who shops repeatedly online."[7]

Online store sales accounted for about half of all direct sales in 2007 and Fuller expects that sales generated by the Web, telephone call centers, and retail stores eventually will be equally divided. He believes that catalogs are primarily an advertising vehicle, driving customers to online and brick-and-mortar stores as well as the telephone.[8]

> Focus on Customer Service

Renowned for thorough training of its call center personnel, L.L. Bean prides itself on its high level of customer service. Telephone representatives are unfailingly welcoming, knowledgeable, and efficient on the phone. An elite corps of associates is trained to provide extended service, for example, when a customer needs help selecting the right apparel or fishing lure for an outdoor adventure.

L.L. Bean offers a branded Visa card. Users are eligible for many benefits, including free standard shipping and monogramming on all credit card purchases. Customers earn "coupon dollars" that can be applied toward future purchases when they use their L.L. Bean card.

Originally L.L. Bean used Bank of America as its Visa affiliate. In 2008, a new agreement was struck with banking partner Barclay's. In return the financial institution has agreed to set up a customer call center in Maine. L.L. Bean alerted customers to the change through letters, e-mail, and Web announcements.[9] The company also included information through special catalog inserts.

Some of L.L. Bean's allure stems from its policy of keeping its flagship store open 24 hours a day, 365 days a year. It has been honoring this tradition since 1951—long before it was practical to grant customers access around the clock, as online stores now do. The company considers this practice part of building brand equity. Extended hours draw nocturnal wanderers from all over the world. Celebrities including Garth Brooks have been spotted shopping the Freeport store in the wee hours. When his group was on tour in Maine, the country music star was observed handing his road crew monetary bonuses to shop in the store.[10]

Certainly not meant only for insomniacs or celebrities, L.L. Bean is a pit stop for many visitors to Maine. Several employees have made a career out of working the night shift. The indoor trout pond, friendly folk, amenities, and quality merchandise draw customers and employees back for more—even if it is at 11:00 p.m. Such are the stories that make retailers legends in their own time.

> Points to Ponder

1. What characteristics make L.L. Bean stand out from its competitors?
2. How has the company evolved into a multichannel retailer? Is its path similar or dissimilar to those of other multichannel retailers of which you are aware?
3. Do you expect L.L. Bean's growth strategies will be successful? Why or why not?
4. What unique branding and operational strategies does L.L. Bean use?
5. Do you expect L.L. Bean to be successful in implementing its brick-and-mortar store growth strategies? Why or why not?

> Notes

1. "Top 100 Web Retailers, 23. L.L. Bean, Inc.," *Internet Retailer 2008 Top 500 Guide,* 130.
2. Chantal Todé, "L.L. Bean Builds on Core Brand," *DM News,* May 12, 2008, 2.
3. David Moin, "L.L. Bean to Open First Midwest Store," *Women's Wear Daily,* February 26, 2008, 2.
4. Chantal Todé, "Crossing the Divide," *DM News,* October 15, 2007, 16, 18.
5. Chantal Todé, "L.L. Bean to Open First Store in China This Month," *DM News,* September 17, 2008, www.dmnesa.com/LL-Bean-to-open-first-store-in-China-this-month/Print/Article/11.
6. *Internet Retailer,* 130.
7. Tode, "Crossing the Divide," 16, 18.
8. Ibid.
9. Lauren Bell, "L.L. Bean Offers New Loyalty Card," *DM News,* July 1, 2008, www.dmnews.com/LL-Bean-offers-new-loyalty-card/PrintArticle/112021.
10. Kevin Rousseau, "Night Shift," *Boston Sunday Globe,* December 3, 2006, M7, M9.

Unit III

TECHNOLOGY SOLUTIONS

Chapter 7

Designing Effective Online Stores

Objectives

> To review characteristics of effective retail Web sites.
> To explore a framework for Web site design.
> To enumerate the steps of e-commerce Web site development.
> To survey advanced graphic and interactive technologies.
> To examine online communication tools.
> To investigate aspects of search engine selection and assess their impact.

> Creating a sticky site is the objective of Web developers. **Stickiness** is the degree to which customers become engaged on a Web site. This chapter probes the physical aspects of Web design, essential components of product presentation, and inclusion of customer service tools—all of which contribute to the stickiness of a site. The impact of color, type styles, and digital images is considered—evidence that basic design principles are adhered to when developing graphic formats. Factors contributing to the functionality of a site are addressed, because users who cannot navigate a site will quickly abandon it. Rich media deserves special consideration as Web 2.0 and 3.0 have set the standards for interactive capabilities and online communication. Search engine options are probed more deeply, and guidelines regarding their selection are identified. The issue of stickiness comes first, as we identify what it takes to attract and keep customers.

Characteristics of Effective Retail Web Sites

The length of time that users stay on a site, shop, and use the site's resources contributes to the stickiness of the site. From a retailer's perspective, the stickier the site, the better. Retailers redesign their Web sites or add new features in their quest to drive traffic and enhance the customer experience. Consider the following examples:

> - Wet Seal, an apparel retailer of choice for many young women, has embraced their penchant for social networking and introduced a fashion community aspect to its Web site at wetseal.com. Visitors to the site can experiment with wardrobe building by mixing and matching styles to create their own looks—then share them with others. Fashion mavens can communicate with stylists, and rate and purchase outfits designed by fellow shoppers using a tool aptly called "The Runway."[1] By developing participatory sites like this, retailers can gain an edge over the competition.
> - Eddie Bauer has expanded its renowned customer service from its stores to the online sector. Its spiffed-up site features easier navigation requiring less scrolling, larger images, and immediate inventory status reports before customers reach the checkout stage.[2] When Web sites perform well, as in this case, momentum builds to the point-of-sale, discouraging shopping cart abandonment.
> - Vera Wang, known for her bridal wear and design affiliation with Kohl's, launched a linen and bedding line that was released exclusively through her newest Web site, verawangonweddings.com.[3] Usually new lines debut in brick-and-mortar stores first; this tactic positions Wang as an innovator.

Let these examples whet your appetite for more. The redesign, revamping, and remerchandising of retail Web sites is an important part of business development for all multichannel retailers.

> Winning the Customer

From avatars to zoom, the working Web is a thing of pleasure, profit, and sometimes profundities encumbered only by a few unscrupulous practitioners. The use of avatars as a means of enhancing the Web experience was touched on in Chapter 6 and is elaborated on later in this chapter. Developing a distinctive online presence that quenches customers' thirst for relevant products delivered in record time at competitive prices while having fun can sound like an insurmountable task for a retailer. But high-performing retailers have been doing this all along. The common goals of customer satisfaction through sales and meaningful contribution to the community remain constant across channels—e-commerce simply provides new opportunities to connect with customers. In the sections that follow, we'll explore the quirks and dedicated technologies of retailing on the Web, which has been witness to some of the most dynamic changes in retail history.

Web sites that over time score high points on consumer polls are those that employ the industry's best practices. Looking at the apparel sector, top e-retailers do well in categories that measure merchandising, customer service, and overall image as judged by analysis of preselected Web pages. According to Lauren Freedman, president of the e-tailing group, "People need to see the use of video, color, and whether or not the page is merchandise-heavy."[4] The merchant scores for the top 10 Web sites that feature apparel are listed in Table 7.1. Notice that retailers on the list range from pure-plays like Amazon, to home shopping channels, department stores, discounters, and specialists. In other words, excellence is not bound by type of retailer, type of primary channel, or pricing policy.

> ### Common Traits of Effective Sites

Think about the Web sites you like to visit repeatedly. Chances are the sites you find the stickiest are not those found by simply surfing or doing a quick pricing comparison. The sites we gravitate toward and spend time on are those that perform well across several criteria. High-performing retail Web sites share several characteristics:

> > They are well-designed, incorporate advanced graphic techniques, and are highly interactive.
> > If they represent multichannel retailers, brand image is consistent with other selling channels.
> > Sites are easily navigable, and products are easy to find.
> > Technology solutions are well chosen to meet the demands of retailers and customers.
> > Customized customer contact methods, product offerings, and service preferences are in place.

Winning the Customer: The Top Retail Web Sites Featuring Apparel — Table 7.1

RANK	COMPANY	SCORE	KEY ATTRIBUTES OF SITE
1	QVC.COM	86.5	Live TV feeds, multilanguage capabilities, focus on brands
2	HSN.COM	82.0	Interactive and stimulating shopping experience, video content
3	REI.COM	80.5	Strong brand emphasis, customer service focus, "how-to" help
4	NORDSTROM.COM	80.0	Customer-service intensive: free returns and exchanges across channels, live chats with experts
5	POLO.COM	76.0	Full-spectrum experience: video-streams, custom-made programs
6	AMAZON.COM	76.0	Top-tier technology: one-click ordering, product recommendations, wish lists; strong apparel brand focus
7	NEIMANMARCUS.COM	75.5	Full service features: shop by trend, designer, silhouette, or occasion; accessories suggested
8	WALMART.COM	75.5	Innovative online approach: introducing new labels, site-to-store shipping, reviews, and ratings
9	ORVIS.COM	75.5	Special section for travel wear; suggestions for all climates, locations, and activities; use of photos, videos, or writing to rate products
10	TARGET.COM	75.0	New product section; free shipping on orders over $50 for apparel and accessories

Source: Adapted from the e-tailing group as published in *Women's Wear Daily,* February 28, 2008, 16.

> **Box 7.1   What's the Buzz?**

> *Tommy Bahama: Beaches and E-commerce*

Situation

Luxury resort brand Tommy Bahama wanted to increase its presence and product availability online while also being able to translate the brand's offline philosophy of "life is one long weekend" to the Web. Although the brand already had a Web site for some time, until recently it was "basically a billboard for the company," says Doug Wood, COO of the Tommy Bahama Group. Its target demographic is men and women age thirty-five and older.

Approach

Tommy Bahama partnered with Escalate Retail and used a Blue Martini e-commerce suite software platform to launch a new Web site at www.tommybahama.com. The site features men's and women's apparel, locators for the brand's stores and restaurants, as well as Tommy Bahama event listings. A section called Paradise Nation provides items to help visitors live an island lifestyle, including tropically inspired recipes, screensavers of various destinations, downloadable wallpapers, island-inspired articles, and forums.

The imagery on the site is very important, according to Wood. "Tommy Bahama spent a lot of money on photo shoots" for the relaunch, which has had "tremendous impact on the effectiveness of the site as a branding and messaging vehicle, he says. Many of the images are presented in a scrapbook-like format on the home page. The site was promoted with in-store collateral, window displays, and Tommy Bahama shopping bags.

Results

The investment appears to be paying off, with the average user viewing eleven pages per visit and spending more than five minutes on the site. The site has received 200,000 monthly unique visits and 150,000 unique visitors since relaunch.

Source: Adapted from Mary Hurn, "The Work, Showcasing Creative Solutions,"
DM News, *April 14, 2008, p. 27.*

> Sites are kept up-to-date and in good working order.
> Retailers monitor and quantify online shopping behavior and act on the information they gather.

Quick, simple, and fun summarize the desired traits expected by customers. It takes tenacity, talent, and technology to build upon these traits. To that end, Tommy Bahama re-launched its Web site with a strong brand-building focus, as described in Box 7.1.

Framework for Web Site Design

Before starting Web site construction, several aspects of design are considered. Aesthetic components create a backdrop for content that includes all technology systems and product information. In addition, commercial, communication, and performance standards are formulated. Various viewpoints are sought as the planning process unfolds.

> Web Page Layout and Design

As in many other areas of life and work, on a Web page you have a very limited time in which to make a good first impression. The choices made regarding theme, color, and image greatly influence the first visit to a Web site. Principles of design include balance, proportion, emphasis, and rhythm. Eye movement follows the flow of art elements as they work together to engage the viewer. Elements of design including line and color are used to convey visual branding messages. Typography selection also has an impact on the design process.

Although it is not an objective of this text to turn readers into artists, it is important for retail executives to have a basic knowledge of design in order to make decisions that reflect brand, image, and company viewpoint. Some art background is helpful when critiquing work done on your Web site and for conversing with professionals who are engaged in creative fields. To begin, let's review several principles of design.

Principles of Design

Artistic approaches to the positioning of objects in a painting or on a Web site rely on a variety of design principles. Several types of balance as well as emphasis, proportion, and rhythm are highlighted here. These are the building blocks of aesthetic understanding.

Balance In an art form, **balance** is the arrangement of components in a work so that they appear to be in harmony. Whether the work is a painting, advertisement, or Web page, the principle remains the same. Balance can be achieved through symmetrical or asymmetrical arrangement of elements. **Symmetrical balance** describes art elements that are equally weighted on left and right sides or top and bottom of the work. This is also known as formal balance. **Asymmetrical balance** describes

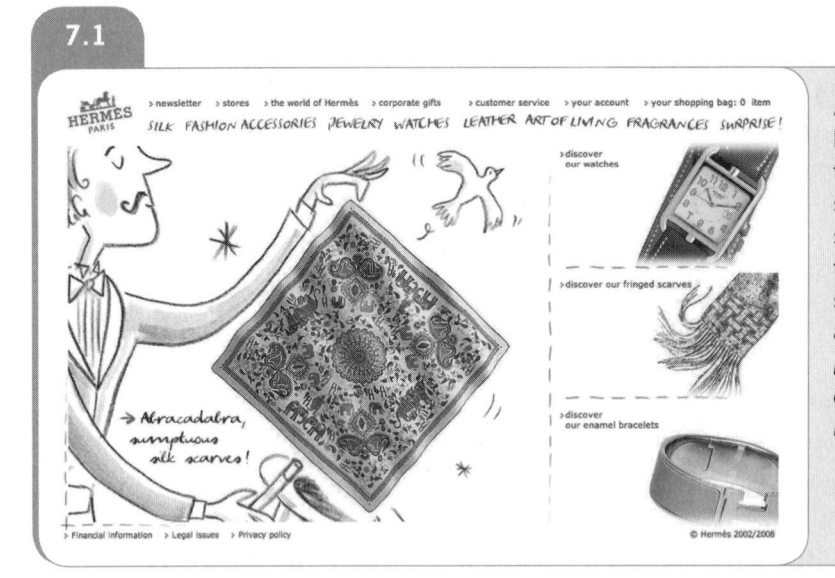

7.1 Asymmetrical balance used on the Hermes Web site suggests a sense of whimsy to the display of signature scarves and accessories. [Source: Courtesy of Fairchild Publications, Inc.]

art elements that are not distributed with equal weight in a work. This is also called informal balance. Although a symmetrical arrangement of illustration, copy, and other decorative items usually is technically correct, an asymmetrical format creates more visual interest and excitement for the viewer. Balance is considered when constructing three-dimensional (3-D) in-store and window displays as well. Use of asymmetrical balance on the Hermes Web site is illustrated in Figure 7.1.

Other types of balance including repetition, alternation, progression, and radiation draw the eye. Several forms that present art elements well include:

> **Repetition** When a single element is replicated to create a pattern, and therefore create more visual impact, this is called **repetition.**
> **Alternation** When repetition is used with an interchange of two or more components that are different from each other in size, shape, or color, this is called **alternation.** For example, a Web page set up to show illustrations of swimsuits might feature a bikini, followed by a one-piece swimsuit, then a bikini, then another one-piece. This technique is used to break up the monotony and interject more visual appeal.
> **Progression** When art components are arranged so they show change, this is called **progression**. Shifting from light to dark shades of color, and small to large shapes—or visa versa—represents the use of progression. A bottle of men's cologne that begins at the top left side of a Web page and cascades

7.2 On this Net-a-porter Web site, the element of repetition is evident by the selection of three models, but the emphasis is on the model in the center, who wears a red dress. *[Source: Courtesy of Fairchild Publications, Inc.]*

down with the containers becoming gradually larger until they reach the lower right of the page uses this tactic.

> **Radiation** When art components are placed to create a sunburst effect from a central point, this is called **radiation**. This technique is used in window displays, print advertising, and also in Web design. Ridged geometric forms are used often on Web sites and might be separated or softened by the use of radiation.

Emphasis Not all components of a painting, advertisement, or Web page are treated equally. **Emphasis** denotes the focal point or primary component of a work. Once the focal point is designated, subordinate components should draw attention to the main feature. For example, depending on the goals of the retailer, the merchandise itself is usually the focal point of a print advertisement. If the home page advertisement is the critical draw in a Web site, it is emphasized at that point in the search process. Under other circumstances a logo might have prime position. If the company is having a sale, a price or sale announcement may warrant more attention. Emphasis is achieved through use of color, image positioning, size, and unique illustrative features. Figure 7.2 illustrates the use of emphasis in determining focal point on a Net-a-porter Web page.

Proportion The relationship of art components to each other and to the space surrounding the components is called **proportion**. The relative size of each piece of the work is considered as designers grapple with the integrity of the entire advertisement or page. For example, using a two-inch high banner ad on a Web page along with a one-inch fashion figure would cause the fashion figure to appear dwarfed. Better proportion is achieved by using a two-inch banner ad with a five-inch fashion figure.

Rhythm The mechanism that guides the eye from one art component in a work to all others is called **rhythm**. The use of line, shape, color, and direction contribute to the flow within the work in a harmonious way. This is the concept that drives eye movement when you view a piece of artwork. Usually eye movement progresses from left to right and from top to bottom—at least among viewers in most Western cultures. The use of progression, such as a change from large to small or light to dark colors, also contributes to the rhythm within a work. Direction can be suggested by the use of a photo or illustration in which a human figure appears to be looking into rather than off a Web page, for example. Eye flow is directed by the artful positioning of other components in an advertisement.

Elements of Design

Elements of design include shape, form, line, color, and optical weight. These are the workhorses of the design world. An overview of color and line, two fundamental elements, follows.

Line The element **line** refers to the use of the artist's stroke to convey design, motion, direction, or graphic details. Line is used subtly in curved or scrolled forms, or boldly and expressively in broad, strong, linear strokes. A horizontal line suggests peace, quiet, and the natural edge of earth and sea. A vertical line connotes power, reliability, stability, and uprightness. Curvilinear lines express femininity and geometric lines, masculinity. Angled lines express motion, speed, and excitement. The subtle messages suggested by line underscore why designers carefully weigh their options when creating ads or Web materials.

Color No other design element reaches the ranges of human emotion as well as color. Used strategically, color is a powerful extension of branding. Color forms the basis for visual merchandising and print advertising decisions and is also the mainstay of Web design. Knowledge of color theory and the psychology of color helps retailers better understand customer behavior. Selective use of color helps organize groups of merchandise, identify a theme, or evoke a mood.

Color is kept consistent when a retailer elects to organize apparel styles by color. For example, in featuring spring merchandise, T.J. Maxx gave visitors to its site the option of viewing groups of merchandise in four different color stories. By clicking on a pink, blue, yellow, or green daisy, customers accessed a preview page of coordinated apparel in their chosen color scheme. A convenient locator tool was available, of course. Even when a site is nontransactional, as in this case, color, sound, and motion can be effective in urging customers to visit a store.

When considering colors for a home page, ask these questions:

> What color "front door" do I want for my online store?
> What would my customers like to see?
> Who are they and what do they relate to?
> What image should the online store convey?
> Do the color choices reflect the schemes used across other selling channels?

Although this text will not go into detail about color theory, realize that it is the foundation for selection of Web components as well as merchandise for display in catalogs and online stores.

Selecting and Using Typography

From logotypes to body copy, choices of typefaces, also called fonts or styles, are a major consideration in Web page design. Decisions about type style and size also reflect image; therefore, they have an impact on target markets. Every piece of descriptive copy that is written, all eye-catching headlines, the borders on an advertisement, banner and boxed ads, and even the graphic exclamations contained therein are designed to represent the image of the retailer graphically.

Type Categories Fonts are broken down into two basic categories, serif and sans serif. **Serif** typefaces feature small appendages on the letters. They are a design touch that makes type look more formal, nostalgic, and ornate. **Sans serif** typefaces are

Table 7.2 Samples of Serif and Sans Serif Typography Styles

TYPEFACE NAMES	SERIF STYLES	SANS SERIF STYLES
Times New Roman	Standard document text; notice appendages on capital letters; more condensed than Courier New	
Courier New	Commonly used for body copy; easy to read; more extended than Times New Roman	
Garamond	Typical textbook type; well designed and spaced letters; style lends itself well to formal logos; elegant but hard to read in small point size	
Arial Black		Bold stroke form for headline use; notice no "doodads" or appendages
Tahoma		Clean and contemporary, but does it shout "Sale"?
Lucida Console		Here is a cool hybrid: basically sans serif but with a design flourish on "i" and "l" and varying width to curved letters; use sparingly for emphasis

less formal, simply stroked letters without appendages. These lend a more contemporary flavor to print and digital projects. Samples of serif and sans serif typefaces are illustrated in Table 7.2.

Sizing Type When viewing the copy on a Web page as a whole, or in an individual advertisement, size of type font is considered in the same way as proportion and emphasis. From your use of word processing and graphic computer programs, you know that type size is based on the point system. A point is 1/72 of an inch. Therefore 72-point type is one inch high, although in actuality it is slightly less than one inch. The original measurement was based on the size of a whole metal "slug" used in old, manual printing processes, and not on the exposed portion of the letter itself.

<u>Using Type Effectively</u> A few general guidelines regarding size and use apply. Usually larger type sizes are used in headlines and smaller sizes in body copy. Anything below 8-point type is usually considered too small to be easily read across all print and digital formats. Some styles can be used in condensed, regular, and extended forms, depending on the demands of space, degree of artfulness needed, and mission. Unless creating a distinctive application, regular type works best in most situations. Extended type styles are too dispersed to be easily legible, and condensed faces too compacted to be useful marketing tools.

As a general rule, no more than two or three different typefaces should be used in the same piece of work. However, there are always exceptions, depending on the image sought, the purpose of the advertisement or Web site, and the skills of the graphic artist. The objective is to avoid having the page become too cluttered or confusing to viewers. Very ornate type styles are best avoided or used sparingly because they are hard to read or too fancy to warrant close inspection by the viewer.

As with every rule, there are exceptions to this "less is more" approach to using type effectively. A visitor to the Costco site found an e-mail from the company initially disconcerting from a design perspective. The e-mail was cluttered with unrelated products, contained many different type styles, and seemed to bombard his senses. When the reader realized the image put forth in the e-mail was identical to the store experience, he changed his assessment and applauded the company for maintaining consistency.[5] Selection of type does delineate image, and when used consistently in this context, rules can be broken.

<u>Type and White Space</u> Total area used for type is another issue. White space increases the readership of ads and gives a more upscale touch to an advertising pitch. When a luxury goods retailer advertises, it does not usually overemphasize type. **White space** is the portion of an advertisement, Web page, or catalog page that is not taken up by illustration, type, or decorative elements. Information on writing copy appears later, in the section on online communications.

> Essentials of Web Content

From corporate home page to transactional Web site, developers craft the online encounter with resolute input from retailers. All digital material that appears on a Web site is considered **content**. Technological content differs from merchandise-centered content such as product information and for this reason is treated separately in this section. An examination of navigation tools and other Web content that ensure the efficacy of site traffic, communication options, and user interface standards rounds out the section.

Product Information Content

Merchandise must speak clearly to the online community. How products appear on the Web is as important as how they look in a print catalog or in a store. Well-chosen merchandise justifies outstanding presentation on a site. The Web site home page is the equivalent of a steel or glass door to a store. In addition, descriptive information on products, including use, benefits, guarantees, and warranties, are all part of content.

Transactional Capabilities and Functionality

Navigation systems ensure the smooth flow of traffic from one part of the site to another. Site maps, drop-down menus, sidebars, and links are carefully engineered to be fully functional. Organizing the Web site in a logical way that allows unfettered user access is crucial. Several key components are considered here.

<u>Site Maps</u> Web components enhance the customer experience just as much as signs and maps, and planograms do for stores. **Planograms** are explicit directions that map and illustrate the placement of fixtures and merchandise in a store. Used by store visual merchandisers, the executed plans ensure consistency across all stores in a chain. Using some creative license, site maps are the online equivalent of store planograms because they combine organizational qualities with Web page layouts that display merchandise. An effective site map should outline every page on the Web site from home page to checkout, company history to merchandise selections. Site maps should indicate how customers get from one page to another, and ideally access to the site map should appear in the same areas on each Web page for easy access by users. Site maps also help Web planners identify the needs of retailers and design pages that present merchandise and information in an organized way, often using drop-down menus.

<u>Menus</u> Drop-down menus are one of the tools Web designers use to make the site tour an expedient one for customers. Headings and topics must be as well chosen as the headlines and body copy in an advertisement. They should relate the content listed on the site map with ease and fluency. Hitting the navigation button for "women's fashion" should bring up every category of goods that the retailer carries: knit tops, sweaters, woven tops, jeans, dress pants, skirts, dresses, suits, eveningwear—if that is the scope of the online store's merchandise.

<u>Links</u> Carefully chosen links to external sites and those within a retail Web site can enhance the online experience for customers. Links to related sites should be relevant, interesting, and workable. Internal links should be both functional and timely. Both types should not detract from the main objectives: building the brand and selling merchandise.

Neiman Marcus Direct sells fashion items that have a brief shelf life. Because of this the company must carefully manage and maintain internal links on its Web site. Nothing frustrates a customer more than to click through to a desired product to find that there is no information on the other end of the link. According to firms that monitor links for retail clients, 7 percent of all links are broken. This means that customers are not served efficiently 7 percent of the time. The problem is averted when retailers redirect traffic to an appropriate Web page as soon as the broken link is discovered.[6]

<u>Side Bars</u> Side bars serve two major functions. First, they serve as an extension to or enhancement of drop-down menus. Second they provide a hosting area for advertising, widgets, and relevant external links. When designing a site, keep in mind that sidebars should be supportive—not subordinate—to the primary message and merchandise presented.

<u>Shopping Cart Functions</u> Shopping cart systems smooth the checkout process, but if they are slow or complex, the customer will abort the sale. Therefore, the fewer clicks it takes to get to the checkout, the more likely it is that shoppers will not give up their quests. Payment systems are chosen for their universality, ease of use, and security online. Because customer convenience is the main goal, they are particularly relevant to the planning process. Shopping cart abandonment is reduced when customers experience smooth sailing to checkout and discover that their payment method of choice is available.

Several ways to reduce shopping cart abandonment are covered later in this chapter. More on customer preferences regarding payment systems is discussed in the next section and in Chapter 8.

Well-designed menus, side bars, carefully chosen links, and other Web page elements contribute to the overall impression of a Web site and its functionality. They also serve as the locus for extended online communications.

Online Communications

Communication has different guises on the Web including:

> - Contact between retailers and customers, via the Web site itself or through targeted e-mails promoting products, conducting surveys, or handling transactions and customer service.
> - The language used on the Web site; the careful selection of words, phrases and information crafted by copywriters. Words that are finely honed to suit the target market and crafted to close the sale.
> - Integrated communication within the greater online community. Tools that enable Web users to shop together, customer reviews, blogging, and user-to-user marketing events are examples. No longer interesting add-ons, these options are expected by online guests.

The importance of communication between channels was covered in Chapter 6. All forms of communication must be used to impart clear, concise product content and customer interface.

Web Site Performance

Navigability, functionality, choices of customer-friendly features, and communication are all important, but so is performance. All "moving parts" must work efficiently. The following statements summarize key Web site performance requirements:

> - Speed and reliability are mandatory aspects of any Web site.
> - Appropriate technology platforms ensure that customers are not thwarted in their attempts to access a site.

> Supportive media such as streaming video, sound, and full-dimensional views of products must function well.

User-friendly engagement online is the consequence of technological choices made well before the Web site's inaugural date. The importance of maintaining all working elements of the Web site is emphasized.

Setting Up an E-commerce Site

Once the essential content areas have been determined, it's time to establish the new e-commerce site. An overview of the basic steps involved in setting up an actual site follows. A survey of technologies that transform the average Web site and elevate it to high stature concludes this section.

> Eight Steps of Web Site Planning

Although not meant to be an exhaustive list, the following guidelines are useful to students or retailers contemplating online stores.

Step 1: Find the Best Address

Living on Hyacinth Lane sounds just a bit more appealing than finding a house on Bacon Street, and the same applies to buying Web "real estate." The choice of URL is a big one, especially now that so many great ones are already taken. The **Uniform Resource Locator (URL)** is the Web site address that includes complete access protocol and the domain name. The **domain name** is the portion of a Web address that contains the business name and the identifier, such as .com, .net, or .biz. Most major companies have owned their Web names and addresses for some time, but new companies take special pains when making this decision. When possible the URL should include the business name, reflect a key product line, or define an attribute that is important to the company. It should be difficult to duplicate and simple to search. Being short and memorable helps.

When the online apparel retailer Bluefly.com set up its new boutique site, b*fly, it was mindful to extract part of the root URL with which many Web users are familiar. Because the new site carries contemporary fashion for young men and women, the name and home page identify with this target market.[7] The b*fly and the original Bluefly.com home pages are illustrated in Figure 7.3.

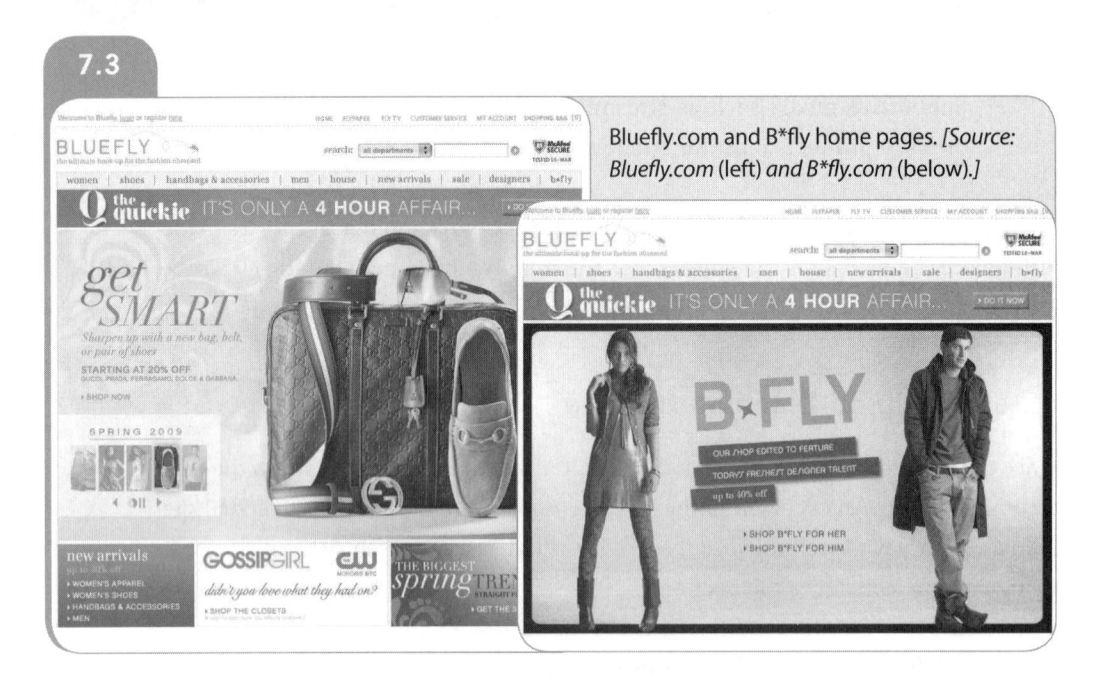

Bluefly.com and B*fly home pages. *[Source: Bluefly.com (left) and B*fly.com (below).]*

Registering a name is neither difficult nor very time-consuming. Several companies, including Network Solutions, a domain name registrar, perform this service. Network Solutions also provides a research tool that indicates the availability of the name you have chosen. Registrars also automatically list your site with major search engines. Even if your first choice is taken, it is possible that the name is for sale. Network Solutions maintains a domain name marketplace site for this purpose.[8]

Step 2: Construct the Site

Make the easier decisions first by deciding whether the site is going to be transactional or nontransactional. Detail your specific goals. If it is a commercial site, you will want to provide for the collection and database housing of customer information. If you are replacing or enhancing an existing print catalog, you will need to decide which aspects transfer well to the Web and which do not. Most companies include a company information section—usually called "About Us"—as well as a frequently asked questions (FAQ) page. All product information should be accurate, and illustrations portrayed well. Adding testimonials, customer reports, press releases, community involvement, environmental platforms, and ethical policies is useful. Customer service aspects and company contact information should be prominently featured and easy to access.

Step 3: My Site or Yours?

Another decision involves whether you will own your own server or participate in shared hosting with an established Internet service provider (ISP). An **Internet service provider (ISP)** is a company that provides a gateway to the Internet. **Shared hosting** indicates that a Web site is hosted by an ISP on the same server as several other Web sites. A **dedicated server** is a special computer connected to the Internet that houses a Web site exclusively. Smaller businesses usually opt for shared hosting because it is less expensive and because the ISP also provides e-mail service, security, and support. Large firms prefer their own server because of the control aspects of purchasing, managing, and maintaining their own hardware and software. Some host companies are Verio, Navisite, and Critical Path.

Step 4: Safe and Secure

When you are dealing with monetary transactions, having tight online security is of the essence. Despite the growing body of security systems and safeguards, hackers, imposters, and other scam-driven reprobates scour the Internet on a daily basis. Security systems should be chosen to protect customers from spoofing, unauthorized disclosure or action, eavesdropping, and data alteration and theft.

To ensure a high level of trust online, industry digital SSL certification standards have been established. **SSL certification** allows customers to determine if a Web site is authentic and if their communications on the site are secure. Certification is based on the Secure Sockets Layer (SSL) protocol developed by Netscape and is a part of all major browsers and Web servers. The company VeriSign provides security for sensitive data on the Internet. Its Secured Seal certification is available in 13 languages and is viewed 150 million times per day by Internet users. Companies using the service have the option of portraying the seal as animated or static graphic on their sites.[9] Verifying Web site server authentication, and ensuring the encryption of transmitted data are chief advantages of SSL certification to online retailers and their customers.

Step 5: Pay Me Now or Pay Me Later?

Payment systems are an understandably sensitive issue to customers. Privacy and security systems online are monitored and modified to ensure maximum safety standards for customers. Wary individuals are wise to do business with firms that have a proven reputation, but even then customers are not completely safe. Data breaches have become more common and affect service providers, retailers, and customers alike.

Many users are apprehensive about giving information over the Web. Consumer advocates suggest these precautions to Web users:

> When in doubt do not use a credit card number online.
> Change passwords frequently and never give them out.
> Never give out your social security number, banking information, or other personal identification numbers.
> Be aware of scam e-mail designed to look as if your bank sent it. Scam scoundrels unscrupulously use the names of reputable financial institutions in their lead lines.

Being a somewhat paranoid online customer, this writer had the unsettling experience of carefully guarding her online transactions only to be caught short in an ATM scam. None of us is immune from some form of identity theft. Retailers work to gain the trust of their customers by providing secure connections and impeccable technological solutions.

Decisions regarding online payment systems are part of the Web site planning process. Major credit card companies and prescreening payment systems such as PayPal are among the most reliable. PayPal has upgraded its online payment system as commercial transactions have become more complex due to the need to protect against fraud. More information on identity theft and fraud appears in Chapter 8.

Step 6: Promote, Promote, Promote

Getting word out that you are in business to sell sounds easy, and it is to a certain extent. When running an online operation, marketing activities are commonly spread over many old as well as several new options, as discussed in Chapter 6. Drawing from that information, the next section examines new ways to get Web sites noticed. This involves using alternative as well as established media. Most tactics require unswerving exposure to advertising messages. There are few promotions—if any—that fully inform prospective customers about your venture in one fell swoop.

Step 7: Sell, Sell, Sell

You have selected your merchandise carefully, priced it fairly, promoted it well. Now it had better sell! To achieve this goal, you need to make it easy for your customers to peruse and purchase online. Shopping cart abandonment was mentioned in other chapters; here we'll consider how to prevent it. Shopping card abandonment is reduced and sales increase when:

> Customers are provided with ample merchandise choices.
> Customers have a clear path to checkout.
> There are few clicks from product selection to order confirmation.
> Multiple payment options are available.
> Return policies are clear.
> Obstacles involving fit, color, and touch are dealt with before the sale is finalized.
> Tools like My Virtual Model, and software from OptiTex International, and Webcom, Inc., are used to help customers make appropriate size choices, thus avoiding many returns.

Sales follow-up techniques include thank-you e-mails, unconditional product guarantees, and loyalty programs. These techniques affirm that your customer made the right choice when shopping on your Web site and go a long way toward building trust and encouraging repeat business.

Step 8: Evaluate and Update

Just as apartments and houses always seem to need repair, renovation, or redecorating, so does a Web site. Retailers that best serve their customers are those that are proactive when it comes to Web site revitalization. If new visual merchandising tactics are needed in brick-and-mortar stores, why should touch-ups to online stores be any less important? A fresh public face and new merchandise are always welcome. Getting customers involved in the process is beneficial. At the very least, customers who share feedback with retailers regarding what is wrong with a site, what is lacking, or what is not customer-friendly have become connected with the company. Conversely, customers should not be expected to tell retailers how to improve their sites; that is up to the Web experts.

> Advanced Graphic and Interactive Technologies

New technologies, enhancements, and devices have made the Web more complex as well as more enjoyable for users. Not a week goes by without the unveiling of more sophisticated graphics, interactive features, and communication options. Included in this discussion are embellishments of what was originally called rich media. **Rich media** is a collective term for early Web tools that enabled animation and interactivity on Web sites. Now vast modifications in systems are cataloged as Web 2.0 and Web 3.0. Both identify transforming features that make the Web experience more exciting and also add value to retailers' efforts to reach and service their customers.

Rich Media and Web 2.0

When Adobe's Flash software became available, Web users cheered that graphic animation had been added to their entertainment and shopping experiences. However, Flash has its limitations because some search engines cannot read it. Fortunately, Adobe, Google, and Yahoo! are working on technology that will make Flash images searchable.[10]

When viewers access a page that uses Flash, usually they are given the option of using pages written in HTML code that gives the same information in a way that is discernable to search engines. **Hyper Text Markup Language (HTML)** is a popular computer code for documents created and used on the Web. Encoded in an HTML document are content, layout, and formatting information.

When building their vast indexes, search engines use HTML coding that provides information about a Web site, including which keywords represent the content. The special HTML code used for marking keywords and other components is called a **meta tag**.

Other rich media technologies such as AJAX were the vanguard of interactive innovation. **AJAX** stands for Asynchronous JavaScript and XML. **XML** stands for eXtensible Markup Language and is an advanced version of HTML code. The user interface between AJAX and XML allows for single-page browsing and checkout processing and has the capacity to offer customers options and product add-ons based on their online behavior.[11] For example, a shopper on a fashion site may be interested in a simple red dress. Through interactive technology like AJAX, an appropriate belt or other accessory could be presented. AJAX also helps speed up cumbersome processes and allows users to move cursors to view maps faster and in more detail. Unlike HTML code, which is used primarily for word document applications, XML is designed for widespread Web use.

Rich media is engaging, but users wanted more. The advent of broadband Internet access paved the way for more rigorous Web graphics and interactive options. Without high-speed connections, however, the grandeur of advanced technologies is lost.

Providing advanced action, motion, and a host of customer service options adds zest to Web sites and keeps visitors at sites longer. It makes sites stickier. These functions form the core of Web 2.0 e-commerce, which was introduced in Chapter 5. A composite term for many advanced technologies that make a Web site interactive, Web 2.0 encompasses applications that let viewers zoom, rotate products, see different views, integrate video, use avatars, and combine images for easier shopping. Personalized functions, blogs, wikis, podcasts, color identifiers, high-quality streaming video, and RSS feeds also are part of Web 2.0. **Wikis** are interactive Web sites that encourage collaboration among multiple users. Drawn from the popular Wikipedia concept, wikis are used to help employees collaborate on projects by originating, revising, and storing ideas and working documents. Some of the most effective Web 2.0 tools are graphed in Figure 7.4.

Some Web 2.0 applications that use XML-based meta data make search more effective. **XML tags** use code to describe information used by search engines when compiling their indexes. Mentioned earlier, meta tags that identify which keywords indicate content on a Web page are one example of tagging. **Tagging** is the process of marking a desired characteristic of a Web user and is a broader concept. Tagging is used to collect geographic, demographic, or behavioral data.[12]

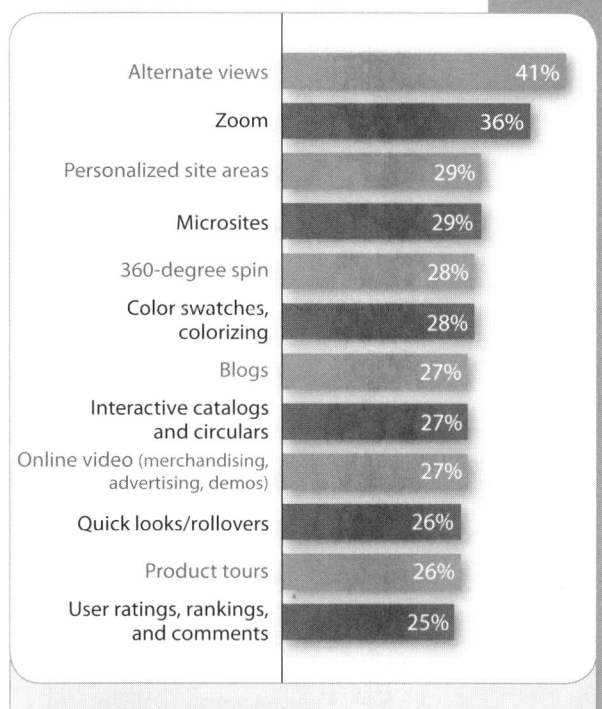

7.4

Tool	%
Alternate views	41%
Zoom	36%
Personalized site areas	29%
Microsites	29%
360-degree spin	28%
Color swatches, colorizing	28%
Blogs	27%
Interactive catalogs and circulars	27%
Online video (merchandising, advertising, demos)	27%
Quick looks/rollovers	26%
Product tours	26%
User ratings, rankings, and comments	25%

Most effective web 2.0 tools (percent of companies citing tools as effective). *[Source: Internet Retailer, March 2008.]*

Because it is more powerful than HTML, XML is used to customize tags that enable data interpretation between Web-based applications and organizations. One of the early users of XML technology was GlobalNetXchange, an organization for retailers all over the world. Using collaboration-enabling technology, companies could purchase business supplies and services through an auction-based system from a global marketplace. Many leading retailers including Walmart, Carrefour of France, and Metro AG of Germany were partners in this initiative.

Why is Web 2.0 so important? About 50 percent of online businesses surveyed intended to add Web 2.0 features to their sites in 2008 and over 93 percent said they would do so within a year.[13] Box 7.2 looks at the way Philosophy Cosmetics has implemented Web 2.0 technologies. Several examples of Web 2.0 applications follow.

Three-Dimensional Graphics Technologies using 3-D capabilities bring a broad range of services to customers and retailers alike. On the consumer side, shoppers relate well to virtual stores that closely resemble real ones and create avenues between brick-and-mortar and online experiences. Three-dimensional technology also makes examining automobile interiors or the front and back of garments much easier on the Web.

On the retail side, companies use 3-D internally to test store designs, floor plans, and merchandise placement. Brookstone, the unique gadget and gift merchant, was an early adopter of software developed by the Kinset Company. Kinset helped Brookstone create a believable rendition of its stores online. Some retailers expect to see virtual store applications used for human resource training and recruiting. Three-dimensional interactive training simulators could be more effective learning tools than those that are document based. Having 3-D virtual tours of headquarters or stores available for employee recruitment programs would be beneficial.[14]

Roaming virtual aisles may not quite replicate the experience of browsing in a store. But the requisite technology is well on its way to becoming a viable alternative as retailers reshape their marketing efforts.

360-Degree Rotation This activity is indispensable when attempting to view a product that requires close inspection. Nike features this option in the custom design section of its Web site. Customers are asking for details like this as their tastes in Internet technologies evolve and their desire for personalized products increases.

What's the Buzz?   Box 7.2

> *Philosophy's Doctrine on Multichannel Retail*

Philosophy Cosmetics may be a niche beauty brand, but the launching of its new Web site with Web 2.0 capabilities places it in the same league with some of the most sophisticated retailers. The company integrated its call center and store into a cross-channel platform employing technology from IBM and Coremetrics. As a result, Philosophy hopes to drive cross-selling opportunities, improve customer service, and send more targeted e-mail.

The site aims to be similar to real retail shopping. Devon Montoya, Webmaster at Philosophy, said that traditional Web pages are very serialized, as browsers move from one page to the next. By employing Web 2.0 technology, visitors to the site will be able to rotate through products on the same page. While scrolling through products, customers can hover over something they would like to get a sneak peak of, or drag and drop it directly into the shopping cart. In fact, the shopping cart is displayed on every page.

Philosophy also replaced its former customer service system, which used separate applications to support its site and call center, with IBM's WebSphere solution. With this, Philosophy can create a promotion and apply it across channels. When a customer contacts the call center, the promotion will automatically pop up on the screen in front of the agent if the customer qualifies. Philosophy will be able to collect data that will show total sales across channels and sales broken out by channel. The solution will eventually be integrated with Philosophy's retail store.

The company also expects to create e-mails that will complete the sale without being too intrusive. The e-mail solution enables retailers to create e-mails by choosing a template and adding images or links in WebSphere. Concurrently Coremetrics is automatically appending tracking so that when the e-mail goes out, all activity related to that e-mail is recorded. In addition, retailers can go into Coremetrics to form a segment and import that information into WebSphere to create an e-mail. For example, a retailer can define a segment based on all the customers who have abandoned a particular product, put an image of the item in the e-mail and send a message to those customers.

So what does Philosophy expect will happen as a result of these changes? "We enjoy a conversion rate and shopping cart abandonment rate that is far better than the average," Mr. Montoya said. "What we're really hoping to pull off is that we decrease those [abandonment] numbers. [Our ideal site] compels customers to complete the sale."

Source: Excerpted and adapted from Chantal Todé, DM News, May 21, 2007, p. 31.

With help from a technology called 3DVO, which is an abbreviation of three-dimensional virtual objects, the company OGIO offered its utility and sport bag customers 3-D modeling on its Web site. The company believes this imaging makes its site stickier. OGIO began with a line of golf bags and expected to extend the 3-D capabilities to its skating and snow sport products.[15]

Embedded Image Recognition Software The Hong Kong company MyClick Media Limited developed technology that allows users to access information about an image embedded in a MyClick frame—irrespective of the type of media—using an Internet-enabled digital camera phone. The frame acts like a bar code, sending users to a specially created Web site for more information or downloads. For example, a cell phone could be used to link photos to a related Web site.

One's imagination can run wild brainstorming potential image locations—magazines, transit advertisements, brochures, e-mails, garment hangtags, or television programs—all would work. Links to contests, coupons, and social networking affiliations are probable. Cosmetic giant Estée Lauder embedded a MyClick image on a brochure directed to Chinese customers. The link led to a site containing information on the company's products, and an offer that encouraged recipients to visit in-store counters for a free makeover.[16]

Mashup Applications Today's Web shoppers expect to be able to review similar items on one Web site. Now they can also compare merchandise from several other sites with an item they discovered initially. To make this happen, mashup technology is needed. **Mashups** are applications that allow aspects of one Web site to be integrated into the workings of another site. The technology behind this option is called an application programming interface (API). The use of mashups may help avoid shopping cart abandonment by customers who are unsure about a purchase. If shoppers can pull items out of their cart and compare them side-by-side with those of other retailers, it may turn the lengthy decision-making process into a sale rather than an experience ending in total frustration.[17]

Fashion sites that want to allow customers to add a scarf or a piece of jewelry to a dress that has already been selected use this technology. It also simplifies comparison shopping in an imaginative way.

Content-Enhancing Microsites **Microsites** are independent Web sites that provide value-added information or activities that enhance the customer experience. For example, a kitchenware company could set up a cooking school or design a site where users could exchange recipes or post video demonstrations.

Arby's, the quick-serve chain, set up its www.arbysrescuebrigade.com microsite to engage users to "save the world from ordinary fast food." Participants can share their own videos in a contest to have their work used on a commercial.[18]

Partnering with Univision.com, Home Depot launched an instructional Web show called Handyman Al Rescate. Using the title as a keyword, customers can access the microsite and learn how to create a patio or renovate a bathroom. Additionally, Home Depot expanded its market by bringing useful information from its in-store clinic to its Hispanic customers online.[19]

Streaming Video Improved technology and broadband access have refined streaming video. YouTube has successfully commercialized the protocol and brought new meaning to user interaction. Everyone can be a star, director, producer, or part of the audience. In fact, 75 percent of us watch online video during a typical month, according to comScore.[20]

Retail businesses benefit from video. It is easier than ever to install a video feature on a Web site and within the financial grasp of smaller firms. The company Fliqz specializes in customized video and offers several player versions. Some include tools that chart the number of plays, videos shared with others, and those that tie-in to advertising serving systems.[21]

Many people would rather watch video than read an advertisement—especially when the content is exciting. To learn how Saks Fifth Avenue used streaming video to bring its catalog to life, go to Box 7.3.

YouTube's *Insight* program has features that show potential for retail use. Insight lets video uploaders use the free service to track the numbers of viewers per day and the geographic region—including states and foreign countries—from where they emanate. Some marketers place commercials on the site, alongside movie trailers and other advertising.[22] Because of the popularity of Google's YouTube, it is expected to draw more attention from retailers as the pace of Web site enhancement quickens.

RSS Programs RSS feeds form the core of a group of online communication methods, including those involving news and social network links. **Really Simple Syndication (RSS)** is the technology behind major news providers as well as quasi news sites, community sites, and blogs. There are several versions of RSS and no definitive industry standard. Anything on the Web that requires change or revision may benefit from RSS.[23] The syndication aspects of this technology have retail applications such as revising online catalog pages and refreshing podcasts.

> **Box 7.3 What's the Buzz?**

> ***Saks Adds Streaming Video, Vaults Online Catalog to Next Level***

Saks Fifth Avenue is stepping up its Web game, launching a new video catalog—and industry first—on its Web site. The company describes the new "Fashion in Action" as "the industry's first ever dynamic fashion catalog," and the effort—a test—went live on its Web site in early 2008.

"We've been thinking about how to take catalogs to the next level," says Denise Incandela, president of Saks Direct. "People have been seeing deterioration in direct mail catalogs, and so we put a lot of thought into how we can combine our catalogs with the Internet, and make it much more like interactive TV."

The test focuses on Saks's three best-selling departments: contemporary ready-to-wear, handbags, and shoes. Because Saks knows that about 99 percent of its shoppers have broadband access, "It's been great for us," she says. "You can have movement, voice-over, music and information, with narrators talking about what's important in each look."

Runway commentary details not just the outfit, but also the shoes, jewelry, and handbags that work best. Incandela says the company chose the seventeen looks in partnership with its vendors, and that like all of its catalogs, this one has specific sales goals.

Although other retailers—even the luxury category—have been struggling as the economy has softened, Saks has consistently shown strong same-store sales performance.

The chain based its marketing on its "Want It!" campaign, which boils a whole season's worth of fashion into a handful of key trends for both women and men. Many of those trends—bangle bracelets, bright colors, and florals—star in the new video treatments.

Source: Adapted from Sara Maloney, Media Post Publications, March 25, 2008, © 2008 MediaPost Communications, New York. Available at: http://publications.mediapost.com.

<u>**Avatars**</u> We either love them or hate them, or so it seems. However, given the right target market, iconic characters, animals, and human-like avatars can enhance the Web experience. Human-like attributes somewhat breach the gap between real and impersonal. "Anna," the avatar on the IKEA site, lends a personal touch to the site's help center. Customers who are comfortable with social interaction in stores find this level of customer service gratifying. As well as personalizing a transaction, avatars are used to expedite sales and even become collectible products.

A new printing technology developed by MIT and adapted by Z Corp. lets individuals print their own 3-D avatar. Used initially by companies like Reebok to make prototype products, the technology has new retail applications. Players of Rock Band 2 can order full-color plastic figurines based on the virtual characters that

7.5 Iconic fashion avatars are used to elucidate the image of L'Oréal, the global beauty products company. [Source: Reuters/Suzanne Miller.]

they create while playing the game. Orders can be placed with Z Corp. using the Rock Band Web site.[24]

Sometimes the person behind the avatar is real, sometimes not. Candy Pratts Price, fashion director for Style.com, is portrayed in avatar form for the site's online video series called CandyCast that is sponsored by companies like Guess, for example. The avatar provides insight on fashion and pop culture using Ms. Price's own voice.[25] Examples of avatars that do not represent real people are illustrated in Figure 7.5.

If avatars are sounding a lot like Second Life, you are correct. Some companies are looking at that virtual reality model to develop meetings that encourage collaboration in workplaces. This format may be suitable for companies that have remote branches or stores with which they need to interact more frequently. If you would like your own avatar to personalize your e-mail, try making one at Meez.com.

Web 3.0 Evolution

The evolution of **Web 3.0** will merge advanced customer-oriented interactive capabilities with artificial intelligence. This fusion is the key difference between Web 2.0 and Web 3.0. Customer behavior will be studied in depth using social networking sites and virtual worlds that are ripe for the collection of data.[26]

Taking a step beyond social networking, the product graph is a tool that tracks complex correlations between products and users across several possible types of interaction. A **product graph** is a filter that helps merge product information with other constructs using Web 3.0 technology. Forward-thinking marketers believe the use of product graphs is integral to the selling process.[27] The technology incorporates product search, other shoppers' reports, and peer recommendations in one useable format. It implies that there will be constructive, ongoing dialogs between retailers and consumers, manufacturers and retailers, and peers with peers. This initiative goes beyond social networking and is the wave of the future to many online observers.

As the industry moves toward Web 3.0 technology caution is advised. Many people are concerned about the capture of consumer behavior intelligence via Web sites and the resultant use of personal information for marketing purposes. One study determined that about 60 percent of adults in the United States were uncomfortable with sites that use online activity as the basis for targeting of advertising.[28]

Some Web 3.0 activity is expected to occur in the mobile Web area. Yahoo! has constructed its own mobile site called Yahoo! Go 3.0.[29] This example is indicative of many more developments in Web 3.0 and further defines the next face of the Internet.

Foundations of Online Communications

The principles of copywriting remain the same whether the vehicle is print, broadcast, or online. However, the length and type of written communications are changing just as customer contact methods are in a state of flux. Let's begin by reviewing the fundamentals of copywriting. From that base, we can go on to examine contemporary methods of communication, including e-mail, live chat, and mobile contact.

> Copywriting Across Channels

Copywriting is itself and art and a science. Facts must be well represented, but presented in an appealing way so that customers will act on the message.

Structure and Preliminary Activities

Words flow freely when writers are feeling comfortable or spontaneous. When the pressure to perform is intense or deadlines loom, words become difficult to find and procrastination ensues. Nevertheless, the quest for clear communication continues. Different types of copywriting require different thought processes, and numerous facts and figures that are compiled before making the first stroke on the keyboard.

<u>Types of Copy</u> There are two general types of copy—headlines and body copy. A **headline** is an attention-getting word, phrase, or statement. **Body copy** is the descriptive collection of words that give detailed information about a product. Body copy can be very brief, comprising a sentence or two, or longer using several paragraphs to convey a comprehensive idea.

<u>Precopywriting Preparation</u> Marketers work closely with copywriters to impart accurate product knowledge, insight regarding sales objectives, and target market analysis. Merchandisers and product developers know the facts about products and services. They become part of the team responsible for content. Some of the material gathered in preparation for writing includes:

> All details that apply to items being advertised—colors, sizes, prices, materials used, and options.
> The type of advertisement that is to be done—product or institutional.
> Whether the merchandise is on sale or regularly priced.
> Who makes up the target market.
> Special selling points; benefits to the customer.
> Seasonal or newsworthy tie-ins.

Thinking about these facts and figures is crucial to the results of copywriting efforts. Some ideas that help to invoke the creative writing muse follow.

Hints for Creative Writing

At one time or another, most retailers and marketers are called upon to write some descriptive copy. The following suggestions are meant to spark your creative process:

> Jot down or type everything that comes to mind regarding the item that is to be advertised—even words that ultimately may not be used.
> Put yourself in the customer's shoes and ask: Why do I want, need, or have to own this item?
> Browse through Web sites, magazines, marketing communications materials, a museum, hot spot, or anything that helps trigger new ideas.
> Try to personalize copy and write on a one-to-one basis, using the word *you* whenever possible.

> Use your word-processing program's spell-checker and thesaurus to help find the perfect words.
> Write, rewrite, and rewrite the copy.
> Use a copywriter's checklist, but remember that all criteria need not be met. Some rules are meant to be broken.

Approaches to Copywriting

Selecting a style of writing that suits your target market is important. Using hypothetical product and retailer examples, here are three approaches to copywriting for print:

1. *Factual.* Using clear, uncontrived language, the writer elaborates on what the headline states. Emphasis is on describing the item, identifying the benefits, and urging the reader to purchase the product:

    Sale! Back-to-School Backpacks…Cool colors, tough canvas and microfiber materials, lots of room for books, lunch and your iPod. Get 'em while they're hot! $29.99 at www.its my backpax.com.

2. *Narrative.* Using this approach the writer uses a story, or narrative form, to impart the information. The message is subtle, yet eventually conclusive:

    Sooner or later it will happen to you. The perfect wave at Malibu and you're not prepared. Visit us soon at Malibu Dude Surf Shop or suffer the consequences of a day wasted. There is a little bit of surfer in all of us so coast in when the sun goes down. Boards . . . wet suits . . . apparel . . . repairs. We're open until 10:00 p.m. most nights. Or check out our Web site at www.malibududesurfshop.com for tomorrow's forecast. We're ready, are you?

3. *Emotional.* Now it is time to bring out the explosive words. State your message in a way that resonates with your target market. Creating a mood and playing on a person's innermost feelings embody an emotional approach:

    "Little Lukas lies in his mother's arms, she loves him."[30] *We want his future to be bright, fulfilling, and healthy. That's why we only buy organic cereals from Grandma Rose's Garden. It's a catalog for all of us who value the goodness of nature, no artificial additives, and buying the very best for our families. Call our toll-free number today for our free catalog or shop online at grandmarosesgarden.com. Nighty-night, Lukas.*

Online Copy Guidelines

Online copy poses some unique challenges for copywriters. The frenzied pace of online shoppers demands that copy get to the point fast. The typical three seconds that a retailer has to make an impression on a customer through a window display or print advertisement is probably lessened when viewing a Web site. The following suggestions apply specifically to Web-based copy:

> Put the most important piece of information, usually the headline, near the top of the Web page.
> Keep body copy to a minimum. If you do need to convey more information, break up the blocks of copy into smaller units, use more white space, or provide a "go to" link for further elaboration.
> Use bullets, headlines, and subheads carefully to organize copy, draw attention to key points, and keep eye flow circulating on the page.
> For most online copy, the factual approach is probably better than the narrative approach.
> Don't be afraid of hyperbole if its use accurately reflects your product line or image. If you honestly have the largest selection of motorcycle seat covers in the world, don't be afraid to say so at the top of your page.
> Include links in copy only when they greatly enhance the message. Many readers find multiple links tiresome.
> Think carefully about whether to include an opening advertisement or "welcome" screen before viewers reach a home page or landing page. The urgency with which most viewers approach a site makes this practice annoying even when the technology, imagery, and copy are superior.
> When in doubt, say what you have to say and then get out of there!

When developing words for broadcast media, including radio, television, and some Internet applications, the need to be heard or seen creates other challenges. The dialog method uses verbal banter between two people and is effective when reaching out to customers through the auditory sense. Question-and-answer formats fit this approach to information exchange and are equally useful in print on the Internet. Testimonial ads in which a person—often a celebrity—endorses a product are used extensively and are most effective if the star can be seen or heard. No matter what approach or channel is used, always ask for the sale.

Chapter 7 > **Designing Effective Online Stores** 281

7.6

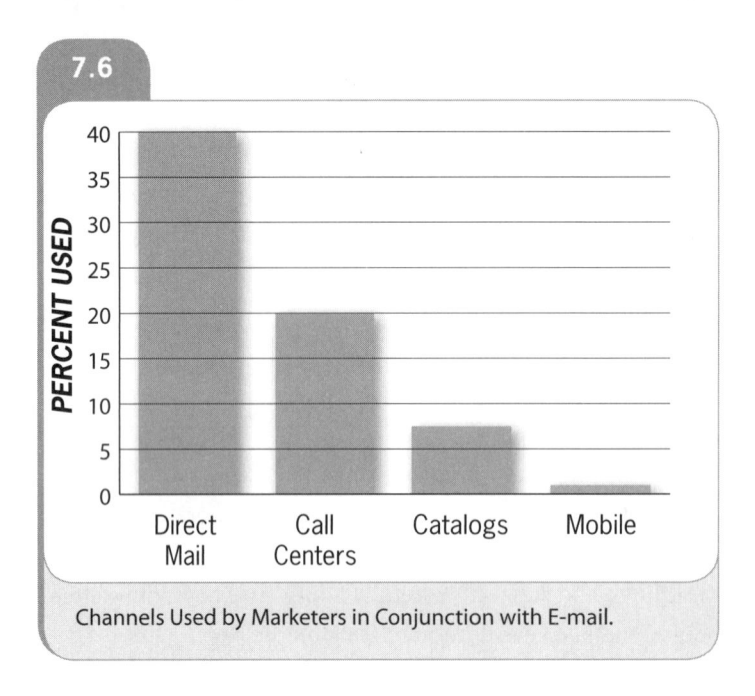

Channels Used by Marketers in Conjunction with E-mail.

Channel	Percent Used
Direct Mail	40
Call Centers	20
Catalogs	7.5
Mobile	1

> **E-mail Communication**

The use of e-mail has blossomed, and fortunately the mechanics are part of most Internet service providers' infrastructure. Retailers must make a determination about how to use e-mail as a Web site service, along with other complementary contact methods. Transactional and marketing-oriented e-mails, text messaging, live chat, and mobile communications are other options to consider.

<u>E-mail, Text Messaging, and Twittering</u>

Marketers are using e-mail across all channels as they segue from transaction-based contact to applications that embellish customer services and promote their products. A recent study looked at the direct marketing channels used by marketers in conjunction with e-mail. About 40 percent of respondents specified that their direct-mail initiatives were linked to e-mail contact.[31] This finding and the impact of other direct marketing methods are graphed in Figure 7.6.

Customers who have an existing relationship with a retailer generally look forward to receiving an e-mail from a company—especially when a special offer, contest, coupon, or event is involved. Retailers that manage their e-mail tactics well understand when e-mail inundation can be a problem. Bass Pro Shops, the outdoor sporting goods supplier, uses e-mail successfully and is careful of the

282   Unit III > **Technology Solutions**

amount and content of the e-mails it sends its regular customers. The company adopted software that lets it track not only what products a customer looked at on its Web site but also the items the customer put into a shopping cart. In that way, Bass tailors future e-mails more succinctly to its customers. After implementing the system, the company earned a 10 percent increase in sales over the prior year.[32]

Text messaging, with which we are all familiar, and twittering are briefer but socially engaging forms of Internet contact, and therefore ultimately important to retail communicators. **Twittering** is a short burst of news updating a person's present status or intentions. Twittering is done on social networking sites and is roughly the equivalent of a text message sent on a mobile device.[33] Using www.Twitter.com, participants can type up to 140 characters to get their messages across using PCs or mobile communications.

What is important is not the present context of casual personal communication like twittering, but the potential for brief but important contact in commercial applications. During the presidential primaries in 2008, both Hillary Clinton and Barack Obama used Twitter.com to send campaign announcements to supporters.[34] The CEO of online shoe retailer Zappos.com uses twittering to communicate with employees.[35] Although the service is presently underused on the Web, the fact that the power of word-of-mouth is now being conveyed in brief text messages or social network-based communications means that retail relevance is not far behind.

There is a downside to e-mail marketing. Much is considered spam and deleted by finely tuned filters. Even opt-in e-mails find it difficult to land in the inbox. On average about 24 percent make it as far as the junk folder in the United States. Europe fares better with junk mail delivery at 19 percent, Canada at 14 percent, and Australia at 10 percent. The percentage of e-mails lost varies greatly by Internet service provider.[36]

Live Chat

Live chat, also called live support, is a useful mechanism when retailers are identifying ways to improve customer contact. **Live chat** involves contacting a real person for further conversation while simultaneously using a Web site. The results of a study done by the e-tailing group surveying 100 top Internet retailers showed that 32 percent offered live chat as a customer service option.[37]

One of the benefits of live chat is the ability to direct a customer to a part of the Web site that he or she may have initially overlooked. Using live chat, the company representative can send a customer an appropriate link to a Web page. Live chat is one of the leading factors in increasing conversion rates. Customers participating in the practice are significantly more likely to make a purchase compared with those who have simply used e-mail.

Customers or retailers can initiate chat sessions but a measure of empathy from the retailer is involved. Retailers offer live chat to visitors when they have been online for a period of time and do not appear to find what they are looking for. Some use fifteen seconds as the point at which to initiate chat, others wait almost two minutes before offering help. Some retailers recognize that customers view an unsolicited chat session as too aggressive. Companies use other criteria for eligibility as they offer chat services. Dollar thresholds based on past sales or monitoring how a visitor has arrived at the site are other options. Limiting chat offers to individuals who are shopping for big ticket or high margin items or those in specific geographic areas are parameters that are sometimes used.[38]

Live chat services usually are not managed by retailers, but are contracted out to a number of providers. Successful live chat is a product of careful planning and selecting employees who are at ease using voice and e-mail communication—often simultaneously and frequently juggling more than one customer. Equally imperative is that retailers provide consistent, timely, and knowledgeable service to customers who want to chat.

> Mobile Commerce Communication

We can already transfer money, buy music, and order merchandise on our cell phones. Why not extend those options further? Mobile commerce is growing as improvement in mobile Internet technologies makes shopping easier. Wireless application protocol is the technology behind the rapid progress. **Wireless application protocol (WAP)** is the platform used to enable communication between cell phones and the Internet. The mobile services most used by consumers are listed in Table 7.3. The following examples highlight the myriad initiatives in m-commerce:

> Apple iPhone updates have made top-quality video and audio possible.
> More retailers are engaged in developing Web sites that are compatible with mobile applications.

> More companies are advertising on the mobile Web.
> Two-dimensional bar codes on products facilitate scanning by cell phones in stores so customers can compare products and seek more information.
> Texting is used between customer and retailer for rapid-fire answers and orders.
> Spoken commands for text messages and Web surfing are forthcoming.
> More geographical positioning systems will be used with mobile communications.

Partnerships between cell phone companies and search engines are reworking the industry. For example, T-Mobile and Yahoo! have joined forces.[39] By the end of 2007, Google, Inc., had formed affiliations with thirty-three companies ranging from mobile operators to handset manufacturers and software providers.[40] Many more mergers and acquisitions are anticipated.

In the retail sector, Best Buy made a concerted effort to dominate the sales of cell phones and related apparatus. The company represents most major carriers and opened a specialty division called Best Buy Mobile in New York City in 2007.[41] Niche marketing efforts like this are likely to be replicated.

Retailers, manufacturers, service providers, and search engines are pooling their interests and services to change the face not only of telecommunications but of retailing. Glitches are to be expected along the way. Just as Flash is incompatible with many search engines, Flash Player is not friendly with iPhones. Videos meant for the iPhone must be specially formatted to work in Apple's product. So far, Google's YouTube is the only video source doing this.[42]

Most Used Mobile Services   Table 7.3

MOBILE SERVICES	PERCENTAGE OF SUBSCRIBERS WHO USED SERVICE*
Text Messaging (SMS)	64
Multimedia Messaging (MMS)	39
Mobile Internet	14
Ringtone	6
Premium SMS	4
Game	4
Software/Application	3
Video	2

* Estimated percentage of U.S. subscribers who used the services in the fourth quarter, 2007.
Source: Nielsen Mobile, a service of the Nielsen company.

Mobile Marketing Association president, Laura Marriott offers this statement on the importance of mobile marketing: "Mobile works best when it is integrated into a multichannel campaign." She goes on to say, "As the medium grows, the playing field is similar to the Web fifteen years ago—the potential seems endless."[43]

The promise of mobile commerce is boundless. We have all heard that there is now more power in a cell phone than there was in the computers used during the first space flight decades ago. At the very least better communication with retailers online and offline is anticipated.

> **Contemporary Personal Communication**

Captivating customers in the first place involves listening to them and augmenting services that keep them coming back. Product reviews by customers and independent panels on retail or blogging sites are standard information sources for many online shoppers. Customers also request personalized sites, products, and services.

Blogging

Bloggers are influencing and driving retail traffic to Web sites and beyond. In the fashion industry, independent bloggers create buzz and communicate priceless information that is shared with other like-minded individuals. Although not yet a fully utilized tool, some blogs are making inroads in molding brand acceptance and strategy while providing useful product information to shoppers. Professional blogger Tina Craig of Bag Snob spent time with Oscar de la Renta as she prepared a piece on the designer. As a result Bag Snob and de la Renta partnered for events in the Dallas and Los Angeles stores. Craig does not accept free products from companies; she would rather purchase the fashion items she chooses to discuss on her blog.[44] This ethical stance imparts a measure of impartiality and objectivity to blogging.

Individuals who write blogs for the beauty industry are becoming more numerous and powerful as they share knowledge and how-to information with readers. Feeling pressure from some beauty product manufacturers and distributors to tout their products, most bloggers strive for objectivity as they evaluate products and services for their readers. Total Beauty is an online resource for disseminating beauty information. Based in Beverly Hills, the beauty product specialist has a network of about 125 bloggers.[45] The trustworthiness and timeliness of bloggers' reports is important to consumers. Blogging is a useful communication tool with great promise for multichannel retailers.

User-Generated Reviews

It is not a lack of confidence that motivates shoppers to seek outside opinions on what to buy, but rather the knowledge that they will be better informed regarding purchases that they make and that they will get better value for their money. Customers are using product reviews to endorse a purchase they are considering but also using it to learn about new products in the marketplace.

Software providers like Bazaarvoice and PowerReviews are enabling retailers to provide user-initiated product reviews for their customers. The online computer retailer Newegg has been successful in building connections with shoppers by implementing a review system. It believes reviews intensify its relationship with customers.[46]

Retailers recognize the benefits of user reviews and are integrating them on product pages rather than in a separate section of the Web site as has been customary. This makes it even easier for shoppers to compare notes with other customers. Called social navigation, this process is expected to help retailers increase sales.[47] **Social navigation** provides the impetus for shoppers to investigate products or reviews in a more intuitive and user-friendly way on a Web site.

Web Site Personalization

Layout and design are crucial aspects of Web site design, but so is personalization. Progressive sites learned that many customers like to control content. Some like to choose their own screen colors or designs. Others like to set up personal profiles, address books, and reminder dates should new product become available.

Many like seeing their first names when they log into a site, in the same way they like to be welcomed into a store as a regular customer. Through the use of log-ins, customers further tailor and secure communications with retailers.

Retailers use customer information obtained by cookies—benign spyware placed on users' computers for the purpose of gaining insight on behavior. Companies direct promotions tied to specific preferences of customers who have agreed to accept cookies. Personalization for or by customers appears to be equally useful and welcome, creating a dyadic communication model.

Today's shoppers seek recognition—whether through the written word in a piece of advertising copy, by e-mail, cell phone, or Web page greeting. Personalization will continue to be valued by customers and supported by retailers.

Search Engine Selection and Maximization

You have heard this before and you will again: the best products go unsold if customers do not know of their existence. If you are selling the most magnificent soccer ball in the world and cannot find a way to get your equipment to student, recreational, and professional athletes, what good are you? Search is of course the modern equivalent of target marketing, advertising, and marketing with high-tech capabilities all rolled into one magnificent machine.

> The Power of Search

Most online retailers use a variety of search tactics concurrently. The objective is to secure the best possible keywords and positions in paid listings in order to make contact with potential customers. Shoes.com has refined its Web site in several ways by adding customer interface tools and improved search functions. Read more in Box 7.4, What's the Buzz? The goal is brand building through repeated exposure and the development of a presence on the Web. The value is in the incremental increases in sales that are derived from search engine marketing strategies. The mechanics of search were introduced in Chapter 5. This section elaborates on the power of search in driving business and offers suggestions for search engine maximization.

> Types of Search

Several types of search engine marketing exist, and hybrids are evolving all the time. In Chapter 5 you learned the difference between natural and paid search. Natural—also called organic—search is free. This is the type of search undertaken when we research a particular name, word, phrase, topic, or company. However, as mentioned in Chapter 5, retail companies pay search placement specialists for the privilege of having their ads or messages seen by us when we conduct natural search.

The basic forms are further broken down into two broad categories: external or internal. External search refers to the practice of using a major search engine such as Google. External search can be paid or nonpaid.

Internal search is done directly on a company Web site, as, for example, when we hunt for something of interest. About half of all shoppers will type in a product or brand in a search box; the other half will navigate through a site at their own pace—and some use a combination of both methods.[48] Important to all types is that responses to keyword queries are drawn from the number and relevance of page links in a Web site.

> **What's the Buzz? Box 7.4**

> *Shoes.com Steps Up Its Site with Consumer Q & A*

Online footwear retailer Shoes.com, a subsidiary of Brown Shoe, is revamping its Web site as part of an ongoing initiative to enhance the customer experience on the site. After a one-year partnership with Bazaarvoice, Shoes.com is now tapping into user-generated potential by using Bazaarvoice's Ask & Answer tool, a social commerce service that lets shoppers post and respond to specific product questions on e-commerce sites. These Q & A conversations run alongside standard product information.

"When customers are shopping for shoes, they want to know how they are going to fit and what other customers have to say about them, " said Meg Armstrong, VP, direct-to-consumer at Brown Shoe. "This gives consumers a voice and a community."

The service is available for every product. Customers are encouraged to participate via an e-mail that thanks them for the purchase and includes a link to write comments about the shoes, and answer other customer questions. According to Armstrong, some example questions include "Do they run wide or small?" "What is the material like?" or "Would these heels look good with a cocktail dress at a wedding?"

This is one of a number of upgrades to the site that Shoes.com is doing. Although she declined to go into detail about specific campaigns, Armstrong said that Shoes.com has updated its product search feature and enhanced product descriptions and is trying to make the site overall more customer friendly. "Our strategy is to encourage a sense of community and interaction for people that are passionate about shoes," Armstrong said.

Source: From Dianna Dilworth, www.dmnews.com, March 24, 2008.

Several search engine marketing options are included in the commercial category:

> *Natural or Organic Search Paid Listings* These are text advertisements that usually appear above or on either side of organic search results. Costs are based upon the desirability of the key word and are charged to advertisers on a pay-per-click (PPC) basis (also known as cost-per-click, CPC).
> *Contextual Ads* These are boxed advertisements—often with graphics—that are placed near related printed content. In this case, keywords are charged for on a cost-per-thousand (CPM) basis.
> *Paid Inclusion* Most large search engines publish directories of Web sites. Some listings are free, such as in Google's directory, called Froogle; others charge on a PPC basis.[49]

> **Making Search Work**

Guidelines are helpful when working with specialized search marketing agencies known as search engine optimizers (SEOs). Web professionals select descriptors that are picked up easily during general, unpaid searches made by prospective customers. Researchers have learned that users generally click no more than the four top search results after employing a search engine. Here are several suggestions for maximizing the use of search engines:

> Choose key words carefully; there is magic in key words and sometimes subtle changes in emphasis are what get companies noticed.
> Avoid overused words or phrases.
> Use industry- or product-specific jargon and vocabulary with which customers are familiar.
> Allow for common misspellings when you establish keywords and Web site addresses.
> Construct a tight, cogent description of the company and its products; customize, customize, customize.
> Put yourself in the shoes of your customers: What do they intuitively type in when searching for products similar to the ones you carry? If they know only part of your company name, which part might they enter in the search box?
> Extend the search field by adding related links to your Web site. More exposure means more hits, but links must be meaningful to your target market.
> If you run a regional business, consider using local search engines.
> Use an SEO for the most professional insight available. Full and limited services are available for all budgets and search objectives.
> Seek publicity and other media coverage for you and your business. Anything that appears in print or broadcast media may be picked up by search engines and will advance your cause.
> Tap into free services offered by some of the major search engines. Google's Analytics software tracks key metrics including hits, keywords used, and customer conversion rates.[50]

Money paid to search engines such as Google was $10.7 billion in 2008 and was expected to reach $19.5 billion in 2013.[51] More than 60 percent of Internet users in North America use searches daily or several times per week.[52]

These statistics record significant spending and use, but all is not effortless in the world of high technology. In fact some companies are using humans to help reduce spam in the search process. This occurs when Web sites inveigle their way into top search results under false premises or when users get results that do not answer ostensibly well-phrased questions asked of search engines. People are employed by companies like Mahalo.com to sort this all out.[53] Despite the untold conveniences, short cuts, and wealth of resources brought to us by the Internet, it is refreshing to learn that there is still the need for the human touch.

Summary

Web sites that really grab us share several characteristics. They are inevitably easy to access and navigate and are astounding in their use of color, illustrations, and sensory elements. But most importantly, they bring us to retail products and services that we seek in record time. If merchandise is presented well, we may purchase more than we expected because online shopping carts are fun and simple to fill to the brim. Or we might chuck the whole thing and start over at another site. Making a site sticky helps alleviate this dire prospect.

Action, animation, sound, video, and interactivity entertain us while we shop and bring us back to a site. Social connectedness also helps encourage the sharing of good—and bad—experiences, hot merchandise, and upcoming events sponsored by a retailer. Activities might include an online forum or an in-store fashion show, and chances are some of our friends will have heard about it first. Communication on the Web is pungent, varied, and inventive.

Many tools are available to create artful and effective Web sites. Drawing from art principles and elements, Web designers plan appealing online stores. The selection of typefaces and the placement of merchandise in relation to other components on a Web page can make or break the customer experience.

Several guidelines help retailers implement or at least better understand the process. Selecting the right name and address starts the process, followed by technical site construction. Retailers decide how the site will be run, managed, and hosted. Customer security and a variety of secure payment systems are imperative. Promoting the site effectively ensures that visitors will turn into customers. Constant evaluation and renovation of Web sites are necessary.

Key Terms

AJAX	Mashups	Social navigation
Alternation	Meta tag	SSL certification
Asymmetrical balance	Microsites	Stickiness
Balance	Planograms	Symmetrical balance
Body copy	Product graph	Tagging
Content	Progression	Twittering
Dedicated server	Proportion	Uniform Resource Locator (URL)
Domain name	Radiation	
Emphasis	Really Simple Syndication (RSS)	Web 3.0
Headline	Repetition	White space
Hyper Text Markup Language (HTML)	Rhythm	Wikis
	Rich media	Wireless application protocol (WAP)
Internet service provider (ISP)	Sans serif	
Line	Serif	XML
Live chat	Shared hosting	XML tags

The array of interactive graphics and applications now available can help make a Web site popular and successful. The use of 3-D tools, image recognition software, mashups, RSS feeds, and avatars certainly helps customize a site. The evolution from Web 2.0 tools to Web 3.0 intelligent software is expected.

Copywriting is a useful skill and an essential ingredient in the preparation of product content for a site. Copy for online use relies on general copywriting rules and approaches as well as those specific to the Web. Copy is usually shorter, crisper, leaner, and selected for brief bursts of attention from Web site viewers.

E-mail, mobile, and contemporary online communication methods alter the way customers relate to retailers, their merchandise, and the services they provide. Personalization, customization, and shared product reviews are vital to keep online customers satisfied.

Understanding the process of search, the difference between free search and search engine marketing, and the thrust of search engine optimization brings Web planning full spectrum. Retailers whose Web sites demonstrate full knowledge of their company mission, how it serves the public, why it is better than the competition, and where it can be found succeed online.

> ## Questions for Discussion and Reflection

1. What does it take for an online retailer to attract and satisfy a customer today? Which of the common traits contribute most to the success of top performing sites?
2. Visit two of your favorite retail Web site home pages. Referring to the principles of design discussed in this chapter, what kind of balance is used? What component on the page is emphasized?
3. Discuss two ways in which selection of typography can enhance or detract from branding or company image.
4. Explain the two dimensions of Web content. What specific components are found in each and what is their significance to the Web site design process?
5. Review the eight steps of Web site planning and select the one aspect that you believe is most important to the overall success of the retail Web site. Justify your position.
6. What is the essential difference between Web 2.0 and Web 3.0 technologies?
7. What are the advantages of using interactive technologies such as embedded image recognition and mashup applications? Give a text example of each in your answer and use others from your own experience.
8. How does copywriting for traditional print and broadcast use differ from writing for Web site use?
9. What types of e-mail communication are most effective for retailers to use when providing customer service? Justify your choices.
10. Personalizing the online experience is one of the popular consumer trends today. What tools are retailers using to customize content and reach customers more effectively? What personalization tools have you used?
11. Search engine selection and management is critical to the selling effort for online retailers. In what ways can retailers optimize the search experience?

Notes >

1. "Wet Seal Announces Launch of New Online Fashion Community," Wet Seal press release, April 28, 2008, http://biz.yahoo.com/bw/080428/20080428005238.html.
2. "Newly Designed eddiebauer.com Delivers an Exciting Hands-On Shopping Experience," Eddie Bauer press release, March 17, 2008, http://biz.yahoo.com/prnews/080317/aqm116.html.
3. Staff, "Luxury Bedding Next Move for Vera Wang," *Home Textiles Today*, April 18, 2008, www.hometextilestoday.com/index.asp?layout=articlePrint&articleID=CA6552968.
4. The e-tailing group, "Winning the Customer," *Women's Wear Daily*, February 28, 2008, 16.
5. Ann Alden, "Costco Newsletter Mirrors In-Store Experience—But Could Be Improved," *DM News*, April 21, 2008, www.dmnews.com.
6. Ellen Keohane, "For Neiman Marcus, Dead Link Maintenance Is Not a Luxury," *DM News*, June 16, 2008, 7.
7. David Moin, "Bluefly's New Launch," *Women's Wear Daily*, April 10, 2008, 4.
8. VeriSign, Inc., "How to Create an E-commerce Site," ©2002, www.verisign.com/resources/gd/ecommerceSite/ecommerceSite.html.

Notes

9. www.verisign.com/ssl/secured-seal/faq/index.html.

10. Michael Estrin, "Will Searchable Flash Revolutionize Web?" *iMedia Connection*, July 1, 2008, http://:imediaconnection.com/news/19844.asp.

11. David Fry, "Web 2.0 E-commerce: A New Era of Competition," *E-Commerce Times*, August 6, 2007, www.ecommercetimes.com/story/58640.html.

12. Yoav Arnstein, "Elevate Interactivity With XML Tags," *iMedia Connection*, November 12, 2007, www.imediaconnection.com/printpage/printpage.aspx?id=17262.

13. "Web 2.0 Experience on 93% of Marketers' To-Do Lists for 2008," *Scene 7 Web 2.0 Experience 2008 and Beyond,* www.marketingcharts.com, © 2007-2008 Watershed Publishing LLC and Media Buyer Planner LLC.

14. Paul Korzenlowski, "Around the E-commerce Corner: More 3-D, Avatars," *E-Commerce Times*, March 11, 2008, www.ecommercetimes.com.

15. Rebecca Logan, "Spin Control," *Stores*, January, 2008, 52, www.stores.org.

16. Cate T. Corcoran, "MyClick Hopes Marketing Idea Clicks in U.S," *Women's Wear Daily*, April 2, 2008, 10.

17. Fry, Ibid.

18. "BrandNew: Curly Fries to the Rescue," *DM News*, May 5, 2008, 3.

19. John Consoli, "Univision, The Home Depot Create Web Series: New Web Show Called Handyman Al Rescate," *Mediaweek.com,* July 2, 2008, www.mediaweek.com/mw/content_display/news/national-broadcast/e3ib9d450805b496f0e53983ae3ca0824b0.

20. James A. Martin, "Don't Add Video Just to Add It," *Web Site Design Dos and Don'ts*, March 24, 2008, www.ecommerce-guide.com/solutions/design/print.php/3736196. ©2008 Jupitermedia Corporation.

21. Jason Del Rey, "Give Your Website the YouTube Treatment," *Inc.*, November 7, 2007, www.inc.com/news/articles/200711/products1107_Printer_Friendly.html.

22. Dianna Dilworth and Ellen Keohane, "Intrigue Grows Over YouTube Tracking Tool," *DM News*, March 31, 2008, 1.

23. Mark Pilgrim, "What is RSS?" O'Reilly Media, Inc., © 1998-2006, www.xml.com/1pt/a/1080.

24. Scott Kirsner, "Figure Friendly," *Boston Sunday Globe*, September 7, 2008, G1, G5.

25. Dianna Dilworth, "Style.com Debuts Video Series With Avatar Host," *DM News*, August 6, 2007.

26. Dianna Dilworth, "Shop.org Offers Web 3.0 Insight," *DM News*, September 24, 2007, 6. (Excerpted from presentation by Donna Hoffman at Shop.org Annual Summit: "The Evolution of Customer Experience: 10 Trends You Can't Afford to Miss."

27. Gordon Gould, "Shopping 3.0 in a Web 2.0 World," *MediaPostPublications*, April 22, 2008, http://publications.mediapost.com.

28. Antone Gonsalves, "U.S. Adults Wary of Web-Use Tracking," *InformationWeek*, April 10, 2008, www.informationweek.com/shared/printableAtrivleSrc.jhtml?articleID=207100981.

29. Dianna Dilworth, "Mobile Rising," *DM News*, April 14, 2008, 19.

30. "Something to Love," © EDG, Phatsac Music, 2005. All rights reserved. Used with permission.

31. "Channels Used by Marketers in Conjunction With Email: Data Bank, the Week in Stats," *DMNews*, April 28, 2008, 8. Statistical source: eROI.

32. Mylene Mangalindan, "Web Sites Want You to Stick Around," *Wall Street Journal*, April 15, 2008, B5.

33. Rob Pegoraro, "To Wit: Twittering," *Washington Post*, May 1, 2008, www.washingtonpost.com.

34. Ben Detrick, "The Social Hour," *American Way*, August 15, 2008, 20.

35. Don Steinberg, "Zappos Finds a Use for Twitter. Really!" *Inc.com,* www.inc.com/articles/2008/06/zappos_Printer_Friendly.html.

36. Dianna Dilworth, "Lyris Report Finds Email Getting Junked," *DM News*, April 22, 2008, www.dmnews.com/Lyris-report-finds-opt-in-email-getting-junked/PrintArticle/1092.

37. Don Davis, "10 Tips for Employing Live Chat Profitably," *Internet Retailer*, March 2008, www.internetretailer.com/printArticle.asp?id=25539.

38. Ibid.

39. Cassell Bryan-Low and Donna Kardos, "T-Mobile, Yahoo in Search Deal," *Wall Street Journal*, February 13, 2008, B7.

40. Kevin Delaney and Amol Sharma, "Google, Bidding for Phone Ads, Lures Partners," *Wall Street Journal*, November 6, 2007, 1, 16.

41. Samar Srivastava, "Best Buy Moves to More Mobile Selections," *Wall Street Journal*, July 12, 2007, B3.

42. Ben Charney, "Adobe, Apple Hit Flash Point," *Wall Street Journal*, February 21, 2008, B3.

43. Dillworth, "Mobile Rising."

44. Irin Carmon, "Bringing Bloggers Into the Club," *Women's Wear Daily*, March 28, 2008, 12.

45. Rachel Brown, "Beauty Bloggers Gain Credibility in Industry," *Women's Wear Daily*, June 6, 2008, 22.

46. Jesse Goldman, "A Rave Review for Social Navigation," *E-Commerce Times*, April 23, 2008, www.ecommercetimes.com/rsstory/62695.html.

47. Ibid.

48. Corey Lebow, "Searchandise Your Way to Success," *E-Commerce Times*, December 12, 2007, www.ecommercetimes.com/story/SearchandIse-Your-Way-to-Success-60696.html.

49. Excerpted from Shar VanBoskirk, "Search Basics and Best Practices: The Direct Marketer's Essential Guide to Search Engine Marketing," *DM News*, July 25, 2005, 8, 15. Material source: Forrester Research.

50. Kelly K. Spors, "In Search of Traffic," Wall Street Journal, April 30, 2007, R1, R4.

51. eMarketer, "E-Mail Performance Steady," January 30, 2009. Source: "U.S. Online Advertising Spending by Format, 2008–2013," emarketer, November 2008, www.emarketer.com/Articles/Print.aspx?id=1006890.

52. Kevin J. Delaney, "Start-Up Adds a Human Touch," *Wall Street Journal*, May 31, 2007, B4.

53. Ibid.

Chapter 8

Multichannel Customer Service

Objectives

> To define a framework for customer service planning.
> To outline customer expectations regarding service.
> To identify customer service characteristics that are shared by top retailers.
> To illuminate strategies that enable effective customer service across channels.
> To recognize the impact of crime on customer service.

> In Chapter 3 many changes in customer behavior were described. Here specific services sought by customers regardless of the channel shopped and those tied to individual channels are discussed. Multichannel customer service requires planning and execution—just like other retail strategies.

Parameters for Effective Customer Service Programs

Planning of customer service programs is multifaceted. Two essential ingredients are providing customer satisfaction to existing customers and trying to attract new ones. Many companies achieve respectable accolades from customers who shop their primary channel. But although established tactics may work well initially, they may not address customer idiosyncrasies as channels are added. One size does not fit all.

The conundrum when offering service through one channel and then expanding to multiple channels is a curious one. On one hand, many customers trade through all channels offered by a retailer. Their overall experience should be seamless and compelling, encouraging not only repeat business but lifetime value. On the other hand, retailers must adapt their customer service practices when they add channels. It is a daunting task to satisfy all customers across all channels at least some of the time. In this section, we'll first look at basic categories of services and then examine a mnemonic device for customer service decision making.

> Levels of Customer Service

When service is addressed in retailing, there are two general connotations: providing service to customers and offering retail services as a business.

Whether a company is a pure-play Web retailer or a multiunit specialty store chain that also operates a catalog and an online store, the basic types of service remain true. Customer relationship management plays a chief role in the delivery of services to customers by providing an ideology and framework for decision making. These topics are discussed in turn.

Macro and Micro Views of Retail Service

The **macro viewpoint** looks at retailing in the broader context of retail service businesses. As examples, a computer repair and installation firm, a dry cleaning establishment, and a hair salon are service businesses. The **micro viewpoint** looks at services that are provided to customers through multiple channels. Gift wrapping, in-house jewelry repairs, e-mail follow-up to a catalog sale, and do-it-yourself learning modules on a home improvement Web microsite are customer services. Customer amenities are sometimes free and often paid services. In this respect many retailers routinely charge for gift-wrapping, but others include it free with purchase.

Basic and Augmented Services

There are two levels of customer services: basic and augmented. **Basic services** are fundamental customer services offered by retailers. Generic greetings, department or merchandise location information, and checkout help are considered basic services. Accepting credit cards and handling returns are also ground-level customer service procedures. Customers expect and rarely question the availability of basic services. **Augmented services** are comprehensive, value-added services offered by retailers. These include but are not limited to gift-wrapping, delivery, personal shoppers, gift registries, loyalty programs, alteration and installation services, and the availability of electronic kiosks. Saying "good morning" to a customer who has entered a store or "welcome" to a new visitor to a Web site is a basic service, but greeting that customer by name personally or in print on a Web site is a form of extended service.

In brick-and-mortar stores the practice of personal shopping, including delivering extensive merchandise assistance and fashion or technical direction, is called **clienteling.** Clienteling is practiced by trained sales specialists who keep detailed records of select groups of customers with whom they have developed a relationship over time. Augmented services form the core of competitive customer service strategies. Sales associates for Men's Wearhouse practice clienteling, especially for professional men who comprise the retailer's target market. The company's database contains a wealth of information about customers' past purchases, and sales associates embellish this information with personal notations. Some hold wardrobing consultations in clients' offices or personally deliver freshly tailored suits to the customer.

All stores offer basic services, and upmarket retailers such as Nordstrom, Neiman Marcus, and Saks Fifth Avenue usually offer high levels of augmented services. Figures 8.1a and 8.1b illustrate customer services available at Saks Fifth Avenue stores. Not surprisingly there are exceptions to this generalization that high service levels are experienced only at upper-end stores. For instance, Target, a discounter, is known not only for its good values but also for its customer services. If shoppers cannot locate a sales associate, one can be summoned within a minute using a call button or internal telephone. All team members and leaders are expected to pitch in if customers need help. With their carefully developed merchandise and customer information databases, many multichannel retailers like L.L. Bean are capable of delivering detailed product information that is beyond the scope of average brick-and-mortar sales associates.

Saks Fifth Avenue offers basic and augmented services: The customer service desk offers information and provides for simple pick-up and deliveries, but the upscale store bridges the gap between basic and augmented services by offering concierge services. *[Source: Photograph provided by Lynda Poloian.]*

The on-premises Bridal Salon in some SFA locations goes beyond the expected with private consultation services available in a self-contained, grandly appointed area. *[Source: Photograph provided by Lynda Poloian.]*

Customer Relationship Management Practices

The expectations of customers have risen as rapidly as multichannel retailing itself. Retailers keep pace with the competition by offering more, better, and meaningful customer services. Customer relationship management (CRM), introduced in Chapter 2, plays a major role in the development of customer service strategies.

This management practice embraces not only basic customer demographic and sales data, but also more important lifestyle, psychographic, and attitudinal information. Retailers use a variety of statistical software and other technology tools to capture useable customer information. In an annual study for the National Retail Federation (NRF), 68 percent of retailers surveyed reported that they use data mining tools and 84 percent of respondents use Web site statistics. More than half use dedicated CRM software, and 78 percent use information for customer service purposes.[1]

Three tenets underscore the ideology of CRM: Know your customer, document customer behavior through capture of database information, and use that data to develop winning strategies that keep customers satisfied.

> S-E-R-V-I-C-E with a Smile

Single and cross-channel customer service strategies depend on good communication and programs tailored to target markets. Several key points from previous chapters are revisited here in the context of customer service as we explore how retailers answer the big question, "What do customers want?"

S: Superior Service Across Channels

Retailers increase the amplitude of their retail mix and the probability that customers will return when they design winning customer service strategies. When service tactics are multichannel, customers like to have a menu of choices. Retailers respond with loyalty programs, gift registries, and gift cards that are useable in their channel of choice. Customer-centrism is not new, yet the magnitude of customer options accompanied by vast technology support makes the viewpoint appear very innovative.

Among the cross-channel services expected by customers are the following:

> Researching in-store merchandise availability while online.
> Using online coupons or promotions in-store or with catalogs.
> Reviewing or confirming in-store events online.
> Researching online; buying in-store.
> Buying online; picking up in-store.
> Visiting a store; buying from extended inventory via electronic kiosk.
> Selecting from a range of wrapping papers online for second-address gift delivery.
> Comparing prices in-store; placing an order via mobile phone.

The scope of this summary reminds us of the challenges faced by retailers once they depart from standard customer services. We are a long way from, "Will this be cash or charge?" Consumer interest in various multichannel contact points is graphed in Figure 8.2.

E: Exceptional Content

Customer service plans are not successful unless product and pricing concerns are addressed first. This mandate touches the heart of the retail mix—merchandising. Many customer problems revolve around disappointing product assortments,

> **8.2**
>
> **81%** want the ability to *return merchandise to a store* even if purchased via telephone or online
>
> **56%** want the ability to *pick up merchandise at a store* after ordering online
>
> **56%** want *gift registry information* in the store, online, and over the telephone
>
> **37%** want access to an *online kiosk in-store* to conduct product research
>
> **36%** want access while shopping in a store to *view items they have tagged online*
>
> **32%** want call center personnel *to have a record of what they have been researching online*
>
> Consumer interest in multichannel points of contact.

stock-outs, wrong colors, and poor-quality fabrics or materials. Without the right products, the best customer service programs are doomed. Pricing should be current and consistent across channels. If inventory is not consistent across channels, pertinent product information should be accessible to customers—and retail associates—from any channel available.

R: Relationship-Driven Programs

Reaffirmation of the importance of lifetime value to retailers is evident on every selling floor—even if that floor is in cyberspace. Catering to existing customers is just as important as gaining new ones. Over time, the contribution to revenue from regular customers is ten-fold that of those who are more transitory. Relationship-centered programs go beyond frequent-shopper and rewards programs that are based only on money spent. Loyalty programs belong to a new breed of customer incentives that celebrate longevity and monetary value.

Relationships are nurtured across all customer bases. As an example, Dairy Queen is offering online games and other treats to some of its youngest customers, hoping that like previous generations of soft-serve devotees they, too, will become loyal customers. Read about DQ's initiatives in Box 8.1.

V: Visionary Tactics

Social networking and online communities provide a theater for shopper engagement and loyalty building. From individualized advertising placement, to reviews

Box 8.1 What's the Buzz?

> *Dairy Queen Launches New 'Tween Site*

With the goal of engaging the age 8–12, or 'tween, market, Dairy Queen has launched a character-driven campaign that includes a new online game called "Unite the Deeqs."

"Everybody knows—especially in today's world—that if you're going to engage tweens online, you'd better have a gaming component to that online experience," said Michael Keller, chief brand officer for American Dairy Queen Corp.

Dairy Queen worked with Space150 on the campaign, which consists of the online game at Deeqs.com, as well as an in-store "Deeqs" kids meal bag, posters, table tents, and trading cards. The campaign is more about the brand experience and it's also a way for Dairy Queen to extend its relationship with kids after they leave the store, Keller said.

Dairy Queen has promoted the Deeqs within its own properties since the site's soft launch in January, 2008. Since then the site has received more than 90,000 visits with an average visit consisting of 8.16 minutes, said John Grudnowski, director of modern media, Space150. "We're seeing about 300 searches a day on Google for Deeqs," he added.

The hard launch took place in June 2008, and the company planned to update and expand the site throughout the summer. There are also plans to make media buys and form partnerships to drive more traffic to the site.

Source: Adapted from Ellen Keohane, DM News, *April 14, 2008, 4.*

and recommendations, new media are changing customer expectations. Better options in emerging technologies also have an impact on innovative retailers.

Community Web sites such as "mommy sites" are fertile ground for messages geared to a large population of women who are online more than the average user. Statistics from a Pew study showed that 87 percent of all parents use the Internet. That usage rate was significantly higher when women who were expecting to have their first or second child within the following year were polled. In that population, 94 percent of women were online. In families with no children, the usage rate was about 73 percent.[2] Acknowledging and serving this market is visionary and productive.

The use of click-to-call services, mentioned in Chapter 7, is expected to evolve rapidly, optimizing retail efficiency and customer satisfaction. In addition to providing real-time contact between customers and retailers, advances in click-to-chat services help segment customers into good-better-best categories. For example, using a bronze-silver-gold system, retailers would offer gold customers click-to-chat options throughout their online shopping session whereas silver and bronze customers would be offered chat only when their shopping carts reach a certain monetary worth.[3]

Retailers with foresight are those that understand the implications of communication methods and market dynamics for future customer service programs. Changes in the technological infrastructure also affect the depth and scope of customer service and retailers' ability to envision more useful methods of contact and data management.

I: Infallible Follow-Up

Delivering goods on time and in optimal condition, keeping the shopper informed of changes in expected deliveries, handling returns well, and following through on customer inquiries in a timely fashion are the aspects of customer service that have the most impact on customer retention. Although these actions may sound simple, they can be challenging to implement.

A study measuring customer satisfaction derived from using catalog call centers identified strengths and areas for improvement. Catalog call centers achieved the highest marks across six different industry groups, scoring 80 out a possible 100 points on the American Customer Satisfaction Index. However, across all industries almost 20 percent of callers hung up before resolving service-oriented issues. Another finding emerged from the data: respondents who believed a call center was located outside the United States ranked their customer service experience lower than if they knew the call center was in the United States. As a result of poor service rendered by offshore call centers, respondents indicated that they were twice as likely to never do business with the catalog company again.[4]

Customers expect flawless follow-up on prepurchase inquiries and transactions across all channels. However, several factors retard retailers' efforts to deliver first-class follow-up. Heavy turnover of personnel, inadequate training or supervision, and faulty customer service practices interrupt the flow of services and contribute to the consequent decline in customer satisfaction.

C: Confidence-Building Communication

Hassle-free, clear communication helps build customer confidence in a retailer and satisfaction with the services provided. Some customers relish the personal touch provided by brick-and-mortar retailers. When customers find it more convenient to pick up goods themselves rather than reschedule their lives to be available for home delivery, traditional stores excel. The growing ranks of customers who prefer to order online and pick up purchases at a store attest to this tendency. Despite inroads made by online retailers to refine the return process, it is easier to return unwanted goods to a store than to a catalog or online company—unless they are multichannel. Retailers with brick-and-mortar stores experience greater customer loyalty because of strong brand identity exuded by a physical presence.[5]

Building trust in a multichannel environment is a complex endeavor as customers gain experience with new retail options. Confidence increases as risk is reduced. This confluence is affected by many factors. For example online customers view larger retail organizations as more trustworthy than small ones and also consider them more reputable. Privacy concerns are a more stringent risk factor for online than for offline retailers.[6] These and other aspects of online customer behavior are reflected in the graph in Figure 8.3.

E: Empowered Customers

Delivering optimal customer experiences requires finding new ways to empower customers. Through several types of personalization and customization, shoppers are finding their voices. For many people having choices of transaction and contact points is empowering. Shoppers find satisfaction in controlling the retail process and engaging in price negotiations when they are well prepared. Customers' increased awareness of product attributes goes hand in hand with a feeling of confidence about their ability to conduct business on their own terms.

If S-E-R-V-I-C-E sounds a lot like the song R-E-S-P-E-C-T, that is no coincidence. After all, mutual respect is what customer service is all about.

Leading Customer Service Providers

Culled from several resources, this section highlights distinctive viewpoints regarding assessment of customer service. Information is based on the e-tailing group's Mystery Shoppers Report, *Stores* magazine data from interviews with thousands of actual online customers, a study by the NRF and American Express that reaches across channels, and a synopsis of *Business Week* magazine's Customer Service Elite. A ranking of top retailers by sales volume appeared in Chapter 1; other criteria are used to evaluate customer service proficiency.

> Online Evaluation Using Mystery Shopping Reports

One method of obtaining information about customer service is to undertake objective reporting of data collected by mystery shopping reports. **Mystery**

8.3

Aspects of online customer behavior.

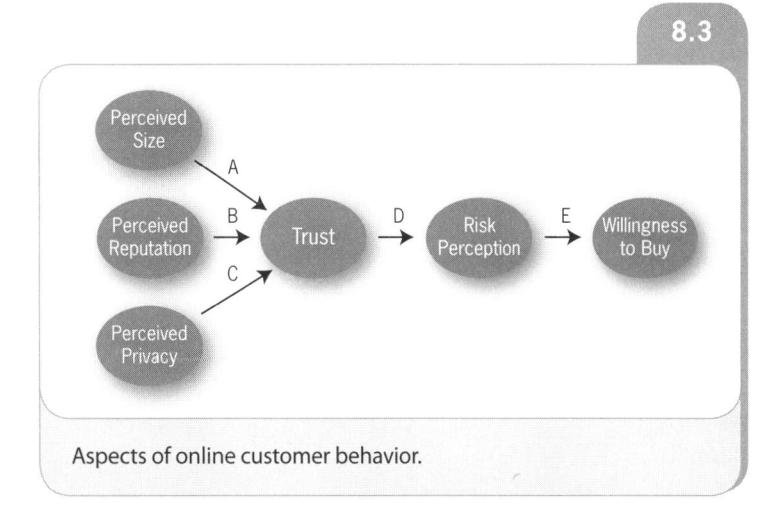

shopping reports are studies completed by retail research firms using specific observable benchmarks. Direct input from consumers and retailers is not sought.

The e-tailing group selects top online retailers on the basis of 12 customer service attributes. Some of the criteria include:

> Ease of keyword search.
> Toll-free telephone number included on home page.
> E-mail response to customer inquiries within 25 hours.
> Deliveries within 4 days.
> Six or fewer clicks needed before checkout.
> Real time inventory information available.
> Shipping status and order confirmations displayed in the shopping cart section.
> Service hours and holiday shopping deadlines available.

When performance of the Top 11 online retailers was compared with that of the Top 100 online retailers in terms of search page relevancy, response times, smoothness of transactions from product selection to checkout, and fulfillment efficiencies, BlueNile.com, the jewelry retailer, was number one.[7] The Top 11 retailers are listed in Table 8.1.

> Online Assessment by Customer Reports

Trade organizations, research firms, and retail companies implement research studies using data collected directly from customers. Participants are chosen at random or preselected to fit prescribed demographic and psychographic criteria.

Table 8.1 Online Customer Service Leaders Compared to the e-tailing group Top 100 Sites

COMPANY	SEARCH PAGE RELEVANCY (1–5; 5 = BEST)	E-MAIL RESPONSE TIME (HOURS/MINUTES)	NUMBER OF CLICKS (SELECTION TO CHECKOUT)	BUSINESS DAYS TO RECEIVE GOODS
1. Blue Nile	5.0	00:21	5	1
2. Container Store	4.5	25:00	6	4
3. Crutchfield	5.0	00:19	5	4
4. Discovery Channel Store	5.0	00:46	5	2
5. Fossil	5.0	00:43	3	2
6. Goldsmith	5.0	07:46	3	2
7. Lands' End	5.0	02:20	4	3
8. Polo	5.0	09:44	6	3
9. Pottery Barn	5.0	01:17	5	4
10. REI	4.5	06:37	4	3
11. Zappos	3.0	00:19	4	1
AVERAGE OF ALL SITES SURVEYED	4.8	31:23	5.26	4.2

Source: The e-tailing group 10th Annual Mystery Shopping Study, 2007.

In partnership with BIGresearch and Microsoft, *Stores* magazine conducted such a survey to learn which e-commerce sites customers use most frequently. Questions were open-ended, and no retailers' names were mentioned. The ranking was compiled using the number of times a retailer was mentioned in the survey process. The assumption is that frequency of response equals favoritism.

The "Top 25 Online Retailers Shoppers Like Most" are listed in Table 8.2. Notice that search engines Google and Yahoo! appeared frequently enough to warrant top ranking. This shows that search engines are the point of departure for many consumers who use search to find their favorite online retailers. At the time of this study, Google listed 2,300 beauty sites and 3,392 consumer electronics sites.[8] It is not surprising that Google is a gateway to sartorial delights for many people.

The study identified several other attributes of online retailers and customers. For example, six of the top ten online retailers are brick-and-mortar retailers that have successfully integrated their online channels. Had they not, being included on this online retailer superlatives list would have been impossible. When customers were

The Top 25 Online Retailers Shoppers Like Most — Table 8.2

RANK	COMPANY	HEADQUARTERS	MAIN PRODUCT
1	Amazon.com	Seattle, WA	General merchandise
2	eBay.com	San Jose, CA	Auction
3	Walmart.com	Bentonville, AR	General merchandise
4	BestBuy.com	Richfield, MN	Electronics
5	JCPenney.com	Plano, TX	Apparel
6	Target.com	Minneapolis, MN	General merchandise
7	Kohls.com	Menomonee Falls, WI	Apparel
8	Overstock.com	Salt Lake City, UT	General merchandise
9	Google.com	Mountainview, CA	Information
10	Sears.com	Hoffman Estates, IL	General merchandise
11	OldNavy.com	San Francisco, CA	Apparel
12	CircuitCity.com	Richmond, VA	Electronics
13	LandsEnd.com	Dodgeville, WI	Apparel
14	LLBean.com	Freeport, ME	Apparel
15	QVC.com	West Chester, PA	General merchandise
16	Yahoo.com	Sunnyvale, CA	Information
17	Blair.com	Warren, PA	Apparel
18	Macys.com	Cincinnati, OH	Apparel
19	LaneBryant.com	Bensalem, PA	Apparel
20	HomeDepot.com	Atlanta, GA	Home improvement
21	VictoriasSecret.com	Columbus, OH	Apparel
22	Chadwicks.com	Boston, MA	Apparel
23	AE.com/American Eagle	Pittsburgh, PA	Apparel
24	Haband.com	Oakland, NJ	Apparel
25	ColdwaterCreek.com	Sandpoint, OH	Apparel

Source: *Stores,* October 2007, F5.

asked which Web site they go to first when researching products online, 26 percent said they went to Google. However 1.8 percent of respondents chose Walmart.com in this category. The discounter was the only retailer in the top ten responses to this question. When consumers were asked about the importance of particular services, 62 percent gave the strongest vote for low prices.[9]

Going directly to the source has its advantages when researching customer behavior. Data is primary, not secondary, and is relatively objective if the survey is designed and implemented well. Disadvantages include possible bias of the interviewers or within the survey instrument, reliance on respondents who may not be representative of the intended sample, and misinterpretation of questions by respondents. Sometimes the most important questions are not asked. However, the rewards far outweigh the risks when surveying the actual users of a product or service.

> Evaluation Across Retail Formats

Assessing performance across more than one selling channel gives a full perspective of the marketplace, competition between pure-play and multichannel retailers, and how different types of retail formats measure up.

The NRF Foundation and American Express examined customer service across all retail formats as opposed to considering only online retailers. The survey, again conducted by BIGresearch, asked the question, "Which retailer delivers the best customer service?" Customer attitudes regarding service were also measured. In general, respondents expected the best service from restaurants and specialty stores and the poorest service from discounters. The results of the survey were announced at the annual NRF Convention and Expo in New York. The 2007 Customers' Choice Award Winners were:

1. L.L. Bean
2. Zappos.com
3. Amazon.com
4. Overstock.com
5. Blair Corporation
6. Lands' End
7. Coldwater Creek
8. Nordstrom
9. Lane Bryant
10. Newegg.com

The four pure-play online retailers on the list are Zappos, Amazon, Overstock, and Newegg. The others are all multichannel retailers.[10]

> Excellence Across Business Disciplines

Another approach to conducting research on customer service focuses on how retail customer service compares with service delivered through a variety of other industries. Rounding out our overview of customer service assessment are the results of a survey completed by *Business Week*. The news magazine's listing of "50 Customer Service Champs" includes insurance companies, automobile manufacturers, hotels, airlines, and retailers. In this study, companies were given letter grades for people and process categories. They were also ranked using a point-based service index. Responses regarding probability of brand recommendation and repurchasing were also included. At the top of the list is USAA, the insurance and financial services provider to military personnel. Retailers fared well, and L.L. Bean earned second place in the ranking.[11] Table 8.3 lists the retailers appearing on the *Business Week* master list, including the positions held by each retailer in the total standings.

A comparison of the results of several assessment tools and ranking tables shows that several retail brands rank high in multiple surveys. High performers have in common strong branding, customer recognition, and consistency in the multichannel marketplace.

Optimizing Customer Service

Customers are satisfied when retailers identify their needs, implement meaningful services, and provide effective follow-up. Several examples drawn from the ranks of high performers illustrate the convergence of customer expectation and retail delivery.

> Cross-Channel Services

It is becoming difficult to separate services that are distinctly cross-channel. This shows that multichannel retailing is working. Loyalty programs, payment options, self-service options, fulfillment tactics, and personalization are practiced across all sales channels.

Loyalty Programs

Rewarding customers for consistent patronage is not a new concept. Several types of frequent shopper programs are in place including:

> *Immediate Rewards*—Make a purchase and instantly receive a coupon good for a dollar amount or a percentage off a future purchase

Table 8.3   Retailers on the *Business Week* Customer Service Champs List

RANK	COMPANY	PEOPLE GRADE	PROCESS GRADE	REPURCHASE PROBABILITY (IN PERCENTAGE)	RECOMMENDATION PROBABILITY (IN PERCENTAGE)
2	L.L. Bean	A+	A+	47.47	36.96
5	Trader Joe's	A	A	78.10	64.71
6	Starbucks	A	A	60.40	57.28
9	Lands' End	A+	A−	59.00	42.00
10	Ace Hardware	A	A	58.32	52.10
16	Nordstrom	B−	B−	45.05	34.82
21	Apple	C+	B	60.40	54.74
22	Chick-Fil-A Quickserve	A−	B+	65.05	50.00
23	Amazon.com	A	A	66.67	66.07
25	True Value Hardware	B+	B+	46.31	38.92
33	Whole Foods Market	B	A−	63.11	57.43
39	Neiman Marcus	C	C+	39.91	32.43
44	Lowe's	B−	B+	56.74	55.19

Source: Excerpted from "The Customer Service Elite" Customer Service Champs Annual Listing, *Business Week*, http:bwnt.businessweek.com/interactive_reports/customer_service. © 2000–2008. The McGraw-Hill Companies, Inc.

> *Extra Incentives*—Credit card holders get preferential treatment for using their in-store charge during specified time periods, often before a general sale is announced. Customers who opt for a retailer-sponsored card usually are frequent shoppers.
> *Targeted Promotions*—Some retailers specifically target their high spenders, typically the top 10 or 20 percent of the customer base, for preferred customer shopping days, special events, or gifts.
> *Point Systems*—The more you spend, the more points per dollar purchase you accumulate. Rewards are as humble as a savings coupon or as opulent as a trip to Tuscany—if you are a member of Neiman Marcus's InCircle program and spend many thousands with the retailer annually.
> *Credit Card Points*—Retailers that offer Visa- or MasterCard-sponsored universal credit cards may extend special cash-back incentives or other point-based rewards for purchases charged to the card. Often extra points can be earned for purchasing preselected products.

What's the Buzz? Box 8.2

> Nordstrom Upgrades Loyalty Program Experience

With the average U.S. household belonging to twelve loyalty programs, many best-of-breed retailers are revamping their retention efforts in order to stand out from the crowd.

Nordstrom realized that offering cash back on purchases to frequent customers isn't enough to build the elusive quality of "loyalty." Instead Nordstrom's new program lets customers design private shopping trips to Chicago or San Francisco and gives them access to a 24-hour fashion emergency hotline, among other privileges. The new loyalty program "puts Nordstrom in the Neiman Marcus category," said Michael Greenberg, vice president of marketing at Loyalty Lab Inc., San Francisco.

Neiman Marcus's renowned InCircle program is twenty-five years old and considered the gold standard of customer loyalty programs with offers such as the Condé Nast experience. In addition to hotel and airfare, it includes lunch at the Condé Nast headquarters in New York, a visit to the Vogue fashion closet, a private tour of the Metropolitan Museum of Art Costume Institute's fashion closet, and a $500 shopping spree at Bergdorf Goodman.

"[Major retailers] can no longer go with a basic rewards program—they have to add experiential benefits to stay ahead of all the other options that are in the marketplace," Mr. Greenberg said. He said that many more retailers now have formal loyalty programs. According to a report from customer loyalty research firm Colloquy, the total number of U.S. loyalty memberships in 2006 was 1.3 billion, up from 973 million in 2000.

Retailers are also turning their attention to retention. Customer acquisition is increasingly more expensive, thanks to the rising cost of search engine marketing and postage. At the same time, the cost of launching and managing a customer loyalty program has declined, Mr. Greenberg said.

It is expected that the Nordstrom loyalty program will benefit from the new offerings. The retailer has not completely done away with more traditional rewards. Earned points can still be used toward the purchase of any Nordstrom product or service. Better participation rates are expected with the blending of hard and soft benefits.

The retailer's level of commitment to the program, and not just the offerings, also helps determine its success. "There are companies that are doing more sales from loyalty programs and it is usually companies that have incorporated loyalty into their overall marketing," Mr. Greenberg concluded.

Source: Excerpted and condensed from Chantal Todé, DM News, May 7, 2007, 1, 30.

Contemporary loyalty programs have taken rewards to higher levels, merging those tied only to accrued sales with more meaningful and often exciting and participatory incentives. Long-term customer satisfaction is the goal, not short-term gain. Nordstrom's loyalty program is profiled in Box 8.2.

In addition to formal programs, retailers are adding a variety of new services and experiences to the classic rewards roster.

Relationship building takes time. Successful retailers recognize that it is necessary to pique customers' interest through many different activities.

Payment Options and Preferences

The more options, the better, appears to be the consumer sentiment regarding payment plans. Retailers and payment system providers are complying as methods of payment stretch to meet demand. Security is the keynote when subscribing to a payment plan or simply giving a credit card number online or over the telephone. Payment services are categorized in three ways: e-mail-based services, mobile payments, and other options.

E-mail Payment Services Shoppers first register with payment service providers on a secure Web site, giving billing and shipping information. From that point on, personal information need not be re-entered on retail sites that participate. Most e-mail payment services offer customers deferred billing. One of the popular online payment services is Bill Me Later. Customers are e-mailed an invoice and then have the option of paying electronically, through bank-sponsored payment programs, or by mailing a paper check. Cost to the retailer for the service is fifteen cents per transaction plus a small percentage of the amount of the transaction.[12]

Since Amazon.com adopted Bill Me Later, the payment service has seen rapid growth. During the holiday season, 22 percent of online shoppers used Bill Me Later. The company found that the simplicity of its service, lower merchant charges, and affinity for older and affluent customers have given it resilience in the market.[13]

Mobile Payment Services As more customers use mobile commerce, the demand for mobile-based payment systems grows. Using services like Bill2Phone, customers enter basic information and are billed through their telecommunications provider. Retailers pay twenty cents per transaction and approximately 4 percent of transaction value plus a fee for facilitating software code. Mpayy's service is somewhat less expensive for merchants and serves customers who want to have purchase transactions deducted from their checking accounts.[14]

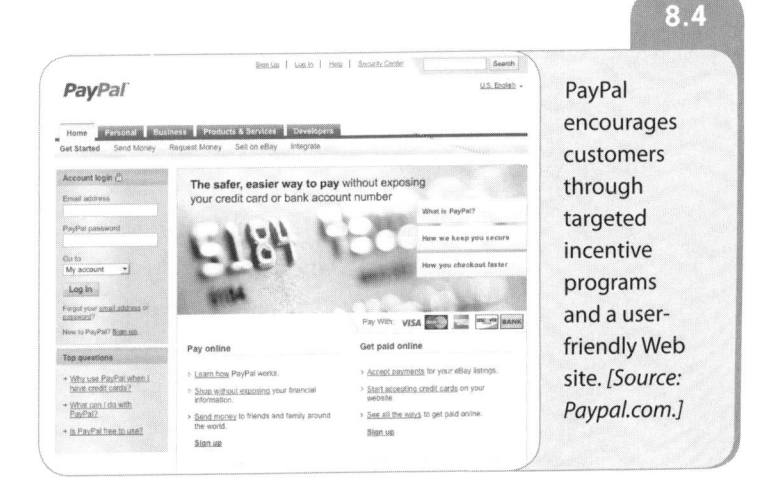

8.4 PayPal encourages customers through targeted incentive programs and a user-friendly Web site. [Source: Paypal.com.]

<u>Other Payment Programs</u> eBay's digital payment system, PayPal, is a third-party service and a pioneer in online payment. Online shoppers register at the PayPal site and are then equipped to submit invoices from online retailers to PayPal. Encouraging customers to use its service during the holiday season, PayPal offered a 20 percent cash-back incentive.[15] PayPal's Web site is featured in Figure 8.4.

It is not surprising that Google has its own payment system called Google Checkout. Users pay with credit or debit cards that have been registered with Google. Less expensive for retailers than many payment services, Google charges twenty cents per transaction, 2 percent of transaction value, and no set-up charges. Retailers that use Google AdWords search program pay lower transaction fees.[16]

Most customers find payment services more convenient and secure than divulging credit card numbers repeatedly as they shop. Retailers comply by providing secure sites with appropriate authentication technology. Technologies that are more prevalent in Europe and Asia, including one-time passwords, are being used to secure mobile phone applications, for example. **One-time password (OTP) devices** are secure portable credentials that simplify and increase the speed of online transactions. Credentials may take the form of key-fob tokens, credit cards, or enabled cell phones.[17]

Retailers have their work cut out for them. One poll showed that 38 percent of those surveyed do not trust online payment services.[18] Sentiment will change as customers become more confident about online retailers and extend their trust to payment systems.

Chapter 8 > **Multichannel Customer Service** 313

8.5a

Electronic kiosks located in Cabela's stores enhance the customer's experience by offering access to many more products. *[Source: Photograph provided by Lynda Poloian.]*

Self-Service Options

Some customers view self-service tactics with a jaundiced eye while others enthusiastically participate. Self-service checkouts are commonplace in supermarkets, home improvement, and some discount and specialty stores. Cabela's, the superstore for serious outdoor enthusiasts, features Internet access from departmental kiosks as well as specialty kiosks strategically placed in high-traffic areas. Sales associates encourage customers to go online for an even larger assortment of merchandise than is found in the impressively stocked stores. A kiosk in Cabela's—directly across from its mountain-like display of woodland creatures—is illustrated in Figures 8.5a and 8.5b.

Some customers prefer assistance in completing the sale; others are happy to do it themselves if it speeds the process. The computerized voice that insists you have not placed your product on the scanner, when you have, can be a source of

8.5b

The kiosk shown above is located directly across from the company's adventuresome wildlife display in the center of its store. *[Source: Photograph provided by Lynda Poloian.]*

Unit III > **Technology Solutions**

8.6

Reason	%
Lack of courteous service from humans	2.6%
Customer demand for privacy	5.3%
Customer demand for large selection of products	7.9%
Customer demand for low price	18.4%
Customer demand for complete/accurate product information	23.7%
Desire for branding opportunities	31.6%
Competitors are using self-service	34.2%
Desire for increased profitability	44.7%
Customer demand for convenient service	68.4%
Customer demand for fast service	76.3%
Desire for increased efficiency	79%

Reasons for deploying self-service.

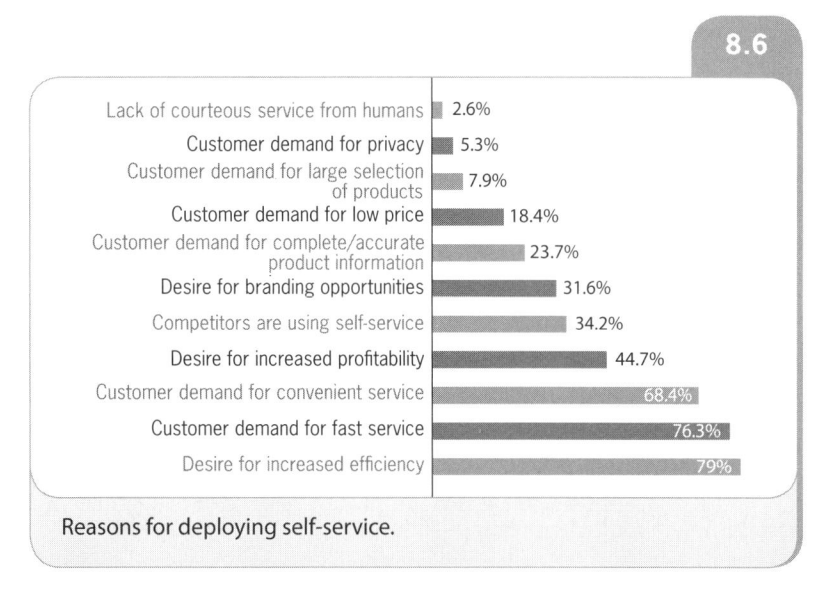

frustration for still other customers at the self-service checkout. But self-service encompasses more than just a do-it-yourself checkout counter. When we use an online shopping cart, we are using self-service. Kiosks enhance an acceptable means of transaction for most shoppers. The reasons why businesses use self-service and the uses of electronic kiosks to extend customer service are discussed in this segment.

Retailers have different objectives as they adopt self-service systems; the foremost reason is the quest for greater operational efficiency. Also important is the fact that customers are requesting speed and versatility as they complete transactions.[19] Each year the trade publication *Self Service World* surveys retailers and other business and industry sources about their use of and plans for self-service. The graph in Figure 8.6 depicts several reasons for deploying self-service drawn from these survey results.

Several examples in previous chapters looked at some of the self-service applications for electronic kiosks in retail stores or remote locations. Here the focus is on kiosks that extend customer services in convenience stores.

Kiosks were not used extensively in convenience stores until 2008 when new developments answered the needs of customers looking for faster service, particularly during rush hours. The solutions were not found in standalone kiosks but in those that are used by employees behind the counter to expedite food orders. The kiosk function is part of the store's point-of-sale system in this case.[20]

The company Coinstar has rolled out rental kiosks to several hundred convenience stores in the United States. Coinstar and McDonald's own Redbox, the supplier of self-service DVD rental units in McDonald's restaurants. Other new applications include kiosks for prepaid gas vouchers, advanced banking functions, and movie theater tickets.[21]

The volume of customer traffic generated by convenience stores makes the location a valid one. Customer service enhances one-stop shopping for families on the go. Kiosks provide effective self-service when placed for maximum visibility and use.

Personalization

From custom newsletters to design-it-yourself shoes and apparel, customers are captivated by personalization and view it as an extended service. Most of us gravitate to communications, products, and services provided just for us. It is human nature to like to see our names in print or hear our moniker spoken. Several examples illuminate multichannel applications:

> *IStorez E-mail Newsletters*—Collecting and organizing e-mail shopping newsletters for customers is the mission of online service provider iStorez. Customers design their own virtual shopping malls, so that they can view weekly specials from many of their favorite retailers all in one place.[22] Many individuals complain about lack of time—iStorez to the rescue.
> *Ripple AdCenter*—Empowerment is central to this unique service. Customers visiting any one of several retail locations where the Ripple media network is available can design their own television ads and select the specific retail venue where they want to view them. The company now operates through 400 stores in California, Arizona, Nevada, and Hawaii and expects to expand to 2,000 locations. Present locations include Jack-in-the Box quick-serve restaurants, juice bars, and coffee shops. In a study done by the company, the recall for content on Ripple programming in California was 90 percent and the recall for advertisements was 25 percent.[23] The technique is a passive yet powerful way to engage customers in the advertising process and increase viewership of the commercials.
> *Localized Display Advertising*—Personalization comes in many forms. Bonobos Pants, an online retailer of men's apparel, used Facebook's self-service ad program to create promotional pieces targeting Chicago Cubs baseball fans. The ad featuring pants was seen over 250,000 times and the "Clarks" pants sold out.[24] North Clark is the name of the street behind the right-field fence at Chicago's Wrigley Field.

> *Personalized Catalog Greetings*—When printing technology evolved so that customers could be greeted by first name on the cover of a catalog, retailers discovered a useful marketing tool. Jordan's Furniture is a retailer of good repute in New England. Its stores are testaments to shoppertainment and ties to the local community. One of the company's personalized catalogs is featured in Figure 8.7.
> *Customizing Apparel and Shoes*—Several online retailers offer customers ways to tweak available designs or start from scratch on their own. Zafu uses shoppers' measurements to guide them to retailers that sell jeans for their body types. At SteveMadden.com, shoppers can design their own high heels.[25]

8.7 Seeing our name on a catalog cover lifts our spirits and makes us more amenable to the retail sales pitch within. Jordan's Furniture runs destination stores in Massachusetts and has strong ties to the Red Sox Nation. *[Source: Jordan's Furniture; original catalog cover from Lynda Poloian.]*

The more engaged the customer, the more likely he or she is to make purchases. The service implications of personalization are profound as shoppers find gratification in the creative process. For some retailers, personalization is a competitive advantage. It distinguishes their company from others by providing services that few customers can resist.

> In-Store Services

Traditional stores serve as role models when it comes to brand building. Services that are rendered one-on-one thrive in an inviting store environment. Excitement raises the pulse of veteran shoppers as they touch products and sniff out bargains. Types of customer services offered in stores and several examples typify the brick-and-mortar experience.

Front-End and Back-End Services

Retailers distinguish between front-end and back-end customer services. **Front-end services** take place on the retail selling floor. Examples of front-end services include cashiers, customer information, returns, and concierge services. A specialized front-end service booth in Walmart's Neighborhood Market is illustrated in Figure 8.8. **Back-end services** take place behind the scenes or off retail store premises. They include alteration and installation services, deliveries, and repair work. As multichannel options expand, the distinction between in-store and online services lessens. For example, when we think of personal shoppers, it is usually in a store setting, but personal shopping services are available online also. Selling and fulfillment-related customer services also are considered.

Selling Tactics

Some services provide close contact with customers. Others coax customers into remaining in the store longer by providing features that are fun, thoughtful, and entertaining. All provide customer-centric features and ultimately are designed to increase sales.

<u>Personal Shoppers</u> At one time personal shoppers were available only to wealthy customers. Shoppers of average means fended for themselves or hoped a knowledgeable sales associate was available to lend an honest opinion. Twenty-first century personal shoppers run the gamut from reasonably well-trained sales associates to the epitome of personal selling specialists. Personal shoppers are available for teens shopping for prom gowns and tuxes, college students looking for interview wear, young professionals climbing the corporate ladder, and retirees looking for iPhones.

Any of the above-mentioned selling situations could be intimidating for shoppers. Sorting through a raft of possibilities is a formidable task even for the well initiated. Benefits of personal shoppers to consumers and retailers include:

> Saving valuable time, because personal shoppers preselect items from the myriad merchandise available.

8.8

Medicare information is readily available to customers close to the entrance in Walmart's Neighborhood Market. This is considered a front-end service and, for Walmart, an augmented one. *[Source: Photograph provided by Lynda Poloian.]*

> Minimizing the hassle of frequent trips to the dressing room; reducing stress for customers.
> Extending customers' knowledge base by presenting merchandise and brands of which they had not been aware.
> Educating customers when they are purchasing items with which they have little experience.
> Presenting more opportunities for multiple sales to retailers.
> Cultivating long-term relationships with customers.
> Enhancing self-esteem and sense of status for some shoppers.
> Increasing customer spending per visit and annually.

Personal shopping services in most large stores are set up by appointment, but some offer on-the-spot consultation services. Appointments could be made on the Internet, lending a cross-channel communication dimension to yet another originally store-based service. Retailer service providers retain well-trained personal shoppers. Having deep product knowledge, an affinity for helping people, as well as good listening and time management skills, are elemental characteristics of personal shoppers. Waiting too long for an appointment or having difficulty setting one up in the first place deters potential customers from becoming preferred customers. The service provides ample opportunity for retailers to develop deeper relationships with their customers.

Shoppertainment Features Combining shopping with elements of entertainment defines **shoppertainment**. Department stores do this well by adding a host of events, demonstrations, and participatory activities. Sitting in a massage chair on display near a health and beauty aid counter, fiddling with the controls, is an irresistible pastime and just might allow a shopper to linger longer and make a purchase. It does make us consider whether a virtual experience could ever replicate an authentic trial run in a department store. See an example of in-store shoppertainment in Figure 8.9.

Fulfillment-Related Tactics

Kiehl's is a retail chain that sells luxurious skin care products and makeup. The company offers curbside pick up at its Newbury Street store in Boston, a city where convenient parking is hard to find. Customers call in advance to place an

8.9

Brick-and-mortar department stores create participatory environments for their customers. Experiencing a sensory break in a massage chair is more pleasurable in person than in a virtual setting. *[Source: Photograph provided by Lynda Poloian.]*

order and then give another quick call when they pull up at the front of the store. A sales associate with package greets them and brings their credit card receipt. As this example shows, successful retailers go to extremes to fill orders, create a buzz through word-of-mouth, and fulfill customer expectations.

Fulfillment is principally a back-end function, but Kiehl's has elevated it to a promotional level as well. Customer deliveries and returns are important parts of the distribution process but behind-the-scenes aspects play equally important roles.

> Online-Centered Services

Several online-specific services are available for customers, and many are used frequently. Some are oriented to the individual whereas others are centered on social networks. Customers return to online stores for a variety of reasons. Heading the list of services is the availability of product recommendations. Other drivers of return visits are graphed in Figure 8.10.

Communication-Enhancing Services

Contact methods that help retailers provide online customer services are highlighted in this section. Included is an example of the power of product recommendations and insight regarding the impact of e-mail and chat services.

Product Recommendations Shoppers use recommendation services to help them make product decisions. In one study, 41 percent of online consumers aged 18 to 24 years stated they were likely to return to a site that offers customer recommendations.[26]

Other customers are responsible for recommending half of all new customers to the Newegg.com site. The online retailer depends greatly on peer-to-peer interaction and communication for feedback on its products and services. More than 250,000

320   Unit III > **Technology Solutions**

8.10

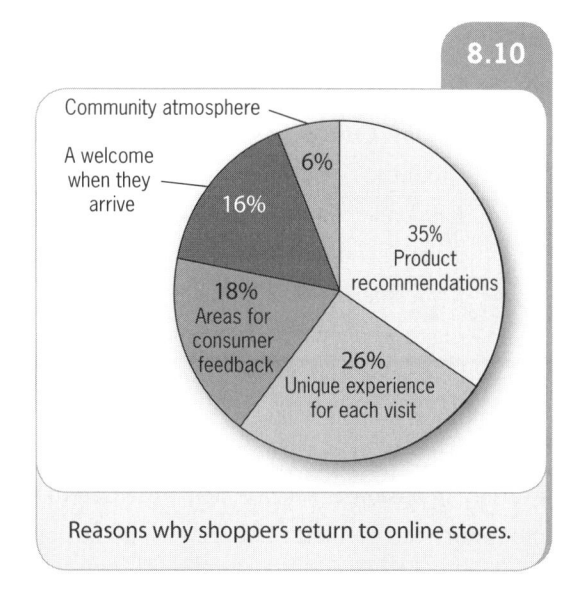

Reasons why shoppers return to online stores.
- 35% Product recommendations
- 26% Unique experience for each visit
- 18% Areas for consumer feedback
- 16% A welcome when they arrive
- 6% Community atmosphere

product reviews were posted to the site in 2007. According to Bernard Luthi, vice president of merchandising at Newegg, "It's about getting closer to the customer, making sure we're giving them every opportunity to give us feedback. That's what drives our business." The company has a presence on MySpace and Facebook where its customers gather. Newegg targets men between 18 and 35 who are technophiles.[27]

Customers trust other customers as well as independent experts, retailers, friends, and celebrities. Consequently, most retail Web sites now offer review capabilities.

E-mail and Chat Services Customer service is magnified when e-mail and chat communications are designed with customer convenience as the central focus. When communication is face-to-face each partner reads the other verbally and visually. It is more difficult to discern emotional nuance on the Internet. Wise online retailers interpret the immediate and long-term needs of their customers. This is done in several ways:

> *Being cognizant of the customer relationship life cycle.* Just as products have life cycles, so do customer relationships. New customers require different e-mail and chat services than returning customers, for example.
> *Monitoring and measuring response patterns of customers.* Being continually aware of response times, reasons for contact, and methods of resolving problems that have been effective over time improves contact with individual customers and development of e-mail and chat programs.

> *Recognizing that e-mail and chat are not always cause-and-effect communications.* Customer service communications need not always sell, but they should always deliver the brand in a positive light.
> *Reinforcing that e-mail and chat are integrative techniques.* Neither is used in isolation; rather, they are used in tandem with other forms of customer service.
> *Remembering that timing is everything.* Develop online empathy by listening to what customers want, and doing so as close to the moment they need help as possible.

Online Community-Oriented Services

A variety of customer service tactics are tied to social networking and other online community involvement. Private events, fan networks, advertising targeting, and blogging present unique forms of customer services.

Private Event Retailing A concept said to have originated in Europe is a version of online targeted promotion based on affinity group identification. **Private event retailing** uses invitation-only, limited time sales that enable a retailer to build viral excitement and a sense of urgency.[28] These attributes are useful to retailers of luxury goods. The aura of scarcity and exclusivity compels fashion-forward individuals and those with aspirational needs to buy. The process is participatory, and customers share information with other users within the social networking realm.

Fan Networks Rather then narrowly segmenting customers, some retailers are using a broader approach through fan networks. **Fan networks** are online social communities set up by retailers to provide interaction between regular customers for the purpose of increasing sales. They work like familiar social networks because they depend on customer profile information and the ability to form groups and invite others to join. However, the content is retail specific. Users can obtain more in-depth knowledge of merchandise, trends, reviews, blogs, and lots of insider information. Because the fan networks are operated through the company's Web site, users are on the premises and able to order merchandise while they are fully immersed in the experience.[29]

Advertising Targeting Advertisements generated by using information gleaned from social networking profiles are promoted as benefiting users of these sites, but it might also be argued that they are simply an invasion of privacy. Retail advertisers believe carefully targeted advertisements provide less clutter because they specifically address customers' interests and shopping preferences. Some customers do not want to opt-in to advertising programs whereas others welcome promotions and view them as a form of customer service.

The version used by MySpace is called HyperTargeting, and if preliminary tests are an indication of success, the system will become widespread. Travis Katz, senior vice president for MySpace International indicated that HyperTargeting tests produced a 300 percent increase in click-through on advertisements.[30]

Blogging Blogs are one way that information about products and services is disseminated, usually in the context of peer-to-peer or expert-to-consumer. However, some retailers are using blogs to promote their companies. Although not an objective source of information and not subject to ethical scrutiny, this is not an illegal practice.

The investigation conducted by the U.S. Securities and Exchange Commission into the actions of John Mackey, chief executive of Whole Foods, illustrates the legal position of retail blogging. A flamboyant individual, Mr. Mackey had posted glowing comments regarding his company's financial status under a pseudonym. The SEC determined that Mackey had broken no laws and was within his rights to practice free speech.[31]

When information from a blog is used to help customers build their knowledge base in preparation for making purchases, it is a customer service tool. Retailers find blogging useful for sharing product information and building brand reputation. Customers are obliged to separate the positive from the negative, the biased from the unbiased viewpoints.

The use of social media in conjunction with e-retailing is expected to grow. It will emerge as an avenue for customer service, relationship building, and brand identification.

There is no lack of imagination in the development of customer service solutions, and benefits are apparent for customers and retailers. In many situations, the more personal the information disclosed or extracted, the more vulnerable customers become. The next section explains the many ways customer confidence is diminished due to criminal activities.

Impact of Crime on Customer Services

Providing customer service adds value to the shopping experience. Unfortunately there are burdensome occurrences that have a negative impact on both retailers and consumers. Retail loss due to shoplifting, employee theft, and internal administrative error is called **shrinkage** or, alternately, shrink. Approximately 47 percent of all shrinkage is attributed to employee theft. Shoplifting accounts for almost 32 percent of losses and administrative oversights account for14 percent. The remaining percentage of shrink stems from vendor error, according to the NRF.[32]

Shoplifting and employee theft contribute to inventory shrinkage, but it is organized retail crime that is of most concern to the retail industry. Information on criminal practices that affect retail planning and productivity across channels is detailed in this section.

> Organized Retail Crime

The NRF reported early in 2008 that 85 percent of retailers were affected in some way by organized retail crime (ORC). Another 66 percent of retailers perceived an increase in such activity in the previous year. Organized retail crime was introduced in Chapter 1. Groups of criminals operate in multiple locations and legal jurisdictions, often on the same day, bilking retailers of merchandise. Companies and the customers they serve are victimized by ORC.

Influence on Retailers

In 2006 retailers reported losses of $41.6 billion due to ORC.[33] The financial loss is staggering, but the criminal activity affects other facets of business, among them:

> Lost tax revenue in states when stolen goods are resold.
> Losses incurred by supply chain and other business partners, including banks and transportation carriers.
> Losses in taxpayer dollars used to support deployment of local, regional, and national law enforcement agency personnel.
> Compromised customer safety and security.
> Reduced brand equity due to disturbing events experienced in stores when crimes are in progress.
> Negative effect on brand due to resultant press coverage.[34]

Individual retailers grapple with the aftermath of ORC, which greatly affects performance. The Gap Stores, Inc., recorded a $30 million loss due to organized retail crime in 2006. That figure represented 25 percent of total shrinkage. Jason Adams, organized retail crime manager for New England, said that by 2008 the percentage of shrink attributed to ORC could reach 60 percent.[35]

Allocation of funds to help deter ORC varies greatly by size of organization. According to the NRF's 2008 *Organized Retail Crime Survey Results*, retailers surveyed spend, on average, $230,000 per year in labor costs, although 8 percent of retailers spend more than $1 million per year.[36] Most large retailers have loss protection directors or organized crime specialists in their executive ranks—some at the vice presidential level.

Types of Organized Retail Crime

People are involved in all criminal activities against retailers, and crimes occur across all selling channels. Some scams are carried out only in brick-and-mortar stores whereas others are limited to the Internet. Distribution centers and other supply chain members are prime targets, as discussed in Chapter 9. Many crimes depend on technology—masterminded by corrupt individuals. Major types of ORC are cyber intrusions, credit card fraud, identity theft, and in-store theft.

<u>Cyber Intrusions</u> This category includes data breaches that compromise personal and business information. **Data breaches** describe the theft of sensitive customer and retail data that may involve fraudulent charges on credit or debit accounts. Cyber intrusions have received extensive media coverage in recent years, but only 5 percent of all data breaches involve retailers.[37]

Since 2005 retailers that have been affected include Ralph Lauren Polo; DSW Retail Ventures; Dollar Tree Stores; TJX Corporation, owners of T.J. Maxx; Marshall's; and Hannaford Supermarkets, a division of Belgium's Delhaize Group.

The TJX breach was discovered in early 2007, although the scam began in the summer of 2005. Criminals lifted 45.7 million credit and debit card numbers from the company's database, making the loss one of the largest in cyber crime history. It was surmised that hackers, using an antenna and a laptop computer, captured data from hand-held scanners, transaction terminals, and store computers.[38]

By early 2008 the Federal Trade Commission had investigated the TJX case and determined that the retailer did not provide proper security for customer data. The company was instructed to develop new security programs and is required to comply with security audits for the next 20 years.[39]

In 2007, Privacy Rights Clearinghouse estimated that 67 million customer and employee records in the United States were susceptible to fraud because of data breaches.[40] This growing problem is not expected to abate until better safeguards are built into computer systems.

Phishing is also a cyber crime, but one in which unsuspecting individual consumers and those on susceptible list serves are targeted, rather than entire databases. Because phishing offers arrive via an e-mail, the responsibility is on the recipient to judge their authenticity. Many offers are very realistic, even imitating the graphics on an authentic site that is being used as a guise for pseudo-governmental agencies, banks, and, with a minimal stretch of the imagination, retailers.

The best consumer defense from cyber intrusions is vigilance, common sense, and a bit of paranoia. Retailers benefit from understanding that their communications—particularly to new customers—may be met with a jaundiced eye.

<u>Credit Card Fraud</u> Devious minds go to great lengths to swindle honest citizens. Using hand-held devices at the point-of-purchase in retail stores, crooks steal credit card numbers directly from the cashier station terminal. Some offenders have replaced the stores' card-swipe terminals with others equipped with skimmers. **Skimmers** are small electronic devices that are embedded in card-swipe devices for the purpose of accessing information from a remote site. Scam artists use the data to tap ATM machines or fabricate fake credit cards.

Point-of-sale instruments that rely on magnetic stripe technology—omnipresent in the retail industry—are especially vulnerable. One study showed that credit card account number theft was highest in restaurants, representing 62 percent of incidents. Retail store organizations accounted for 12 percent.[41]

Retailers guard against credit card fraud by increasing internal security and being more vigilant during transactions. Sometimes laws work against these initiatives, because retailers cannot turn down a sale if a customer refuses to produce a second form of identification when using a credit card in a store.[42]

<u>Identity Theft</u> We have all seen the commercials in which an actor depicts a sweet-looking senior citizen out of whose mouth issues the voice of a tough-sounding character—or vice versa. The dramatization is amusing, but the reality of identity theft is not. A fraud survey showed that most identity theft occurs through mail, telephone calls, and as a result of stolen personal property. Identity

theft from telephone calls accounted for 3 percent of identity thefts in 2006, but that number had risen to 40 percent in 2007. The average out-of-pocket loss per consumer in 2007 was $691.[43]

Identity theft has two forms: high-tech and low-tech. High-tech crimes dupe the public through the use of online spyware, phishing, and bogus e-mails, for example. Low-tech crimes involve capture of customer information via automobile dealers, restaurants, and other retail stores. Other illegal low-tech activities include dumpster diving—examining garbage for personal information—and scanning personal and health care files. In another common practice, called "shoulder scanning," crooks eyeball personal data and access codes as shoppers punch them into card-swipe boxes at checkout.[44]

When crimes against consumers use the mail to reach unsuspecting individuals, the U.S. Postal Service (USPS) steps in. Some of the common scams include false applications for credit cards disguised as preapproved solicitations and merchant fraud, whereby goods are shipped to a false address. Cases in which a scam artist assumes someone else's account using stolen statements are called "mail diversions." Crimes of this nature make a strong case for vigilance by multichannel merchants. The USPS recommends shredding unnecessary paperwork, checking computers for security holes, and carefully handling transactions in which credit cards are not physically presented, such as online and over the telephone.[45]

<u>In-Store Criminal Activity</u> Thieves are at work in brick-and-mortar stores. Some in-store crimes are committed by employees or nonprofessional shoplifters, others by organized crime groups. Several techniques are used, including concealment, team theft, break-ins, and push-outs. Examples of each are highlighted:

> *Concealment*—Booster bags and hidden pockets are part of the repertoire of professional shoplifters. Booster bags include remodeled conventional shopping bags, diaper bags, plastic containers masquerading as legitimate merchandise, or large tote bags—some with false bottoms. People who steal by concealing merchandise in bags and hidden pockets are called **boosters**. Usually they line bags with duck tape or other materials that defy electronic article surveillance sensors. The "green" shift toward reusable shopping bags has also made it easier for booster bags to be bought into stores. Occasionally baby strollers are used as props for the concealment of goods.

> *Team Theft*—One of the distinguishing characteristics of ORC when contrasted with nonprofessional shoplifting is the well-planned group effort behind organized crime. Criminals use teams to conduct merchandise sweeps. **Sweeps** occur when teams enter a store, create diversions, and then grab as much merchandise as possible before making a speedy exit. Speed, not necessarily stealth, is the objective. When caught unaware, retailers and customers unknowingly place themselves in jeopardy as a team makes its getaway. Sadly for society, families comprise many of these professional criminal teams.
> *Break-ins*—Intentional invasion of locked display cabinets is another ORC specialty. Crooks are adept at breaking into showcases containing susceptible products, such as iPods, liquor, and medications.
> *Push-outs*—Placing one or more team members inside the store—occasionally overnight—teams work together to move products like LCD televisions out to a waiting van.[46]
> *UPC Code Switching*—Individuals switch UPC codes on products, either with existing merchandise in the store, or by bringing in their own pre-printed UPC codes. The thief, usually at a very busy time, picks a checkout line with an inexperience cashier, who never notices the switch.

Despite well-trained security staffs, video and electronic article surveillance, and other theft deterrents, criminal minds challenge retailers. Thieves use various methods to move goods through the underground supply chain. The resale market for stolen goods is intricate and elusive.

Methods of Reselling Stolen Goods

Offenders have several means of reselling or disposing of merchandise scoffed from retailers. Tactics have changed since the birth of online and multichannel selling. Prevalent methods include fencing, e-fencing, and fraudulent returns.[47]

Fencing A common way of reselling stolen retail goods through pawnshops or flea markets is called **fencing**. A fence is a person who agrees to knowingly purchase stolen goods. Criminals make approximately thirty cents on the dollar fencing goods.

E-fencing The contemporary version of fencing, aptly named e-fencing, primarily is done through online auctions. **E-fencing** is the criminal practice of reselling stolen goods on the Internet, usually after altering their bar codes. Participants in this illicit practice make about seventy cents on the dollar through e-fencing.

Many retailers believe that e-fencing could be prevented if stronger safeguards were put in place. For example, when an online seller tries to move many cases of a product at well below cost, reputable auction companies should be able to intercede. Most legitimate merchants believe laws must be changed to combat these transactions.

The most common type of e-fencing is auction fraud. The impact of this and other cyber crimes is highlighted in Box 8.3.

<u>Fraudulent Returns</u> Iniquitous perpetrators go to great lengths to alter receipts and merchandise tickets, and return goods to the retailer. Some print their own sales tickets or receipts from their truck-offices in nearby parking lots. Ironically, depending on retail policy, sometimes receipts are not needed to make a return. Most fraudulent returns occur during holiday periods. The NRF estimated that $3.7 billion worth of goods were fraudulently returned during the 2007–2008 holiday period in the United States.[48]

Fraudulent returns are the most profitable means of disposing of goods; offenders recoup 100 percent of the price of goods plus tax using this method. For huge states like California, the loss of sales tax due to return fraud is $250 million annually.[49]

Barry Joyce, manager of national investigations for the MarMaxx division of TJX Corporation, said that over a two-year period, $175,000 was lost on illegal refunds alone. TJX takes a proactive approach to ORC, with full-time ORC personnel on staff, partnerships with law enforcement agencies, and policies to prosecute and incarcerate guilty persons.[50]

Certain questionable returns are unethical if not illegal. Some customers purchase merchandise for one-time use and then return the goods soon after. Called "renting" or "wardrobing," this return practice is routine when the need for an expensive outfit for a wedding or prom arises. Returned merchandise that has been worn or used cannot be put back in stock and therefore is a loss to the retailer. Some research firms estimate that about half of all fraudulent returns are wardrobing returns.[51] What appears to most people an unethical practice or a crime is considered socially acceptable in some consumer circles. Retailers walk a fine line as they offer customer services yet must protect their assets.

Box 8.3 What's the Buzz?

> *Losses Rise in Online Scams*

Money lost in Internet-related crimes hit a new high last year, topping about $240 million, according to a government report showing increases in scams involving pets, check-cashing schemes, and online dating.

The number of reported Internet scams dropped slightly from previous years, but the total lost jumped $40 million according to the report by the FBI and the National White Collar Crime Center. The report, based on data from the Internet Crime Complaint Center, shows men lost more than women on average—$765 compared to $522 for women. The report also shows the amounts lost increased with age. Victims in their 20s lost $385 on average whereas people over 60 reported an average loss of $760 per scam.

The most common crime reported was auction fraud, in which consumers did not get the right merchandise they paid for. A customer might "pay $25 for a DVD that somebody actually recorded in the back of a movie theater," said FBI spokeswoman Cathy Milhoan. The second most common crime was nondelivery of a purchased good, followed by confidence fraud, in which scammers ask consumers to rely on them, resulting in a financial loss. About half the losses involved amounts less than $1,000 and one-third involved amounts between $1,000 and $5,000. The jump in money lost online might be due to new scheming techniques and generally more expensive electronic items being purchased online, said John Hambrick, a spokesman for the Internet Crime Complaint Center.

The report cites repeated increases over the years in pet scams, online dating fraud, spam e-mail, and "phishing," in which scammers send phony e-mails to retrieve consumers' personal or financial information. "The scam changes, but ultimately they're preying on the good will of people," said Milhoan.

Source: Excerpted and condensed from Christine Simmons, Associated Press, Washington, DC, April 5, 2008.

> Retailers Fight Back

To stem the tide of ORC, retailers deploy many tactics:

> *Loss Prevention Teams*—Retailers form their own loss prevention teams using in-house expertise. Most draw from security staff and management as well as employees from functional areas that interface with merchandising, sales, and distribution.

> *Employee Screening and Training*—Preventative measures include more intense reviews of prospective employees. Several psychological testing programs are available for this purpose. Enhanced training can alert

staff to potential problem areas and raise the awareness of loss prevention substantially.

> *ORC Working Groups*—Many companies form interdisciplinary groups made up of retailers, law enforcement, and fraud experts. An example of this is the **Law Enforcement Retailer Alliance of New England (LERANE)**, a working group of retailers and law enforcement formed in 2008 that will be sharing information on ORC in New England. There been a disconnect between retailers talking to one another, and retailers and law enforcement communicating with each other. In addition, different jurisdictions of law enforcement have been distributing information without informing each other. With help from the offices of the attorneys general of New Hampshire and Maine, LERANE hopes to solve this problem by sharing information with over 400 retailers and law enforcement officers.

> *Law Enforcement Training*—Workshops and seminars are held across the country to help law enforcement officers learn about the unique characteristics of retail crime. Conversely it benefits retailers to learn more about the legal process.

> *Public and Retail Industry Awareness*—Communication inside and outside the retail industry raises the level of awareness. This in itself is a preventative measure. Through trade associations, retailers learn how to cope with the aftermath of incidents and impede OCR.

> *Legislation*—Lawmakers respond to lobbyists who are knowledgeable regarding the impact of ORC on retailers and work to influence legislators. Drafting and passing legislation that helps prosecute criminals and protect retailers and consumers is the goal.

> *LERPnet Initiative*—The **Law Enforcement Retail Partnership Network (LERPnet)** is a system that logs major crime incidents and shares that information with law enforcement agencies and retailers. LERPnet is designed to help track, prevent, and apprehend criminal networks.[52] Some of the retailers using LERPnet include Coach, Kohls, Limited Brands, Office Depot, Safeway, Supervalu, Walmart, Williams-Sonoma, and Walgreens.[53]

Counterfeiting, intellectual property copyright and trademark infringements, and fraudulent check manufacturing are other criminal acts that affect multi-channel retailers, their suppliers, and customers. ORC compromises the ability of

Key Terms

Augmented services
Back-end services
Basic services
Boosters
Clienteling
Data breaches
E-fencing
Fan networks
Fencing
Front-end services
Law Enforcement Retailer Alliance of New England (LERANE)
Law Enforcement Retail Partnership Network (LERPnet)
Macro viewpoint
Micro viewpoint
Mystery shopping reports
One-time password (OTP) devices
Private event retailing
Shoppertainment
Shrinkage
Skimmers
Sweeps

retailers to provide services and is a major deterrent both to the smooth functioning of retail organizations and to their fiscal performance. Consumers are also victims as ORC losses ultimately contribute to higher retail prices. Retailers, law enforcement agencies, service providers, and legislators work together to thwart criminals.

No single channel can deliver all retail services to customers effectively. Multichannel service providers orchestrate their customer service policies with this fact in mind. Despite obstacles, including nonprofessional and professional crimes against retailers, customer-centricity is paramount to multichannel retailers.

The delivery of exceptional customer service is dependent upon the synchronization of all aspects of the supply chain. If customers purchase, take possession of, or return products through their favorite combination of channels, systems that encourage multichannel activities must be in place. Participating suppliers, manufacturers, distributors, and transportation providers need easily accessible data to reach optimal levels of service. These topics are explored in Chapter 9.

Summary

Customer service is rendered to provide satisfaction for customers and long-term selling relationships for retailers. All retailers deliver basic services such as handling sales transactions and returns courteously. The more upscale the retailer, the more likely it is to add augmented services such as personal shopping and loyalty programs.

The letters S-E-R-V-I-C-E identify areas that deserve reflection when planning customer service programs. The letters stand for Superior service across selling channels; Exceptional content, including merchandise and fulfillment practices; Relationship-centered programs for customers; Visionary planning techniques; Infallible follow-up at all levels of retail transactions; Confidence-building contact with customers; and Empowered customers who require involvement in the retail process.

There are several ways of assessing customer service programs. Several focus on reporting methods and some go to the source—the customer—for input. Others focus on one channel while some take a cross-channel approach. It is useful to see how customer service is rated in industries other than retailing.

Certain customer services have validity across channels while others are appropriate for specific retail formats. Those that work well across channels are loyalty programs, payment services, self-service, and personalization options. Personalization is one of the key directions for retailers today.

In-store services celebrate the physical presence of their stores in various ways, including the selling and fulfillment-related services. Personal shoppers and shoppertainment features are important for retailers to consider as they create an exciting environment from which to trade. Online-centered services revolve around online communications, including product recommendations, e-mail and chat services, and social networking.

The negative aspects of organized retail crime put a damper on retail efforts to serve customers. The problem is a large and complex one. Many parties are involved in finding solutions to rampant cyber intrusions, data theft, identity theft, and in-store theft. Shoplifting and internal theft detracts from retailers' efforts to trade profitably and provide a safe and pleasant environment for customers. Retailers, customers, security experts, legislators, and law enforcement agencies work together to improve the working and shopping environment.

> **Questions for Discussion and Reflection**

1. What is the essential difference between basic and augmented services? Give several examples of each in your answer.
2. Based upon the S-E-R-V-I-C-E principles, how would you answer the question: "What do customers want?" Include three points in your answer.
3. When assessing customer services, what are the benefits of mystery shopping reports compared with actual customer interviews?
4. Several cross-channel services were identified. Which payment methods seem most attuned to customer security? Justify your answer.
5. Customer loyalty is an elusive concept. What key policy shift has occurred in the planning and implementation of loyalty programs?
6. State and elaborate on three reasons why retailers are using self-serve tools? Use some examples from the text and your own experience in your answer.

7. What are two distinct differences between the delivery of customer services online and in brick-and-mortar stores?
8. How are retailers using e-mail and chat to enhance customer services?
9. Many new customer options have emerged from social networking and other online community resources. Discuss two tactics that you believe will most benefit customers and two that will benefit retailers.
10. How does organized retail crime differ from shoplifting and internal theft? Why is ORC a growing concern for retailers?
11. Discuss why and how fraudulent returns can be classified by different people as unethical, criminal, or somewhat socially acceptable. How are retailers fighting fraud?

Notes >

1. National Retail Federation and Ogden Associates Inc., "Return on Innovation," Presentation at the CRM Retail Conference, © 2006.
2. "How Many Moms Online?" *eMarketer*, May 6, 2008, www.emarketer.com/articles/Print.aspx?id_1006260. Statistical source: Pew Internet & American Life Project, 2006.
3. John Federman, "Creating Opportunities to Chat With Online Customers," *E-Commerce Times*, August 7, 2007, www.ecommercetimes.com/rsstory/58692.html.
4. "Issue Resolution and Offshoring Have Major Impact on Customer Pleasure and Pain with Contact Centers in Six Industries, Call Center Satisfaction Index," CFI Group press release, Ann Arbor, Michigan, June 12, 2007, www.cfigroup.com.
5. Keith Burgess, "Stores Are Increasingly Important in Multichannel Retail Supply Chain," October 4, 2007, www.supplychainbrain.com.
6. DMS Retail, "E-tailing and Multi-Channel Retailing," www.dmsretail.com/etailing.htm, modified April 28, 2008.
7. "Online Customer Service Excellence: Top Performing E-sites Deliver Exemplary Customer Service," *E-Tail Detail* report, January 17, 2008. Based on *10th Annual Mystery Shopping Study*, e-tailing group, Chicago, IL, km@e-tailing.com.
8. Peter Johnston, "Favorite 50 The Online Retailers That Shoppers Like Most," *Stores*, October 2007, F5.
9. Ibid., R6, R11, R12.
10. "L. L. Bean Number One in Customer Service, According to NRF Foundation/American Express Survey," National Retail Federation press release, www.nrf.com.
11. "The Customer Service Elite: Customer Service Champs, Annual Listing," *Business Week*, http://bwnt.businessweek.com/interactive_reports/customer_service/. © 2000–2008 The McGraw Hill Companies, Inc.
12. Paul Demery, "Examining Payment Options to Find More Ways Into Consumers' Wallets," *Internet Retailer*, April 2008, 14.
13. Keith Regan, "Bill Me Later: The 'Frictionless' Online Payment Alternative," *E-Commerce Times*, April 29, 2008, www.ecommercetimes.com.
14. Ibid.
15. Mylene Mangalinden, "Web Shopping: New Perks and Risks," *Wall Street Journal*, December 5, 2007, D1, D8.
16. Demery, *Internet Retailer*.
17. VeriSign, Inc. White Paper, "A Guide to Providing Proactive Protection to Consumer Online Transactions," © VeriSign 2008, 7, www.verisign.com.
18. "U.S. Customers Wary of Online Payments," *eMarketer*, April 10, 2008, www.emarketer.com. Statistical source: Gemalto Digital Touch Barometer.
19. James Bickers, "The End Is Near," *Self Service World*, 2007 Self Service World Market Survey. Graph 2: Why are you deploying self-service? December 2007, 18-19.

20. Patrick Avery, "Kiosks Take Over C-Stores," *Self Service World*, November 14, 2007, www.selfserviceworld.com/article.php?id=18814.
21. Ibid.
22. Keith Regan, "iStorez: Putting a Fresh Gloss on Email Newsletter," *E-Commerce Times*, March 10, 2008, www.ecommercetimes.com.
23. Chantal Todé, "New Online Tool from Ripple Goes Local," *DM News*, May 7, 2007, 28.
24. Shira Ovide, "Do-It-Yourself Display Ads May Reshape Online Marketing," *Wall Street Journal*, May 7, 2008, B3B.
25. Maria Puente, "Online Shopping: Now It's Personal," *USA Today*, www.usatoday.com/life/lifestyle/fashion/2007-07-31-online-shopping_N.htm.
26. "Online Shoppers Will Return to Socialize, Survey Finds," *Internet Retailer,* April 15, 2008, www.internet retailer.com/print/article.asp?id=26062.
27. Don Davis, "Raising the Stakes," *Internet Retailer*, May 2008, 31, 32.
28. David Katz and Marc Osofsky, "Online Communities: What Should a Retailer Do?" Optaros White Paper, © Optaros 2008, 2.
29. Ibid., 3-4.
30. Jeremy Kirk, IDG News Service, "MySpace User Ad Targeting Will Be Optional," *InfoWorld*, April 29, 2008, www.infoworld.com/archives/emailPrint.jsp.
31. Steven Russolillo, "Whole Foods CEO Returns to Blogging as Probe Ends," *Wall Street Journal*, May 28, 2008, B3.
32. Joseph LaRocca, vice president of Loss Prevention, National Retail Federation. Presentation at the New England Organized Retail Crime Symposium, Worcester, MA, September 13, 2007.
33. LaRocca, NRF.
34. Ibid.
35. Jason Adams, Organized Retail Crime Manager, New England Region, The Gap Panel presentationat the New England Organized Retail Crime Symposium, Worcester, MA, September 13, 2007.
36. NRF Survey Results.
37. LaRocca, NRF.
38. Joseph Pereira, "How Credit-Card Data Went Out Wireless Door," *Wall Street Journal*, May 7, 2007, A1, A12.
39. Lauren Bell, "TJX, Reed Elsevier Data Breach Cases End in Settlements," *DM News*, March 31, 2008, 3.
40. Denise Power, "More Data Safety Issues Expected in Year Ahead," *Women's Wear Daily*, January 3, 2008, 5.
41. Joseph Pereira, "Skimming Devices Target Debit-Card Readers," *Wall Street Journal*.,March 8, 2007, B1-B2. Statistical source: Ambiron Trustwave.
42. Ibid.
43. "Most Identity Theft Occurs Offline," *eMarketer,* February 14, 2008, www.emarketer.com/Articles/Print.aspx?id=1005940&src=print_article_graybar_article. Statistical source: 2008 Identity Fraud Survey, Javelin Strategy & Research.
44. Joseph Kleinberg, Inspector, United States Postal Service. Federal Agency panel presentation at the New England Retail Crime Symposium, Worcester, MA, September 13, 2007.
45. Ibid.
46. Brendan Fitzgerald, Investigator, Assets Protection, Target. Panel presentation at the New England Organized Retail Crime Symposium, Worcester, MA, September 13, 2007.
47. LaRocca, NRF.
48. "Trends: Numbers Worth Counting," *Stores*, January 2008, 22. Statistical source: National Retail Federation.
49. LaRocca, NRF.
50. Barry Joyce, Manager of National Investigations, Marmaxx National Taskforce, Division TJX Corporation. Panel presentation, "Evolution of ORC," at the New England Retail Crime Symposium, Worcester, MA, September 13, 2007.
51. David Speights and Mark Hilinski, "Return Fraud and Abuse: How to Protect Profits," *Retailing Issues Letter* 17, no. 1 (2005): 2. Center for Retailing Studies, Mays Business School, Texas A&M University. Statistical source: The Return Exchange.
52. NRF 2007 Study and LaRocca, NRF.
53. Ibid.

Chapter 9

Synchronizing the Supply Chain

Objectives

> To explain the function and membership of the supply chain.
> To state the goals of supply chain management.
> To identify key collaborative activities among supply chain members.
> To relate how technology increases effectiveness of the distribution process across channels.
> To discern new forms of strategic partnerships and direction among supply chain members.

> The supply chain is responsive to customer demand from product inception to final sale. The **supply chain** includes manufacturers, suppliers, distributors, and retailers. Members of the marketing channel work to ensure timely delivery of products to ultimate consumers. Efficiencies within the supply chain are fueled by technology, progressive management, and collaboration.

Supply Chain Membership and Function

The entire process is customer-centric, and contributions from each player in the channel are synchronized to meet demand and return a profit. Let's look at the businesses involved and the purposes that they serve in the supply chain.

> Functional Areas and Participants

The supply chain comprises three main functional areas: production, distribution, and customer interface.

Production

Activities such as manufacturing, contracting, and product sourcing are part of production. Manufacturers are full-service companies that are responsible for the construction of finished goods. For example, in the apparel industry designing, pattern making and grading, cutting, sewing, and finishing are part of the manufacturing process. **Product sourcing** refers to the identification of resources such as raw materials, textile goods, and components for manufactured goods or finished products for resale. Product developers who create private-label merchandise engage in product sourcing and use the services of manufacturers and contractors to produce their lines. Contractors perform some manufacturing processes but are not considered full-service companies.

Distribution

Distribution involves logistics: it includes all activities required to physically move the product through the supply chain from manufacturers to final customers, including transportation, warehousing, inventory management, and shrinkage control. Distribution manifests the concept called *place* in the "4 Ps of marketing." (The other three Ps are *product, price,* and *promotion*.) Supply chain members that are part of distribution include transportation companies, wholesalers, and distribution and fulfillment centers.

    Physical distribution is the process of transporting goods from producer to retailer. Physical distribution operations include receiving, processing, storing, picking and packing, shipping, and stock replenishment. The selection of appropriate delivery networks, transportation scheduling, and traffic management are parts of logistics planning.

9.1a Mothers Work, Inc. operates several retail formats including specialty and superstores for expectant mothers. [Source: Photograph provided by Lynda Poloian.]

Warehousing is the process of housing merchandise at various stages of the physical distribution process. Warehouses may be publicly or privately owned. Major retailers rely on a network of strategically placed warehouses called distribution centers. **Automated storage and retrieval (ASR)** refers to warehousing systems that combine the use of computer control of stock records with mechanical handling. In the stock-holding area of a food distributor that uses ASR, one might see pet food next to paper towels and beverages next to cereal because this placement of products has been deemed more efficient. The capital cost of automation can be measured against labor savings, better inventory control, and better customer service.

Distribution centers are football-field-size facilities, fully automated for efficient handling of merchandise. Mothers Work, Inc., a multichannel retailer of maternity fashions, has its headquarters and distribution center in Philadelphia. Design and garment sample making is done on the premises of the large facility. The warehouse conveyer system and preshipment consolidation areas are illustrated in Figures 9.1a, 9.1b, and 9.1c.

As you learned in Chapter 5, cross-docking moves goods in and out of a distribution center with minimal handling of merchandise. Cross-docking and customer-direct shipments are operating methods designed to move goods faster by eliminating unnecessary stops in physical distribution systems.

One of the newer technologies used to automate the distribution process is robotics. Staples and Walgreens both use mobile fulfillment systems in their distribution centers. **Mobile fulfillment systems (MFS)** rely on small robots to move merchandise in distribution centers (Figure 9.2). The robots are quiet and energy efficient, and some of them even look a bit like R2D2.[1]

Customer Interface

Customer interface involves point-of-service people, systems, equipment, and technologies that maximize customer satisfaction. Cross-channel customer service has become more challenging since the advent of multichannel retailing, because inventory problems occurring at any level of the supply chain can adversely affect other supply chain partners and ultimately the final consumer.

Despite good intentions, issues involving inventory management, fulfillment, and promotions cause many retailers to fall short. A study done by the Aberdeen Group concluded that lack of cross-channel integration in these areas is caused by channel inflexibility, inability to replace old systems, and the absence of appropriate customer and process management tools.[2] The magnitude of the problems with which retailers contend is graphed in Figure 9.3. All affect customers directly or indirectly.

> Supply Chain Goals

Supply chain members grapple with numerous obstacles, including inevitable economic ebbs and flows. Skyrocketing fuel costs greatly increase transportation expenses throughout the supply chain. Price increases in raw materials such as petroleum-based synthetic fibers are reflected in the wholesale cost of yarn, fabric, and ultimately apparel and home goods at the retail level. The rise of developing markets such as China, India, Russia, and Brazil tax the market for energy, natural resources, and services. Thirst for merchandise from

Picking and packing reusable canvas totes in preparation for shipping to retail stores cuts down on the use of cardboard cartons. The distribution center has a cardboard recycling center on the premises for paper containers that arrive from vendors. *[Source: Photograph provided by Lynda Poloian.]*

Outbound merchandise is preticketed and hung; allocated by size, color, and style in areas designated to each store; then shipped. *[Source: Photograph provided by Lynda Poloian.]*

emerging middle-class customers in these areas must be quenched. The global demand for more material goods and services places pressure on supply chains.

Regardless of the complexities of business in the twenty-first century, multichannel service providers have several common goals. All members of the supply chain work to meet these goals:

> High levels of automation and flow.
> Timely shipment and handling of goods.
> Complete shipment of orders.
> Accuracy of orders shipped.
> Transparent communication across channels.
> Synchronized physical distribution across channels
> Fine-tuned systems that function well globally.
> Controlled distribution costs.
> Customer satisfaction at all levels.

Robotic fulfillment systems expedite distribution. *[Source: KivaSystems.com.]*

Retailers turn to technology-based supply chain management systems to meet these goals. New systems optimize cost efficiency, physical distribution practices, and information technology. **Collaborative planning, forecasting, and replenishment (CPFR)** is an initiative designed to develop distribution efficiencies throughout the supply chain. CPFR advocates do business in ways that save money and time and increase sales. Distribution costs are reduced by determining the optimum number and location of warehouses, reducing shipment handling to speed deliveries, and implementing more effective inventory management. All mid-size and large retail companies use CPFR to run their businesses effectively and many small companies use this concept to improve distribution practices.

9.3

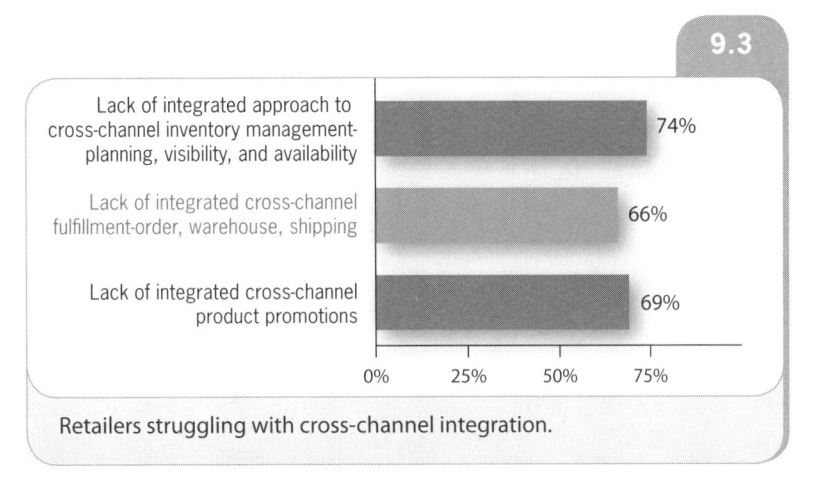

Lack of integrated approach to cross-channel inventory management-planning, visibility, and availability	74%
Lack of integrated cross-channel fulfillment-order, warehouse, shipping	66%
Lack of integrated cross-channel product promotions	69%

Retailers struggling with cross-channel integration.

Supply Chain Synergy

To streamline the supply chain and reduce inefficiencies, supply chain members expedite numerous activities. All depend on cooperation between members, flexibility, and information technology. Several tactical areas including fulfillment, transportation, and inventory management are discussed next.

> Fulfillment

To understand the importance of fulfillment to multichannel retailers, consider your own experience with catalog or Internet purchases. If you were planning a rock climbing expedition next weekend and expected delivery of a North Face jacket three days after placing an order on Monday, but delivery took more than a week, you would be very unhappy with the service. If you were shopping in an electronics store and found the Flip Video Mino that you wanted but not in the color you were hoping for, you would be equally disappointed. Yours are fulfillment issues. However, nondelivery or lack of availability could be caused at any number of junctures in the fulfillment process. Time spent in a distribution center does not equate to customer satisfaction, and the cost to retailers of storing merchandise until it is sorted for delivery to individual stores is high. The solution could lie in improving **lead time**—the period of time that passes between ordering goods and fulfilling orders. Fulfillment systems strive to minimize or eliminate time spent in distribution centers.

Customer Service Standards

Efficient fulfillment contributes to customer satisfaction. Customer service requirements in terms of turnaround time for delivery and minimum acceptable order fill rates

9.4 Shipments that are non-compliant with retail distribution center standards are sent to the vendor quality management area for inspection. Some cartons are relabeled, other merchandise is reticketed while "in hospital" (pending fix-and-recovery). [Source: Photograph provided by Lynda Poloian.]

are guiding factors. **Turnaround time** refers to the passage of time between an action and the response to it, such as the receipt of an order at a distribution center and its shipment to a retail store. **Fill rate** refers to the ability of manufacturers or distributors to ship all goods ordered. It is expressed as a percentage. A fill rate of less than 100 percent means that improvement is needed. Distribution centers use quality management programs to help speed turnaround times. Efficient centers operate at 95 to 98 percent fill rates. Figure 9.4 illustrates a vendor quality management area in a major regional retail distribution center.

Two methods are used to distribute goods to stores. Push and pull strategies were introduced in Chapter 2 to describe customer- or retailer-initiated selling and promotional activities. The same terms are used to describe actions occurring between a distribution center and a retailer. When a push strategy is used, a distribution center initiates shipments to a retailer in anticipation of sales. When a pull strategy is used, a retailer initiates shipment from a distribution facility in response to sales. The method selected depends on the types of goods carried, inventory turnover rates, type of store, channel, and retailer preference.

Using several online retail stores as examples, the article in Box 9.1 suggests five ways to expedite fulfillment. Fulfillment rates also are affected by inventory turnover.

Effect on Inventory Turnover

Advanced information technology has improved distribution practices. Better distribution contributes to increased stock turns, called turnover. **Turnover** is the number

What's the Buzz? Box 9.1

> *Five Ways to Cut Time and Costs Out of Getting Orders to Customers*

With a design for a new sophisticated warehouse and the company's reputation for service on the line, Zappos.com Inc.'s vice president of fulfillment, Craig Adkins, wasn't satisfied. A product fetched from the farthest point in the warehouse under the new design took about 35 minutes to get to a packing station, and that would make it impossible for Zappos, a Web-only retailer, to meet its promise of fast service.

For Adkins, that meant going back to the drawing board. The result: A redesigned system with additional conveyor belts that direct two levels of conveyors and merging points to a new common area—"like a spider web," Adkins says. The time to a packing station is now about 5 minutes. In the world of fulfillment, the Zappos system represents one of the more ambitious and technology-heavy methods of streamlining the flow of orders to get them picked, packed, and delivered to a customer's door as fast and efficiently as possible.

But merchants can take other steps to significantly upgrade fulfillment. Here are five areas of easy improvement that retailers and fulfillment experts recommend:

Better organized warehouses

One of the first and most obvious steps a retailer can take to expedite fulfillment is to maximize the use of space in warehouses and distribution centers. It is difficult to store multiple products, including slow-sellers, in a way that supports fast picking, packing, and shipping.

Outdoor apparel and gear retailer Backcountry.com, acting on recommendations from carrier UPS, arranged its distribution center to place the retailer's most popular products—about 60 percent of a total 800,000 items—in primary locations so they can be more quickly picked. For polo shirts, for example, the retailer sorts them by size, but mixes them by color in the same bin because it's easier for a worker to quickly grab a yellow or black shirt than to search through the labels of individual shirts for the ordered size.

(continued)

of times inventory turns into sales annually. It is an important performance measurement that is tracked by all retailers. Efficient logistical systems allow for reduced inventory levels and timely distribution, resulting in faster turnover and cost savings.

Strategic Partnerships

Retailers and vendors share information in order to provide better fulfillment. They exchange data regarding production schedules, time-to-market predictions, and in-stock availability. Although they have been reluctant to do so, more supply chain members are sharing sensitive financial information such as gross margin figures.

> **Box 9.1 What's the Buzz?** *(continued)*
>
> ### Closely reviewed shipping contracts
> One of the quickest ways to lower shipping costs is through regular monitoring of carrier contracts. With constantly changing shipping rate schedules, including fuel surcharges, and supplementary charges placed on unusual destinations or package sizes, retailers should routinely review carrier services and fees. In one case a retailer reviewed carrier schedules and found it was paying about $23 for expedited shipping to a particular region, when the $8 ground shipping service delivered orders within the same time.
>
> ### Smarter packaging and handling
> Instead of shipping sweatshirts in boxes as it had in the past, GiftsForYouNow.com now sends them in flexible vinyl pouches that it can easily fold to fit a product's size and shape. When it does ship things in boxes, it's replacing craft paper with much lighter plastic air pillows. The result is lower overall packaging weight, plus the ability to load more products into a single truck, leading to an estimated 10 percent savings in shipping fees.
>
> ### Motivating workers
> All the best fulfillment technology and processes still need cooperation from workers to produce the most value. Backcountry.com has taken some of its best steps toward productivity in fulfillment operations by motivating distribution center workers. Inside the building's entrance, photographs of outdoor scenery taken by workers hang along side productivity charts illustrating inventory storage and shipping accuracy and orders processed per hour. The example addresses three common problems associated with unhappy employees—anonymity, irrelevance, and lack of performance measurement.
>
> ### Consolidating shipments
> Overall shipping costs can be reduced by consolidating shipments as GiftsforYouNow.com has done. The company cut costs by 14 percent by hiring a third-party firm to take skids of orders to its facility and sort them by size and weight to designate each order for the least costly local delivery by the U.S. Postal Service.
>
> Regardless of what steps retailers take to improve fulfillment, perhaps the best advice is to never stop rethinking the process, says Adkins of Zappos.
>
> *Source: Excerpted and condensed from Paul Demery,* Internet Retailer, *May 2008, 23, 24, 26.*

Teamwork between channel members is crucial to the success of multichannel retailing. Strategic partnerships vary, depending on the size of the business, degree of involvement, and available technology. Large retailers require more sophisticated information technology systems and distribution methods because of the volume of merchandise they ship, the number of channels they use, and the varied customers they serve.

> Collaborative Transportation Decisions

Four principal means of transportation are used to physically transport goods around the world. They are air, sea, rail, and truck. The distinguishing characteristics of these transportation methods are summarized here. Retailers carefully evaluate transportation options and carriers, and often will use more than one type to move goods to their destination. Ensuring safe, reliable, and speedy delivery at the lowest cost is the objective.

Land Transportation Methods

Participants in land transportation include railroads and trucking companies. Fewer rail and more truck deliveries are the general rule in domestic transportation of retail goods. Larger trucks and specialized vehicles handle all types of merchandise effectively. Stacktrains are used by many transportation firms. These high-speed trains feature rail cars with two piggy-backed freight containers per car.

Transporting merchandise in several small shipments is much more expensive than using a single large one. In the independent trucking and rail industries, **freight forwarders** are firms that consolidate products manufactured by several small firms and transport them as one truck rail, or container shipment to major retailers. (For this reason, they are also sometimes called consolidators.) Their services save shippers and retailers considerable freight costs. To aid in transporting specific types of merchandise, trucks may be customized with fittings, for example, racks that enable apparel to be hung during shipment. Shipping and delivery are more efficient when merchandise is consolidated and shipped appropriately.

Sea Transportation

When time is not of the essence for delivery of goods produced overseas, container ships are the main carriers of cargo. **Container ships** are vessels that are outfitted with large numbers of cargo holders that are roughly 40 feet long and shaped like a tractor-trailer bed. Costs are lower, ocean crossings are slower, but huge quantities of goods are shipped at one time. Container ships carry retail products from and to major ports. Newer ships hold close to 5,000 containers and cross the Pacific in about three weeks.

Air Freight

Although it is the most expensive and the least utilized method of cargo transportation, air freight is safe and efficient for several product categories. Air

Table 9.1 Most Frequently Used Shipping Carriers

COMPANY	PERCENTAGE USED
UPS	44.4
U.S. Postal Service	27.5
Federal Express	18.3
DHL	4.9
Other	4.9

Source: "The Internet Retailer Survey: Fulfillment and Order Management," *Internet Retailer,* February 2008, 40. Responses to the question: "Which carrier do you use the most?"

transportation is cost-effective for small, lightweight merchandise classifications such as silk apparel and accessories like scarves. Jewelry and other high-ticket items travel safely by air.

Much retail-bound merchandise in the United States is shipped via United Parcel Service (UPS), Federal Express, and the U.S. Postal Service (USPS)—all of which maintain their own carriers. The shipment carriers used most frequently are listed in Table 9.1.

A high volume of imported merchandise creates a need for improved transportation logistics. Companies that integrate transportation by land, sea, and air command physical distribution channels. The practice of shipping goods via more than one transportation conveyance owned by the same company is called **intermodal** transport. Several transportation providers have the capability to move freight from Asia to all of North America or Europe using ship, train, and truck.

> Inventory Control

Information technology makes a significant contribution to supply chain management. Merchandise control systems support key functions in all retail organizations. Periodic and perpetual inventory reporting keeps retailers in touch with merchandise status. Cross-channel inventory control systems are selected for their agility, accuracy, and adaptability. Changes in the economy, company goals for return on investment, and customer service demands are reflected as retailers refine technology systems.

Many market variables motivate retailers to improve inventory management systems. In a study done by Aberdeen Research, retail participants identified increased supply chain costs, need to improve return on invested capital, and need to improve service levels as the top three pressures prompting improved inventory management.[3] Merchandise management solutions are diverse and suggest the magnitude of areas in which retailers develop expertise.

Inventory Management Applications

Technology systems make it possible for retailers to:

> Facilitate planning and physical distribution of merchandise.
> Use electronic purchase orders and advanced shipping notices.
> Print sales tickets or replace inaccurate ones.
> Improve replenishment tactics; highlight transfers, fast sellers, and age of stock.
> Indicate slow-selling merchandise and initiate markdowns.
> Compile stock-keeping unit (SKU), classification, and department reports.
> Integrate financial data.
> Extract historical sales data.
> Create online linkages and improve visibility with suppliers.
> Manage cross-channel distribution
> Manage customer databases

Aberdeen found that visibility of inventory in the supply chain improves as companies move from localized to network-level inventory organization. Companies have more knowledge of inventory in company-owned distribution centers than in the facilities that are run by third parties, for example. Inventory in transit in the global marketplace is the most difficult to track.[4]

Despite the downturn in the economy in 2008, about 50 percent of retailers indicated they would invest in inventory management systems that year. One option is vendor-managed inventory systems.[5] **Vendor-managed inventory (VMI)** shifts the responsibility for keeping track of merchandise to the manufacturer.

Inventory Tracking Methods

Most retailers expect real-time capabilities as they monitor in-stock merchandise and track goods that are in transit. Typically retailers use two basic forms of inventory systems, periodic and perpetual. As goods move through the supply chain, retailers need to be aware of their location at all times. When they prepare to receive large quantities of merchandise in their distribution centers, advance notification is mandatory. The globalization of product sourcing brings merchandise from all over the world for distribution to retail stores, catalogs, and online

9.5

Merchandise passing through distribution centers servicing most large retailers in the United States is imported from 50 or more countries, including India. [Source: Photograph provided by Lynda Poloian.]

business. A broader network increases the need to accurately monitor shipments. Shipping labels from myriad countries are apparent when visiting a distribution center. One is illustrated in Figure 9.5. Awareness of this global network reinforces the need to maintain accurate inventory records.

Periodic and Perpetual Systems A **periodic inventory** is a physical count of all merchandise, usually taken annually or semi-annually. A **perpetual inventory** is an ongoing measurement of merchandise in stock as sales and replenishment occur. Most contemporary systems offer real-time access to information. The perpetual system provides retailers with several advantages, including:

> Fewer out-of-stock positions
> Minimized inventory levels
> Indication of slow-selling goods
> Fewer markdowns
> Faster inventory turnover
> More accurate store inventories
> Fewer transfers between stores

The perpetual method remains the basis for inventory software applications used by retailers. Annual physical counts help document shrinkage and serve as a countermeasure to periodic systems.

Advanced Shipping Notification Advanced shipping notices (ASNs) have traditionally been sent by electronic data interchange (EDI) or fax to notify retailers of vendor shipments. Unfortunately for retailers ASNs are often flawed, necessitating an unvarnished look at the practice. Because so many notices are generated, the adage "haste makes waste" rings true. Web-based systems improve the process by

348   Unit III > **Technology Solutions**

allowing retailers to access information at any stage of the shipment process. Companies such as GXS, Inc., and GT Nexus, Inc., provide systems that synchronize distribution data across the supply chain.[6]

Getting participants on the same page is a challenging but worthwhile endeavor. Many retailers are reluctant to relinquish control over the inventory process even when change has a positive impact on performance.

Supply Chain Technology Initiatives

For decades inventory control systems depended on two technologies—UPC and EDI. **Universal product codes (UPCs),** which are found on most products, contain product identification information encoded in a series of printed stripes. The stripes and accompanying SKU numbers identify vendors, departments, classifications, and style numbers, for example. Bar coding is used for data entry. **Bar coding** refers to the capture of information at the point of service by scanning the UPC with an electronic device. **Electronic data interchange (EDI)** is a communications network used by supply chain members. Although these tools are linchpins in retail technology, Internet-based systems now make some classic electronic inventory control and management systems superfluous. One of the technologies being evaluated by retailers, radio frequency identification (RFID), was introduced in Chapter 1 and has been mentioned in several chapters of this book. This method ultimately may supplant earlier technologies.

> Radio Frequency Identification (RFID) Technology

We use RFID applications when we activate payment wands such as Speedpass at the gas pump or trigger highway toll collection devices using EZPass. The technology also is used to control access to buildings, track library books, and obtain information in various settings. For example, using RFID, an art gallery is able to disseminate information about artists and painting styles. By scanning various art objects with a PDA (personal digital assistant), visitors can gain a deeper understanding of the artwork and have more a more satisfying gallery experience.[7]

RFID helps retailers locate products at any given point along the supply chain. Airlines use this technology to find lost luggage, and it is amusing and comforting to know that even livestock and household pets could be tracked in this way.

Although many well-known global retailers have implemented RFID, the practice has not been widely adopted. The next section examines the technology behind RFID, its role as an agent of change, benefits and disadvantages, reasons for the slow assimilation by retailers, and present and future retail applications.

Evolution of Product Recognition Technology

After the development of UPC and EDI, the next technology to evolve was automatic identification devices, called auto ID. **Auto ID** uses wireless devices to capture and identify information. RFID is a form of auto ID that dates back to the 1970s. Working on the premise that computers are adept at sensing each other, the Massachusetts Institute of Technology (MIT) and a consortium of retailers and suppliers created RFID. The technology uses radio waves as the medium and requires a microchip antenna, electronic product code, and a wireless computer. An **electronic product code (ePC)** is the RFID version of the UPC. There is potentially a unique number for every item in the world.

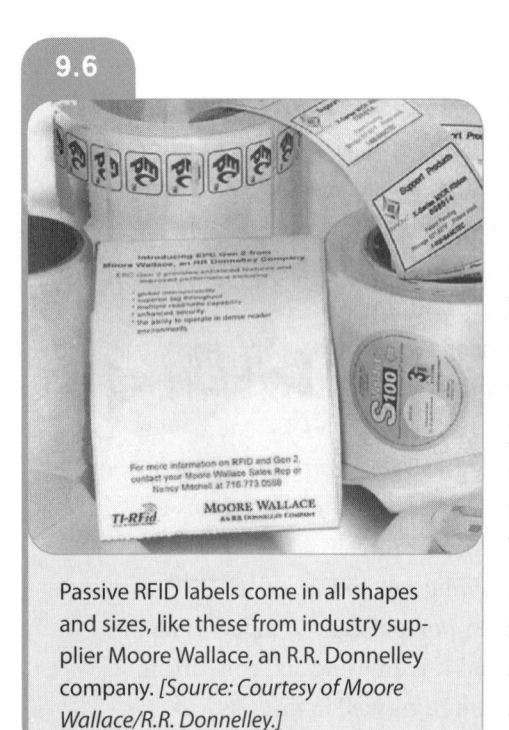

How Does RFID Work?

Products or other items containing an RFID tag are passed in front of an automatic reader called a sensor. The tag transmits the ePC code to the reader via radio waves. There are two basic types of tags, active and passive. **Passive RFID tags** are very small microchips that are attached to a paper-like antenna. Data are read when chips are scanned from a pallet, case, or individual product. The reader converts the code to recognizable data. The code contains information such as producer, manufacturer, or unique number. It can also tell where the item is and where it is going. A diverse group of passive RFID labels is illustrated in Figure 9.6. **Active RFID tags** are larger, have a longer range, require a power source, and are more expensive. EZPass devices use active tags.

9.6 Passive RFID labels come in all shapes and sizes, like these from industry supplier Moore Wallace, an R.R. Donnelley company. [Source: Courtesy of Moore Wallace/R.R. Donnelley.]

RFID technology depends on robust hardware and software solutions, including:

> *Sensors*—temperature, moisture, or position readers.
> *Managing Software*—designed to empower sensors and connections between wired and wireless devices.
> *Support Systems*—plug-and-play devices, read–write tags, and filtering and interpretation tools. Interpretation tools differentiate between actionable and nonactionable data and allow retailers to synchronize and distribute data.

A technologically intelligent ePC network is termed a savant, or more formally, **ePC information services (eIS)**. Servers are the communicator between sensors and business applications. Common eIS business applications include:

> *Eliminating Stock-Outs*—RFID-labeled merchandise is easily distinguished. For example, "smart" shelves can identify which products are missing from a shelf display. The technology also can tell the difference between oranges and bananas in a display.
> *Controlling Shrinkage*—RFID can identify customers who take an abnormally large amount of products from shelves, alerting retailers to possible theft.
> *Integrating the Supply Chain*—Total reporting is possible cross-channel wherever and whenever the need for information arises.

Benefits of RFID Over Bar Codes

For many reasons RFID technology is being adopted by many large retail companies. RFID provides:

> 360-degree capture of information over a relatively wide range, not limited to line of sight. Data are transferred without physical contact.
> Distinct identification of items that can be distinguished from one another in groups, as in a shopping cart.
> Lost or inaccurate shipment protection; the technology increases shipping efficiency and aids distribution center management.
> Faster product recalls.
> Reduced wastage and spoilage of perishable goods.

> Ability to rewrite, reuse, or destroy tags.
> Reduced labor costs.

Challenges to RFID Adoption

Several factors discourage the adoption of RFID technology. Cost and customer privacy concerns head the list:

> *High Cost of Implementation*—Average cost per passive RFID tag in 2000 was $1 and by 2006 about 12¢ to 20¢, depending on the quantity ordered. However, by 2010 the average cost of an RFID tag is expected to be less than 5¢,[8] and many retailers expect the price to fall to 1¢ to 2¢ per tag eventually.
> *Consumer Privacy Issues*—Some customers and consumer advocacy groups fear invasion of privacy. They believe RFID tags would remain active not only in the marketplace but after purchase. Although retailers have countered these reservations, the issue remains a sensitive one. When RFID was beginning to gain ground, Benetton, the Italian apparel company, planned to test RFID tags on 15 million sweaters. After the company announced its intentions in the media, customers objected. Anticipating loss of privacy some said, "I'd rather go naked."[9]
> *Lack of Standardization*—Several providers make RFID devices, and retailers are concerned about compatibility unless industry-wide standards are adopted.
> *Environmental Restraints*—Green-thinking consumers and retailers question the environmental impact of millions of discarded RFID tags dispersed into landfills.

Present and Future Retail Applications

Several retailers have tested or are conducting ongoing testing of RFID technology. Among the first to develop and use retail applications were supermarket and superstore retailers Metro AG of Germany, Tesco of the United Kingdom, and Walmart in the United States. Other retailers involved in RFID programs include Target, Home Depot, Lowe's, Ace Hardware, Best Buy, and Costco. Retailers often work in partnership with key vendors including Proctor & Gamble, Gillette, Johnson & Johnson, Purina, and Kimberly-Clark.

Walmart sets the pace for RFID research and development and has been on a technological spurt of its own. The company attained RFID compliance with 200 vendors in 2005. By 2007 Walmart had added another 500 vendors.[10] Walmart's partnership with major university research programs is advancing RFID programs globally.

Walmart's Involvement in Research In 2005 the University of Arkansas opened the RFID Research Center and Information Technology Research Institute in Fayetteville, Arkansas, in conjunction with Walmart. The center operates under the auspices of EPCGlobal, Inc. **EPCGlobal** is the organization that develops and monitors standards involving the ePC. Work is done in a "'live-entertainment' laboratory put together for creation and dissemination of RFID knowledge in the retail, consumer product goods, and supply chain fields."[11] The center looks at questions of public policy involving RFID as well as technical issues.

Studies in several sectors, including product, pallet, and portal readability, have shown that RFID technology is not effective for some common retail applications. For example, radio waves do not work well on metal containers that reflect waves, or on liquid that absorbs waves. Conversely, oil helps transmit an RFID signal. It is expected that breakthroughs will come at the nano structural level of materials and that these advances are 5 to 10 years away.

Other experiments have involved reading RFID numbers from packages on a conveyer and then transforming the data into printed product labels. During this process, researchers found that RFID reading is easier than label printing. Food products have been tested for readability. Researchers found that cans of soda are difficult to read when radio waves hit on top of cans. To alert personnel to a malfunction, a red light spot indicates a difficult read. Soup, saltine crackers, cooking oil, and moist wipes were other products observed in the laboratory during different phases of testing.[12]

Walmart's primary reasons for using RFID are to reduce stocks-outs, track defective products, and reduce theft. The company expects to have RFID tags on all products sold at its Sam's Club division by 2010. The company has reassured customers that product labels will contain only product information and that for those who want them removed at the point-of-sale, employees will provide the service. However, some of Walmart's 60,000 suppliers have expressed concern that they will not be able to comply by 2010 and that the initiative is too costly for their companies.[13]

Apparel Sector Progress The retail apparel sector has been slower to implement RFID, largely due to the cost involved. Eventually the technology will provide detailed information on sizes as well as what, where, when, and to whom merchandise is sold. Wardrobe-building technology that enables customers to find the perfect match for favorite outfits in their closets by accessing the data stored on RFID tags is now available. This service would only be used by customers who opt in and would not compromise personal security.

Levi Strauss & Co. has adopted RFID in 40 of its stores in Mexico. This initiative is considered one of the largest uses of RFID tags in apparel retailing. Wireless readers are used at checkout, allowing associates to transact sales and then deactivate tags in one operation. Prior to this Levi's had tested RFID with the Mexican retailer Liverpool. Tests showed that inventory accuracy was increased from 80 percent to 99 percent by the use of RFID.[14]

Innovation and the Future An innovator in the implementation of RFID, Metro Group of Germany will expand the use of RFID to 200 of its Real Hypermarkets by installing RFID portals from Checkpoint Systems, a U.S. supplier of technology.[15] Using these portals, complete pallets of product or shopping carts full of groceries can be scanned simultaneously. The portals look like large, illuminated arbors or archways.

Future RFID applications could include tracking workplace attendance, monitoring hand washing by food service workers in rest rooms, and identifying underage liquor purchasers in liquor stores or drinkers in bars. It may seem futuristic, but one day a chip embedded in your wrist or other body part could serve as an electronic wallet.[16] RFID also has asset protection applications. A mannequin embedded with an RFID tag is illustrated in Figure 9.7.

9.7 An RFID-enabled "watch mannequin" serves as a display fixture as well as a loss-prevention tool. [Source: Photograph provided by Lynda Poloian.]

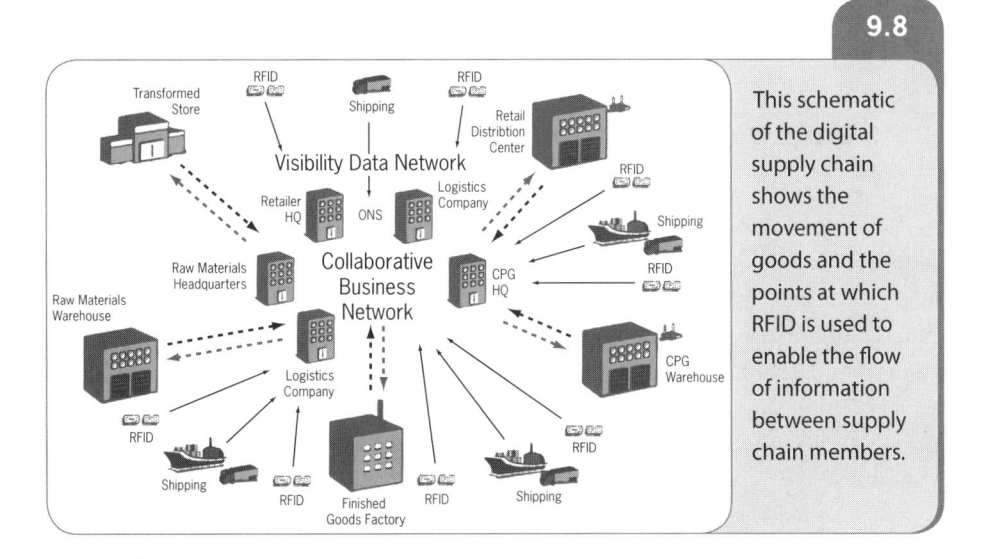

9.8 This schematic of the digital supply chain shows the movement of goods and the points at which RFID is used to enable the flow of information between supply chain members.

The main reason for escalating the adoption of RFID is better collaborative planning, forecasting, and replenishment, made possible by this technology. Cooperation, trust, and synergy throughout the supply chain are essential to its successful implementation. Costs of implementation vary greatly, depending on the size and type of company and degree of RFID involvement. The recent economic downturn and supply chain reticence have pushed RFID adoption lower on the priority list, yet many industry insiders believe RFID technology eventually will replace UPC bar coding. The digital supply chain map in Figure 9.8 indicates the movement of goods facilitated by RFID technology.

> Merchandise Management

With the advent of multichannel retailing, companies are forced to reevaluate merchandise management initiatives and find new ways to be competitive. This is nowhere more apparent than on the Web. Savvy merchants use niche sites, create new brands when necessary, and find that new factors drive merchandise decisions.

In a study done by the e-tailing group, 60 percent of retailers said that inventory data drive decision making, and 86 percent said Web analytics are the primary influence. Knowing what was happening merchandise-wise across all channels was another important factor.[17]

Technology has helped Cabela's plan and achieve more accurate merchandise forecasts with lower inventories. Learn more about the multichannel business practices of this outdoor lifestyle retailer in Box 9.2.

Box 9.2 What's the Buzz?

> ### Multichannel Experience: Cabela's Defined Business Process, then Deployed Technology

A larger-than-life shopping experience is what outdoor lifestyle retailer Cabela's seeks to provide across every consumer channel. Translating the unique experience and ambience of its physical stores, which have an average footprint of 170,000 square feet and include in-store attractions such as aquariums and dioramas, across multiple channels was no small feat. However, the true measure of successful multichannel retailing is the ability to deliver the desired product to the end consumer—in-store, online, and through the call center.

In addition to 26 stores located in 19 states, Cabela's publishes 120 catalogs annually, each with a circulation of 130 million households. The company also maintains a dynamic e-commerce business at cabelas.com.

Speaking at the National Retail Federation annual conference, James Landsman, senior applications channel manager, described how his company has successfully developed and implemented a set of business practices and support technologies to achieve optimum supply chain execution for each sales channel.

Cabela's commitment to customer service is unwavering. Landsman noted, "If product is not available at the distribution center, we'll ship overnight from another location to where it needs to be." Supporting this commitment is complicated by the challenges of a complex global supply chain, with vendors in multiple countries and product in-transit around the world. Landsman estimated that Cabela's has more than 4,000 active vendors.

Landsman advised retailers that many challenges are posed by a global supply chain, including the integration and replication of data and maintaining executive-level commitment to the ongoing change-management process. The most critical key to success, advised Landsman, was to define the desired business processes and decide how they should operate within the organization before investing in technology to support the processes. The technology Cabela's implemented to support its new processes included a merchandise-management system, an order-management suite, and a warehouse management system with an advanced planning and replenishment application.

The retailer's three distribution centers, which typically process more than 100,000 orders a day, have to strike a balance between store and direct-to-consumer fulfillment. Landsman reported that Cabela's has already achieved more accurate forecasts with lower inventories held in stores and increased inventory turns. The Nebraska-based company planned to open seven stores in 2008.

Source: Excerpted and condensed from Connie Robbins Gentry, Chain Store Age, *March 2008, 74, 76.*

> Strategic Partnerships and Direction

Throughout the supply chain, strategic partnerships of many dimensions are under way. Online retail exchanges are a type of collaborative project first created to organize group purchasing on a worldwide basis, thus effecting economies of scale. Another strategic direction involves business-to-consumer (B2C) relationships that effectively reduce the number of supply chain members engaged in the distribution process.

Online Retail Exchanges

Business-to-business (B2B) organizations wield influence over the supply chain by providing buying efficiencies, cost savings, online auctions, and a forum through which members communicate with other retailers. **Online retail exchanges** are electronic marketplaces through which large companies establish trading partners and build relationships within the retail industry. GlobalNetXchange (GNX), mentioned in Chapter 7, was one of the first. The early incarnations of online exchanges did not meet all expectations of member companies although they reduced some costs and encouraged data sharing. The evolution of retail exchanges continues.

In 2005 GNX and its competitor, Worldwide Retail Exchange (WWRE), merged. The new company included more than 60 food, drug, and apparel retailers. Many services are directed to food retailers. The list of invited members reads like a smorgasbord of international retailers: Aeon Group of Japan, Lotte of Korea, Metro of Germany, Ahold of the Netherlands, Carrefour and Auchan of France, El Corte Ingles of Spain, Tesco and Sainsbury of the United Kingdom, and Sears, Walmart, and Walgreens from the United States are examples.[18]

The retail exchange organization partnered with VeriSign to provide point-of-sale data to members of the supply chain. The platform allows users to share information among thousands of individual stores and vendors.[19] Eventually the name Agentrics was selected for the new entity. Ultimately, collaboration of this type helps identify retailers with staying power in a complex, stimulating, and often unpredictable global marketplace.

B2C Disintermediation

In a discussion of the supply chain, it would be remiss not to include information about B2C selling initiatives that bypass the retail channel. **Disintermediation** occurs when manufacturers sell directly to consumers on the Internet. Apple, Nike, and Dell at points in their development would have qualified as disintermediators.

Although all began as manufacturers, they now sell through stores, catalogs, the Internet, or a combination of these channels. Disintermediation occurs primarily when consumer product companies that sell to retail stores also engage in direct-to-customer business.

<u>Viewpoints on Disintermediation</u> Is disintermediation detrimental to retail objectives or is it simply another way to bring products to customers when and how they want them? Many manufacturers have maintained Web sites only for customer information purposes or to expose their brands to more potential customers. Now some are actively engaging their customers in sales.

Paradoxically the practice doesn't hurt large retail companies that consider manufacturers' online sales too meager to constitute real competition. Small manufacturers savor the opportunity to sell online and extend their brands into underserved or new markets.

Conversely some manufacturers were lured to the retail side and have opened store chains. Both Oakley, the sunglass company, and Tommy Bahama, the tropically inspired apparel firm, have gone this route.

<u>New Partnerships</u> In certain situations liaisons between manufacturers and retailers encourage customers to order from the manufacturer's Web site, then pick up their merchandise in retail stores. This plan twists the traditional supply chain in a new direction.

A service called Shopatron enables manufacturers to tap retail markets painlessly by eliminating the fulfillment function on their premises. The doll company Pretty Ugly used Shopatron to expand its primarily urban footholds to smaller locales. Online customers order their faddishly ugly dolls online and pick them up at toy stores that are part of Pretty Ugly's established network. [20]

Sales are increased for both manufacturer and retailer using this approach. Creative solutions surface when retailers and fellow supply chain members relinquish some control for maximum gain. Box 9.3 offers a fresh viewpoint on how fashion companies can learn about supply chain practices from convenience store retailers.

> Web-Based Private-Label Management

The nature of buying and design has changed in the last decade to meld product development, design, and technology. Many new initiatives are occurring at this

What's the Buzz? Box 9.3

> *Learning to Take Cues from Other Industries*

What can Seven-Eleven Japan teach the fashion industry? A lot when it comes to how supply chains and sales information, used intelligently, can rev up a business, said Stanford University professor Hau Lee, who offered insight in fast-food mode. The convenience store was just one example of how apparel brands and retailers can learn from firms that sell everything from fresh food to computer games, but have similar supply chains.

"We are dominated by three major drivers," said Lee. These drivers are: increasing uncertainties in demand and supply, changes in technology and markets, and the need to partner with companies in the supply chain. To meet these challenges, Lee said companies must be agile and able to deal with change.

Seven-Eleven Japan manages to pull in sales of about $23 billion annually by reacting to who is in their stores and when, he says. It is a responsive company that masters information, knows what people want, and builds its logistics system accordingly. By knowing what school kids want in the morning, what housewives want in the afternoon, and what their husbands pick up on their way home from work, the company became the country's number one seller of fast food, and pantyhose. Through research the company learned that it was men who were buying the pantyhose on their way home from work, probably upon request of their wives. Accordingly, Seven-Eleven moved the pantyhose display closer to the beer.

Lee also believes that supply chains are broadly understood by answering two questions: Is the production done by the company or outsourced and are the goods made near the market or far away? In the case of popular Crocs shoes, the company does a bit of each in both cases. "You do not want to have a one-size-fits-all supply chain," said Lee.

According to Lee, supply chains are like people and have two personality types. Type A is responsive and flexible but costs more. Type B is cheaper but may be slower. Successful companies combine the two types so that they have cost efficiency, flexibility, and speed.

Source: Excerpted and condensed from Evan Clark, Women's Wear Daily, *March 18, 2008, 17.*

level, and collaboration is taking place not in exotic locations but on the Web. Manufacturers that specialize in private-label merchandise are working closely with retailers on these projects. Specification sheets—which hold a mound of details—are shared with all constituents in the production process. This enables designers, product developers, contractors, technical experts, and logistics personnel to communicate together more easily. Among the providers of Web-based collaborative services are Agentrics, mentioned earlier, and GenNovation, discussed below.

The average time to bring a new private-label line to market is diminishing. What used to take 12 to 18 months to deliver now takes between 6 and 12 months. In a study done by RSR Research, 47 percent of retailers stated that it took them 6 to 12 months to get a new product into the pipeline, and 24 percent reported that it took them only 3 to 6 months to get their new private-label lines to market.[21]

The British retailer Marks & Spencer (M & S) uses Web collaboration for development of its private-label (St. Michael's) grocery products. Flowers, wine, and household products account for about 6,000 SKUs in the company's private-label program. M & S's use of the GenNovation system for product lifecycle management has reduced data retrieval, sorting, and processing time from days to hours or minutes.[22]

More teamwork is expected as retailers realize the benefits of online team interaction and the ability to speed goods to market in a demanding and competitive retail environment.

Meeting customers' expectations is inevitably easier when systems and processes are in place across the supply chain. Distribution, fulfillment, inventory management, and a host of related functions benefit from an integrated approach to supply chain management. Creating value for customers is still at the root of decisions made everywhere within the supply chain. The supply chain that feels the pleasure and pain of all participants and acts to correct imbalances and celebrate advances contributes to the high performance of the whole.

Summary

Lithely maneuvering goods through the supply chain is foremost in the minds of multichannel retailers. Those that are successful recognize that the formation of strategic partnerships is essential. In a highly competitive retail world, and particularly in difficult economic times, there is power in numbers.

The supply chain begins with the purchase of raw goods and materials and ends with shipment of the finished product to the ultimate consumer. Key members of the supply chain include the providers of raw goods and materials, manufacturers, distributors, and retailers. Areas for planning and decision making include production, distribution, and customer interface.

Essential services, systems, and applications that make the supply chain perform effectively should work in harmony. Decisions involving fulfillment, transportation, and inventory control affect the level of service provided to customers.

Technology enables the supply chain to function at peak efficiency. New innovations have made it possible to run complex multichannel operations effectively and profitably. Radio frequency identification (RFID) is a pivotal technology that is expected to change existing product recognition methods as support, funding, and momentum builds. Some of the advantages of RFID are full capture of more information from any direction, the ability to track goods throughout the supply chain, and opportunities to share information with other supply chain members with the vital goal of serving customers better. Some of the challenges to RFID adoption include costs of tags and implementation of facilitating technological infrastructure. Privacy concerns of customers regarding the types of data gathered and how data are used constitute another issue. Many large retailers around the world are testing and implementing RFID. Walmart and Metro AG are considered two of many leaders in the field.

Merchandise management systems benefit from new technologies. The movement toward greater sharing of pertinent data between supply chain members is a key direction.

Several new directions in supply chain management and use are evolving. Online retail exchanges allow large retail companies to share data and expertise, make advantageous purchases, and communicate with other retailers worldwide. Manufacturer-to-consumer direct selling is creating new challenges and opportunities for supply chain members. The use of the Web for private-label management is enhancing

Key Terms

Active RFID tags
Auto ID
Automated storage and retrieval (ASR)
Bar coding
Collaborative planning, forecasting, and replenishment (CPFR)
Container ships
Disintermediation
Distribution
Distribution centers
Electronic data interchange (EDI)
Electronic product code (ePC)
EPCGlobal
ePC information services (eIS)
Fill rate
Freight forwarders
Intermodal
Lead time
Mobile fulfillment systems (MFS)
Online retail exchanges
Passive RFID tags
Periodic inventory
Perpetual inventory
Physical distribution
Product sourcing
Supply chain
Turnaround time
Turnover
Universal product codes (UPCs)
Vendor-managed inventory (VMI)
Warehousing

the collaborative efforts of designers, product developers, manufacturers, and technology partners.

An integrative approach to global supply chain management drives multichannel retailing today. Retailers best serve their customers by developing substantive and sustaining relationships with supply chain members.

> **Questions for Discussion and Reflection**

1. What types of businesses belong to the supply chain? What is the ultimate goal of all activity generated by the supply chain?
2. The distribution function of the supply chain includes several elements that provide necessary links between manufactures and retailers. State and elaborate on three key services that are performed in this area.
3. How does fulfillment affect inventory turnover? Why is this a crucial metric for retailers?
4. Decisions regarding transportation consider speed, flexibility, cost, and convenience. If your company needed to ship high-priced silk T-shirts from Asia to the United States, what transportation mode would you use? Justify your decision.
5. Explain two fundamental methods of inventory tracking. Which aspect is of primary concern to multichannel retailers? Why?
6. What are the major benefits and disadvantages of RFID technology? What types of retailers benefit most from RFID?
7. How is Cabela's using technology to integrate merchandising and customer service across the three channels that it operates? How does the company make multichannel decisions?
8. Explain the concept of disintermediation. Why is this practice both a concern and an opportunity for retailers?
9. Why are private-label developers embracing new Web-based systems?

Notes

1. Connie Robbins Gentry, "Transformers: The Movers," *Chain Store Age*, March 2008, 76.
2. Sahir Anand, "Technology Strategies for Multi-Channel Integration," April 2008, 4, www.aberdeen.com. Research report by the Aberdeen Group, Boston, MA.
3. Aberdeen Group, "Technology Strategies for Closed Loop Inventory Management," April 2008, 5, www.aberdeen.com. Research report.
4. Ibid., 18.
5. Ibid., 24.
6. Paul Demery, "For Retailers, Collaboration with Carriers Has Come a Long Way Thanks to the Web," *Internet Retailer*, January 2008, 58.
7. Jonathan Collins, "RFID for the Art Shy," *RFID Journal*, April 28, 2005, www.rfidjournal.com/article/print/1540.
8. Lauren LaCapra and Rich Franconen, "Surveying the Field: RFID in Retail," *Wall Street Journal*, July 13, 2006, B4. Statistical sources: various business and research companies.
9. James Covert, "Down But Far From Out," *Wall Street Journal*, January 12, 1004, R5.
10. Dan Scheraga, "Wal-Smart," *Chain Store Age Retail Technology Quarterly*, January, 2006, 20A.
11. Fact Sheet, RFID Research Center/ Information Technology Research Institute, Fayetteville, Arkansas, April 6, 2006.
12. RFID Research Center/ Information Technology Research Institute. Fayetteville, Arkansas. Staff presentations during visit to center April 6, 2006.
13. John Gambrel, "Wal-Mart Workers to Remove, Turn Off Tags," Associated Press, April 23, 2008, www.boston.com. © The New York Times Company.
14. Cate T. Corcoran, "Levi's Adopts RFID in 40 Stores," *Women's Wear Daily*, August 21, 2007, 2.
15. Karen Willoughby, "New RFID Phase for Metro," *Elsevier Food International,* April 3, 2008, www.foodinternational.net/articles/news/1136/new-rfid-phase-for-metro.html. ©Reed Business Food and Horeca.
16. www.NRFSmartBrief.com, July 2004, and Cisco white paper, 2003.
17. Paul Demery, "Finding the Focus in Merchandising Can Make All the Difference," *Internet Retailer*, May 2008, 22.
18. Worldwide Retail Exchange, "GNX and WWRE Boards Agree to Landmark Merger, Creating the Definitive Business Platform and Industry Forum for the Global Retailing Community," press release, April 26, 2005, www.worldwideretailexchange.org/cs/en/pres_room/wr0787.htm.
19. Worldwide Retail Exchange, "VeriSign and Worldwide Retail Exchange Partner to Provide Point-of-Sale Data Services to the Retail Supply Chain," press release, www.worldwideretailexchange.org/cs/en/press_room/wr0790.htm, October 26, 2005.
20. Chantal Todé, "New Shopatron Feature Tested," *DM News*, January 2, 2008, www.dmnews.com/New-Shopatron-feature-tested/PrintArticle/100379/.
21. Paul Demery, "How Web-Based Private Label Management Helps Merchants Turn Merchandise," *Internet Retailer*, May 2008, 101-104. Statistical source: RSR Research.
22. Ibid.

Chapter 10

Business Intelligence and the Future of Multichannel Retailing

Objectives

> To investigate business intelligence systems.
> To determine how retailers use analytics to chart performance.
> To survey metrics used by multichannel retailers.
> To explore legal impediments to online selling.
> To identify future directions and challenges for multichannel retailing.

New methods of reaching customers have melded with the old, bringing more options than ever before to retailers, along with higher expectations of performance. Retailers have responded to the complexities of emerging contact methods, media, and channel choices by executing innovative strategies. Establishing performance criteria and selecting appropriate metrics are critical to meeting expectations. The best business intelligence systems are those that are adaptable to changes in the retail environment.

Aspects of technology, the economy, law, sustainability, and customer lifestyles intertwine as we look ahead to the evolution of multichannel retailing. A glance into the future identifies several areas of growth and challenge for multichannel retailers. Many of today's technologies will segue into new solutions while others will become obsolete. Although change takes many forms, customers are expected to retain their supremacy in the retailer–customer relationship.

Business Intelligence

A recurring query in business is this: What does a company need to help it run smoothly, stand by its employees, serve the common good, and turn a profit? The answer is really good research, data, analysis, people, and solutions. **Business intelligence (BI)** is the information gathered from a variety of internal and external sources to help a business make sound decisions. A system of business-wide integrative services is called **service-oriented architecture (SOA)**. The word "architecture" used in this way means a business structure. It is represented graphically as a flow chart or diagram. To multichannel retailers, SOA signifies investing in a technological infrastructure that is equipped to handle the demands of diverse selling channels simultaneously. The flow of information, content, services, and people depends on shrewd thinking and the development of facilitating systems that support decision making.

> Adaptive E-commerce Architecture

Some of the first e-retailers who opened their virtual doors more than a decade ago are updating their e-commerce platforms. E-commerce architecture that has been in operation for many years is called a **legacy system**. Integrated out of necessity rather than design, older structures are less efficient. Justifiably they were pieced together rapidly as needs grew even faster. Legacy systems are being replaced by reference assembly architecture. **Reference assembly architecture** is an operational platform that breaks down key functions into logical service centers that can be analyzed from a variety of perspectives.

Figure 10.1 illustrates contemporary reference assembly architecture. The separation of retail functions and services into areas of expertise that transcend individual channel emphasis is noteworthy. This new approach makes it easier for retailers to adopt new business practices or add a new channel more efficiently than with the legacy architecture.[1]

Aberdeen Group has studied cross-channel technology priorities and lists several that retailers say they currently have or were planning to embellish in 2008. The top priority for enhancement of existing platforms is for cross-channel marketing management followed by multichannel fulfillment and on-demand full spectrum multichannel platforms.[2]

10.1

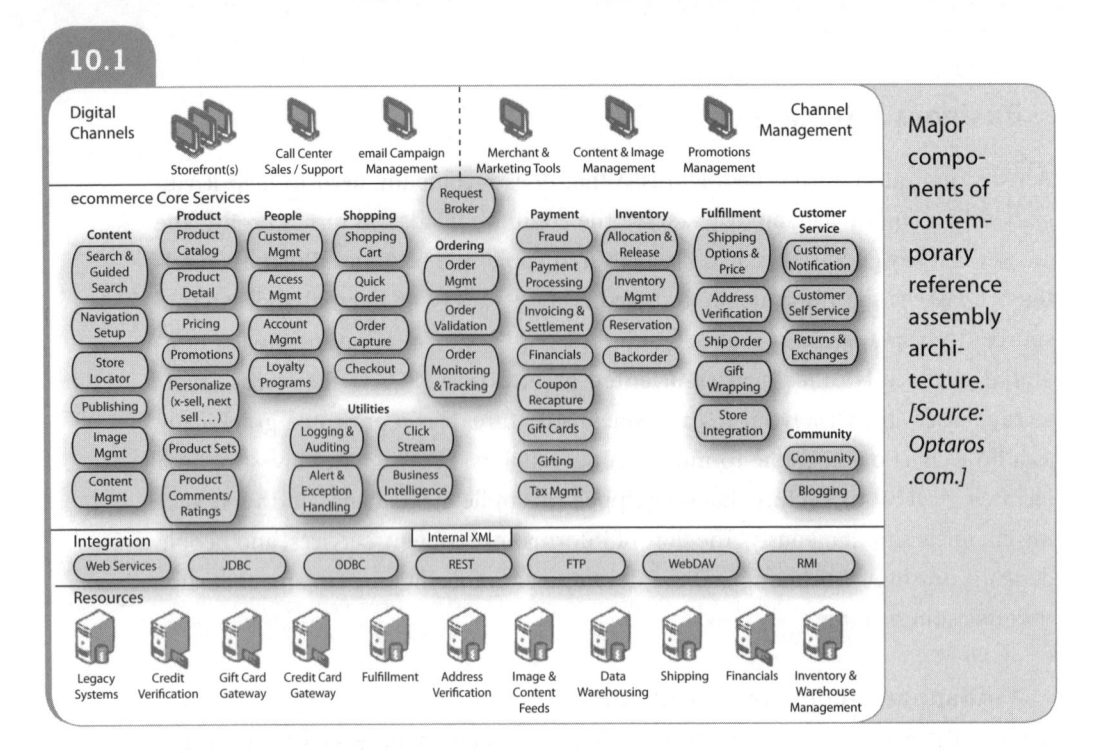

Major components of contemporary reference assembly architecture. [Source: Optaros.com.]

> **Performance Metrics**

The metrics of multichannel retailing determine whether stores, catalogs, and Web sites are independently and collectively reaching their goals and generating revenue and profits. Customer value and shopping behavior are quantifiable. Using the best analytical tools available, retailers measure performance across channels. Metrics vary for brick-and-mortar, catalog, and online stores. To begin, we'll consider some general tendencies—by no means an exhaustive list—before surveying various metrics:

> Online measurement tools are dependent on integrated information systems; customer conversion rates and multidimensional online traffic analysis tools are useful.

> Advertising hits, store traffic, or quantities of catalogs mailed provide important information, but a deeper knowledge of the factors influencing conversion rates is better.

> Direct marketers measure response rates and time, average order size and value, and customer retention; catalog retailers also want to know how many catalog drops are necessary to increase sales.

> How e-mails convert to sales or how customer service influences return rates is useful information, as is how e-mails drive traffic to other channels.

Unit III > **Technology Solutions**

> Store productivity is traditionally measured in turns of sales per square foot or linear foot; metrics are applied storewide, departmentally, or by shelving unit.
> All retailers measure revenue growth, profits, and return on investment independently and across channels.

All scenarios are critical to the multichannel assessment process. Depending on the company's objectives, measuring the impact of supermarket end cap displays may be just as valuable as charting annual sales for a convenience store or conversion rates for an online apparel retailer.

> Web Analytics

Profit and loss, return on investment, and accountability have never been taken for granted in retailing. However, accountability for sales has become even more vital since the advent of online selling. E-retailers track many metrics in addition to basic financial and traffic reporting, and the options are growing steadily. The information from online stores that is used for statistical purposes emanates from several areas, including customer access and use, accuracy of order fulfillment, efficiency of transactions, post-sale follow-up, and customer security. As with any new medium, online retailers have plenty of data but not always the time, money, systems, or expertise to mine them or perform statistical measures.

The results of a study on Web analytics showed 69 percent of survey participants did not believe people using data actually understood what the data signified. The researchers concluded that Web analytics were underutilized by companies. There is great potential for integration of data into all phases of business and movement, from simple tactical applications to more sophisticated integrated applications.[3]

Web analytics are used to detect and measure levels of engagement with the customer. The level may be as innocuous as a serendipitous click or as evocative as a lifelong relationship with a company. One trend in business intelligence is toward real-time analytics. **Real-time analytics (RTA)** are actionable programs that capture information for immediate use at all levels of a company. Data compiled by the Aberdeen Group verified that 62 percent of multichannel retailers planned to either enhance existing programs or use real-time cross-channel analytics in the future.[4]

Evaluating Web Site Performance
First, what constitutes a good site? How do you differentiate a good one from a mediocre or poor one? Does it all come down to dollars and cents or is there more to consider?

Technology writers, and the discussion of Web site design in Chapter 7, have suggested that site navigation is both a key Web function and a challenge. As sites become larger and more complex, visitors are bewildered by their inability to find products or related information that they need. Here we look at navigation as an aspect of Web performance that should be measured. One example, from Bruce Temkin of Forrester Research, illustrates this point: "Say it's a retail site and we are a user who has a problem with a product and wants to return it. What we would look for on the home page is a specific link that a user could click on for returning products. But some sites might bury that link behind a tab that might say, 'Service and Support.' The key goals for your customers should be obvious from the home page."[5]

Under these circumstances the retailer would want to quantify the number of customers who were inconvenienced. This finding could lead to further assessment of competitors' sites. Solutions to the problem could then be addressed.

Ease of navigation is only one topic that may come under scrutiny. There are many aspects to consider when measuring performance:

> Customer traffic, including hits and click-through rates.
> Home page and branding recognition.
> Navigation efficiency.
> Merchandise availability.
> Stickiness of Web site; likelihood of return by customers.
> Customer service.
> Sales closure rates; positive shopping cart experience.
> Availability of special services.
> Cross-channel shopping options.

One of the best examples of enticing Web sites comes from the Netherlands. Dutch retailer HEMA sells a variety of popularly priced merchandise through a chain of small department stores. It opened its first e-retailing site in 2007 and although customers can order online, they must pick up products in stores. This aspect will be improved in the future, but the site is most appealing and entertaining.[6] A photo of a HEMA brick-and-mortar store and a view of one of its Web pages appear in Figures 10.2a and 10.2b. Learn more about HEMA and its online operation in Box 10.1.

10.2a HEMA, a Dutch retailer, carries apparel, accessories, items for the home, bakery products, and wine. *[Source: Photograph provided by Lynda Poloian.]*

10.2b The HEMA Web site uses high-tech excitement to draw the viewer into the online experience. Visit HEMA at www.hema.nl. *[Source: Hema.nl.]*

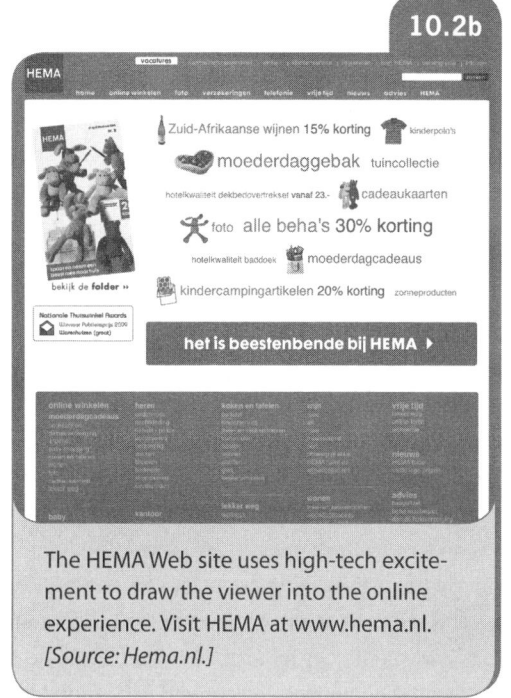

Types of Assessment Tools

Several types of assessment tools are available for Web retailers. Many types of tactical and statistical analysis are options. Some results-oriented metrics, including conversion rates, pay-per-click (PPC), and branding impression metrics such as cost-per-thousand (CPM), were introduced earlier in this text in Chapter 6. Here, additional performance-based measures and predictive analytics are described: A/B testing, multivariate testing, and logistic regression analysis. In addition to these measures, several cognitive analysis tools also are available.

A/B Split Testing From the direct marketing and advertising testing repertoire comes A/B testing. When two variables along the same dimension are compared, the measurement is referred to as A/B or **split testing**. For example using A/B software, two versions of a home page in which only an illustration was different could be compared. Although this technique has been useful for evaluating the effectiveness of catalog or print advertising, where a change in a price or headline could mean increased revenue, it is considered elementary for the needs of the current multichannel marketplace, where deeper analysis is needed.

Box 10.1 What's the Buzz?

> HEMA: Making an Entrance

You don't need to speak Dutch to understand the beauty behind the latest online viral marketing campaign from Amsterdam-based department store chain HEMA. The retailers, known for its affordable and high-quality generic housewares and goods, had expanded its presence throughout the Netherlands, Belgium, and Germany for several decades, but it didn't offer an e-commerce channel until last year. So what better way to let consumers know of its new site than creating a welcome page that is one of the most uniquely engaging and innovative Web introduction the online world has seen in a while: an animated site that brings its products to life.

When shoppers visit, several products for sale appear on screen, such as cups, an outfit for a baby and packaging tape. But after the mouse is left on the page for several seconds, the cups tip over a roll about the page. A domino sequence then occurs and the page scrolls to follow the moving products. For example, one item bumps into and turns on a light (priced at 7.95 euros) that shines on a magnifying glass (1.95 euros). The light sparks a fire from the magnifying glass and eventually heats the teapot listed for sale above it. When the water in the teapot boils, the cork blows and the page scrolls back up to the top for more animated display. Along with sound effects, this action continues for about a minute until the final movement brings the viewer back up to the top of the homepage and confetti falls around the HEMA banner.

At the end of the show—because that is what it feels like—a question box appears and asks if you want to send the page to a friend, similar to that of an e-card. And just like that, an online phenomenon ignites.

In the first few weeks of the viral's debut in October 2007, the site attracted more than several hundred thousand page views. People sent it to inboxes all over the globe, introducing not only the site but also the brand to shoppers worldwide. What makes HEMA's approach stand apart form the others that have taken similar steps in the past is that the style mirrors the very essence of what the company represents. The company calls it "special simplicity."

HEMA, whose acronym translates into English to mean "Dutch Standard Prices Company Amsterdam," is know for adding modern and somewhat designer touches to its products, which are made by and specifically for the chain.

Although shoppers can now make online purchases, the HEMA site does not offer shipping; customers must pick up their purchases in-store. This is its weak spot. The conversion results would have been remarkable of shipping had been available at the time of site launch.

HEMA said it is looking to expand its site by offering shipping in the future. When that happens there should be another viral ready to go. The bar has already been set—and it's certainly pretty high.

Source: From Samantha Murphy, "Web-site Review: Dutch Chain HEMA Introduces New Site with Online Viral Phenomenon," Chain Store Age, *March 2008, 66.*

<u>Multivariate Testing</u> Several types of multivariate testing help retailers compare possible changes or directions simultaneously. **Multivariate testing** is a statistical measure that allows users to investigate several elements in different combinations to find optimal relationships. For example, it can be used to discover what works and does not work to enthrall customers on a Web site. This form of testing is considered more sophisticated than A/B testing because it provides broader reference points and enables users to draw conclusions based on the actual testing of a few possible outcomes, thus saving time and money. One form of multivariate testing used by online companies is called **Taguchi testing**. Taguchi testing enables users to test many variables economically and quickly. For example, several headlines, product photos, prices, or sources of traffic can be tested at the same time. Behavioral dimensions can also be added based on the interpretation of other responses that indicated a greater likelihood that certain customers would purchase over others.[7]

<u>Logistic Regression Analysis</u> Advanced statistics help predict outcomes across multiple product categories or classify customers by type. **Logistic regression analysis** is a statistical tool used to analyze the strength of responses to stimuli. Stimuli might be prices or incentives, for example. Regression analysis can be used to model which factor is responsible for predicting whether a customer buys one of three different products, or to indicate whether a customer might or might not purchase a specific product.[8]

<u>Cognitive Measures</u> Several Web analytical tools center around customer behaviors and physiological responses to marketing stimuli. Researchers at the Sloan School of Management at M.I.T. are working on new technologies that can discern specific traits based on how customers instinctively use a Web site. For example, people who are analytical tend to prefer more detail on a Web site; people-centered individuals prefer peer recommendation options; and those who are visually driven prefer more imagery. By analyzing a user's pattern of clicks, sites could adapt automatically to the customer's individual cognitive style.[9]

If customers are more comfortable as they peruse online retail sites, chances are they will purchase more merchandise. The use of cognitive tools to learn more about customer behavior provides quantifiable data that can aid in developing more effective Web sites and metrics.

Selecting Web Metrics

Examples of specific applications for using metrics online are rich and varied. Heading the category of effective promotional tools is online advertising, followed by Web video, which has expanded rapidly. Here we review methods of assessing the effectiveness of these tools. Tools for assessing e-mail and mobile commerce performance are also highlighted.

Measuring Online Advertising Effectiveness Customer exposure to online advertising has been the key indicator of effectiveness since the advent of the first commercial Web sites. Knowing how many hits a site receives is good, learning how much time is spent on a site is better, but gaining insight into how customers use the time spent on sites is best. Simply counting clicks has been superseded by more meaningful measurements of user interface with advertising messages and Web sites.

Tracking user time spent with several Web site deliverables is the direction most online retailers are taking. Analyzing how customers are viewing Web pages, listening to audio, watching video, and using widgets and microsites is more significant than simply counting visitors to a site. Several companies have developed tools to measure aspects of Web usage that go well beyond the first landing page:

> ComScore is introducing software that enables retailers to measure use of several Web features concurrently. Called "engaged duration metrics," the program tracks when windows become active—even if several are open at the same time.[10]
> Microsoft is testing its Engagement Mapping tool, which attaches values to users' activities preceding the final click and then directs them to an advertiser's Web site. The technology is expected to determine how multiple exposures of a message across many digital avenues may ultimately influence a purchase.[11]

When considering click-stream metrics, a few cautions must be kept in mind. This type of measurement does not include off-line marketing messages that also influence customers. Click-based metrics may be most useful for only a small percentage of online customers because heavy clickers are not representative of the greater population of Web users. It has been shown that only 6 percent of the online population accounted for 50 percent of clicks.[12]

As new information surfaces, at stake is a deeper understanding of Web site use and customer behavior before, during, and after a visit. New metrics may help retail advertisers adjust marketing programs to determine if repeated messages are effective or if fresh approaches should be used.

The top 25 companies ranked in terms of stickiest brands on the Web count several retailers among them. Sites were assessed on the basis of how long customers remained on a Web site. eBay kept customers engaged for almost two hours. Apple Computer kept users interested for just over an hour, and Amazon for about one-half hour. Target kept viewers on its site for 7½ minutes whereas Walmart did so for 13 ¾ minutes.[13]

Assessing Web Video One of the reasons online advertising hits are no longer as effective is that other forms of online advertising like video are gaining a foothold.

Nielson/NetRatings tracks how long visitors spend watching online video content and advertisements. Some pertinent trends emerged from the company's research. Women are twice as likely as men to watch videos on TV network Web sites, for example.[14] Another study determined that teenagers are the largest group of online video watchers. Young people aged 12 to 17 years averaged 74 streaming videos and 132 minutes of online video monthly, according to Nielsen.[15]

Several retailers including Costco use direct-response video to reach their customers. The company HookSell has developed a tool called HookTour that measures which customers respond to video viewing, and encourages customers to stay on the site longer by offering additional relevant video messages. Costco used the technology to increase sales of a small-business telephone system that it usually sold at the rate of one every eight days. After implementing HookTour, the company sold one unit every day.[16]

These types of video viewing measurements are helping retailers target specific groups based on demographics and customer buying habits. Some are tracking multiple behaviors of individual customers. As new media including social networking sites grow, expect that more video metrics will emerge.

E-mail Effectiveness In general, targeted e-mail works best when it its part of a multichannel promotional plan. JupiterResearch found that e-mail campaigns improved results for 74 percent of companies that integrated such campaigns with off-line direct marketing efforts and for 85 percent that integrated the campaigns with Web site analytics.[17]

One of the obstacles to deliverability of e-mails is spamming. Spam accounts for 78.5 percent of all e-mail. About 26 percent of this total is product related, and therefore of particular concern to retailers. Several companies have fallen prey to brand hijacking, sometimes in the guise of gift cards. **Brand hijacking** describes the use of name brands in bogus e-mail messages. Both Target and Dunkin' Donuts have had their brands misused in this way.[18]

To establish e-mail marketing measurement standards, the E-mail Measurement Accuracy Coalition (EMAC) was created in 2007. The first metric it will address is deliverability, which the group has defined as: "total e-mail deployed divided into the total amount successfully delivered."[19] This development supports momentum in the industry to generate operable and customary measurement practices. E-mail is a viable and low-cost way to contact customers and enhances customer service in many ways.

<u>Mobile Metrics</u> Some companies are using multivariate testing to learn more about what works on their Web sites when accessed through mobile networks. Because m-commerce is a relatively new channel, it is important to accurately measure conversion rates. Retailers are testing images that transfer well to small screens, colors, and even specific words and phrases to learn what works best. Measurement in the mobile sphere is more difficult because the technology structure does not yet support JavaScript and cookie placement, which is commonplace on laptop and personal computer delivery systems.[20]

By tracking keywords and text-messaging telephone numbers, advertisers collect information from responses received from calls placed by cell phone users. The company 1 Touch Marketing Service offers applications for generating leads, building databases, and targeting advertising to cell phone users. It can also draw keywords from other selling vehicles such as e-mail and postal mailing lists, for example. The solution is more useful than 800 numbers when presenting offers to customers because keywords reach targeted customers rather than a random population.[21]

M-commerce is expected to grow and follow an adoption pattern similar to that of cell phones. With three times as many cell phone users as Internet users worldwide, the need to track mobile use and develop appropriate transactional methods will grow accordingly.

Whatever metrics are used to measure online services provided by retailers, several commonalities exist. Shopping patterns are changing and assessment tools must keep pace.

Pressure to accumulate as many unique visitors to a site or garner as many one-time sales as possible has subsided. Prevalent objectives now are to serve and retain existing customers while being profitable. Providing quantifiable information to help retailers make informed decisions about their business is the goal of metric selection and use.

> Catalog Fulfillment Measurement

Most catalog retailers are now multichannel. The metrics used to measure effectiveness of catalog retailing are also used in slightly different guises on the Web. Five common metrics used by catalog retailers are highlighted:

1. *Costs–Sales Relationship*—Improvements in fulfillment practices such as inventory tracking, receiving, shipping, and transportation management lower costs of doing business. Inefficiencies increase them. Fulfillment costs are monitored as a percentage of total supply chain costs and sales.
2. *Cash-to-Cycle Time*—This metric measures efficiencies of processes, including forecasting, planning, timing, and reliability. Cash-to-cycle is calculated as follows: Inventory days of supply *plus* days of sales outstanding *minus* days payable.
3. *Perfect Order Index*—This assessment tool combines several metrics, including complete shipments, on-time delivery, damage-free delivery, and accuracy of pricing and invoicing. The perfect order index is a fusion of performance ratings in each of the four categories expressed as a percentage.
4. *Back Order Fulfillment*—When customers are given "rain checks," it means that goods are not in stock. Every effort is made to get back-ordered merchandise out to customers. The speed at which this is accomplished is another important measure for catalog operations.
5. *Fill Rates*—Reaching the customer at the time when goods are requested is another dimension of catalog metrics. Retailers track and evaluate order fill rates.[22]

Catalog companies use data analytics extensively as they sharpen their understanding of customer behavior. Measuring value by viewing customers' complete purchase history is an option used by the Vermont Teddy Bear Company and its catalog operations Calyx, Corolla, and PajamaGram. Formerly the company only had access to first and last purchase data. Using new technology, the gift and toy company has been able to leverage its relational database and gain valuable new information on its customers.[23]

Technology providers use artificial intelligence to sharpen the impact of catalogs on customers. Catalogixx applies the personal shopper mindset to direct-marketing pieces that are specifically tailored to customers. The application uses customer purchase history information to build a model, and draws from that database to customize catalogs, direct-mail pieces, or e-mails to the customers.[24]

Companies respond differently to increased competition between channels and the rising costs of postage and print stock. Many catalog retailers continue to build their multichannel businesses. Others have discontinued one channel in order to concentrate on more productive alternatives. For example, in order to better service its online business, Bloomingdale's will cease distribution of its mail catalogs by the end of 2009. Bloomingdale's online sales have exceeded catalog sales for the last several years.[25] In this case, the measurement of performance dictated the change in approach.

Many of the performance measurement tools in use today across all channels originated within the catalog industry.

> Brick-and-Mortar Productivity

Retailers look at classic determinants of productivity, such as annual sales, profitability, and breakdowns by sales per square foot storewide and departmentally. Units per transaction and sales per hour are other metrics used by brick-and-mortar chains to measure sales force productivity.

Retailers also look to new measures of performance. Some are using video-based technologies, including traffic counters, to monitor not only the ebb and flow of traffic in the store, but also other useful metrics. Traffic information is used to compare different measures of return on investment for stores within the chain. Through this analysis, staffing utilization and advertising effectiveness can be determined. Read about how Anna's Linens uses video traffic counters in Box 10.2.

A study by Opinion Research Corporation reaffirmed other research showing that multichannel customers tend to spend twice as much as customers who shop only one channel. Multichannel shoppers are very price conscious and perhaps because of this are not the most loyal customers. The research also showed that customers who use multiple channels shop more frequently at big box retailers such as Lowe's or Staples, mass merchants such as Walmart, and department stores such as Macy's than they do specialty retailers and high-end department stores like Saks Fifth Avenue.[26]

What's the Buzz? Box 10.2

> *Stuck on Traffic: Anna's Linens Uses Video-Based Technology to Generate "The Metric that Measures Potential"*

Executives at Anna's Linens are counting far more than threads these days. The California-based bed, bath, and home decor chain has been installing traffic-counters at the entrances of all its stores. Management expects to track how many people have walked through any of Anna's 253-plus stores.

Anna's executives have crunched plenty of numbers, like sales volume and units per transaction, "but we recognize that we are missing a tool that would allow us to measure a store's potential, the effectiveness of our marketing, and whether or not we had effectively aligned payroll and staffing," says COO Scott Gladstone.

Anna's signed up for I-Count, a video-based technology with shape recognition from the company CountWise. Average shoppers might mistake the modules for smoke detectors, but they can shed valuable light on conversion rates.

The company is not alone of course: 35 percent of 168 North American retailers surveyed for a 2007 AMR Research report were using some form of traffic-tracking technology, and another 32 percent were in the evaluation stage.

The decision to deploy the video technology solution throughout the chain followed a five-store test. The test stores were selected based on a variety of factors including climate. One of the stores that were not performing to plan was in the test group. The first month of testing showed that in terms of traffic, the store was within 6 percentage points of the chain's highest performing location. "We realized that our marketing efforts and customer traffic in that store were more than acceptable . . . so we looked at staffing. Anna's executives learned that, "WE had pulled hours out of that store and that sales had responded accordingly." An analysis of traffic versus sales showed that the conversion rate at this particular store was the lowest when it was the most crowded. "We weren't staffed to handle those spikes and peaks in traffic," Gladstone says.

Gladstone likes the traffic-counting data because it empowers management at the store. Accountability is always a challenge so Anna's is tying bonuses and incentives to traffic-counting related improvements. The soft economy makes the kind of ROI data the chain is now gleaning through traffic-counters especially important, Gladstone says.

Other retailers using the technology are H&M, Gucci, and Lord & Taylor. Some stores track traffic in individual checkout lines or within specific departments as well as at the entrance. Amir Chitayat, president of CountWise, says that retailers want detailed video information: "They want to see, 'How long did they stay here?' And, did they just pass by or did they browse?"

Source: From Rebecca Logan, Stores, April 2008, 74.

Stores contribute most significantly to the gross margin of multichannel retailers, reinforcing the import role played by the brick-and-mortar channel. Stores comprised 62 percent of total gross margin across all multichannel retailers' Web-influenced store sales, and e-retail direct sales are expected to continue on a growth trajectory through 2012.[27]

> Maximizing Multichannel Return on Investment

"The whole is worth more than the sum of its parts." This sentiment has merit when discussing productivity in multichannel organizations because progress is measured in many ways. Productivity not only reflects the drive for revenue growth but also the goal of long-term customer retention and value. Classic return on investment calculation could be construed as return on innovation as well as investment.

Creating a multisensory experience on the Web challenges retailers, but the task is being accomplished. Initiatives to transfer key characteristics that have made brick-and-mortar stores popular are being approximated by online stores and have met with some success. The comfort level among consumers is rising as they adjust their shopping approaches and convenience levels and find that all channels may work for them some of the time. In the online sector, improvements in interactive and graphic design are occurring continuously. Smelling the aroma of coffee or our favorite fragrance online, sampling the texture of a fabric sample, or tasting a new gelato flavor seems out of reach—for the moment. Could this happen? Can this be measured? Wait and see.

The major realignment that is currently under way among retailers, from collecting figures to searching for the underlying behavioral patterns that translate to repeat visits, represents a key direction for today's multichannel retailers. There are, however, several legal issues relating to this trend that may compromise online selling efforts.

Legal Impediments to Multichannel Retailing

Legal aspects of the retail environment that are of concern to retailers and customers are those that involve taxation, privacy, and Internet regulation. A greater issue is whether there should be federal or state government regulation or no regulation at all. Anticipated changes in customer interface are expected as a result of legislation in the following areas.

> Online Sales Tax Legislation

Since the dawn of Internet retailing, the legality of sales tax has been in dispute, and the industry is in a state of flux regarding the matter. Although only five states (Alaska, Delaware, Montana, New Hampshire, and Oregon) do not impose sales tax on most products purchased in stores, other states invoke different tax percentages, making standardization complicated.

A Supreme Court decision in 1992 suspended sales tax collection for direct-mail and online purchases as long as retailers did not have a store, office, or distribution center in that state.[28] Subsequently the federal Internet Tax Freedom Act was passed in 1998.

New York State served as the poster child for embracing online taxation when the state passed legislation requiring online sellers to pay sales taxes even if they do not have a physical presence in New York. In 2008, Governor Patterson signed the bill, making it a law.[29] Pure-play online retailers including Amazon.com were adamantly opposed to passage of the law, and the Direct Marketing Association was not supportive. Proponents stressed revenue generation and the opportunity to reduce unfair advantages to retailers that do not pay taxes over those that already are contributing to state coffers.[30]

> Privacy Bills

New York State is also attempting to make online advertising networks illegal. Rather than bidding on advertisements, as is the current practice, retailers would have to establish contracts between publishers and their companies. Detractors believe requiring contracts would be the equivalent of returning to the stone age. Online bidding is speedy; contract negotiation and writing takes longer.

Promoters of the proposed legislation believe that advertising benefits customers and is what keeps potential costs of other online services—like free e-mail—at bay. Many online retailers would rather encourage easier opt-outs by customers than tamper with the existing advertising bidding process.[31]

> Network Neutrality Debate

Internet service providers (ISPs) that allegedly compromise the speed with which customers access Web sites are coming under legal scrutiny. A concept called network neutrality is at stake. **Network neutrality** is the understanding that Internet users should be able to go where they want on the Web without intrusion from ISPs.[32]

Hearings were held in Congress to discuss possible legislation that would prevent ISPs from slowing down or tampering with the delivery of content over their networks. ISPs believe such cease-and-desist legislation would defeat the purpose of high-speed broadband and is unfair regulation. Some users who believe regulation of controversial peer-to-peer sites like BitTorrent is needed welcome the proposed Internet Freedom Preservation Act.[33] Other users cited possible discriminatory practices based on how much money was paid to put questionable content on the Internet.

> Retailer and Consumer Rebuttals

Strong sentiments on the issue of Internet taxation emanate from all constituencies. States insist they need the revenue brought by online sales taxes. Uncollected taxes are estimated to total between $15 and $18 billion annually. In 2008 the U.S. Congress debated a bill allowing at least 22 states to require most online retailers to collect taxes.

Customers do not take a strong position regarding taxation, probably because most reside in states where sales tax is customary. The state of the economy is considered a more valid indicator of shopping reticence.

There is some movement to protect small retailers from having to collect sales tax because many could not absorb more costs of doing business. Larger retailers are equally concerned, and Amazon has filed a lawsuit challenging New York State's law regarding mandatory compliance. The company disputes the law, emphasizing that its many affiliates that feature Amazon products on their Web sites and blogs would be unfairly disadvantaged.[34]

Online privacy is not a new issue. In 2007 the Federal Trade Commission (FTC) met with several consumer advocacy groups about creating a do-not-track service. It would be similar to the existing telephone marketing do-not-call lists now in effect. FTC cookies are available for consumers who want to install them on their computers. Presence of the cookie allows individuals to see which Web sites track their behavior.[35]

Activity in large states such as New York could influence federal legislation on these and other retail trade-related issues. That is why all parties involved watch the legislative progress carefully. Proregulation and antiregulation debates will continue.

Environmental Influences Shaping the Future

Predicting trends for the next year, much less the next five, is difficult. Several trends mentioned throughout this text are expected to continue, including personalization, shoppertainment, and extended customer services.

There is deeper concern that deserves reflection. The yin and yang of social and physical needs to shop in a real world rather than experience virtual fulfillment is at the crux of many retail initiatives. It is reasonable to expect that malls will remain sacred sartorial spots for those individuals who want to shop and savor the experience. On occasions when only the personal touch will suffice, brick-and-mortar stores will be the destination of choice. Online stores will fare well if customers need essentials, grocery commodities, or replacement products. Those who are particularly time-challenged will continue to shop online from home late at night when most brick-and-mortar stores are closed.

The online world—by virtue of its vast array of products and services—has captured an A-to-Z market, judging by research done by trusted academics and research firms. The desire to discover a specialty store where one can find that perfect avocado or the best zebra-striped throw pillow remains strong.

The many ways in which aspects of the retail environment affect businesses and individuals were discussed in Chapter 4. Bridges to the future can be detected by revisiting some of these key areas. In the discussion that follows, technology, the economy, "green" practices, and social change are pinpointed as we see what the future has in store for multichannel retailers and customers.

> Technological Innovations and Solutions

In this section we'll explore new products and services in our search to identify extensions to existing technologies. Limited windows of time exist for retailers to react as new technologies emerge to tempt customers and increase revenue streams for manufacturers and retailers.

Hot Products and Cool Services

Planned obsolescence is a factor that must always be considered in retailing. To keep up with and attempt to surpass Blackberry, Apple introduced its touch screen iPhone—touch an icon and the world is yours. New services and product releases inundate the industry as trends coalesce in a few areas.

10.3

Designer cell phone from Prada. *[Source: AP Photo.]*

<u>Mobile Phones: Designer to Discount</u> If you want a new touch screen iPhone, consider one by Dior. If Apple isn't selling them, try the French manufacturer ModeLabs Group, which produces designer mobile phones priced at € 3,500—about $6,000, depending on the exchange rate. Elegantly styled, the "My Dior" phone is about the size of a small USB device and can be used worldwide, except in Japan and Korea.[36] It was only a matter of time before top global fashion designers crossed over to extend their brands to cell phones. Dolce & Gabana earlier developed a line, and other designers are expected to follow suit. The cellphone-as-art is a trend that is expected to grow. A Prada cell phone is illustrated in Figure 10.3.

For the budget conscious, Apple has introduced the less expensive iPhone3G. Selling for $199 or $299, depending on gigabyte capacity, the phone provides faster Internet access than its predecessors and has built-in global positioning system (GPS) capability. Overseas distribution has accelerated with the arrival of this model, and Apple set a goal of 10 million iPhone sales in 2008.[37]

It is evident that all levels of the cell phone market are covered as the product eases into the maturity phase of the product life cycle. Look for rapid innovation within the m-commerce realm as key players fight for market share.

<u>Touch Screen Displays</u> In 2006 Ralph Lauren Sport unveiled a 67-inch image touch screen on the window of its store on Madison Avenue in New York City.[38] Macy's had experimented with an interactive window display a few years earlier, but Lauren's application included all the contemporary accoutrements. Customers could make a selection, insert their credit card in a special slot, arrange to have the item

shipped, or have the invoice sent via e-mail so that they could transact business in the privacy of their home. Touch screen displays are expected to augment most Internet, kiosk, and m-commerce applications. See the Ralph Lauren window in Figure 10.4.

You were introduced to the amazing electronic mirror in Chapter 3. Although not yet widely in use, the concept will evolve. Expect this vital linkage involving customers, fitting rooms, peer assessment, and multichannel fulfillment to escalate, and expect customers to adopt the technology as readily as they would a new appliance.

Eye Tracking Consumer goods manufacturers are learning more about the supermarket product selection process and making shopping easier for customers. In a laboratory setting, Kimberly-Clark learns subtle perceptual cues that affect shopping behavior. Its virtual shopping aisles are designed to approximate a typical grocery shopping experience. But there the similarity ends. A retinal-tracking device measures customer eye movement. The master touch screen allows participants to tap for a different view of shelving. Interiors are designed to replicate actual retail stores. The technology is used as a tool to help manufacturers secure prime shelf space—a competitive process in the stores they supply.[39]

10.4

Ralph Lauren Sport touch-screen interactive window display lets customers order merchandise and make shipping and payment arrangements at any time of day in New York City. [Source: Courtesy of Fairchild Publications, Inc.]

Eye tracking also is used to gain more insight into the habits of online users as they view a Web page. Apparel retailer Charlotte Russe used eye tracking to learn more about how visitors to the site related to lifestyle photographic images. Actual customers were used in the test, which was done in 50-minute one-on-one sessions using the actual Web site. The company selected the technique in

Chapter 10 > **Business Intelligence and Multichannel Retailing** 383 order to maintain objectivity and not be influenced by moderators. Charlotte Russe learned that viewers spent time looking at the images but had no way to link directly to the merchandise. This was subsequently corrected on the Web site so customers would have immediate access to all items shown on models.[40] Techniques like these will remain on the cusp of innovation.

Holographic Sales Associates and Digital Signage The esoteric figure in front of you says, "Welcome to the store of the future," and you respond with thanks and ask for directions to the virtual dressing room. No, you weren't speaking to a human sales associate or personal shopper, but you might as well have been. Holographic service providers are well under development and will serve key functions in the stores of tomorrow.

Digital out-of-home (OOH) advertising provides still and video images using plasma, liquid crystal display (LCD), and high-definition (HD) screens. In juice bars, restaurants, or gyms, or while in transit, promotional and informational content is delivered while individuals are engaged in other activities—such as waiting.

Taste Bud Tempters The five senses have not been fully utilized in multichannel retailing, but companies are breaking barriers that involve taste and smell. First Flavor, Inc., specializes in sensory marketing and has developed small edible strips that melt in your mouth. The film-like Peel 'n Taste strips are saturated with flavors representing many food, beverage, and health-related products. A package of strips might be fastened to a liquor display to allow customers to sample fruit-flavored vodka. The product was successfully used for a popular mouthwash brand, and helped introduce a new coffee flavor for a convenience store chain. The applications are vast. Samples easily can be included with direct-mail pieces or even catalogs, stretching the limits of sensory marketing and heightening brand awareness.

Customization Creating a fully functional virtual self is well on its way to reality. Think about My Virtual Model, combine this with an avatar, add your exact measurements, and what do you have—virtual you. Sears comes close using the newest 3-D version of My Virtual Model. Shoppers enter pertinent size data and can now add a photo of themselves to customize their virtual selves. As well as drawing from Sears's digitized merchandise, users can also scan styles from a favorite fashion magazine to virtually try on their models.[41] One of the keys to customization is to transfer intimate details of your body (honestly and objectively) to Web sites so that you can benefit from shopping without the need for a fitting room.

There are many other modes of customization. Think about the vitamin-enriched waters that are now commonplace on supermarket and health food store shelves and in our own refrigerators. Our favorite brand gives us triple the antioxidants we need in a day and twice as much vitamin C. What more could we want? Perhaps vitamin water customized to our own DNA. This may well be part of future consumption habits.

Enterprise Solutions

Business systems are taxed by the demands of multichannel retailing, and suppliers are meeting requests for efficiency, better access to technology, and supportive infrastructures. A variety of solutions are available for retailers of all sizes.

Virtualization Finding solutions to the overwhelming amounts of hardware that advanced technologies demand has created a space problem for some retail companies. To buffer the shrinking floor space for servers and other computer equipment, retailers are turning to virtualization. **Virtualization** is the consolidation of numerous electronic applications on less, and better utilized, hardware.

Retailers are deluged by electronic applications that have taxed available infrastructure. Supporting kiosks, self-service checkouts, mobile personal digital assistants (PDAs), electronic signage, and computerized shopping carts are examples of the applications that have maximized use of square footage. Applications stretch from headquarters to stores and warehouses. Virtualization increases efficiency and lowers power consumption, increasing company participation in green programs.[42]

Wine Online Shopping for wine has always been a hassle for customers and retailers because states have different rules regarding interstate shipping. Software is now available to sort out the maze of regulations; some companies are taking on the responsibility for providing services for wine companies. This exemplifies progress that changes the way retail business is done.

> Sustainability

As discussed in Chapters 1 and 4, sustainability is a key factor influencing the retail industry. Many new products for building and maintaining green stores in the future have resulted from material developments and a resurgent use of natural, sustainable products. Shopping mall developers are turning to new construction methods and are taking leadership in creating energy-efficient malls and green outdoor marketplaces. Attitudes about spending extra for environmentally safe products are varied and are affected by the economy as well as by individual perspectives on the green movement.

Green Building

Green developers have a fresh outlook regarding design and construction of lifestyle shopping centers. Forest City Enterprises of Cleveland, Ohio, is an industry leader in environmentally sound project development. The company has built several green properties, including The Village at Gulfstream Park in Hallandale Beach, Florida. It features more community areas and green space than other contemporary projects. The developer is seeking LEED certification. **LEED** stands for Leadership in Energy and Environmental Design and is the program that sets environmental standards for builders. The U.S. Green Building Council (USGBC) is an agency that works to guide shopping center developers and help initiate pilot programs in the United States.[43]

Green construction projects are apparent worldwide. All details of development from heating, ventilation, and air conditioning (HVAC) to the energy-efficient controls that run them are part of the greater environmental consciousness. One of energy-efficient units of the French hypermarket retailer Auchan in China is illustrated in Figure 10.5.

Green Products

Product developers continue to take the initiative to develop environmentally friendly products and to source and specify sustainable raw material for the manufacture of consumer products and apparel. Separating green hype from practices that are truly environmentally sound is an aspect of the movement that deserves reflection. For example, many manufacturers claim their products are made from organic cotton, yet fail to realize that most cotton has always been organic. It is the nature of the fiber. But because the product bears the organic label, some feel it deserves a higher price tag and, automatically, more respect. Ethical dilemmas must be worked out if sustainability is to be integrated into our lives and not construed as just another earth-friendly movement. Customers accept products that are authentic in their claims and truthful in their marketing statements.

10.5

This environmentally conscious Auchan hypermarket is one of ten that the French company has opened in China. Stores use state-of-the-art energy management control systems by T.A.C., a division of global company Schneider Electric. *[Source: Courtesy of TAC Times.]*

Green Customers and Their Wallets

Will consumers of the future open their hearts and wallets to support green initiatives or will they loose the momentum built over the past decade and succumb to inertia? That is the question confronting environmentalists and retailers alike. Many green products are pricier than nonenvironmentally approved items. Some people believe that this price differential, coupled with difficult economic times, will adversely affect the green movement. Others believe that environmental consciousness has been raised during this decade and that sufficient education has transpired, leading to greater awareness of the fragility of Earth and support for green initiatives. People around the globe have different perspectives regarding the outlay of money for eco-friendly items, as shown in Table 10.1.

> ### Economic Volatility

The price of a barrel of oil was $100 in early 2008. At the time the nation was aghast. Only a few months later it topped $140, a record high, as stocks tumbled and middle- and lower-class families became more cautious in their spending habits. Gasoline reached over $2.50 per gallon in the summer of 2006, the price documented at

Table 10.1 Percentage of Customers Willing to Pay for Eco-Friendly Products

COUNTRY	PERCENTAGE OF CUSTOMERS
Thailand	94
Brazil	83
United States	53
United Kingdom	45

Source: TNS as published in *DM News*, "Data Bank, The Week in Stats," May 5, 2008, 8.

Walmart in Bentonville, Arkansas, and illustrated in Figure 10.6. By June 2008 it hit $4 for the first time in history. Commuters complained about burgeoning fuel bills, vacationers cancelled planned trips to stay home, and homeowners cut back on spending.

The shock and awe that U.S. consumers are experiencing is rather geocentric. The price per liter of petrol in London converted from pounds sterling into dollars was the equivalent of $4—*20 years ago*. Growing awareness that other countries have experienced shortages and price hikes and have dealt with apoplexy at the pump long before American customers did gives new meaning to these prognostications. It is difficult to interpret exactly how abnormal, disparate increases in the cost of energy affect retail sales.

The mortgage loan crisis, banking crisis, housing slump, deflated real estate market, and rising food and grocery prices have taken an increasing toll on families and businesses. Retailers that provide furniture and home furnishings, decorative products, and appliances were the first to suffer. The reality is that the convergence of negative aspects will continue to take the zing out of the ka-ching until well after this book is published.

10.6

Summer 2006 found gasoline prices rising as Walmart advertised regular unleaded gas for $2.55 per gallon. Customers with a Walmart credit card or shopping card could purchase fuel for 3¢ less per gallon. By 2008 prices had topped $4 but then fell to $2 in early 2009. *[Source: Photograph provided by Lynda Poloian.]*

> **Impact of Social and Lifestyle Changes**

If they are not already, generations X and Y will be running the retail show in the years to come. Consider that the biggest users of blogging, mobile phones, fast food, and other consumables are young people. These and other changes will affect choice of shopping venues and service availability in the future.

10.7 Thinking beyond the traditional, this mall of the future is designed to target different age and interest groups in pod-like clusters. *[Source: Chain Store Age magazine.]*

Changes in Attitudes and Latitudes

The attitude toward products on retail shelves changes as society embraces new values, priorities, and ways of living. Some people, dubbed "locavores," have become much more conscious of purchasing products close to their homes. Whether it is fresh produce from local farms or handmade soaps from cottage industries, many prefer to shop close to market.

Shopping destinations are adapting to our growing needs for mixed use centers where we can live, work, socialize, shop, and sometimes go to medical appointments or attend a class. Another shopping center trend is the growth and new direction of lifestyle centers. Originally, these centers were designed to replicate old downtown areas in small cities where everyone knew each other and shopping areas exuded a sense of nostalgia for customers. Rather than fit a narrow theme or single market, lifestyle centers of the future will be geared to different age and interest groups within the same facility. Great expectations of service will be fulfilled in a harmonious environment. An illustration of a lifestyle center of the future appears in Figure 10.7.

Incongruence in Service Supply and Demand

Many predictions speak to the growing importance of enhanced retail services. One area of note is retail concierge service. A concierge is considered a provider

Box 10.3 What's the Buzz?

> *Unlocking the Store of the Future*

Today we have malls where it can take days just to window-shop and hypermarkets where shoppers can buy everything—including the kitchen sink. We can even take convenient trips to cyberspace, day or night, where we browse through online stores and malls without leaving the comfort of our homes or hotel rooms. With all this variety, it seems like there would be no new frontier for retailers to explore. But this is far from the truth.

For retailers the future has always been an unpredictable mix of customer taste, changing fashion, store inventory, and disconnected supply chains. With the arrival of the Internet and other technological and social advances and the collapse of trade boundaries, the daunting challenge for many retailers is how to cater to the specific, fast-changing tastes of local customers while fighting competition from every corner of the globe.

One thing is certain. To be successful, retailers must be flexible and agile, and that capability is all about an integrated supply chain. Conversely, nothing can kill flexibility like a lengthy and rigid supply chain.

The next frontier for retailers involves finding the fastest and most efficient way to transform traditional business models at the breakneck speed of market shifts. Successful retailers will continually find ways to differentiate their products and services from those of their competitors. Retailers have to provide a compelling experience to compete with proliferating buying channels, growing demand online, one-stop shopping alternatives, and the ever-faster introduction of new products and services. They must offer a more personal and focused venue with a shopping experience that combines the right products with a personalized level of service that goes beyond shoppers' expectations and inspires them to come back for more. A strong knowledge of past buying habits is the key to understanding future demands that will in turn drive merchandising decisions throughout the enterprise.

(continued)

---

of superior service and is knowledgeable and skilled in many areas. The addition of concierges to the retail service mix will become common and expected, but who will fill their shoes? Where are the experts who will dispense information, arrange bookings, multitask, and do it all with a gracious countenance? Today's retail organizations have difficulty finding reliable, skilled employees. It is hard to foresee how retailers will be able to implement recruitment and training methods to induce high-level service providers to work at low-paying jobs with high status.

Despite economic upheaval, retailers are satisfying customers as their shopping instincts adapt to new channels and opportunities. The essay in Box 10.3 presents a

> **What's the Buzz?** *(continued)* **Box 10.3**
>
> Retailers will find ways to enhance or expand the business processes that support intelligent demand planning and merchandising and provide a distinctive shopping experience for their customers. Ultimately, these processes should help create a shopping environment that suits customers' needs dynamically by leveraging technologies like RFID, mobile self-checkout, and high-speed payment. All these capabilities will be used to help customers find what they are looking for in their own time frames.
>
> With today's savvy shoppers being inundated with product and shopping channel choices, retail growth and profitability will demand a deeper understanding of consumers, quantitative data to anticipate and fulfill their needs, and insight to inspire them to return to the stores, whether brick-and-mortar or virtual.
>
> To achieve this superior real-time enterprise management, a scalable, reliable, and future-proof technology platform is required. Retailers of the future must be able to implement emerging services, processes, and technologies on their installed technology platform. Quick response, enabled by a platform designed for change, can help retailers define excellent experiences for customers that will rapidly translate into customer satisfaction, customer loyalty, and increased sales.
>
> *Source: From Verlin Youd, senior vice president of trading industries for SAP, Stores, April 2008, 105.*

view of the future that incorporates many of the topics put forth in this book along with the insights of an industry participant.

Multichannel Retailing: A Final Word

Moody's Investors Service now includes online sales as an important factor in determining retailers' credit ratings. The service noticed that for many retail companies, online sales are driving performance in a poor economy and are offsetting diminished sales in brick-and-mortar outlets. Online sales have reached critical mass for retailers when credit rating services acknowledge their importance.[44] For every dollar spent online, the Internet influences $3.45 of brick-and-mortar sales.[45] Multichannel retailing influences these changes and is affected by others.

Just as mergers and acquisitions have affected traditional retail organizations in the past, they will continue to shape multichannel retailers and the organizations that power and serve the Internet. Rumors of tentative agreements between companies such as Microsoft, Google, Yahoo!, and others play heavily in news reports. Activity in this sector will continue to shape business liaisons and power structures. An analyst has predicted that Google and Amazon will be the major forces on the Internet as Yahoo!, IAC InterActiveCorp, and eBay decline.[46]

New leadership in many multichannel retail companies is another hallmark of change that can be interpreted in several ways. Change in executive ranks is natural as company executives reach goals and move on. In tough economic times, change in leadership is often precipitated by disenchantment of shareholders who are dismayed by performance results. New leadership can herald a new direction for a company—particularly one that is increasingly dependent on technology and proactive about growth strategies, whether they entail global expansion or multichannel direction. Among the companies that have experienced changes in key leadership are Home Depot, Lord & Taylor, and Talbots. Speculation is that other large retailers will follow suit.

Many developments in retailing come full cycle over time, whether reinvigoration of department stores or emergence of the next great specialty concept. Although we tend to credit technology for changing our world, access to the Internet has only accelerated trends that were well established a generation ago.

We are close to having the technological capabilities to provide an electronic mirror over our vanity sink, reporting the weather for us as we prepare for work. It could even tell us what type of sun protection we would need that day. It might remind us when we forget to take our medication, or suggest what we should have for breakfast based on a quick nutritional analysis of our bodies and then prepare a shopping list for perusal. "Smart" refrigerators that could detect household stock levels, automatically order from a food provider, and accept delivery in our absence are not far from reality—if we want that level of service. If we do not, many supermarket products will be available for purchase prepacked in refrigerated materials for protection from extreme heat and cold. These features will add a welcome element of stress reduction to our harried lives, a key aspect of many innovations, both today and tomorrow. Customer acceptance remains the threshold upon which success will be measured.

Summary

In the future, customers will continue to wear crowns and be treated like royalty—just as they are today by high-performing, customer-centric multichannel retailers. Retailers will continue to provide meaningful services and positive shopping experiences. They will quantify data gathered through interaction with their customers using opt-in methods. They will do this regularly because nothing stays the same in retailing and that aspect is not expected to change.

Web analytics are tools that help retailers reduce risk, plan more effectively, and make keener decisions. Many types of metrics depend on channels used, business objectives, and level of information needed.

Most legacy platforms that are the underpinnings of the business architecture are in the process of being upgraded or changed to keep up with the demand for more fluid operations, more effective channel integration, and economies of merchandising, fulfillment, and service.

Changes in the retail environment have an impact on many future trends. Technology, the economy, sustainability, and societal shifts are drivers of change. Insightful retailers react well to change because they face it proactively.

Multichannel retailing is already an established practice and philosophy of conducting business. Increased globalization and the growth within developing countries such as China and India will change the marketplace further. Technological capabilities and business intelligence will keep up with increased demand. These are concurrently arduous and exhilarating times in which to trade.

> **Key Terms**

Brand highjacking
Business intelligence (BI)
Digital out-of-home (OOH)
LEED
Legacy system
Logistic regression analysis
Multivariate testing
Network neutrality
Real-time analytics (RTA)
Reference assembly architecture
Service-oriented architecture (SOA)
Split testing
Taguchi testing
Virtualization

> ## Questions for Discussion and Reflection

1. What is the difference between legacy systems and reference assembly architecture? What do retailers expect to gain from this aspect of business intelligence?
2. Sales are not the only metric used to evaluate online store performance. State and elaborate on three other customer activities that are quantifiable.
3. Why do retailers choose eye tracking rather than more conventional methods to assess customer behavior? What does eye tracking measure?
4. What is the pure-play retailers' position regarding online sales taxation? How does it differ from the consumer viewpoint?
5. Attempts to make online advertising networks illegal have raised objections by retailers. What are the pros and cons of this position?
6. Several trends are expected to gain momentum in the next few years. Drawing from your reading and personal observations, what technologies will benefit retailers and customers the most?

7. Why has virtualization become an important tool for retail information technology departments?
8. Designer and touch screen mobile phones, electronic gadgets and gizmos—which devices have the potential for a long product life cycle? Justify your choice.
9. What can be learned about the economy by studying the radical price increases in basic commodities such as fuel and groceries? How do consumers and retailers cope with this issue?
10. Environmental movements have waxed and waned in the United States over the last several decades. The resurgence of interest in sustainability and green retailing is on the rise. Do you believe this movement is a short-term phenomenon or a genuine agent of change?

Notes >

1. Adam Michelson and Marc Osofsky, "Read Before Ecommerce Re-Platforming: A New Agile Option," Optaros White Paper, © Optaros 2008, 2-5.
2. Sahir Anand, "Technology Strategies for Multi-Channel Integration," White Paper. © Aberdeen Group 2008, April 2008, 16.
3. Giselle Abrahamovich, "Companies Lack Web Metric Know-How: Study," *DM News*, June 11, 2007, 6.
4. Anand, 17.
5. Lee Gomes, "Talking Tech: Good Site, Bad Site: Evolving Web Design," *Wall Street Journal*, June 12, 2007, B3.
6. Samantha Murphy, "Making an Entrance," *Chain Store Age*, March 2008, 66.
7. Rober W. Bly, "Taguchi Testing Can Triple Conversion," *DM News*, December 4, 2006, 16.
8. "SPSS Regression Models 16.0," Decisions, SPSS Product Catalog 11 (2007): 16.
9. Erica Naone, "Adapting Websites to Users," *Technology Review*, (Cambridge, MA, Massachusetts Institute of Technology, June 9, 2008), www.technologyreview.com.
10. Josh Chasin, "Better Measures for Web Ads," *Washington Post*, January 14, 2008, www.washingtonpost.com/wp-dyn/content/article/2008/01/13/AR2008011302701.
11. Brian Morrissey, "Marketers Seek Better Ways to Measure Online Ad Hits," *Brandweek.com*, March 3, 2008, http://www.brandweek.com/bw/news/recent_display.jsp?vnu_content_id=1003718448.
12. Ibid.
13. Nielsen Online, as reported in "Top U.S. Parent Companies and Stickiest Brands on the Web, March 2008," April 22, 2008, www. Clickz.com/showPage.html?page=clickz_print&id-3629238.
14. Emily Steel, "Nielsen Online Takes a Look at How People Use Web Video," *Wall Street Journal*, February 14, 2008, B7.
15. Mike Shields, "Nielsen: Teens Biggest Users of Online Video," June 9, 2008, www.mediaweek.com/mw/content_display/news/digital-downloads/metrics/e3i32a6c4ade2dd7b238403192b9ee8b8e0?imw=Y.
16. Anne Zieger, "Click Me, Baby…One More Time," *Media Post Publications*, April Issue 2008, 3-4, http://publications.mediapost.com.
17. Tanya Lewis, "In Perfect Harmony," *DM News*, April 7, 2008, 15. Statistical source: Jupiter Research, 2007 Study.
18. Rebecca Logan, "Impersonators in the Inbox," *Stores*, May 2008, 50.
19. Dianna Dilworth, "Deliverability Defined by EMAC," *DM News*, February 28, 2008,

www.dmnews.com/Deliverability-defined-by-EMAC/PrintArticle/107187/.

20. "ToolBox: Why Is Multivariate Testing Important for the Mobile Web?" *DM News*, April 14, 2008, 39.

21. Jim Emerson, "Text-Messaging Service Ties Keywords to Targeting," *Direct*, April 8, 2008, www.directmag.com/disciplines/lists/Text-messagi040808/index.html.

22. Kate Vitasek, "5 Most Useful Fulfillment Metrics," *Catalog Success* (Philadelphia: North American Publishing Company, © 2008), www.catalogsuccess.com/story/print.bsp?sid=94398&var=story.

23. Lauren Bell, "Database Strategy Drives Vermont Teddy Bear Sales," *DM News*, May 12, 2008, 3.

24. Fred Minnick, "Getting Personal," *Stores*, May 2008, 46.

25. "In Brief: Bloomingdale's to Stop Sending Catalogs," *Wall Street Journal*, May 12, 2008, B9.

26. "Multichannel Shopping Changing Retailing," *eMarketer*, June 12, 2008, www.emarketer.com/Articles/Print.aspx?id1006364.

27. Ibid.

28. Bob Tedeschi, "Days of Tax-Free Online Sales May Be Numbered," *New York Times*, June 27, 2005, www.nytimes.com.

29. Saul Hansell, "Amazon Sues Over State Law on Collection of Sales Tax," *New York Times*, May 2, 2008, www.nytimes.com.

30. Dianna Dilworth, "Proposed Tax Rocks Retailers," *DM News*, April 21, 2008, 1, 26.

31. Dianna Dilworth, "NY Bill Threatens Online Ads," *DM News*, March 24, 2008, 1, 26.

32. John Dunbar, Associated Press, "Senators Debate Future of Web," *Washingtonpost.com*, April 22, 2008, www.washingtonpost.com/wp-dyn/content/article/2008/04/22/AR2008042200386>p.

33. Kenneth Corbin, "House Takes Up Net Neutrality," May 6, 2008, www.internetnews.com/government/article.php/3745181.

34. Hansell, "Amazon Sues."

35. Dilworth, "NY Bill…," 26.

36. Christina Passareillo, "Dior to Unveil Line of Mobile Phones," *Wall Street Journal*, May 21, 2008, B9.

37. John Markoff, "Apple Aims for the Masses With a Cheaper iPhone," *New York Times*, June 10, 2008, www.nytimes.com/2008/06/10/technology/10apple.html.

38. Lisa Lockwood, "Ralph Lauren Makes Window Shopping Interactive," *Women's Wear Daily*, August 7, 2006, 2.

39. Ellen Byron, "A Virtual View of the Store Aisle," *Wall Street Journal*, October 3, 2007, B1, B12.

40. "Eye-tracking Helps Charlotte Russe Tie Online Merchandising to Impulse Buys," *Internet Retailer*, February 4, 2008, www.internetretailer.com/printArticle.asp?id=25274.

41. Sandra Guy, "Shopping for Clothes Online Goes 3-D at Sears," *Chicago Sun-Times*, September 15, 2008, www.suntimes.com/technology/1163480,CST-FIN-sears15.article.

42. Geoff Thomas, "What Virtualization Has in Store," *Stores*, May 2008, www.stores.org/Current_Issue/2008/05/POV.asp.

43. Katherine Field, "Green Spaces and Places," *Chain Store Age*, March 2008, 152, 156.

44. Jennifer Saranow, "Moody's Includes Online Sales in Rating Retailers," *Wall Street Journal*, June 16, 2008, B9.

45. Clickz, News Headline, www.shop.org SmartBrief, June 3, 2008.

46. Reuters, "U.S. Internet Will Shrink to 2 Strong Players: Report," *New York Times*, June 3, 2008. Source Jeffrey Lindsay, "U.S. Internet: The End of the Beginning," www.nytimes.com/reuters/technology/tech-internet-research1.html?sq=ebay&st=nyt.

Multichannel Retail Profile > Amazon.com

> Overview

If any Web site could be called the grandparent of all online retailers it must be Amazon.com. From its humble roots as a seller of books to its present incarnation as an online department store, Amazon has become a household word since its inception in 1995. Headquarters are in Seattle, Washington.

When the company filed an initial public offering (IPO) in 1997, it stated sales of $511,000 for 1995. At the time of the IPO, founder and Chief Executive Officer Jeffrey Bezos indicated that he and his family would control a minimum of 52 percent of common stock. Sales grew to $15.7 million in 1996.[1] Amazon sold $610 million in books and music in 1997.[2] By 2001, revenue for the pure-play retailer reached approximately $3 billion.[3]

More than half of Amazon's revenue is derived from its North American operations. The company's sales reached $14.8 billion in 2007, representing a 38 percent growth rate over the previous year. Average monthly visits to the site were 207,671,000, the sales conversion rate was 3.5 percent, and the average ticket was estimated at $193. It is the top online retailer in the world.[4]

Competition comes from many sectors but apparently no online business performs quite as well as Amazon. Multichannel booksellers Barnes & Noble and Borders are chief competitors in book, video, and music categories. However, these products are not the only revenue generators for the more diversified Amazon. Extensive diversification of products and services may dilute the power of conventional retailers, but for online retailers it tends to be an advantage.

Amazon did not turn even a scant profit until the fourth quarter of 2001, and then experienced sporadic performance until the third quarter of 2003 when it became profitable.[5] Several strategic initiatives, timely decisions, and a high level of innovation have contributed to its strong position today.

> Strategic Direction

Amazon's aggressive expansion into vast products, services, and partnerships is at the core of its success and is noted in many chapters of this text. Tracing the movement from books to videos, music, toys, electronics, drugs, jewelry, handcrafts, food, apparel, and much more is indicative of the foresight of Bezos and a cadre of internal expertise.

Early in its history, Amazon embraced smaller online merchants by creating an affiliate program called zShops. Many third-party retailers signed on for a nominal monthly fee and a percentage of credit card transactions conducted on the Amazon site.[6] Independent merchants generate about 25 percent of all sales on the site. All types of products are sold—even used books.

The company continually looks for strategic advantages by fully exploring new product line opportunities, acquiring other online businesses, and developing new concepts in-house. Amazon opened an office supply store featuring about 500,000 products in

2008.[7] Despite an assortment of prohibitive interstate-shipping laws, Amazon has not given up hope that it will eventually add wine to its merchandise mix.[8]

Retail partnerships, media linkages, product development, and international expansion are tactically significant areas for Amazon. All are undertaken with the goal of providing more and better services for customers.

Partnership Programs

The company has formed several types of partnerships over the years, including those with affiliates, vendors, and other retailers. Among the more notorious retail partnerships was an arrangement with Toys "R" Us that was meant to last for ten years. Under the agreement, which was signed in 2000, Toys "R" Us was to pay Amazon an annual fee, transaction fees for sales emanating from Amazon.com, and a small percentage of Toysrus.com sales. In 2002 the agreement was renegotiated—ostensibly to decrease cash payments incurred by Toys "R" Us.[9] Despite efforts to sustain the partnership, by 2006 it had been prematurely terminated.

In 2001, Amazon entered into an agreement with Borders for which it provided online services, including customer service, inventory, and other fulfillment functions. Amazon gained revenue from these sales and in turn paid Borders a commission on all online sales.[10] The agreement expired in 2007, and Borders launched its own e-commerce site in 2008.[11]

Other partnerships involve media companies and retail services. Amazon is working with TiVo on a product purchase feature. Knowing how TiVo users tend to skip commercial messages, Amazon believes it will benefit from installing mechanisms that will allow viewers to buy CDs, DVDs, and books touted by guests on programs such as the Oprah Winfrey and David Letterman shows.[12]

Innovative Products and Services

Amazon moved into new turf when it launched its Kindle reader in 2007. Who would have believed that people would be content to read a book by holding the palm-fitting device in their hands? Yet sales of the device were growing steadily by 2008, prompting some market analysts to hail the Kindle a success paralleling Apple's launch of its iPod.

In another innovative spurt, Amazon has extended an open invitation to digital entrepreneurs and is investing in several compatible online companies. Amazon recognized the potential of AmieStreet.com, a site that combines the benefits of downloading music with customer ratings, and invested in the young company. The digital download site specializes in independent artists and lets user reviews help determine the price of songs.[13]

Amazon is also offering its "Checkout by Amazon" payment service to other online retailers. Customers need only enter their contact and credit card preferences once at Amazon.com to be able to use the secured information while shopping on other sites. About 81 million Amazon customers have provided data to the company.[14]

Multichannel Retail Profile > Amazon.com

International Expansion

Amazon has a global presence through operations worldwide. It entered the United Kingdom in 1998, followed by Germany and France in 2000.[15] The company then set its sights on several other European countries and entered Japan.

Amazon acquired the Chinese Internet company joyo.com in 2004 and considers China its fastest-growing division. Bezos said that similar to the U.S. operation, he did not expect the Chinese site to become profitable quickly. One significant difference in fulfillment is that in China goods are routinely delivered by bicycle rather than by postal services. In a branding shift, the company renamed the Chinese site JoyoAmazon in 2007.[16]

> Web Presence

Amazon accounts for 9 percent of total U.S. consumer-based sales—a commanding share far beyond that of any other single Web site. Only twenty-one online retailers earned $1 billion or more in 2007 and Amazon ranked at the top of the list.[17]

Very few of its Web site, fulfillment, marketing, or design services are outsourced, making Amazon one of the few online sellers to use substantially fewer outside vendors. This practice may indicate both strength and weakness in the long run. Companies that rely on inside expertise—especially in a technology driven company—may find they lack the fresh approach brought by outsiders. On the other hand, when a company is at the top of its industry it is possible that increased control over operations, and decision making derived from internal strength and experience, contributes to high performance.

Amazon is the place consumers go to fulfill needs. The company ranks at or near the top of natural search rankings in most merchandise categories in which it participates. Of fifty Web sites ranked, Amazon was first in Web site performance metrics, receiving a 99.97 percent rating for site availability. In other words, Amazon is always open and accessible.[18]

> Future Direction

Amazon is the online channel of choice for many consumers and dominates sales generated on the Web. Promotional incentives and discount pricing keep customers coming back for more. Free shipping offers and carefully structured annual fee policies encourage repeat business. Building loyalty takes time, and many retailers have required decades to build a strong customer base. Amazon has accomplished this in only fifteen years.

Amazon projected revenues of about $20 billion for 2008.[19] The company is not satisfied with past or current successes and carefully monitors the retail environment, constantly looking for new opportunities as it invests in emerging technologies and fresh content. Diligence, tenacity, and the ability to think of customers first in every decision are qualities that solidify the status of the top online retailer.

> **Points to Ponder**

1. Amazon has been in business for fifteen years and has only been profitable for approximately half that time. What factors have contributed to its significant annual revenue gains but slowly developing profitability?
2. Amazon has participated in many partnerships with other retailers. Judging from current and past examples, what does Amazon gain from these relationships? How do they benefit the partner retail companies?
3. Reflect on the evolution of Amazon from bookseller to online department store. What are the benefits and disadvantages of this strategic direction?
4. What is the purpose of Amazon's affiliate merchants? Would you be interested in selling products on Amazon's site? Why or why not?
5. Comment on Amazon's outlook for the future. Why has it chosen to expand globally?
6. Visit Amazon.com. Do you believe it serves customers as well as it says it does? What features appeal to you? Why?

> **Notes**

1. G. Bruce Knecht, "On-line Book Retailer Amazon Sees Profit in Later Chapters, Files for IPO," *Wall Street Journal,* March 25, 1997, B7.
2. Ross Kerber, "Taking a Page from Amazon.com's Playbook," *Boston Sunday Globe,* March 28, 1999, F1, F5.
3. Nick Wingfield, "Amazon Cuts Jobs, Posts Sales Warning," *Wall Street Journal,* January 31, 2001, A3, A6.
4. "Top 100 Web Retailers, 1. Amazon.com, Inc.," *Internet Retailer 2008 Top 500 Guide,* 86.
5. Nick Wingfield, "Amazon Has First Off-Season Profit," *Wall Street Journal,* October 22, 2003, A3.
6. Steven Zeitch, "Amazon.com to Host Private E-commerce Retail Sites," *Publishers Weekly,* October 4, 1999, 12.
7. Bryan Yurcan, "Amazon.com Launches New Office Supplies Store," *DM News,* June 30, 2008, 3.
8. "In Brief: Amazon Wine-Buyer Posting Has Subtle Hints of Product Expansion," *Wall Street Journal,* March 7, 2008, B3.
9. Nick Wingate, "Amazon Finds Partners Toys R Us, Expedia, Hotwire Are Growing Restless," *Wall Street Journal,* March 15, 2002, B2.
10. Nick Wingfield and Erin White, "Border's Deal Bolsters Amazon's Strategy," *Wall Street Journal,* April 12, 2001, B13.
11. Dianna Dilworth, "Borders Plans Its Latest Online Sales Debut," *DM News,* September 24, 2007, 2.

Multichannel Retail Profile > Amazon.com

12. Brad Stone, "TiVo and Amazon Team Up," *New York Times,* July 22, 2008, www.nytimes.com.
13. Scott Martin, "Amazon Stakes Social Music," *Red Herring,* August 6, 2007, www.redherring.com/PrintArticle.aspx?a=23057&sector=Industries.
14. Brad Stone, "Amazon Offers Other Sites Use of Its Payment Service," *New York Times,* July 30, 2008, www.nytimes.com.
15. Amy Barrett, "Amazon.com to Launch French Website with Four Lines Simultaneously," *Wall Street Journal,* August 30, 2000, B12.
16. Jason Dean, "Bezos Says Amazon Will Boost Investment in China," *Wall Street Journal,* June 6, 2007, A12.
17. Mark Brohan, "Overview," *Internet Retailer 2008 Top 500 Guide,* 10.
18. Andrea Mulligan, "The Online Experience and Sales—Connecting the Dots," *Internet Retailer 2008 Top 500 Guide,* 26.
19. Mylene Mangalindan, "Amazon's Net Doubles on Strong Sales," *Wall Street Journal,* July 24, 2008, B1.

Multichannel Retail Profile > Apple

> Overview

Someone who first encountered the company's engaging mall stores and witnessed the architecturally wondrous Apple superstores opening in major cities might be amazed to learn that Apple began as a computer manufacturer and not a retailer. Reaching for the top by successfully contending with competition and carefully merging form and function, Apple has reached #7 in the *Internet Retailer 2008 Top 500 Guide*.[1] From laptops to iTunes, Macs to iPhones, the company is a force in manufacturing and retail entertainment.

Based in Cupertino, California, Apple dealt skillfully with the consumer perception of being the smaller, but cooler and more artsy, computer company. By moving into online services such as iTunes, opening retail stores, and developing products like the iPod and iPhone, the company enhanced its multichannel presence. Not only is iTunes the top music store online, but it also has the highest sales of any music retailer in the United States—including Walmart.[2]

Apple has worldwide distribution and is planning to increase its share in the personal computing market in China through a brick-and-mortar network. The first of the planned stores, in Beijing, opened in 2008 just prior to the Olympics. The store is called Ping Guo—Chinese for Apple. In 2008, the iPhone was not officially distributed in China, but many people purchased them in resellers' markets.[3]

> Retail Store Expansion

Apple opened its first brick-and-mortar store in 2001 at a shopping center in Virginia. In 2005 sales from its store division had reached $2.3 billion. By mid-2006, the company had 147 stores and stated that its stores had been profitable for years. By this time, Apple had expanded to Canada, Japan, and the United Kingdom.[4]

The early stores were refreshingly light and bright with minimal contemporary décor. Customers were invited to try out new products in an open and participatory environment. The larger superstores combine art and function, deriving much media attention prior to grand openings.

In Boston, customers lined up for blocks waiting to get a peek at the three-story glass palace when Apple opened its 210th store in 2008. The Boylston Street location is in the heart of Boston near the famous Prudential Center and several urban malls, shopping districts, hotels, and historic sites. The company has other superstores in cities including New York, Chicago, and San Francisco, and many smaller units in shopping centers.

Typical of its newest showplaces, the three levels are conveniently arranged by product and service. The first floor features Mac computers and related products, the second carries iPod and iPhone items, and the third is dedicated to service and learning. There, classes on many topics are held in the "Pro Lab," the "Genius Bar" staff provides technical support, and customer service is provided. According to analysts' estimates, the $2,500-sales-per-square foot productivity of Apple's stores is well above that of competitors.[5]

Brick-and-mortar stores accounted for 20 percent of total company sales in 2007. Commenting on the Apple Stores position in the marketplace, Michael Gartenberg, vice president and research director at JupiterResearch said, "They've become the Nordstrom of technology."[6] Apple Stores, including iTunes, earned revenues of $6.6 billion in 2007.[7]

> Products and Branding

The iPod need not be introduced, such is the omnipresence of this music storage and delivery product and the brand. The iPhone, adopting the same naming tactic as its iPod cousin, continues to draw market share away from its cell phone and PDA competitors.

When the original version of the iPhone was introduced in 2007, it sold approximately 270,000 units in the first two days. When Apple introduced its next model in 21 countries one year later, the iPhone3G sold 1 million units in the first weekend. The market leader Nokia sells approximately 10 million cell phones a week, so Apple has room to grow despite its impressive iPhone3G launch.[8]

Because the iPhone3G has many more capabilities than the first iPhone, it is competing head on with the BlackBerry, Research in Motion's market leader in the PDA market with 41 percent market share. Apple is expecting that the extended services, mobile, and download capabilities will challenge BlackBerry by drawing more business professionals into its customer ranks.[9]

Multichannel Retail Profile > Apple

In a step away from its customary distribution strategy, Apple shipped its iPhones to 970 Best Buy and 18 Best Buy Mobile stores. Previously the phone was sold only through Apple Stores and through the 2,000 stores of its exclusive carrier, AT&T.[10] Best Buy in many respects is a competitor to Apple Stores. However this co-branding initiative is beneficial to both Apple, the manufacturer, and Best Buy, the retailer. Cannibalization of sales is less likely in this case because Apple has a more highly defined technophile market than Best Buy.

> Online Metrics

With $2.7 billion in online sales in 2007, Apple achieved a 33.3 percent increase in sales over the previous year. The Apple.com site was launched in 1998 and has almost 165 million average monthly visits, a conversion rate of 1.08 percent, and an average ticket of $130.[11]

Being a vertically integrated as well as a multichannel retailer gives Apple many unique advantages in the marketplace. It controls distribution more effectively than retailers that do not manufacture their products. Brand equity is built through its manufacturing base, retail stores, Internet services and sales such as iTunes, and brand extensions of computers, phones, and extensive peripherals. Apple is well poised to dominate its niche this decade.

> Points to Ponder

1. Its manufacturing arm and its multichannel retail presence compound the scope of Apple's reach in the marketplace. What do you believe is crucial to its success?
2. The iTunes online store has helped change the way music is delivered. How does this Web service influence Apple's brand image?
3. By introducing a new, improved iPhone, what is Apple doing to compete more effectively with BlackBerry? What market does it expect to tap? Do you believe the company will be effective in its attempts to gain market share from BlackBerry?
4. Apple's brick-and-mortar showplaces serve as both retail stores and brand builders. Comment on this statement in the context of retail location, store design, and growth strategies.
5. If possible, visit an Apple Store in your area. Compare the in-store experience with a visit to Apple.com.

> *Notes*

1. "Top 100 Web Retailers, 7. Apple, Inc.," *Internet Retailer 2008 Top 500 Guide,* 98.
2. Michelle Quinn and Dawn C. Chmielewski, "ITunes Records a Sales Milestone," *Los Angeles Times,* April 4, 2008, www.latimes.com/business/la-fi-itunes4apr04,1,50828,print.story.
3. Loretta Chao, "Apple Steps Up China Retail Push," *Wall Street Journal,* July 23, 2008, B2.
4. Nick Wingfield, "How Apple's Store Strategy Beat the Odds," *Wall Street Journal,* May 17, 2006, B1, B10.
5. Jenn Abelson, "Opening Day," *Boston Sunday Globe,* May 11, 2008, G1, G4.
6. Katie Hafner, "Inside Apple Stores, a Certain Aura Enchants the Faithful," *New York Times,* December 27, 2007, www.nytimes.com/2007/12/27/business/27apple.htm?th=&emc=th&pagewanted-print.
7. "Top 100 Retailers," *Stores,* July 2008, T9, www.stores.org.
8. "A Million New iPhones Sold in the First Weekend," *New York Times,* Reuters, July 15, 2008, www.nytimes.com/2008/17/15/technology/15apple.html.
9. Nick Wingfield, "Apple Positions iPhone as Rival to the BlackBerry," *Wall Street Journal,* March 7, 2008, B1, B4.
10. "Retailer Best Buy Gets Call to Sell the iPhone," *Boston Globe,* Associated Press, August 13, 2008, C3.
11. "Top 100 Web Retailers, 7. Apple, Inc.," *Internet Retailer 2008 Top 500 Guide,* 98.

Glossary

Active RFID tags Large tags that have a longer range than passive tags, require a power source, and are more expensive.

Advance shipping notice (ASN) Invoice for products scheduled for imminent shipment from a manufacturer to a retailer or distribution center.

AJAX Acronym for **A**synchronous **J**avaScript **a**nd **X**ML.

Alternation In design, the use of repetition with an interchange of two or more components that differ from each other in size, shape, or color.

Aspirational wants Wants that relate to products and services that people perceive will help them achieve higher status.

Asymmetrical balance Art elements that are not distributed with equal visual weight in a work; also called "informal balance."

Asynchronous learning Learning that takes place at different times, usually at the convenience of the online learner.

Augmented services Comprehensive, value-added services offered by retailers.

Auto ID Automatic identification that uses wireless devices to capture and identify information.

Automated storage and retrieval (ASR) Warehousing systems that combine the use of computer control of stock records with mechanical handling.

Avatar A digital representation of a human figure.

Baby boomers The 76 million people born in the United States between 1946 and 1964.

Back-end services Services that take place behind the scenes or off retail store premises. In the direct marketing sector, fulfillment, customer service, and payment are considered back-end services.

Balance In design, the arrangement of components in a work so that they appear to be in harmony.

Banner advertisement A paid electronic message that appears on a landing page, home page, or elsewhere that promotes a product, service, or other Web site.

Bar coding The capture of information at the point of service by scanning the UPC with an electronic device.

Basic customers The majority of fashion consumers who shop in the maturity stage of the fashion cycle.

Basic services Fundamental customer services offered by retailers.

Behavioral targeting The use of information based on affinity groups to identify prospective customers.

Big box retailers Stores of 70,000 to 150,000 square feet or more that are usually operated by large discounters or mass merchants.

Biogenic needs Physiological needs for food, warmth, shelter, and sex.

Blogs Written narratives that convey opinions and solicit reader feedback online.

Body copy In advertising, the descriptive collection of words that give detailed information about a product.

Boosters People who steal by concealing merchandise in bags and hidden pockets.

Brand hijacking The use of name brands in bogus e-mail messages.

Brand image The perception that customers have of a brand.

Branding The integrative process of building, maintaining, and refining strategies that present the total retail concept to the public.

Brand positioning The place in the marketplace held by a brand or retailer as compared to competitors.

Brick-and-mortar retailers Retail stores that do business from traditional physically constructed facilities.

Business intelligence (BI) Information gathered from a variety of internal and external sources to help businesses make sound decisions.

Call centers Company telecommunication facilities from which telemarketers place calls.

Cannibalization The erosion of sales from an original sales channel by the startup of a new channel.

Carry-over The period of time between the receipt of a catalog by a person and when the person takes action by placing the order. Also applies to advertising materials.

Category killers Specialty superstores that focus on limited merchandise categories and great breadth and depth of assortments.

Channels Conduits through which sales are transacted.

Chapter 11 The federal bankruptcy protection statute that allows companies to stay in business while they reorganize under court supervision.

Choice™ Generation Coined term referring to individuals who believe they have the right to choose and control what, when, and how they receive marketing messages.

Click-through Measurement indicating the number of times Web site visitors use a link.

Click-to-chat services Online services that allow customers to click on an icon, add their telephone number, and receive an immediate callback.

Clienteling The practice of keeping detailed records of select groups of customers with whom trained sales specialists have developed a relationship over time.

Collaborative planning, forecasting, and replenishment (CPFR) An initiative designed to develop distribution efficiencies throughout the supply chain by determining the optimum number and location of warehouses, reducing shipment handling to speed deliveries, and implementing more effective inventory management.

Collections Definitive, very expensive apparel lines produced by a designer.

Consultative selling A form of person-to-person selling that is set up by appointment and often done through a referral network.

Container Ships Vessels outfitted with large numbers of cargo holders that are roughly 40-feet long and shaped like a tractor-trailer bed.

Content All digital material that appears on a Web site.

Convenience goods Low-cost items purchased with minimal effort or time.

Conversion rate The metric used to identify the number of visitors to a Web site who have actually made a purchase. Also applies to non-Web purchases.

Cookies Small files placed on users' browsers by Web site servers for the purpose of identifying prospective customers and delivering targeted messages.

CPM Cost per thousand (**c**ost **p**er **m**ille) advertising impressions.

Cross-docking The practice of receiving goods and then rapidly preparing them for shipment from the distribution center.

Customer relationship management (CRM) Gathering and using database information to reach customers more effectively, identify their needs more specifically, and direct selling and promotional initiatives more precisely.

Database marketing Capturing and using observable and quantifiable information regarding customer behavior and aspirations.

Data breaches Theft of sensitive customer and retail data that may involve fraudulent charges on credit or debit accounts.

Dedicated server A special computer connected to the Internet that houses a Web site exclusively.

Deep discounters Big box discount retailers that offer limited and changing product lines in no-frills environments at very low prices.

Demographics Statistics on human populations, including age, gender, ethnic origin, education, income, occupation, type of housing, and other descriptors.

Department stores Retail companies that occupy large facilities and carry broad assortments of hard and soft goods organized by use, function, and brand.

Devaluation A reduction in the international exchange rate of a currency.

Differential advantage The unique attributes of a business that may give it a superior position in the marketplace.

Diffusion lines Merchandise that is produced and sold at lower prices than designer apparel collections.

Digital out-of-home (OOH) Advertising that provides still and video images using plasma, liquid crystal display, and high-definition screens.

Direct mail Sending customers or prospects printed pieces through the mail that are designed to promote a special offer to a customer.

Direct marketing "An integrative process of addressable communication that uses one or more advertising media to effect, at any location, a measurable sales, lead, retail purchase, or charitable donation, with this activity analyzed on a database for the development of ongoing mutually beneficial relationships between marketers and customer, prospects, or donors" (Direct Marketing Association).

Direct selling A personal form of selling that involves meeting with the customer face to face.

Discounters Retailers that buy and sell at low prices and depend on high volume to be profitable.

Disintermediation When manufacturers sell directly to consumers on the Internet, bypassing retailers.

Distressed merchandise Goods sold by deep discounters that were purchased from retailers and manufacturers with surplus or slow-selling stock.

Distribution All activities required to physically move a product through the supply chain from manufacturer to final customer.

Distribution center Football-field-size facility, fully automated for efficient handling of merchandise.

Domain name The portion of a Web address that contains the business name and the identifier, such as *.com*, *.net*, and *.biz*.

Dot-com Contemporary term used to describe Web-based businesses that trade electronically and use the identifier *.com* as part of their domain name in the Uniform Resource Locator (URL).

Dual-channel retailers Companies that operate from two sales channels.

E-commerce All goods and services sold on the Internet and through other electronic means, including business-to-business (B2B) and business-to-consumer (B2C) business transactions.

E-fencing The criminal practice of reselling stolen goods on the Internet.

Electronic data interchange (EDI) Computer-based communications network used by supply chain members.

Electronic kiosks Small display units in stores or other locations that use computer technology and often the Internet to generate sales or provide extended customer services.

Electronic product code (ePC) The radio frequency identification–capable version of the universal product code (UPC).

Electronic spin-offs Companies that originally traded through other electronic means before opening online stores.

Emphasis In design, the focal point or primary component of a visual work.

Environmental scanning The practice by which opportunities and threats outside a company are detected.

EPCGlobal The organization that develops and monitors standards involving the electronic product code.

ePC Information Services (eIS) A technologically intelligent ePC network; also called a "savant."

E-retailing Online and other electronic transactions involving goods and services for personal, nonbusiness use.

Face-to-face selling A form of direct selling in which selling takes place in homes or workplaces.

Factory outlets Company-owned stores that sell manufacturers' overruns, seconds, irregulars, or sample products.

Family life cycle Schematic that traces the progression of family groupings through their lifetimes.

Fan networks Online social communities set up by retailers to provide interaction between regular customers for the purpose of increasing sales (Katz and Osofsky, Optaros white paper, 2008).

Fashion-forward customers Trendsetters who purchase the newest apparel and accessories early in a fashion season.

Fencing A common way of reselling stolen retail goods through pawnshops or flea markets.

Fill rate Ability of manufacturers or distributors to ship all goods ordered.

Franchise A contract by which an individual or group (the franchisee) agrees to operate a time-tested business format for which the owner (the franchisor) charges a fee and percentage of business over time.

Freight forwarders Firms that consolidate merchandise from several manufacturers into truckload, railroad, or container shipments.

Front-end services Services and that occur on the selling floor prior to purchase. In the online sector, front-end areas include Web site design and search capabilities.

Fulfillment The process of satisfying the customer through efficient physical distribution, inventory management, and service technologies.

Full-line department stores Stores that carry both hard and soft lines of merchandise.

Fully integrated structure Multichannel structure in which all key business functions and information are shared across channels.

General merchandise discounters Discount department stores that carry broad assortments of low-priced merchandise in large storefronts with minimal décor.

Generation X People born in the United States between 1965 and 1981.

Generation Y People born in the United States after 1981.

Goals Statements that indicate company aims or end results.

Guerilla marketing Creative street promotions and online events implemented by hired groups of outgoing people to raise brand awareness.

Headline An attention-getting word, phrase, or statement.

Hedonic needs Human needs that are emotionally based and concerned with serving the ego.

Hierarchy of needs theory Developed by Dr. Abraham Maslow, the theory suggests that people seek to satisfy needs in an ascending order of importance: biogenic, social, and psychogenic.

Horizontal competition Competition that pits retailer against retailer.

Hyper Text Markup Language (HTML) Popular computer code for documents created and used on the Web to encoded content, layout, and formatting information.

Impulse goods Items that are purchased spontaneously.

Inbound telephone calls Calls that are initiated by customers or prospective customers.

Independent structure Business structure in which all operating channels are run separately and information is not shared across channels.

Inflation The abnormal increase in the volume of money and credit resulting in a substantial and continuing rise in prices.

Infomercials Television commercials that combine detailed product information, demonstration, and excitement with a sales pitch.

Innovation In retailing, a groundbreaking new product that is developed and brought to market.

Intermodal The practice of shipping goods via more than one transportation conveyance owned by the same company.

Internet service provider (ISP) A company that provides a gateway to the Internet.

Keywords Names, places, words, or phrases that are used by a search engine to seek out pertinent information on the Web.

Lead time The period of time that passes between ordering goods and fulfilling orders; also called "cycle time."

LEED Acronym for **L**eadership in **E**nergy and **E**nvironmental **D**esign; the program that sets environmental standards for builders.

Legacy system E-commerce or other architecture that has been in operation for many years.

Law Enforcement Retailer Alliance of New England (LERANE) A working group of retailers and law enforcement formed in 2008 that will share information on organized retail crime in New England.

Law Enforcement Retail Partnership Network (LERPnet) Partnership designed to help track, prevent, and apprehend criminal networks.

Lifestyle The way people live, work, play, and spend their money.

Lifetime value The amount of money spent by a customer over a long period of time.

Limited-line department stores Stores that focus on upmarket soft lines; also called "department/specialty stores."

Line In design, the use of the artist's stroke to convey design, motion, direction, or graphic details.

Live chat Contacting a real person for further conversation while simultaneously using a Web site.

Logistic regression analysis A statistical tool used to analyze the strength of responses to stimuli.

Macro viewpoint Perspective that focuses on retailing in the broader context of retail service businesses.

Mailing lists Collections of names and addresses of present or potential customers.

Market segmentation The process of breaking down a larger population to find identifiable, manageable, actionable target markets.

Market share The percentage of industry-wide product sales earned by one company.

Marketing mix The unique arrangement of product, pricing, distribution, and promotion tactics selected to appeal to target customers.

Mashups Applications that allow aspects of one Web site to be integrated into the workings of another site through the use of an application programming interface (API).

Meta tag Special HTML code used for marking keywords and other components.

Metrosexual A young adult man who is attuned to a fast-paced urban lifestyle and who is a connoisseur of fine products and services.

Micromarketing Creation of a tailored marketing mix that is delivered to a small group or to even one individual.

Micro viewpoint Perspective that focuses on services provided to customers through multiple channels.

Microsites Independent Web sites that provide value-added information or activities that enhance the user's or customer's experience.

Mission statement Part of a vision statement that speaks to how a company will reveal its vision, its roadmap for performance.

Mobile commerce (m-commerce) Selling through cell phones and personal digital assistants (PDAs) that are Internet equipped.

Mobile fulfillment systems (MFS) Small robots that are used to move merchandise in distribution centers.

Multichannel retailers Companies that sell through two or more channels.

Multichannel retailing A business-to-consumer (B2C) model that integrates store, direct marketing, direct selling, online, and other electronic methods to transact business with customers globally.

Multivariate testing A statistical measure that allows users to investigate several elements in different combinations to find optimal relationships.

Mystery shopping reports Studies completed by researchers using specific observable benchmarks.

Natural search Free search to look up a general topic of interest or do research; also called "organic search."

Need The awareness of a discrepancy between a person's present and ideal states.

Network neutrality The concept that Internet users should be able to go where they want on the Web without intrusion from Internet service providers.

Neuromarketing Technique that uses brain wave function to measure customer response to products or concepts online and offline.

Nontransactional sites Web sites used purely for information or promotion that do not sell products.

North American Free Trade Agreement (NAFTA) Alliance to promote trade among the United States, Canada, and Mexico.

Objectives Specific intentions stated by a company.

Off-price retailers Specialty discount stores that sell branded products at 20 to 60 percent less than traditional specialty or department stores.

One-time password (OTP) devices Secure portable credentials that increase the speed and decrease the complexity of online transactions.

Online retail exchanges Electronic marketplaces through which large companies establish trading partners and build relationships within the retail industry.

Opinion leaders Individuals who shape decisions due to their knowledge of or experience with a product.

Opt-in To accept offers from a company to receive its communications.

Opt-out To decline offers from a company to receive its communications.

Organized retail crime (ORC) The theft of merchandise by multiple people working together to steal large quantities of goods from retail stores with the intent to resell the merchandise (National Retail Federation).

Outbound telephone calls Telephone calls initiated by a company for the purposes of seeking sales, providing customer service, or prescreening prospective customers.

Overstored A retail area where too many stores are selling relatively similar products so that none captures significant market share.

Paid search Advertisements that appear in the sponsored links boxes at the top of a Web page when researching a topic.

Passive RFID tags Very small microchips that are attached to a paper-like antenna; they are smaller and less expensive than active RFID tags.

Pay-per-click Remuneration earned by search engines every time a link is used.

Penetration rate The percentage of the population that purchases a product or service.

Periodic inventory A physical count of all merchandise, usually taken annually or semi-annually.

Perpetual inventory An ongoing measurement of in-stock merchandise as sales and replenishment occur.

Personalization Any relationship-building tool used by online retailers that tailors a message by using a customer's name or demographic characteristic to make an advertising message unique.

Phishing Unscrupulous practice in which individuals who pose as authentic business people try to lure people into disclosing sensitive personal information via the Internet.

Physical distribution The process of transporting goods from producer to retailer.

Planograms Explicit directions that map and illustrate the placement of fixtures and merchandise in a store.

Podcast An audio file used to lend credence, opinion, or detail to Web-based content.

Population density The number of people per square mile or kilometer living in a specific geographic area.

Positioning The perception a customer has of a company, store, or product in relation to others.

Predictive modeling The practice of examining data concerning recency, frequency, and monetary value (RFM) of past sales in order to identify key prospects or future intentions of current customers.

Prime rate Interest rate charged by the Federal Reserve Bank to commercial lending institutions.

Private event retailing Use of invitation-only, limited time sales to build viral excitement and a sense of urgency (Katx and Osofsky, Optaros white paper, 2008).

Private-label goods Goods that are manufactured to store specifications and bear a retailer's name or other brand names created by the retailer.

Product development The process that merges the buying function in a retail organization with product sourcing and technology.

Product graph A filter that helps merge product information with other constructs using Web 3.0 technology.

Product life cycle Schematic that traces the life of a product in the marketplace.

Product sourcing Identification of raw materials such as textile goods and components for manufacturing or finished goods for resale.

Progression In design, the arrangement of art components so that they show change, such as from small to large.

Proportion In design, the relationship of art components to each other and to the space surrounding the components.

Prospecting Seeking qualified potential customers through screening and analysis of database information.

Protectionism Government policy that supports domestic manufacturers by placing restrictions on foreign producers of the same goods.

Psychogenic needs Needs that stem from the socialization process and involve intangible aspects, such as status, acquisition, or love.

Psychographic segmentation A classification of people on the basis of their lifestyles, activities, interests, and opinions.

Pull strategies Used when customers initiate the selling process, or when a distribution center initiates shipment to a retail store.

Pure-play retailers Companies that do business through one predominant sales channel.

Push strategies Used when retailers initiate the selling process with a customer, or when a retailer initiates shipments from a distribution facility.

Radiation In design, the placement of art components to create a sunburst effect from a central point.

Radio frequency identification (RFID) Use of radio waves to detect merchandise, people, and other discernable elements.

Reach The number of viewers exposed to an advertising message in a specified period of time.

Really Simple Syndication (RSS) The technology that enables major news providers, as well as quasi news sites, community sites, and blogs, to transmit continually changing content over the Internet.

Real-time analytics (RTA) Actionable programs that capture information for immediate use at all levels of a company.

Recency, frequency, and monetary value (RFM) The set of measurements used by direct marketers to judge how recently customers have placed orders, how often customers do business with the firm, and how much they spend per order.

Recession A period in which there is less money in the economy than previously.

Reference assembly architecture An operational platform that breaks down key functions into logical service centers that could be analyzed from a variety of perspectives.

Reference groups Social and professional associations with which a person identifies and that he or she values when forming opinions.

Remote selling A type of direct selling done on the telephone or Internet to extend store sales.

Repetition In design, the replication of a single element to create a pattern, and thereby more visual impact.

Rhythm In design, the mechanism that guides the eye from one art component in a work to all others.

Rich media A collective term for early Web tools that enabled animation and interactivity on Web sites.

Same-store sales Measurement of sales growth in stores that have been operating for at least a year.

Sans serif Typeface that consists of simply stroked letters without appendages.

Scrambled merchandising The practice of carrying products unrelated to a customary or predictable retail merchandise assortment.

Search The process of using information technology to identify pertinent Internet resources on a topic of interest.

Search engine A computer program used to seek, find, and index all the information that is available on the Web.

Search engine marketing (SEM) Paid search activities.

Search engine optimization (SEO) The industry term for harnessing ways to increase the number of visitors to a site by increasing the site's ranking within the search engine.

Semi-integrated structure Multichannel structure that shares some but not all operational and informational tools across channels.

Serif Typeface with small design appendages on the letters.

Service-oriented architecture (SOA) A system of enterprise services for business integration.

Shared hosting A Web site that is hosted by an Internet service provider on the same server as several other Web sites.

Shoppertainment Combining shopping with elements of entertainment.

Shopping cart abandonment The practice of selecting but discarding merchandise before completing an online transaction.

Shopping goods High-priced items purchased after considerable deliberation and consultation.

Shrinkage Retail loss due to shoplifting, employee theft, and internal administrative error; also called "shrink."

Situation analysis Determining the current strengths and weaknesses of a company by looking at business practices internally and externally.

Skimmers Small electronics embedded in card-swipe devices for the purpose of accessing information from a remote site.

Slotting fee Money paid by a retailer to a vendor for the privilege of displaying a product.

Social navigation Practices that involve interaction or feedback from other viewers of a site, and when used by retailers provide the impetus for shoppers to investigate products or reviews in a more intuitive and user-friendly way on a Web site.

Specialty goods Products bearing name brands or with special attributes buyers covet and go out of their way to purchase.

Specialty stores Retail outlets that present large selections of highly focused, limited lines of merchandise in small or large facilities.

Spectrophotometers Color-measuring devices that aid the color matching process.

Split testing Analytical method that involves comparing two variables along the same dimension; also called "A/B split testing."

SSL certification Certification standards that enable customers to determine if a Web site is authentic and if their communications on the site are secure. Certification is based on the Secure Sockets Layer (SSL) protocol developed by Netscape and is a part of all major browsers and Web servers.

Stickiness The degree to which customers become engaged on a Web site, or the time spent using a Web site.

Strategic business unit One part or division of a company that is treated as a separate entity in terms of its mission and strategic plan.

Strategic planning The process of gathering and analyzing information from internal and external sources to identify concrete tactics that will reduce risk as business plans are executed.

Strategies Action plans that prescribe tactics used by a company to reach common goals and objectives.

Superstores Huge retail stores—usually over 150,000 square feet—that combine general merchandise and food under one roof.

Supply chain Manufacturers, suppliers, distributors, and retailers who interact to bring goods from the point of production to the point-of-sale.

Sustainability The maintenance and sustenance of Earth.

Sweeps A practice in which criminal teams enter a store, create diversions, and then grab as much merchandise as possible before making a speedy exit.

SWOT analysis Analytical method that lists **s**trengths, **w**eaknesses, **o**pportunities, and **t**hreats in matrix form and use of the information to determine a company's future direction.

Symmetrical balance In design, art elements that are equally weighted on left and right sides or top and bottom of the work; also called "formal balance."

Synchronous learning Learning that involves trainees participating in online leaning activities at the same time.

Tagging The process of marking a desired characteristic of a Web user.

Taguchi testing A form of multivariate testing used by online companies.

Telemarketing Using the telephone to seek prospects or solicit business from existing customers.

Trade embargo Restriction placed on the importation of goods by a government.

Transactional messages E-mails that confirm or check the status of an online order or convey pertinent delivery information.

Triple-plays Retailers that trade through three channels, such as stores, catalogs, and online.

Turnaround time The passage of time between an action and the response to it, such as the receipt of an order at a distribution center and the shipment of it to a retail store.

Turnover The number of times inventory turns into sales annually; also called "turn" or "stock turn."

'Tweens Young people between the ages of 8 and 12 years who are no longer considered small children but are not old enough to be considered teenagers.

Twittering A short burst of news updating a person's present status or intentions; usually delivered via social networking site twitter.com.

Updated customers Customers who dress fashionably and purchase shortly after a trend is introduced in the market.

Uniform Resource Locator (URL) Web site address that includes the complete access protocol and domain name.

Universal product code (UPC) Product identification information encoded in a series of printed stripes found on most products; also called "bar code."

Utilitarian needs Human needs that serve simple requirements such as comfort, body coverage, or maintenance.

Value In retailing, the worth customers place on merchandise.

Vehicles Promotions or other techniques used to reach and inform customers.

Vendor-managed inventory (VMI) System that shifts the responsibility for keeping track of merchandise to the manufacturer.

Vertical competition Competition that pits a retailer against a wholesaler or against a manufacturer that also engages in retailing.

Viral marketing The use of customers to generate excitement called "buzz" to help sell a product.

Virtual franchising An online business ownership format that uses Web pages in place of physical stores and clicks rather than visits.

Virtualization The consolidation of numerous electronic applications on less, better-utilized hardware.

Vision statement Articulation of a company's core business and its differential advantage, usually in a brief sentence or paragraph.

Vlogs Blogs with a video component.

Want The specific form of consumption used to satisfy a need.

Warehouse clubs Large format, bare-bones retail stores that sell diverse merchandise and services to business and individual members.

Warehousing The process of housing merchandise at various stages of the physical distribution process.

Web 2.0 e-commerce Advanced technologies that enable high-level user interaction, and offer rich media, heightened graphics, and 3-D capabilities.

Web 3.0 Web technologies that merge advanced customer-oriented interactive capabilities with artificial intelligence.

White space The portion of an advertisement, Web page, or catalog page that is not taken up by illustration, type, or decorative elements.

Widgets Embedded code in an HTML page that users can insert into Web sites, blogs, or social networking pages to provide information, interactive activities, and items for sale.

Wikis Interactive Web sites that encourage collaboration among multiple users.

Wireless application protocol (WAP) Platform used to enable communication between cell phones and the Internet.

Word-of-mouth Passing of positive or negative information from one person to another.

XML Acronym for e**X**tensible **M**arkup **L**anguage, an advanced version of HTML code.

XML tags Special code that describes information used by search engines when compiling their indexes.

Index

Page numbers in italics refer to figures or tables.

AbeBooks
    text messaging as marketing device, 91–92
Abercrombie & Fitch, *43*
    Gilly Hicks, *181*
    new concept development, 180
acquisitions and divestitures, 162–64
advanced shipping notices, 189, 348–49
advertising
    banner advertising, 227–29
    data mining to facilitate advertising, 232–34
    digital out-of-home (OOH) advertising, 384
    e-mail, 226–27
    legal issues, 379
    online advertising effectiveness, 372–73
    online advertising spending, *223*
    personalization, 316–17
    search engines, 290
    social networking, 225–26, 322–23
AJAX, 270
alternation, 256
Apple Inc., 21
    profile, 400–2
Amazon.com, 87
    global expansion, *16*
    overview, 19–20
    partnering with other companies, 14
    product development, 185
    profile, 396–98
    Toys "R" Us partnership, 216
Anna's Linens
    traffic-tracking technology, 377
aspirational wants, 89–90
augmented services, 298
automated storage and retrieval (ASR), 338
avatars, 235, 276–77
Avon, *51*

baby boomers, 99–100
balance
    alternation, 256
    asymmetrical, 255–56
    progression, 256–57
    radiation, 257
    repetition, 256
    symmetrical, 255
banner advertising, 227–29
bar coding, 349
basic customers, 108
basic services, 298
behavioral targeting, 234
big box retailers, 44
biogenic needs, 89
Blockbuster, 164–65
    Web presence development, 193
blogs and blogging, 118, 187, 286, 323
Bloomingdale's, 149
Bluefly.com, *266*
Blue Nile, 22
    international expansion, 10
body copy, 279
boosters, 327
Borders, 93, 127
    divestitures, 164
    Web site development, 155
brand hijacking, 374
branding
    brand positioning, 183
    brand image, 183
    customizing retail location, 183
    definition, 183
    private labeling, 185
    product development, 183

brick-and-mortar retailing
   clienteling, 298
   customer behavior, 83–84
   department stores: definition, 37; full-line, 38; limited-line, 38; private-labels, 40; strengths, 40–41; target market and pricing strategies, 39; weaknesses, 39–40
   discount stores: big box retailers, 44; category killers, 45; deep discounters, 47; definition, 37; distressed merchandise, 47; factory outlets, 46; general merchandise discounters, 44; off-price retailers, 46; key characteristics, 44; superstores, 44–45; warehouse clubs, 46
   in-store services optimization: front-end and back-end services, 317–18; fulfillment-related tactics, 319–20; selling tactics, 318–19
   market saturation, 191
   measuring productivity, 376–78
   specialty stores: collections, 42; definition, 37; diffusion lines, 42; strengths, 42; target market and pricing strategies, 42; weaknesses, 43–44
   supplementing limited store space, 190–91
bricks, slicks, and clicks, 3
business intelligence
   adaptive e-commerce architecture, 365
   brick-and-mortar productivity, 376–78
   catalog fulfillment measurement, 375–76
   definition, 365
   future trends: economic volatility; 387–88; social and lifestyle changes, 388–90; store of the future, 390–91; sustainability, 385–87; technological innovations and solutions, 381–85
   multichannel return on investment maximization, 378
   performance metrics, 366–67
   service-oriented architecture (SOA), 365
   Web analytics, 367–75
business practices and theories. *See* strategic planning
buy.com, 66

Cabela's
   merchandise management technology, 356
cannibalization, 13
catalog selling
   carry over, 52
   customer behavior, 84–85
   effectiveness metrics, 375–76
   key attributes, 52–53
   overcoming limitations, 191–92
   weaknesses, 53–54
category killers, 45
CDW Inc., 21
cell phones. *See* mobile phones
channels
   definition, 4
   differentiating from vehicles, 4–5
Chapter 11, 152–53
China
   and global retailing, 28–29
Choice™ Generation, 110–11
click-through, 197
Click-to-chat services, 117–18
clienteling, 298
Club Libby Lu
   and 'tween demographic, *100*
Coldwater Creek
   data integration across channels, *232*
collaborative planning, forecasting, and replenishment (CPFR), 340
color, 258–59
competition
   horizontal, 159
   vertical, 160
consumers. *See* customer behavior
container ships, 345
convenience goods, 96
conversion rates, 67
copywriting
   structure and preliminary activities: approaches, 280; online copy guidelines, 281; precopy-writing preparation, 279; types of copy, 279;
cookies, 232–33
counterfeiting, 29–30
   see also retail crime

credit card fraud, 326
cross-channel collaboration
- channel synchronization significance, 208–9
- Coldwater Creek's experience with, *232*
- collaboration problems and solutions: customer data, 210; customer service procedures, 210, 212; embracing change, 213–15; financial resources, 212–13; information technology, 209–10; internal expertise, 213
- customer relationship management (CRM), 231–34
- distribution practices: customer expectations, 220; fulfillment strategies, 220–21
- Ghirardelli's experience with, 211
- integration struggles, *341*
- marketing strategy integration, 215–17
- merchandise selling and pricing tactics: cross-channel selling, 217; luxury goods, 217–18; pricing techniques, 218–19
- organizational design: fully integrated structures, 207; independent structures, 208; semi-integrated structures, 207; three phases of multichannel structure development, *208*
- organizational leadership, 234–38; human resource management, 235–36; profitability and productivity, 236–38
- promotions, 222; cross-channel exposure consistency, 223–24; modern media trends, 224–31
- Title Nine's experience with, *233*

CPMs, 29, 289
Crime. *See* retail crime
cross-docking, 189
customer behavior
- brick-and-mortar retailing, 83–84
- catalog retailing, 84–85
- economic impact on retailers, 127
- marketing concepts: adoption categories, 94; decision-making process, 96–97; innovation, 94; product life cycle, 93–94; purchasing situations, 95–96
- online customer behavior, *305*
- online retailing, 87

- overview/primer: human needs and wants, 89–90; shifts in customer behavior, 90–93
- value, 83, *88*
- *see also* human needs and wants; marketing concepts

customer expectations
- cross-channel shopping, 113
- communication, 114
- consistent in-stock position, 115
- customization, 115
- gift card use, 114–15
- integrated services, 113
- online-specific amenities: click-to-chat services, 117–18; e-mail alerts and follow-up, 117; social networking availability, 118; secure systems and payment options, 118–19
- personal shoppers, 116–17
- price and value commitment, 112
- promotions, 114
- purchase and return options, 115–16
- telephone and internet options, 117
- what customers do not want, 119–20

customer relationship management (CRM), 25, 26, 51, 297, 299
- cross-channel collaboration: database development and use, 231–32; data mining, 232–34; loyalty programs, 234

customer service
- assessments: evaluation across retail formats, 308; excellence across business disciplines, 309; mystery shopping reports, 304–5; online assessment by customer reports, 305–8
- *Business Week* customer service champs list, *310*
- consumer interest in multichannel points of contact, *301*
- crime impact on customer services: organized retail crime, 324–29; retailers fighting back, 330–32; shrinkage, 324
- customer relationship management practices, 299
- fulfillment standards, 341–42
- levels of customer service: basic and augmented services, 298–99; macro and micro viewpoints, 297

Index   417

customer service *(continued)*
   online customer service leaders, *306*
   optimizing: in-store services, 317–20; loyalty programs, 309–12; online-centered services, 320–23; payment options and preferences, 312–13; personalization, 316–17; self-service options, 314–16
   S-E-R-V-I-C-E principles, 300–4
   see also customer relationship management (CRM)
Cyber Monday, 18

database marketing, 50
data breaches, 325
dedicated server, 267
deep discounters, 47
demographics, 98
   see also market segmentation
Dell, Inc., 20
   partnerships with brick-and-mortar retailers, *21*
department stores
   definition, 37
   full-line, 38
   limited-line, 38
   private-labels, 40
   strengths, 40–41
   target market and pricing strategies, 39
   weaknesses, 39–40
design basics
   elements: color, 258–59; line, 258; typography, 259–61
   principles: balance, 255–56; emphasis, 257; proportion, 258; rhythm, 258
devaluation, 149–50
differential advantage, 144–45
digital out-of-home (OOH) advertising, 384
digital shopping malls, 187
digital signage, 384
discount stores
   big box retailers, 44
   category killers, 45
   deep discounters, 47
   definition, 37
   distressed merchandise, 47
   factory outlets, 46
   general merchandise discounters, 44
   off-price retailers, 46
   key characteristics, 44
   superstores, 44–45
   warehouse clubs, 46
direct mail
   definition, 54
   effective uses, 55–56
   strengths, 56
   weaknesses, 56
direct marketing, 48–61
   definition, 49
   methods: catalogs, 52–54; direct mail, 54–56; telemarketing, 57–59
   terminology: customer relationship management (CRM), 51; database marketing, 50; fulfillment, 51; lifetime value, 51; mailing lists, 50–51; predictive modeling, 51; prospecting, 50; Recency, frequency, and monetary value (RFM), 51
Direct Marketing Association (DMA)
   customer privacy issues, 54
direct selling, 48–61
   Avon, *51*
   definition, 50
   methods: consultative selling, 59; face-to-face selling, 59–60; group sales, 60; remote selling, 59, 60–61
distribution and fulfillment, 187–90, 337–38, *340*, 341–42
   collaborative planning, forecasting, and replenishment (CPFR), 340
   cross-channel issues, 219–21
   distribution center synergy, 189
   fill rate, 342
   lead time, 341
   turnaround time, 342
   turnover, 342–43
   warehouse organization, 343–44
distribution centers, 338, *348*
domain name, 265
dual channel retailers, 6

e-commerce
　　definition, 3
　　see also e-retailing
e-commerce architecture, 365–66
　　legacy system, 365
　　reference assembly architecture, 365
economic indicators
　　buying power, 151–52
　　consumer price index (CPI), 152
　　employment rates, 152
　　gross domestic product (GDP), 152
economic turmoil, 152–54, 387–88
Eddie Bauer
　　reaction to 2008 recession, 153
electronic data interchange (EDI), 349
electronic kiosks, 61–62, 72–73, 118, 214, 314
electronic retailing. See e-retailing
electronic spin-offs, 7
e-mail, 282–83, 321–22, 373–74
emphasis, 257
environmental scanning, 143
e-retailing
　　brand resurrection, 199–200
　　concerns: customer privacy, 68; customer service; taxation, 68; updating Web sites, 68
　　customer conversion rates, 197–98
　　definition, 3
　　designing effective online stores/Web sites, 250–92
　　electronic kiosks, 61–62, 72–73, 118
　　enhancing apparel sales and services, 195–97
　　franchising, 198–99
　　infomercials, 61
　　mobile commerce (m-commerce): strengths, 71; usage and reach, 70–71; weaknesses, 71
　　online advertising spending, *223*
　　online communications: copywriting, 278–81; e-mail, 282–83; live chat, 283–84; mobile commerce communication, 284–86; personal, 286–87
　　online customer services, 320–23
　　online merchandise category performance, *64*
　　performance measures, 15, 17–19
　　popularity of online shopping, 109
　　resellers, 199
　　search strategies and optimization, 192–95
　　strategies: comparison shopping sites, 65; online shopping malls, 63–65; online auctions, 65; push and pull, 62–63
　　tactics: conversion rates, 67; purchase frequency, 68; search engine efficiency, 67; shopping cart abandonment, 67
　　television retailing: infomercials, 74, 76; interactive television, 76; home shopping channels, 74
　　top 10 web retailers, *17*
　　top 25 online retailers shoppers like most, *307*
　　web sales by type of company, *37*
　　see also Internet; online stores
Estée Lauder, 148
eye tracking, 383

factory outlets, 46
family life cycle, 104–5
fan networks, 322
fashion-forward customers, 107
fencing, 328
　　e-fencing, 328–29
fill rate, 342
franchising
　　online, 198–99
freight forwarders, 345
fulfillment. See distribution and fulfillment

gay and lesbian demographic
　　closeted respondents, 103
　　gay mainstream, 103
　　habitaters, 102
　　party people, 103
　　super gays, 102
generation X, 100, 388
generation Y, 100, 388
Ghirardelli Chocolate Co.
　　channel integration, 211
gift cards, 114–15
Giorgio Armani, 41, 42
globalization, 156
　　Amazon.com, *16*
　　global retail expansion, 27–28, 181–82

Index　　419

Godiva Chocolatier, 164
goods. *See* purchasing situations
Google, *193*
   payment system, 313
"green" marketing, 110
guerilla marketing, 122

H&M (Hennes and Mauritz), 23
headlines, 279
hedonic needs, 89
HEMA
   online operations, 369–70
hierarchy of needs theory, 89
Home Depot
   branding technique example, 184
   microsites use, 275
   reaction to 2008 recession, 153
Home Shopping Network (HSN), 75
horizontal competition, 159
HP Home and Office, 20
human needs and wants
   aspirational wants, 89–90
   biogenic and psychogenic needs, 89
   utilitarian and hedonic needs, 89
Hyper Text Markup Language (HTML), 270

identity theft, 126, 326–27
impulse goods, 96
inflation, 147–49
infomercials, 74, 76
innovation (of new service or product), 94
International Council of Shopping Centers (ICSC), 166
Internet
   domain name, 265
   dot-com, 13
   Hyper Text Markup Language (HTML), 270
   internet service provider (ISP), 267
   origins of, 12–13
   really simple syndication (RSS), 255
   SSL certification, 267
   top 10 countries in usage and penetration, *16*
   Uniform Resource Locator (URL), 265
   wikis, 271
   XML, 270–71
   see also e-retailing
Internet Retailer (trade publication), 17, 63
internet service provider (ISP), 267
inventory control
   merchandise management applications, 347, 355–56
   periodic and perpetual systems, 348
   shipping notifications, 348–49
   tracking methods, 347–48

J. C. Penney
   multichannel sales, 11
   profile, 136–38
   reaction to 2008 recession, 153
J. Crew
   search technology, 230

Kriss Cosmetics, 162–63, *164*

Lands' End
   My Virtual Model technology, 196
Law Enforcement Retailer Alliance of New England (LER-ANE), 331
Law Enforcement Retail Partnership Network (LERPnet), 331
Leadership in Energy and Environmental Design (LEED), 386
lead time, 341
learning
   asynchronous, 236
   synchronous, 236
legal and legislative issues
   consumer rebuttals to various legal and legislative issues, 380
   legal and ethical issues, 157
   legislative lobbying practices, 157
   network neutrality debate, 379–80
   online sales tax legislation, 379
   privacy bills, 379
   regulatory laws: antitrust, 158; data privacy, 158; product safety, 158

Levi Strauss & Co.
    benefits from currency devaluation, 150
    radio frequency identification (RFID) technology, 354
lifestyle, 106
Lillian Vernon, 22
    reaction to 2008 recession, 153
line, 258
live chat, 283–84
L.L. Bean, *5*, 309
    profile, 244–46
logistic regression analysis, 371
Lord & Taylor
    acquisitions, 163
Louis Vuitton, *108*
loyalty programs, 234, 309–12

Macy's, 127
    acquisitions, 163
    online business expansion, 23
    reaction to 2008 recession, 153
mailing lists, 50–51
marketing concepts
    adoption categories, 94
    decision-making process, 96–97; steps in, 97
    innovation, 94
    product life cycle, 93-94
    purchasing situations: convenience goods, 96; impulse goods, 96; shopping goods, 95; specialty goods, 95
marketing mix, 171–72
market segmentation
    behavioral segmentation: Choice™ Generation, 110–11; time-dependent, 111–12
    definition, 98
    demographic segmentation: age, 98–101; ethnicity, 104; family life cycle, 104–5; gay and lesbian, 102–3; gender, 101–2; household income, 103–4; social class stratification, 105, *106*
    geographic segmentation, 105–6
    marketing mix, 171–72
    psychographic and lifestyle segmentation: fashion orientation, 107–8; "green" orientation, 110
Marks & Spencer
    Amazon.com, 14
    private labels, 360
mashups, 274
Meow Mix
    online promotions, 4
meta tag, 270
metrosexual, 102
micromarketing, 172
microsites, 274–75
Microsoft
    interactive television, 76
mission statement, 145
mobile commerce (m-commerce)
    communication, 284–86
    definition, 3
    metrics, 374–75
    most used mobile services, *285*
    strengths, 71
    usage and reach, 70–71
    weaknesses, 71
    see also AbeBooks
mobile fulfillment systems (MFS), 338
mobile phones, 382
Montgomery Ward, 199–200
multichannel customer experience
    influencers: guerilla marketing, 122; media, 123–24; opinion leaders, 121; reference groups, 121; social networking, 122; viral marketing, 122; word-of-mouth (WOM), 121–22
    inhibitors: identity theft, 126; online shopping risks, 124–25; payment problems, 125–26; preference services, 125; privacy and security concerns, 125; shopping cart abandonment, 126; technological malfunctions, 127
multichannel retailers, 7
    customer expectations, 112–20
    key players, 19–22
    Web sites, 250–92
    see also customer expectations; multichannel retailing; Web sites

multichannel retailing
   adopting: benefits of, 7–9; justification, 9–11
   advantages and disadvantages of major channels, 77
   best practice evaluation, 200–1
   contemporary business model development, 14
   cross-channel collaboration, 206–39
   customer behavior across various channels, 83–88
   customer experience: influencers, 120–24; inhibitors, 124–27
   customer service, 296–333
   definition, 3
   deployment strategies, 23
   distribution and fulfillment, 187–90
   expansion issues: cultural differences, 182; global, 27–28, 181–82; international shipping issues, 182; new concept development, 179–81; online payment preferences
   future trends: economic volatility; 387–88; social and lifestyle changes, 388–90; store of the future, 390–91; sustainability, 385–87; technological innovations and solutions, 381–85
   legal and legislative issues, 156–58, 378–80
   marketing and communications, 186–87
   organizational structure, 7
   origins: Internet, 12–13; Sears, Roebuck and Co., 11–12
   return on investment maximization, 378
   technology, 24, 26, 177–79
   terminology overview, 3–7
   see also cross-channel collaboration; customer behavior; customer service; multichannel customer experience; e-retailing; retailing; retailers; strategic planning

multichannel retail profiles
   Amazon.com, 396–98
   Apple, 400–2
   J. C. Penney, 136–38
   L.L. Bean, 244–46
   QVC, 133–35
   RedEnvelope, 242–44

multivariate testing, 371
MySpace. *See* social networking
My Virtual Model, 196, 269, 384

National Retail Federation
   shop.org, 14
needs. *See* human needs and wants
Neiman Marcus, 127
   catalog operations, 54
Netflix.com, 165
network neutrality, 379–80
neuromarketing, 215
newegg.com, 10
   as a pure-play company, *6*
nontransactional retail sites, 7
Nordstrom
   loyalty program, 311
North American Free Trade Agreement (NAFTA), 154
Nutrifilter, 180

Office Depot. 20
Office Man, 20
off-price retailers, 46
one-time password (OTP) devices, 313
online selling. *See* e-retailing
online stores. See Web sites
opinion leaders, 121
opt-in, 125
opt-out, 125
organized retail crime, 29–30
overstored, 8

PayPal, 313
pay-per-click, 197, 289
penetration rate, 15
personalization, 225
personal shoppers, 116–17, 318–19
Philosophy Cosmetics
   Web 2.0 technology implementation, 273
phishing, 30
physical distribution, 337
Pier 1, *159*
   use of nontransactional retail site, 7
planograms, 262

podcasts, 118
Polo Ralph Lauren, *40*
    touch screen displays, 382, *383*
positioning, 145
population density, 159
Prada, 41
predictive modeling, 51
pricing techniques, 218–19
private event retailing, 322
private labeling, 40, 185, 358–60
product graph, 277
product life cycle, 93–94
product/market expansion grid, 168–71
    diversification, 171
    market development, 170
    market penetration, 169–70
    product development, 171
product sourcing, 337
progression, 256–57
proportion, 258
prospecting, 50
protectionism, 155
psychogenic needs, 89
psychographic segmentation, 106
purchasing situations
    convenience goods, 96
    impulse goods, 96
    shopping goods, 95
    specialty goods, 95
pure-play retailers, 5
push and pull strategies, 62–63

QVC
    profile, 133–35
    QVC.com as electronic spin-off, 7

radiation, 257
Radio frequency identification (RFID), 27, 167, 349–54
    Walmart's involvement in research, 353
Really Simple Syndication (RSS), 275
real-time analytics (RTA), 367
Recency, frequency, and monetary value (RFM), 51

recessions, 147
    industry professional advice on coping with, 148–49
    2008 recession reactions of various retailers, 153–54
Red Envelope, 22, 195
    profile, 242–44
reference groups, 121
REI, *221*
repetition, 256
Restoration Hardware, 23
retail crime, 29–30
    influence on retailers, 324–25
    losses rising, 330
    prevention methods, 330–32
    reselling stolen goods, 328–29
    types of organized retail crime: credit card fraud, 326; cyber intrusions, 325; identity theft, 126, 326–27; in-store criminal activity, 327–28
retailing
    brick-and-mortar, 37–48
    consolidation, 25
    and crime, 29–30
    customer dynamics, 25
    customer privacy, 30
    customer service, 296–333
    distribution and fulfillment, 187–90
    expansion issues: cultural differences, 182; global, 27–28, 181–82; international shipping issues, 182; new concept development, 179–81; online payment preferences
    marketing and communications, 186–87
    merchandising polarity, 26–27
    supply chain initiatives, 27
    sustainable business practices, 30–31
    technological advances, 24, 26
    see also brick-and-mortar retailing; e-retailing; retailers
retailers
    brick-and-mortar, 5
    dual channel, 6
    global top 10, *28*
    multichannel, 7

Index 423

retailers *(continued)*
    organizational structures: brick-and-mortar retailers, 5; dual-channel, 6; electronic spin-offs, 7; multichannel, 7; nontransactional retail sites, 7; pure-play retailers, 5–6; triple-plays, 6
    pure-play, 5–6
    Web sites, 250–92
    see also retailing; Web sites
rhythm, 258
RobotGalaxy, 49

Saks Fifth Avenue, *38, 84*
    customer services, *299*
    Web presence, 276
same-store sales, 237
Sam's Club, *47*
scrambled merchandising, 160
search engine marketing (SEM), 194
search engine optimization (SEO), 192–93, 290
search engines, 192, 306
    selection and maximization, 288–91
    visual search engines, 194
searches
    keywords, 194
    natural, 194
    paid, 194
    search drive sales, 229–30
Sears Holdings Corporation, 21
    "Wish Book," catalog, *12*
Sears, Roebuck and Co.
    early multichannel retailer, 11
    My Virtual Model, 384
service-oriented architecture (SOA), 365
Seven-Eleven Japan, 359
shared hosting, 267
Sharper Image
    reaction to 2008 recession, 153–54
shipping (of goods)
    air freight, 345–46
    land methods, 345
    most frequently used shipping carriers, *346*
    sea, 345
Shoes.com
    customer Q&A, 289

shoppertainment, 319
shopping cart systems
    abandonment, 67, 126
    functions, 263
shopping goods, 95
shop.org, 14
skimmers, 326
slotting fees, 187
social navigation, 287
social networking, 118, 122–23, 322–23
    advertising, 225–26
    fan networks, 322
    see also blogs and blogging
specialty goods, 95–96
specialty stores
    collections, 42
    definition, 37
    diffusion lines, 42
    strengths, 42
    target market and pricing strategies, 42
    weaknesses, 43–44
spectrophotometers, 196
SSL certification, 267
Staples
    overview, 20
Starbucks
    reaction to 2008 recession, 153
store of the future, 390–91
strategic business units (SBUs), 167–68
strategic planning
    competition, 159–60
    decision-making tools and market strategies: growth–share matrix, 167–68; market segmentation strategies, 171–72; product/market expansion grid, 168–71; strategic business units (SBUs), 167–68
    definition, 142
    external tactics: acquisitions and divestitures, 162–64; market share, 164–65; unpredictable events, 165–67
    internal tactics: advantageous location, 161; product differentiation, 162; scrambled merchandising, 160
    legal and legislative issues, 156–58

strategic planning *(continued)*
    monitoring the retail environment: currency volatility, 149–50; economic indicators, 151–52; inflation, 147–49; interest rate fluctuations, 150–51; recessions, 147, 152–53
    political influences: globalization, 156; trade agreements, 154; trade restrictions, 155–56
    population dynamics, 159
strategic planning process
    differential advantage, 144–45
    environmental scanning, 143
    goals and objectives, 145–46
    mission statement, 145
    positioning, 145
    situation analysis, 143–44
    strategies, 146
    SWOT analysis, 143; sample analysis, *144*
    vision statement, 145
superstores, 44–45
supply chain
    B2C disintermediation, 357–58
    definition, 336
    fulfillment, 341–44
    functional areas and participants: customer interface, 339; distribution, 337–38; production, 337
    goals, 339–40
    initiatives, 27
    inventory control, 346–49
    online retail exchanges, 357
    technology initiatives: merchandise management, 355–56; radio frequency identification (RFID), 349–55
    transportation decisions: air freight, 345–46; land, 345; sea, 345
    web-based private-label management, 358–60
sustainability, 30–31, 385–87
    percentage of customers willing to pay for eco-friendly products, *388*
sweeps, 328
SWOT analysis, 143
    sample analysis, *144*

tagging, 271
Taguchi testing, 371
Talbots
    brand positioning, 184
Target
    Pizza Hut partnership, *45*
technology
    catalog-oriented, 178
    cross-channel IT concerns, 209–10
    enterprise solutions, 385
    graphic and interactive technologies, 270–78
    internet-centered, 178–79
    store-centered, 177–78
    supply chain initiatives: bar codes, 349; Radio Frequency Identification (RFID), 349–51
    see also Web analytics; Web sites
telemarketing
    advantages, 57–58
    inbound telephone calls, 58
    outbound telephone calls, 58
    weaknesses, 58–59
television retailing
    infomercials, 74, 76
    interactive television, 76
    home shopping channels, 74
    QVC profile, 133–35
Tesco, 190
    online grocery service, 48
Title Nine
    data integration across channels, *233*
Tommy Bahama
    online development, 254
touch screen displays, 382–83
trade embargo, 156
transactional messages, 226–27
triple-plays, 6
Tupperware, 60, *61*
turnaround time, 342
turnover (of inventory), 342–43
'tweens, 100–1
    Dairy Queen 'tween-focused Web site, 302
twittering, 283
2008 economic turmoil, 152–54, 387–88

typography
   sizing type, 260–21
   type categories: serif, 259; sans serif, 259–60
   using type effectively, 261
   white space, 261

Uniform Resource Locator (URL), 265
Universal product codes (UPCs), 349
updated customers, 107–8
utilitarian needs, 89
value, 83
   aspects of customer value provided by major channels, 88
vehicles
   definition, 4
   differentiating from channels, 4–5
vendor-managed inventory (VMI), 347
vertical competition, 160
Victoria's Secret
   cross-channel brand building, 216
visual merchandising, 48
viral marketing, 122
virtual franchising, 198
vision statement, 145
vlogs, 118

wage gap, 104
Walmart
   electronic kiosks, 73
   fulfillment strategies, 221
   radio frequency identification (RFID) technology, 353
wants. See human needs and wants
warehouse clubs, 46
   Sam's Club, 47
warehousing, 338
   organization, 343–44
Web analytics, 367–75
   assessment tools: A/B split testing, 369; cognitive measures, 371; logistic regression analysis, 371; multivariate testing, 371
   e-mail effectiveness, 373–74
   evaluating Web site performance, 367–68
   real-time analytics (RTA), 367

Web video assessment, 373
Webkinz.com, 24
Web sites
   communications, 264
   design and layout: design elements, 258–59; design principles, 255–58; typography, 259–61; see also design basics
   graphic and interactive technologies: avatars, 276–77; embedded image recognition software, 274; mashup applications, 274; microsites, 274–75; rich media and Web 2.0, 270–72; RSS programs, 275; streaming video, 275; three-dimensional graphics, 272; 360-degree rotation, 272–73; Web 3.0 evolution, 277–78
   online communications: copywriting, 278–81; e-mail, 282–83; live chat, 283–84; mobile commerce communication, 284–86; personal, 286–87
   performance, 264–65
   product information content, 262
   search engine selection and maximization, 288–91
   setting up/planning, 265–69
   stickiness, 250
   top apparel retail sites, 253
   traits of effective sites, 252, 254
   transactional capabilities and functionality: links, 263; menus, 263; shopping cart functions, 263–64; side bars, 263; site maps, 262
   winning the customer, 251–52
Web 3.0, 277–78
Web 2.0, 270–72
   e-commerce, 178–79
white space, 261
widgets, 228
wikis, 271
wireless application protocol (WAP), 284
word-of-mouth (WOM), 121–22

XML, 270–71

YouTube
   as promotional tool, 231